Revealing Structure

CSLI
Lecture Notes
No. 219

Revealing Structure
Papers in Honor of
Larry M. Hyman

EDITED BY

Eugene Buckley, Thera M. Crane, and Jeff Good

CSLI
PUBLICATIONS
Center for the Study of
Language and Information
Stanford, California

Library of Congress Cataloging-in-Publication Data

Names: Buckley, Eugene, 1964- editor. | Crane, Thera M., editor. |
  Good, Jeff, editor.

Title: Revealing structure : papers in honor of Larry M. Hyman / [edited by]
  Eugene Buckley, Thera Crane and Jeff Good.

Description: Stanford, California : CSLI Publications, [2017] | SSeries: CSLI
    lecture notes ; number 219 | "Center for the Study of Language and
    Information." | Includes bibliographical references and index.

Identifiers: LCCN 2017030674 (print) | LCCN 2017044968 (ebook) | ISBN
        9781684000319 (Electronic) | ISBN 1684000319 (Electronic)
        paper) | ISBN 9781684000302 (hardcover : acid-free paper)
        | ISBN 1684000300 (hardcover : acid-free paper) |
        ISBN 9781684000296 (softcover : acid-free paper) | ISBN 1684000297
        (softcover : acid-free paper)

Subjects: LCSH: Grammar, Comparative and general–Phonology, Comparative. |
    Mathematical–Languages. | Phrase structure grammar. | Hyman, Larry M.

Classification: LCC P217.52 (ebook) | LCC P217.52 .R48 2018 (print) | DDC
        414–dc23

LC record available at `https://lccn.loc.gov/2017030674`

CIP

CSLI was founded in 1983 by researchers from Stanford University, SRI International, and
Xerox PARC to further the research and development of integrated theories of language,
information, and computation. CSLI headquarters and CSLI Publications are located on the
campus of Stanford University.

Visit our web site at
`http://cslipublications.stanford.edu/`
for comments on this and other titles, as well as for changes
and corrections by the author and publisher.

Contents

Contributors

FIRMIN AHOUA: Unité de Formation et de Recherche de Langues, Littératures et Civilisations, Université Félix Houphouët-Boigny
fahoua2003@yahoo.fr

ỌLÁDIÍPỌ̀ AJÍBÓYÈ: Department of Linguistics, African and Asian Studies, University of Lagos
oladiipo@yahoo.com

EUGENE BUCKLEY: Department of Linguistics, University of Pennsylvania
gene@ling.upenn.edu

FARIDA CASSIMJEE
cassimjee4@gmail.com

THERA CRANE: Department of Languages/Helsinki Institute of Sustainability Science, Faculty of Arts, University of Helsinki
thera@berkeley.edu

JEFF GOOD: Department of Linguistics, University at Buffalo
jcgood@buffalo.edu

REBECCA GROLLEMUND: Department of English, University of Missouri
grollemundr@missouri.edu

CARLOS GUSSENHOVEN: Department of Linguistics, Radboud University
c.gussenhoven@let.ru.nl

JOHN HARRIS: Department of Linguistics, University College London
john.harris@ucl.ac.uk

JEAN-MARIE HOMBERT: Laboratoire Dynamique du Langage, Université Lumière Lyon 2
jeanmarie.hombert@gmail.com

SHARON INKELAS: Department of Linguistics, University of California, Berkeley
inkelas@berkeley.edu

CHARLES W. KISSEBERTH: Emeritus Professor of Linguistics, Tel Aviv University
kisseber@hotmail.com

WILLIAM R. LEBEN: Department of Linguistics, Stanford University
leben@stanford.edu

SOPHIE MANUS: Laboratoire Dynamique du Langage, Université Lumière Lyon 2
sophie.manus@univ-lyon2.fr

JOYCE T. MATHANGWANE: Department of English, University of Botswana
mathanjt@mopipi.ub.bw

NGESSIMO M. MUTAKA: Department of African Languages and Linguistics, University of Yaoundé 1
pmutaka@gmail.com

JOHANNA NICHOLS: Department of Slavic Languages and Literatures, University of California, Berkeley
johanna@berkeley.edu

JOHN J. OHALA: Department of Linguistics, University of California, Berkeley
ohala@berkeley.edu

GÉRARD PHILIPPSON: Emeritus, Département Afrique, Institut National des Langues et Civilisations Orientales and Laboratoire Dynamique du Langage, Université Lumière Lyon 2
Gerard.Philippson@ish-lyon.cnrs.fr

DOUGLAS PULLEYBLANK: Department of Linguistics, University of British Columbia
douglas.pulleyblank@ubc.ca

RUSSELL G. SCHUH†: Department of Linguistics, University of California, Los Angeles

IMELDA I. UDOH: Department of Linguistics and Nigerian Languages, University of Uyo
icheji@gmail.com

JOHN R. WATTERS: SIL International
John_Watters@sil.org

ALAN C. L. YU: Department of Linguistics, University of Chicago
aclyu@uchicago.edu

1

Revealing Structure in Languages and Grammar

JEFF GOOD, EUGENE BUCKLEY & THERA CRANE

1 The Range and Influence of Larry Hyman's Work

Few linguists in the last half century can be said to have influenced as diverse a range of scholars, and subfields of linguistics, as Larry Hyman.[1] In North America, he is perhaps best known for his work in phonological theory. This work includes his textbook *Phonological theory and analysis* (Hyman 1975), published just three years after completion of his dissertation (1972a) and still cited today; his monograph establishing the mora as a significant tool for phonological theory (Hyman 1985a; republished as Hyman 2003a); and his research on tone (Hyman & Schuh 1974), harmony (Hyman 1988, 1995), and abstractness in phonological representations (Hyman 1970a)—just to mention a few of his papers in these areas (with others to be cited below). More recently, he has used his deep knowledge of phonological patterns to consider high-level questions of phonological typology (Hyman 2006, 2008, 2009, 2011a), and he has built on his extensive knowledge of African tone systems to shed light on tonal languages in other parts of the world (Hyman & VanBik 2004, Daly & Hyman 2007).

Moreover, the influence of his work extends well beyond phonology. It has also had a significant impact within Africanist linguistics and other lin-

[1] We would like to thank Robert Hepburn-Gray and Timothy Jowan Curnow for their assistance in preparing this book. Most contributions to this book were first presented to Larry Hyman on the occasion of his sixty-fifth birthday in 2012.

guistic subfields. Hyman & Watters (1984), a seminal contribution to our understanding of the encoding of information structure in African languages, has seen renewed attention as other scholars have increasingly turned their attention to this topic in languages of the continent (see e.g. Güldemann, Zerbian & Zimmermann 2015). Hyman & Katamba (1993) remains one of the most detailed available studies on the syntax and pragmatics of the augment vowel, an important feature of many Bantu languages (see de Blois 1970), and Hyman (1971) is still widely cited as a reference on the predicate combining strategy of consecutivization. His work on African languages has had a significant historical dimension as well. Hyman (2003b), for instance, is an illuminating study on how complex synchronic morphophonological patterns result from the interaction of specific sound changes and subsequent analogical change. Hyman (2011b) extends his more usual emphasis on the analysis of structural patterns in grammars to the domain of prehistory, critiquing the extent to which contemporary areal patterns should be used to reconstruct proto–Niger-Congo.

He has also produced a number of grammatical descriptions of African languages (Hyman & Magaji 1970, Hyman 1979a, Hyman 1981, Crane, Hyman & Tukumu 2011) and conducted significant comparative-historical studies of Bantu languages (Hyman 1980b, 1999). In addition, his work has been influential in the study of morphology (Mutaka & Hyman 1990, Hyman 2003c) and syntax and semantics (Hyman & Comrie 1981, Hyman & Duranti 1982, Hyman 2012), as well.

Classifying a linguist like Larry Hyman within the usual schemes used by the field hardly seems possible. Instead, in this volume dedicated in his honor, we present a selection of papers that are unified by a method or "style" of investigation rather than a specific linguistic subfield. We categorize this style as *revealing structure*. This phrase deliberately encompasses two meanings. On the one hand, it invokes the detailed language-internal investigation required to insightfully reveal grammatical patterns—that is, work that reveals structure. On the other hand, we also use it to refer to work that emphasizes the exploration of those patterns' special theoretical interest—that is, work that shows how a given structure reveals something about grammar. This is the theme which we believe unifies Larry Hyman's body of work and which runs through the papers in this volume.

In the rest of this introduction, we summarize and contextualize the papers found in the following chapters, connecting them to those aspects of Larry Hyman's work that they draw on. One point that will become evident—in case it is not already clear from the above citations—is that he has not only been a prolific author, but also a prolific and generous coauthor, and many of the contributors to this volume have written papers with him.

Indeed, since we began planning this volume he has added to his list of co-authors (see, for instance, Harry & Hyman 2014), and given his productivity, we would not be surprised if, in a couple of decades, another volume like this one will be needed.[2]

2   The Nature and Representation of Tone

Not surprisingly, studies on tonal phenomena are well represented in this volume, and they cover topics ranging from the role of phonetic data in understanding phonological representations, to the ways in which loanwords can serve as a probe into a language's abstract phonological patterns, to consideration of different prosodic domains where tonal generalizations apply.

Leben and Ahoua examine the phenomena of downstep and downdrift using new phonetic evidence to explore their phonological relationship. In particular, they are interested in the extent to which these processes may or may not be distinct in phonetic terms. Hyman (1979b), in fact, suggests that downstep and downdrift can both be modeled phonologically in similar ways. For instance, the lowering of the second high tone in an HLH sequence, typically treated under the heading of downdrift, could instead be understood as the downstepping of a high tone after the L. This would be comparable to what is found in a more canonical H!H downstepping sequence, where a high tone is downstepped immediately after a preceding high. Such a phonological approach can be tested by looking at the phonetics of downstep and downdrift within languages exhibiting both phenomena. Ahoua and Leben's study draws on data from two Kwa languages, Abron and Adioukrou, and they consider whether downstep and downdrift in these languages both involve a similar drop in the pitch of high tones targeted by the phenomena. Most significantly, they find that there is less variability in the realization of downstep than downdrift, which is consistent with results of previous phonetic studies. This suggests that downstep and downdrift may be more phonologically distinctive than impressionistic observations suggest, pointing to the need for a more subtle typology of these tonal lowering phenomena than presented in earlier, phonologically-oriented work.

The paper by **Gussenhoven** also considers data where tonal realization is distinct depending on its phonological environment. He provides evidence for a noteworthy divergence between unassociated, or floating, tones (see Hyman & Tadadjeu 1976: 59–65) that are present due to an intonation-

---

[2] We should also point out that this is not the first volume written in Larry Hyman's honor. Mutaka & Chumbow (2001) is another volume dedicated in his honor.

al boundary and those that are present for other reasons, for example, due to lexical specification or accent-sensitive phrasal tone placement. He presents compelling evidence from Japanese, French, and Cantonese that intonational boundary tones are not subject to deletion due to lack of association, but are instead always realized, whereas tones from other sources can be deleted depending on the details of a language's tonal association rules. He further demonstrates that looking at intonational tone in parallel with other kinds of tone can reveal significant generalizations. While focused on the realization of tones rather than stress, the results of Gussenhoven's study recall Hyman's (1977: 39) consideration of the morphological versus demarcative function of stress, where phenomena with comparable phonetic realization play distinct structural roles.

Cassimjee and Kisseberth consider topics that are important themes of some of Larry Hyman's earliest work: concreteness in phonology (Hyman 1970a) and the ways in which phonological patterns in loanwords can help reveal important aspects of a language's sound system (Hyman 1970b). They look at prosodic patterns in the Bantu language Shingazidja, focusing on the prosodic properties of loanwords from French into the language. A novel aspect of their study is to consider the phrasal phonological properties of these borrowings. They identify a general principle in Shingazidja that assigns a high tone to the vowel in the loanword whose French equivalent would have borne stress. In French loanwords ending in a consonant cluster, epenthesis in Shingazidja can result in the antepenultimate syllable receiving a high tone in the citation form, as in *shámburu* from French *chambre*. In native words, this HLL surface pattern corresponds to an abstract underlying representation HHL, with specification of both a penultimate and an antepenultimate high tone. Phrasal patterns show that the French loanwords are put into this phonological class as well, providing strong evidence that the abstract analysis is not merely a linguist's convenience but represents a synchronically active feature of Shingazidja's sound system.

Mathangwane presents another phonological study of a Bantu language, looking at tonal patterns in Chisubiya, also known as Kuhane and spoken in Botswana, Namibia, and Zambia. She presents a general overview of the language's tonology. As is typical for a Bantu language, the language presents a two-tone system (high and low). She focuses on two topics in particular. The first is the realization of tone on verbs in different tense-mood-aspect (TMA) configurations, taking into account that some verbs are associated with a lexical high tone and others are not. The facts can only be accounted for via the interaction of phonological and morphological factors, and the discussion enriches our database on the complex nature of TMA realization in Bantu. Her second area of focus is reduplication, and she finds, among other things, that Chisubiya is among those Bantu languages where reduplicants retain the tones associated with their base form. While this pattern is also attested, for instance, in Chichewa (Hyman & Mtenje 1999), it appears to be relatively rare, at least in Central Bantu languages (Hyman, Inkelas & Sibanda 2009: fn. 14). It is not found, for instance, in Haya (Hyman & Byarushengo 1984) and has raised theoretical interest (Myers & Carleton 1996), making its description in another language a clear contribution to the literature.

Mutaka continues the discussion of tonal patterns in Bantu, presenting a detailed account of the tones of Kinande imperatives and hortatives. Somewhat counterintuitively, even verbs associated with a lexical high tone in Kinande surface with low tones in imperative forms, though in other contexts, such as hortatives, the high tone surfaces, and these verbs then contrast tonally with lexically toneless verbs. Even more striking is the fact that objects of imperative verbs whose last two vowels are underlyingly toneless also surface with low tones rather than the more usual phrasally assigned penultimate high tone. Mutaka proposes that the imperative is marked with two different low tones, one assigned to the verb itself and another to a larger intonational domain containing the imperative utterance. The verbal imperative tone displaces any lexical high tone, while the intonational imperative can affect the tonal realization of a word at the end of the intonational phrase. In devising this analysis, he builds on work such as Hyman (1990), which also assumes an analysis where Kinande distinguishes underlyingly between vowels specified for high tone /H/, low tone /L/, and unspecified tone /Ø/. Mutaka's paper thus considers both issues of underlying representation, as found in Cassimjee and Kisseberth's, and the importance of distinguishing tones associated with different levels of phonological constituents, as considered by Gussenhoven.

The contribution by **Schuh** continues a line of investigation represented by Hyman & Schuh's (1974) influential paper on typological patterns in tone rules. He looks at tonal alternations in a number of Chadic languages of Yobe State, Nigeria. While there are broad similarities among them, they also show enough differences to allow a comparative approach to yield interesting generalizations. In particular, he finds that the major source for tonal alternations in these languages is tone spreading, which he understands as the tendency for the pitch of a tonal domain to "leak" into the following domain, a claim which is consistent with Hyman & Schuh (1974: 87–90; see also Hyman 1978: 262, 2007b). Thus, for example, in the closely related languages of Ngizim and Bade, a high tone will spread left-to-right across word boundaries in most types of phrases. This process, though seemingly grounded in a universal tendency, is nevertheless realized differently across the phonologies of the languages surveyed. Thus, even though the high tone spreading processes in Ngizim and Bade are similar in many respects (e.g. not particularly sensitive to syntactic boundaries and blocked by a modally voiced obstruent), they differ in their phonological domain of application. In Ngizim, spreading only goes to the following mora, while in Bade it can go as far as an intonational phrase boundary. Schuh's study therefore further adds to our understanding of the ways that a single phonetic pattern can become phonologized (Hyman 1976, 2013a).

3 Prosodic Phenomena and Phonological Structure

While Larry Hyman is especially well known for his descriptive and theoretical work on tone, he has also done significant research on issues connected to prosodic phonology and phonological structure more generally. As a result, work on prosodic phenomena involving segmental alternations is well represented in this volume as well.

Ajíbóyè and Pulleyblank, for instance, examine patterns of nasal harmony in the Mọ̀bà dialect of Yorùbá. Standard Yorùbá has a well-studied pattern of nasal harmony, but the Mọ̀bà dialect has not been subject to detailed investigation and shows a number of interesting features. Like Standard Yorùbá, Mọ̀bà has a set of nasal vowels in its inventory, with seven oral vowels and three apex nasal vowels. The mid vowels lack nasal counterparts, following a pattern in this part of the world discussed by Hyman (1972b). The consonant inventory of Mọ̀bà can be divided between obstruents, which are always oral, and sonorants, which may be oral or nasal. Standard Yorùbá exhibits syllable-based nasal harmony: adjacent sonorants in a syllable must be either both nasal or both oral. Thus, *rì* 'drown' and *r̃ĩ̀* 'walk' are both possible words, but a form like **r̃ì̃* is disallowed. Mọ̀bà extends this pattern of nasal harmony to high vowels that precede a nasalized vowel. Other vowels are not affected by this pattern, and oral obstruents are "transparent" to this process—that is, they do not block nasal harmony to a high vowel. There are further complications as well, and Ajíbóyè and Pulleyblank describe them in extensive detail and offer a constraint-based analysis of the patterns. Their analysis suggests that, despite surface differences between Standard Yorùbá and the extended harmony patterns of Mọ̀bà, each variety can be analyzed with the same set of formal tools and are, therefore, more similar to each other than they would first appear to be, thereby demonstrating the power of abstract analysis to clarify deep relationships among surface structural patterns.

Philippson also considers cases of harmony in his examination of the vowel height harmony facts of a number of varieties of Chaga, a Bantu language of Tanzania, as well as other Bantu languages in contact with Chaga.

Vowel harmony in Bantu has been carefully explored by Hyman (1999) and, roughly speaking, can be said to involve alternations in suffixes between high and mid vowels depending on the quality of the vowel that precedes them. The examination of vowel height harmony in Bantu languages raises a number of important historical questions, for instance regarding whether it was present in Proto-Bantu, and how to reconstruct the forms of the suffixes observed to undergo harmony. Chaga is of special interest due to the fact that vowel harmony is attested in its dialects with significant, and revealing, variation. For example, the reflex of the Proto-Bantu root *-bón- 'see' in Chaga varieties commonly appears with a so-called neuter (or stative) suffix to create a verb stem that has the conventionalized meaning of 'be born' (i.e. "be seen"). In a number of eastern, western, and central Chaga varieties, this stem has the shape -βon-ek-, which shows the effects of harmony, while in other western and eastern varieties, it has the shape -βon-ik-, which does not exhibit harmony, with no obvious geographic pattern to these differences. Philippson considers various historical scenarios to account for his observations. While he ultimately concludes that an explanation for them is not yet clear, his paper only further emphasizes how the analysis of the synchronic distribution of abstract phonological patterns reveals interesting questions about historical processes of differentiation and convergence within Bantu.

The topic of the paper by **Manus** is a process of vowel shortening found in the Bantu language Símákonde, a variety of Makonde spoken in Tanzania. There is a regular, phrase-final rule in Símákonde which lengthens the penultimate syllable of phonological phrases. Penultimate lengthening is widespread in much of the eastern and southern parts of the Bantu area, though with considerable variation, for instance with respect to its domain of application (Hyman 2013b). Manus is specifically interested in cases where penultimate vowels fail to lengthen within noun phrases, in order to see what patterns emerge with respect to prosodic constituency in the language. For instance, in a clause like *sílóólo síkúmeêne sindiîgwa* 'a big mirror fell', lengthening can be seen in the penultimate vowel of all three words. By contrast, in the phrase *sílóló asiilá* 'that mirror', with a postnominal demonstrative, lengthening is not present in the noun. (As can be seen in this example, these vowel length alternations can involve tonal changes as well.) Among other things, she finds that a noun-phrase-final demonstrative causes all preceding elements to be treated as belonging to the same phonological phrase, even if they would be phrased separately if the demonstrative were not present. This suggests that determination of the prosodic structure of a noun phrase may require consideration not only of very general aspects of its syntax but also its semantic or pragmatic properties, something which is already known to be important in the presence of penultimate lengthening at the clausal level (Hyman & Monaka 2011).

Harris is primarily interested in the prosodic domain of the foot as a locus of phonological generalization, and he discusses data from English where phonotactic patterns which might, at first, appear to be syllable-based are, on closer inspection, better analyzed as being foot-based. The relevant facts are (i) that the sequence *aw* (i.e. /aʊ/) cannot be followed by any non-coronal consonant—thus, *shout* is an attested word in English but one does not find forms ending in a *p* or a *k*—and (ii) that the vowel in the sequence *wa* has generally merged with the vowel associated with historical short *ŏ*, rather than being pronounced the same as other tokens of historical short *ă*, except when followed by a dorsal consonant—thus, *want* now rhymes with *font* (or nearly rhymes, depending on the dialect) while *wax* rhymes with *lacks* rather than *locks*. At first glance, these generalizations might appear to be syllable-based, with a vowel's realization being conditioned (whether synchronically or historically) by a following coda consonant. However, Harris demonstrates that the domain of these generalizations cannot be straightforwardly treated as the syllable since they also apply to words where the relevant postvocalic consonants are followed by unstressed vowels. In the case of *aw*, this means one finds words like *powder*, but not, for instance, */aʊgɚ/. In the case of *wa*, this means that one finds words like *swagger* where the first vowel's pronunciation can be associated with historical short *ă*. Harris's analysis of these English patterns has parallels in work such as Hyman (1998: 62), which examines stem phonotactic constraints in Bantu languages via detailed consideration of the overall prosodic structures in which they occur rather than seeing them as purely syllabic patterns.

Looking at what, at first, seems to be a question of segmental phonology, **Yu** reexamines the status of laryngealized resonants in the Native American language Washo. These are resonant sounds, such as *m̓*, which combine an oral articulation with a laryngeal constriction either resulting in phonetic creaky voice or complete glottal closure. The surface Washo segment inventory overall exhibits a three-way laryngeal contrast for a given place and manner of articulation, with stops appearing as plain, aspirated, or glottalized (specifically ejective), and resonants as modally voiced, voiceless, or glottalized. However, previous studies had suggested that the glottalized series of resonants were better treated as the surface realization of a glottal stop–resonant sequence, in opposition to glottalized obstruents which were treated as unitary segments. Yu argues against this view, instead presenting evidence that treating glottalized resonants as unitary segments as well is a better fit with the overall phonological patterns of the language.

For instance, in a reduplication construction, the glottalized resonants pattern the same way as uncontroversially unitary segments, rather than patterning with clusters, in that the entire glottal-resonant "complex" is copied rather than just the resonant position. Thus, *pʰaˈlolo* 'butterfly' reduplicates as *pʰaloˈlolo* (where the reduplicant is bolded) rather than **pʰaloˈlolo* where the copied consonant lacks glottalization. The study demonstrates the importance of looking not only at contrasts but also prosodic phonology when considering issues of segmentation, in a manner comparable to what has been seen in the analysis of nasal-stop sequences in Bantu languages, which are also open to diverging segmental analyses (see e.g. Hyman & Ngunga 1997).

4   Morphological Encoding and Variation

Morphological structure has been an important theme of much of Larry Hyman's work. His contributions in this area have spanned topics in morphophonology, such as the examination of cyclicity in Bemba (Hyman 1994a); morphosyntax, as found in the development of a syntactic account of alternations in the form of Aghem nouns (Hyman 1985b, 2010); as well as more basic descriptive work (Hyman 1980a) and comparative and historical investigations (Hyman 1973, 1994b, 2003b). Three of the contributions in this volume reflect this dimension of Larry Hyman's work.

The paper by **Inkelas** focuses on noncanonical cases of morphological expression involving overexponence (i.e. when a morphological category is expressed by more than one morpheme in a word) and underexponence (i.e. when a morphological category unexpectedly fails to be expressed). One example of overexponence involves the encoding of the morphological reciprocal category in the Chichewa verb where, under certain conditions, the reciprocal suffix appears twice. For instance, in the form *-mang-an-il-an-* 'tie-REC-APP-REC', meaning 'tie each other for', two reciprocal suffixes are required, before and after the applicative suffix (see Hyman 2003c: 254). She also considers underexponence in Chichewa, discussed in Hyman & Mtenje (1999), involving verbal constructions which require high tones on verb stems. Even if multiple such constructions apply to a single verb stem, only one high tone may surface—thus giving "less" exponence than expected. In order to account for such cases of noncanonical exponence, Inkelas makes use of the emerging framework of Optimal Construction Morphology, which integrates insights from constraint-based and realizational approaches to morphology. This allows her to model cases of noncanonical exponence as the interaction of competing constraints of different levels of morphological structure, and to demonstrate the ways in which disparate surface structures can be related to each other via abstract principles of morphological expression.

Watters is also interested in a problem of morphological exponence, specifically the way time is encoded on the verb in the (Wide) Bantu language Ejagham, spoken in Nigeria and Cameroon. Ejagham has a well-developed system of encoding aspect and mood on the verb, as well as encoding the focus status of clausal elements, including "auxiliary focus" (Hyman & Watters 1984). Ejagham can hardly be said to be morphologically poor, unlike some of its relatives in the Benue-Congo subgroup of Niger-Congo (see Hyman 2004). However, there is a noteworthy gap in what the language expresses morphologically: verbs are not coded for tense in any way. What makes this gap especially striking is that closely related languages within the Bantu group often have elaborate tense systems, such as that found in the Bamileke language of Dschang (Hyman 1980c), spoken fairly close to Ejagham in Cameroon, which distinguishes five past tenses and five future tenses. Moreover, while some of the verbal markers found in Ejagham are relatively new historically, none of them are grammaticalizing in order to encode tense—that is, there is no evidence of any pressure for a tense-marking system to develop. Watters considers this in light of the larger historical and areal picture, for instance noting that the Upper Cross River language Leggbó, spoken in the same general region as Ejagham in Nigeria, also lacks tense encoding (Hyman, Narrog et al. 2002), and concludes that the lack of tense in Ejagham is more likely to represent the conservative situation, with tense in Bantu languages being innovative for the family. His study demonstrates how a detailed analysis of the structure of a language's inflectional system can lead to significant historical results.

Udoh offers a description of compound formation in Leggbó, a language of Nigeria just mentioned above. She considers both the ways that different parts of speech can combine to form compounds and the evidence for a distinction between root and synthetic compounds. Moreover, her paper offers data on interesting morphological patterns found within compounds. For instance, in noun-noun compounds, the second noun generally loses its noun class prefix, resulting in forms such as *yètti-kkpál* 'tree bark' based on the words *yètti* 'tree' and *lìkkpal* 'scale', where the second word has lost its *lì-* prefix as a result of compound formation. This is an instance of a root compound, a class of compounds which are always right-headed. This means that, somewhat surprisingly, the semantic head of the compound exhibits morphological reduction while the modifying element does not. There are, however, exceptions to this pattern, and there is a class of noun-noun root compounds where the prefix of the semantic head word of the compounds replaces that of the first word, as in the form *lè-tti-dùl* 'bundle of sticks', which is based on *ètti* 'stick' and *ledùl* 'bundle'. Root compounds can also be formed from adjective-noun combinations, as seen, for example, in *ètà-kkpon* 'world', based on *ètà* 'big' and *ekkpón* 'land'. Udoh also examines other kinds of compound structures that are right-headed. One group of these involves the creation of agentive nouns from verb-noun combinations where the noun fulfills an argument role for the verb, and she categorizes these as synthetic compounds. An example is *è-ttùì-àtɛèmì* 'farmer', based on *ttùì* 'cultivate' and *àtɛèmì* 'farm'. These compounds also appear with an initial prefix indicating their nominal status. A general lesson of this study is the need to look at morphological, syntactic, and semantic factors in parallel in order to fully analyze the diversity of a language's compound structures.

5 Methodologies in Revealing Structure

Most of the chapters in this volume focus on the analysis of specific grammatical patterns. However, a few also emphasize methodological concerns. This balance is largely reflective of what is found in Larry Hyman's own work. The bulk of his publications emphasize the analysis of specific linguistic facts. However, he has also done important work on just how one should go about "revealing structure". To take a few examples, Hyman (2001) considers the role phonetic generalizations should play in phonological analysis, Hyman (2009) lays out a general model for how to undertake phonological typology in a rigorous fashion, and Hyman (2014) provides a practical "how-to" for working out a description of a language's tonal system.

Hombert and Grollemund make use of a comparatively new approach in linguistics—the application of phylogenetic methods developed for research in biology—to reconsider the classification of Bantoid languages spoken in the Grassfields area of Cameroon, where many of Narrow Bantu's closest relatives are spoken. The complex linguistic situation of the Grassfields has long been of great interest for historical and comparative Bantu linguistics, and this led to various initiatives specifically aimed at collecting comparative data on the region, such as the work reported on in Hyman & Voorhoeve (1980). Hombert and Grollemund, in particular, were able to make use of wordlists collected by these earlier efforts, enhancing it with data from a number of nearby Narrow Bantu languages, in order to analyze their historical relationships using phylogenetic algorithms and, thereby, provide an updated classification of languages of the region. Their results reinforce, and add new detail to, previous proposals and are valuable not only for the contribution they can make to unraveling Bantu prehistory, but also for how they can inform comparative investigation of the distribution of historically significant grammatical phenomena in these languages, such as the presence of noun class prefixes containing nasal consonants (Hyman 1980b).

From a descriptive perspective, the chapter by **Nichols** is concerned with the function of two deictic prefixes in Ingush, a Nakh-Daghestanian language. One of these, *dwa-*, is associated with events involving motion away from the speaker, and the other, *hwa-*, with events involving motion towards the speaker. However, their usage is more complex than simple directionality of motion. They can have conventionalized quasi-derivational functions, such as the use of the *hwa-* prefix to encode transition into a desirable or fully aware state, as seen, for example, in the verb *hwa-soma-d.oal* 'wake up'. More surprisingly, these prefixes also encode a direct/inverse opposition in Ingush. Specifically, in constructions involving a goal or recipient—e.g. 'me' in a clause like 'he'll introduce you to me'— the prefix *hwa-* is almost exclusively used when this argument outranks the subject on the person hierarchy. The prefix *dwa-* is generally used otherwise. Direct/inverse systems are unusual for Eurasia. So, the discovery of a system like this in Ingush is quite remarkable. However, Nichols' paper is not only meant to be relevant for language description and typology. She also makes the methodological point that, in order for her to be able to fully describe this system, it was not possible to rely solely on texts. Elicitation was also required to determine the behavior of certain low frequency patterns and also to uncover semantic and pragmatic nuances unlikely to be revealed by even a relatively large corpus in a documentation project. In this regard, she underscores one of the points made by Hyman (2007a), namely that complete description requires the sort of structured interaction with consultants that is only achieved by traditional elicitation.

Ohala focuses his contribution on elaborating the phonological consequences of the Aerodynamic Voicing Constraint and evaluating how our knowledge about the constraint should impact phonological theorizing. This constraint is not linguistic in nature but, rather, physiological. In short, it is a generalization about the degree of airflow that is required to pass through the vocal tract to allow the vocal cords to vibrate and voicing to occur. Since the presence or absence of voicing in the speech stream is an important feature of spoken language, this physiological constraint has important linguistic consequences. For example, it predicts that obstruents are more likely to be voiceless than voiced because the degree of oral closure required to articulate them impedes airflow in a way that inhibits voicing. It also predicts that voice onset time for voiceless stops will be longer after high vowels than low vowels because the comparatively close constriction associated with high vowels again reduces airflow through the vocal tract.

Moreover, this constraint can play a role in explaining various kinds of sound changes, such as the prenasalization of voiced stops, which can be viewed as a strategy to maintain air flow during a stop closure by allowing some air to pass through the nasal cavity. Ohala then considers what the implications are of the presence of the Aerodynamic Voicing Constraint for phonological analysis, and he concludes that it suggests there is less need to posit specific linguistic constraints to account for sound patterns than is common of many influential phonological theories. While such a claim may not, at first, seem congruous with the strong emphasis on phonological analysis found in Larry Hyman's work, it actually complements arguments made in, for example, Hyman (2001, 2013a) that the relationship between phonetics and phonology is an indirect and largely historically mediated one, rather than reflecting a "deep" integration of phonetic factors into phonology itself.

6 Language Structure and Linguistic Analysis

In recent decades, the increased availability of new kinds of data collection and analysis tools has seen much of the field of linguistics shift towards approaches that do not rely as strongly—as was typical of much of the twentieth century—on rigorous and insightful structural analyses of the kind that are well exemplified in this collection and in Larry Hyman's work. Work on underdescribed languages, for instance, has been greatly influenced by the documentary paradigm that emphasizes the collection and annotation of naturalistic data over exhaustive coverage of a specific grammatical space via elicitation that is commonly associated with traditional description. Also, work in phonology increasingly involves experimental investigation and quantitative analysis over large datasets.

To the extent that these developments help us arrive at a better understanding of language in general, as well as the grammars of particular languages, they should, of course, be welcomed. However, we should not lose sight of the power of structural techniques to reveal the generalizations that govern the grammatical systems of the world's languages, and to provide us with an intuitive framework for modeling typological variation. Moreover, even when linguistic research is not primarily aimed at structural analysis— whether it involves documentary data collection, experimental testing, quantitative analysis, or something else—it is unimaginable that it could be successful without building on the foundations of structurally oriented work, whether this involves relatively old notions, such as the phoneme, or newer ones, such as the autosegmental treatment of tone. The papers here— as well as the many works of Larry Hyman cited below (and those he has yet to write)—make the importance of *revealing structure* abundantly clear.

References

Blois, K. F. de 1970. The augment in the Bantu languages. *Africana Linguistica* 4: 85–165.

Crane, T. M., L. M. Hyman & S. N. Tukumu. 2011. *A grammar of Nzadi [B865]: A language of Democratic Republic of the Congo*. Berkeley: University of California Press. http://escholarship.org/uc/item/846308w2.

Daly, J. P. & L. M. Hyman. 2007. On the representation of tone in Peñoles Mixtec. *International Journal of American Linguistics* 73: 165–208.

Güldemann, T., S. Zerbian & M. Zimmermann. 2015. Variation in information structure with special reference to Africa. *Annual Review of Linguistics* 1: 155–178.

Harry, O. G. & L. M. Hyman. 2014. Phrasal construction tonology: The case of Kalabari. *Studies in Language* 38: 649–689.

Hyman, L. M. 1970a. How concrete is phonology? *Language* 46: 58–76.

Hyman, L. M. 1970b. The role of borrowing in the justification of phonological grammars. *Studies in African Linguistics* 1: 1–48.

Hyman, L. M. 1971. Consecutivization in Fe'fe'. *Journal of African Languages* 10: 29–43.

Hyman, L. M. 1972a. A phonological study of Fe'fe'-Bamileke. Los Angeles: University of California dissertation.

Hyman, L. M. 1972b. Nasals and nasalization in Kwa. *Studies in African Linguistics* 3: 167–206.

Hyman, L. M. 1973. Notes on the history of Southwestern Mande. *Studies in African Linguistics* 4: 183–196.

Hyman, L. M. 1975. *Phonology: Theory and analysis*. New York: Holt, Rinehart and Winston.

Hyman, L. M. 1976. Phonologization. In A. Juilland (ed.), *Linguistic studies offered to Joseph Greenberg on the occasion of his 60th birthday*, 407–418. Saratoga, CA: Anma Libri.

Hyman, L. M. 1977. On the nature of linguistic stress. In L. M. Hyman (ed.), *Studies in stress and accent* (Southern California Occasional Papers in Linguistics 4), 37–82. Los Angeles: Department of Linguistics, University of Southern California.

Hyman, L. M. 1978. Historical tonology. In V. A. Fromkin (ed.), *Tone: A linguistic survey*, 257–269. New York: Academic Press.

Hyman, L. M. (ed.). 1979a. *Aghem grammatical structure: With special reference to noun classes, tense-aspect and focus marking* (Southern California Occasional Papers in Linguistics 7). Los Angeles: Department of Linguistics, University of Southern California.

Hyman, L. M. 1979b. A reanalysis of tonal downstep. *Journal of African Languages and Linguistics* 1: 9–29.

Hyman, L. M. 1980a. Esquisse des classes nominales en tuki. In L. M. Hyman (ed.), *Noun classes in the Grassfields Bantu borderland* (Southern California Occasional Papers in Linguistics 8), 27–35. Los Angeles: Department of Linguistics, University of Southern California.

Hyman, L. M. 1980b. Reflections on the nasal classes in Bantu. In L. M. Hyman (ed.), *Noun classes in the Grassfields Bantu borderland* (Southern California Occasional Papers in Linguistics 8), 179–210. Los Angeles: Department of Linguistics, University of Southern California.

Hyman, L. M. 1980c. Relative time reference in the Bamileke tense system. *Studies in African Linguistics* 11: 227–237.

Hyman, L. M. 1981. *Noni grammatical structure* (Southern California Occasional Papers in Linguistics 9). Los Angeles: Department of Linguistics, University of Southern California.

Hyman, L. M. 1985a. *A theory of phonological weight*. Dordrecht: Foris.

Hyman, L. M. 1985b. Dependency relations in Aghem syntax: The mysterious case of the empty determiner in Aghem. *Studies in African Linguistics* Supplement 9: 151–156.

Hyman, L. M. 1988. Underspecification and vowel height transfer in Esimbi. *Phonology* 5: 255–273.

Hyman, L. M. 1990. Boundary tonology and the prosodic hierarchy. In S. Inkelas & D. Zec (eds.), *The phonology-syntax connection*, 109–125. Chicago: University of Chicago Press.

Hyman, L. M. 1994a. Cyclic phonology and morphology in Cibemba. In J. Cole & C. Kisseberth (eds.), *Perspectives in phonology*, 81–112. Stanford: CSLI.

Hyman, L. M. 1994b. Conceptual issues in the comparative study of the Bantu verb stem. In S. S. Mufwene & L. Moshi (eds.), *Topics in African linguistics*, 3–34. Amsterdam: Benjamins.

Hyman, L. M. 1995. Nasal consonant harmony at a distance: The case of Yaka. *Studies in African Linguistics* 24: 5–30.

Hyman, L. M. 1998. Positional prominence and the 'prosodic trough' in Yaka. *Phonology* 15: 41–75.

Hyman, L. M. 1999. The historical interpretation of vowel harmony in Bantu. In J.-M. Hombert & L. M. Hyman (eds.), *Bantu historical linguistics: Theoretical and empirical perspectives*, 235–295. Stanford: CSLI.

Hyman, L. M. 2001. On the limits of phonetic determinism in phonology: *NC revisited. In E. V. Hume & K. Johnson (eds.), *The role of speech perception in phonology*, 141–185. San Diego: Academic Press.

Hyman, L. M. 2003a. *A theory of phonological weight*. Stanford: CSLI. (Reprint of Hyman 1985a.)

Hyman, L. M. 2003b. Sound change, misanalysis, and analogy in the Bantu causative. *Journal of African Languages and Linguistics* 24: 55–90.

Hyman, L. M. 2003c. Suffix ordering in Bantu: A morphocentric approach. In G. Booij & J. van Marle (eds.), *Yearbook of morphology 2002*, 245–281. Dordrecht: Kluwer.

Hyman, L. M. 2004. How to become a Kwa verb. *Journal of West African Languages* 30: 69–88.

Hyman, L. M. 2006. Word-prosodic typology. *Phonology* 23: 225–257.

Hyman, L. M. 2007a. Elicitation as experimental phonology: Thlantlang Lai tonology. In M.-J. Solé, P. S. Beddor & M. Ohala (eds.), *Experimental approaches to phonology*, 7–24. Oxford: Oxford University Press.

Hyman, L. M. 2007b. Universals of tone rules: 30 years later. In T. Riad & C. Gussenhoven (eds.), *Tones and tunes: Studies in word and sentence prosody*, 1–34. Berlin: Mouton de Gruyter.

Hyman, L. M. 2008. Universals in phonology. *The Linguistic Review* 25: 83–137.

Hyman, L. M. 2009. How (not) to do phonological typology: The case of pitch-accent. *Language Sciences* 31: 213–238.

Hyman, L. M. 2010. Focus marking in Aghem: Syntax or semantics? In I. Fieder & A. Schwarz (eds.), *The expression of information structure: A documentation of its diversity across Africa*, 95–115. Amsterdam: Benjamins.

Hyman, L. M. 2011a. Tone: Is it different? In J. Goldsmith, J. Riggle & A. C. L. Yu (eds.), *The handbook of phonological theory*, 2nd edn., 197–239. Chichester: Wiley-Blackwell.

Hyman, L. M. 2011b. The Macro-Sudan Belt and Niger-Congo reconstruction. *Language Dynamics and Change* 1: 1–47.

Hyman, L. M. 2012. Post-verbal subject in the Nzadi relative clause. *Journal of African Languages and Linguistics* 33: 97–117.

Hyman, L. M. 2013a. Enlarging the scope of phonologization. In A. C. L. Yu (ed.), *Origins of sound change: Approaches to phonologization*, 3–28. Oxford: Oxford University Press.

Hyman, L. M. 2013b. Penultimate lengthening in Bantu. In B. Bickel, L. A. Grenoble, D. A. Peterson & A. Timberlake (eds.), *Language typology and historical contingency*, 309–330. Amsterdam: Benjamins.

Hyman, L. M. 2014. How to study a tone language. *Language Documentation & Conservation* 8: 525–562.

Hyman, L. M. & E. R. Byarushengo. 1984. A model of Haya tonology. In G. N. Clements & J. Goldsmith (eds.), *Autosegmental studies in Bantu tone*, 53–103. Dordrecht: Foris.

Hyman, L. M. & B. Comrie. 1981. Logophoric reference in Gokana. *Journal of African Languages and Linguistics* 3: 19–37.

Hyman, L. M. & A. Duranti. 1982. On the object relation in Bantu. In P. J. Hopper & S. A. Thompson (eds.), *Studies in transitivity* (Syntax and Semantics 15), 217–239. New York: Academic Press.

Hyman, L. M., S. Inkelas & G. Sibanda. 2009. Morphosyntactic correspondence in Bantu reduplication. In K. Hanson & S. Inkelas (eds.), *The nature of the word: Studies in honor of Paul Kiparsky*, 273–309. Cambridge: MIT Press.

Hyman, L. M. & F. X. Katamba. 1993. The augment in Luganda: Syntax or pragmatics? In S. A. Mchombo (ed.), *Theoretical aspects of Bantu grammar*, 209–256. Stanford: CSLI.

Hyman, L. M. & D. J. Magaji. 1970. *Essentials of Gwari grammar* (Occasional Publication of the Institute of African Studies 27). Ibadan, Nigeria: Institute of African Studies, University of Ibadan.

Hyman, L. M. & K. C. Monaka. 2011. Tonal and non-tonal intonation in Shekgalagari. In S. Frota, G. Elordieta & P. Prieto (eds.), *Prosodic categories: Production, perception and comprehension*, 267–290. Dordrecht: Springer.

Hyman, L. M. & A. Mtenje. 1999. Prosodic morphology and tone: The case of Chichewa. In R. Kager, H. van der Hulst & W. Zonneveld (eds.), *The prosody-morphology interface,* 90–133. Cambridge: Cambridge University Press.

Hyman, L. M., H. Narrog, M. Paster & I. I. Udoh. 2002. Leggbo verb inflection: A semantic and phonological particle analysis. In J. Larson & M. Paster (eds.), *Proceedings of the twenty-eighth annual meeting of the Berkeley Linguistics Society: General session and parasession on field linguistics*, 399–410. Berkeley: Berkeley Linguistics Society.

Hyman, L. M. & A. S. A. Ngunga. 1997. Two kinds of moraic nasal in Ciyao. *Studies in African Linguistics* 26: 131–163.

Hyman, L. M. & R. G. Schuh. 1974. Universals of tone rules: Evidence from West Africa. *Linguistic Inquiry* 5: 81–115.

Hyman, L. M. & M. Tadadjeu. 1976. Floating tones in Mbam-Nkam. In L. M. Hyman (ed.), *Studies in Bantu tonology* (Southern California Occasional Papers in Linguistics 4), 57–111. Los Angeles: Department of Linguistics, University of Southern California.

Hyman, L. M. & K. VanBik. 2004. Directional rule application and output problems in Hakha Lai tone. *Language and Linguistics* 5: 821-861.

Hyman, L. M. & J. Voorhoeve (eds.). 1980. *L'expansion bantoue: Actes du colloque international du CNRS, Viviers (France) 4–16 avril 1977, vol. 1: Les classes nominales dans le bantou des Grassfields*. Paris: SELAF.

Hyman, L. M. & J. R. Watters. 1984. Auxiliary focus. *Studies in African Linguistics* 15: 233–273.

Mutaka, N. M. & S. B. Chumbow (eds.). 2001. *Research mate in African linguistics—Focus on Cameroon: A fieldworker's tool for deciphering the stories Cameroonian languages have to tell*. Cologne: Rüdiger Köppe.

Mutaka, N. M. & L. M. Hyman. 1990. Syllables and morpheme integrity in Kinande reduplication. *Phonology* 7: 73–119.

Myers, S. & T. Carleton. 1996. Tonal transfer in Chichewa. *Phonology* 13: 39–72.

2

Mọ̀bà Nasal Harmony

Ọládiípọ̀ Ajíbóyè & Douglas Pulleyblank

1   Introduction

This paper is a case study of nasality in Mọ̀bà, a dialect of Yorùbá. Nasality in Mọ̀bà is of interest for various reasons.[1] In particular, it illustrates how a local and highly restricted pattern of assimilation can develop into a more general pattern of "harmony", and it demonstrates the interaction of conditions on locality and similarity. Nasal harmony in Standard Yorùbá (SY) is quite well understood (Oyebade 1985, Awóbùlúyì 1990, Clements & Ṣọnaiya 1990, Awóbùlúyì & Oyebade 1995). In contrast, nasal harmony in the Yorùbá dialect of Mọ̀bà is virtually untreated. Work such as Bamisile (1986) and Ajíbóyè (1991, 1997, 1999) has examined some aspects of the phonology of Mọ̀bà, but this is the extent of the work on the dialect's phonology. Here, we show that Mọ̀bà exhibits a robust pattern of nasal harmony that is significantly different from SY, though clearly related.

Mọ̀bà nasal harmony has several significant properties. Harmony is unbounded, all eligible targets left of a nasal source undergoing harmony. Two classes of ineligible targets differ in their behavior: voiced and voiceless obstruents do not undergo harmony and are transparent to

---

[1] Mọ̀bà dialect is spoken by about 200,000 people in Òkè-Èró Local Government Area of Kwara State (except Ìdọ̀fin) and Mọ̀bà Local Government Area of Ekiti State, in Nigeria. The first author is a native speaker; he is the primary source of data, with data confirmed by a second speaker.

Revealing Structure.
Eugene Buckley, Thera Crane & Jeff Good (eds.).
Copyright © 2018, CSLI Publications.

harmonic propagation; and nonhigh vowels do not undergo harmony and block propagation.

2 Background

In order to understand nasal harmony in Mọ̀bà, it is crucial to consider the function of nasality in the Yorùbá segmental inventory. Like SY, Mọ̀bà has seven oral and three nasal vowels [i, e, ɛ, a, ɔ, o, u, ĩ, ã, ũ].[2] Minimal and near-minimal pairs establish the contrast: [dì] 'bind/tie' vs. [dĩ́] 'fry'; [dù] 'scramble for' vs. [dũ̀] 'sweet'; [tà] 'sell' vs. [tã̀] 'deceive'. Both high and low vowels exhibit oral/nasal pairs, but mid vowels cannot be nasalized.

(1) Nasalized mid vowel prohibition—*Mid/Nas: *[+nasal, −high, −low]

The constraint is motivated by the frequency of this pattern crosslinguistically (Ruhlen 1975) and in related languages more specifically (Hyman 1972).[3] The constraint must outrank faithfulness to input nasality: *Mid/Nas >> MaxNas (where MaxNas: a nasal specification in the input must have a correspondent nasal specification in the output).[4] This ranking means it is preferable to lose a specification of nasality rather than to have a nasalized mid vowel, hence nasalized mid vowels become impossible.

Mọ̀bà includes two series of consonants that must be distinguished: (i) the obstruents /t, k, kp, b, d, ɟ, g, gb, f, s, h/, which are systematically oral;[5] and (ii) the sonorants /m, r, l, y, w/, which may be nasalized, [m, r̃, n, ỹ, w̃].

3 Basic Syllable-Internal Harmony

Like SY, Mọ̀bà exhibits agreement within the syllable: adjacent sonorants within a syllable must be either both oral or both nasal, as illustrated in (2) (though see below).[6]

---

[2] Nasalization on vowels in Yorùbá is indicated orthographically by a preceding nasal consonant (*ma* = /mã/) or a following *n* (*an* = /ã/). To avoid potential confusion, we give all data in IPA with one exception—rather than use [j] for a palatal glide, we use [y].

[3] Numerous Kwa languages exhibit equal numbers of oral and nasal vowels, including mid vowels (Williamson 1973); numerous Kwa languages allow only retracted mid nasal vowels.

[4] Following work such as Pulleyblank (1996), Lombardi (2001), Zhang (2000), Kim & Pulleyblank (2009), we assume Max[Feature] constraints rather than Ident[Feature] constraints.

[5] Mọ̀bà exhibits a difference from SY concerning /h/. SY exhibits a nasalized variant, [h̃] (Owólabí 1989), whereas in Mọ̀bà, [h̃] is not attested. Also, Mọ̀bà has only one phonemic nasal consonant, namely /m/. Whether SY has one phonemic nasal (/m/) or two (/m, n/) is a matter of debate (Owólabí 1989, Clements & Ṣọnaiya 1990, Awóbùlúyì 1992).

[6] On syllabification in Yorùbá, see Ọla (1995). For the purposes of this paper, two assumptions about syllable structure are important. First, CV sequences constitute syllables. Second, there are no long vowels or diphthongs in Yorùbá; any VV sequence is heterosyllabic.

(2) Standard Yorùbá & Mòbà: syllable-internal sonorant harmony
    a.   rì   'drown'   r̃ì   'walk'
    b.   rù   'carry'   r̃ù   'smell'
    c.   yà   'draw/comb'   ỹà   'choose'

The facts of contrast and syllable-internal sonorant harmony are comparable in SY and Mòbà. Indeed, the forms seen so far are the same in both. Overall patterns of nasalization, however, are strikingly different.

The syllable-internal pattern forms our starting point. Anticipating properties to be discussed below, we propose an analysis based on sequential cooccurrence constraints (Smolensky 1993, Pulleyblank 2002, 2006). For SY, we assume that two constraints taking the syllable as their domain drive harmony. The first constraint requires that a sonorant to the *left* of a nasal segment be nasal; the second constraint requires that a sonorant to the *right* of a nasal segment be nasal. Directionality is motivated below.

(3) Standard Yorùbá: nasal harmony constraints
    a. *[Oral/son Nas/son]$_\sigma$: an oral sonorant incurs a violation if preceding a nasal sonorant (*[O N]$_\sigma$); domain = syllable
    b. *[Nas/son Oral/son]$_\sigma$: an oral sonorant incurs a violation if following a nasal sonorant (*[N O]$_\sigma$); domain = syllable

By ranking these constraints above the relevant faithfulness constraints, the agreement observed in (2) results. An interesting point emerges when we consider the interaction of the syllable-internal harmony constraints and the occurrence of a nasal onset. Within a morpheme, both SY and Mòbà exhibit syllables with two oral or two nasalized sonorants, but combinations of oral and nasal sonorants are not allowed. That is, nasal consonants may occur before any of the vowels [ĩ, ã, ũ] but never before an oral surface vowel. Hence morphemes such as [mũ] 'drink' are attested, while others such as *[mu] and *[mo] are impossible; see also (2) above. It is important to note that there are two different types of impossible nasal + oral sequences. A nasal consonant plus a high or low vowel is possible, provided that the vowel itself is nasalized, as in [mũ].[7] A nasal consonant plus a mid vowel, on the other hand, is impossible whether the mid vowel in question is oral or nasalized, *[mo] or *[mõ]. Such a sequence is ruled out by *Mid/Nas (1) if the mid vowel is nasalized, and by *[N O]$_\sigma$ (3b) if the mid vowel is oral.

Although the facts of Mòbà so far could be derived by the same constraints as those proposed for SY, we show that the relevant constraints are

---

[7] Yorùbá orthography does not show nasalization on a vowel following a nasal consonant. A word like [mũ] 'drink' is orthographically *mu*. This writing convention must not be confused with the issue under discussion: *mu* is a possible spelling, but [mu] is not a possible sequence.

somewhat different in the grammar of Mọ̀bà. We consider it plausible that (3) forms the core from which the pattern of Mọ̀bà developed diachronically. Significantly, we show below that assimilation extends this set of constraints in interestingly restricted ways. We structure the discussion by considering gradually larger domains, from syllable to word to phrase, showing how such domains differ in their properties and therefore analysis in the two dialects. Three variables are crucial to an understanding of harmonic properties: (i) domain size, (ii) the similarity between trigger and target, and (iii) the segmental nature of potentially affected consonants and vowels.

4   Word-Level Harmony: Mọ̀bà

Unlike in SY, Mọ̀bà routinely extends the domain of nasality to high vowels that precede a nasalized vowel. This is true within morphemes, as in (4), and across a prefix-stem boundary, as in (5). Note that the nominal prefix is oral when added to an oral root, such as [ùfέ] 'love' from [fέ] 'like'.

(4)   Mọ̀bà: nasal harmony

a.	ũrĩ	'iron'	d.	ĩỹắ	'pounded yam'
b.	ĩw̃ĩ	'spirit'	e.	ĩỹĩ́	'feces'
c.	ù̃ỹà̃	'famine'	f.	ũw̃ắ	'lie'

(5)   Mọ̀bà: polymorphemic words, nasal roots

a.	rĩ̀	'walk'	ũrĩ̀	'walk'
b.	ỹì	'praise'	ù̃ỹì̀	'praise'
c.	nĩ́	'have'	ũnĩ́	'possession'
d.	à̃	'measure'	ù̃à̃	'measurement'

Since the constraints in (3) hold of syllables, they would be inadequate for the more general harmony observed in Mọ̀bà. We propose modifying the domain to "prosodic word" (Pulleyblank 1996, Orie & Pulleyblank 2002, Perkins 2005) in the constraint in (3), but delay formulating the constraint until discussion of transparency. As with its syllable-restricted cousin in (3), word-domain harmony prevents an oral sonorant from being an onset to a nasal vowel, ruling out forms like *[uwắ]. In addition, word-domain harmony rules out nasal syllables preceded by an oral vowel as in *[uw̃ắ]. The result is therefore a continuous string of nasal segments: [ũw̃ắ]. Note too that harmony is observed in both mono- and polymorphemic forms.

In the following sections, we discuss properties of word-level harmony.

Transparency. As seen in (6), a high vowel before a nasalized vowel must itself be nasalized, even if an obstruent intervenes between the two vowels. Note that the transparent obstruent is itself oral, not nasal.

(6)   Mòbà: transparency of obstruents

a.	ĩdũ	'bed bug'	d.	ĩfũ	'intestine'
b.	ũgũ	'corner (of a house)'	e.	ĩtã̀	'story'
c.	ĩsĩ̀	'worship'	f.	ũ̀kpĩ̀	'KIND OF INSECT'

This pattern of transparency depends on two basic points. First, an obstruent in Mòbà cannot be nasalized—*Nas/Obs: *[+nas, −son]. This constraint is phonetically motivated, since being an obstruent requires constricted airflow while being nasal requires unrestricted nasal airflow. Second, although the obstruents in (6) cannot be nasalized, they do not interrupt the extension of nasality leftwards. That is, obstruents are transparent to nasal harmony. Before proposing a harmony constraint allowing transparency, we briefly address representational issues.

Two representations are conceivable: (i) having two phonetically nasal vowels flanking an oral consonant could mean two nasal specifications (7a); or (ii) a single nasal value might skip over the transparent obstruent (7b).

(7)   a.   n   n   b.   *   n
           | | ⟋⎺⎺⎯|
           V   d   V   V   d   V

While proposals differ in how to impose locality on phonological representations, the gapped structure in (7b) is widely rejected. If phonological specifications are to map straightforwardly onto phonetic targets (Keating 1988, Cohn 1990), then (7b) must be rejected, since its phonetic implementation involves a nasal-oral-nasal sequence, not a single nasal target maintained through multiple segments. For Gafos (1999), Ní Chiosáin & Padgett (2001), and Rose & Walker (2004), (7b) would be ruled out because assimilation must obey a "strict segmental locality" principle whereby multiply linked features can only exist on segments with adjacent root nodes. Even with a less restrictive notion of adjacency (Archangeli & Pulleyblank 1994), (7b) violates a general precedence condition, since both consonants and vowels are nasal anchors in Mòbà and no eligible anchor may be skipped. We conclude that (7a) is well-formed while (7b) is not.

At issue is how to penalize an oral-nasal sequence where the oral segment is not adjacent to the nasal. Consider two options: (i) assume a single nasal domain with the obstruent contained within it, for example by enriching representations (Cole & Kisseberth 1994, Ní Chiosáin & Padgett 2001) or by allowing gapping (e.g. Itô, Mester & Padgett 1995); or (ii) allow nonadjacent segments to be referenced in a constraint (Suzuki 1998). We adopt the latter here.

Assuming that the output of harmony is as in (7a), word-domain harmony holds of two sonorants even if a consonant intervenes (Suzuki 1998).

(8)   *[Oral/son C_0 Nas/son]$_{Wd}$: an oral sonorant incurs a violation if preceding a nasal sonorant, with or without an intervening C (*[O C_0 N]$_{Wd}$); domain = PrWd

According to this formulation, the Mọ̀bà constraint differs in two ways from the constraint in SY: (i) it does not require strict adjacency, and (ii) its domain is the word rather than the syllable. We exemplify with [ũgũ] 'corner'.

(9)   Transparency of obstruents

/ugũ/	*Nas/Obs	*[N O]$_\sigma$	MaxNas	*[O C_0 N]$_{Wd}$
a. [ugũ]				*!
b. [ũⁿgũ]	*!			
☞ c. [ũgũ]				
d. [ugu]			*!	

Any candidate involving a nasal obstruent (9b) is ruled out by *Nas/Obs. Loss of nasality is prevented by MaxNas (9d). A candidate like (9a) with an "oral ... nasal" vowel sequence is penalized by *[O C_0 N]$_{Wd}$, so the optimal candidate is the harmonic one (9c).

Concluding this section, harmony may cause multiply-linked representations where a single nasal specification links to both vowels and an intervening sonorant, and harmony may also cause a "twin peaks" representation (7a), where the obstruent intervening between two vowels is not nasalizable.

Vocalic targets of harmony: high vowels only. As noted above, nasal harmony targets high vowels; mid and low vowels do not harmonize.

(10) Mọ̀bà: mid vowels are not nasal harmony targets

    a.   orĩ   'song'   d.   ogũ   'war'

    b.   ɛ̀sí   'reproach'   e.   ènĩ   'bonus'

    c.   ɛ̀rã   'meat'   f.   ɔmã   'child'

With mid vowels (10), this immunity to harmony is not surprising since Mọ̀bà is like SY in not allowing mid vowels to be nasalized. In contrast, low vowels are perfectly good nasalized vowels, yet do not harmonize (11).

(11) Mọ̀bà: low vowels are not nasal harmony targets

    a.   àgã   'KIND OF CULT'   d.   àkṹ   'KIND OF BEAD'

    b.   àrũ̃   'disease'   e.   así   'KIND OF RAT'

    c.   àfí   'albino'   f.   àkpá   'bachelor'

Yorùbá has a three-way scale for nasalizability (*Hi/Nas: *[+nas, +hi]; *Mid/Nas: *[+nas, −hi, −lo] (1); *Low/Nas: *[+nas, +lo]). High nasalized vowels are both underlying and derived; low nasalized vowels are underlying, not derived; mid nasalized vowels are neither underlying nor derived.

(12) Nasal scale for vowels: *Mid/Nas >> *Low/Nas >> *High/Nas

That nasalized mid vowels are impossible shows that *Mid/Nas is undominated. That both nasalized low and high vowels are attested shows that MaxNas must outrank *Low/Nas and *High/Nas. That word-level harmony derives only nasalized high vowels indicates that *Low/Nas, but not *High/Nas, outranks word-level harmony. These rankings are seen in (13).

(13) Mòbà: low vowels are not harmonic targets

/àrá/	*Mid/ Nas	*[N O]$_\sigma$	Max Nas	*Low/ Nas	*[O C$_0$ N]$_{Wd}$	*High/ Nas
a. [àrá]				*	**!	
☞ b. [àrá]				*	*	
c. [àrá]				**!		
d. [àrá]		*!				

*Mid/Nas is ranked above MaxNas, hence nasalized mid vowels are completely ruled out. Nasalized low vowels, on the other hand, are retained if underlying (13d) but not derived by harmony (13c). Nasalized high vowels are possible both underlyingly and as a result of harmony given the low ranking of *High/Nas. Tableau (13) illustrates an important point. Candidate [àrá] (13a) violates *[O C$_0$ N]$_{Wd}$ twice; both [a] and [r] are oral sonorants, and each of these segments precedes the final nasal vowel. The winner, [àrá] (13b), is better therefore since it violates *[O C$_0$ N]$_{Wd}$ only once.

Restrictions on the location of nasality. In the cases seen above involving two vowels, and in subsequent cases with multiple vowels, either all vowels are nasalized or only the final vowel or vowel sequence is nasalized.[8] This appears to be true of both SY and Mòbà. At issue is how to exclude morphemes with a nasal vowel followed by an oral vowel, such as *[vcṽcv] and *[ṽcṽcv].

Assuming "richness of the base" (Prince & Smolensky 2004), the exclusion of *[...cṽ...cv...] forms must be due to properties of the output grammar, not to some stipulation of impossibility underlyingly. We propose that both SY and Mòbà prohibit nasal-oral sequences within the *morpheme.*

---

[8] There are a very small number of exceptions to this generalization, for example, [àmàlà] 'yam flour paste'.

(14) *[Nas/son C_0 Oral/son]$_{Morph}$: an oral sonorant incurs a violation if following a nasal sonorant, with or without an intervening C (*[N C_0 O]$_{Morph}$); domain = morpheme

This constraint must not require adjacency between the nasal and oral segments, since the constraint holds even if there is an obstruent intervening between two sonorants. As this constraint is only ever in very exceptional cases violated, we assume that the constraint is undominated.

By ranking this constraint above MaxNas, two cases are ruled out: (i) it is impossible to have a morpheme where the first vowel is nasalized and the second is unnasalizable (*[ĩwe]); and (ii) a morpheme with two nasalizable vowels cannot have nasality solely on the first vowel (*[ãda]).

The effects of *[N C_0 O]$_{Morph}$ overlap significantly with *[N O]$_{\sigma}$. The two constraints are different, however: the former applies to tautomorphemic segments that are not within the same syllable; the latter applies to heteromorphemic segments that are tautosyllabic. This becomes relevant below where a class of derived nasal-oral sequences is discussed.

To conclude this section, we have accounted for the apparent location of nasality, when present, on the final syllable of a morpheme. Word-level harmony in Mọ̀bà is derived by prohibiting oral sonorants before nasals; the mirror-image constraint, taking the morpheme as its domain, prohibits oral sonorants following nasals. The combination of these two constraints locates nasality on the rightmost segment in the morpheme, from which it extends leftwards as far as possible within the word.

Opacity of nonhigh vowels. Although nasal harmony skips over obstruents, harmony is blocked by any vowel that cannot itself undergo harmony. We illustrate this vocalic opacity with trimoraic forms. Note that there is nothing unusual in the basic trimoraic harmonic patterns. Sequences of high vowels may be oral or nasal: [isùkù] 'corn stalk' or [udidi] 'whole' vs. [ũmũmĩ] 'drinking cup' or [ìsũ̀gbĩ̀] 'traditional singers'. When a nasal vowel is present, as in [ìsũ̀gbĩ̀], word-domain harmony forces all the vowels to be nasal.

Similarly, the presence of an initial mid or low vowel does not prevent harmony from applying when a high vowel precedes a nasalized vowel (see (15)). A medial nonhigh vowel, however, blocks the spread of nasality from the final vowel to the initial one (see (16)); that is, nonhigh vowels are opaque.

(15) Mọbà: trimoraic sequences involving initial nonhigh vowels

a.	egbìgbò	'root'	d.	egígú	'masquerade'
b.	adití	'deaf person'	e.	èrĩrũ	'KIND OF SPONGE'
c.	akúrí	'dullard'	f.	àgũfã	'giraffe'

(16) Mọbà: nonhigh vowels are nonundergoers and opaque

a.	ìrègũ	'reproaching'	d.	ùrɔ̃rũ	'peace of mind'
b.	ilègũ	'NAME OF COMPOUND'	e.	ìgósũ	'NAME OF TOWN'
c.	ìranũ	'unserious'	f.	ìkpákũ	'climber'

Opacity follows from our analysis. Word-level $*[O\ C_0\ N]_{Wd}$ enforces nasality on a sonorant at most one syllable away from the nasal source. In a form like [ù-gbádũ] 'enjoyment', the low vowel cannot nasalize ($*Low/Nas$) and there is no pressure from $*[O\ C_0\ N]_{Wd}$ to nasalize the initial vowel. A form like $*[\tilde{ù}$-gbádũ] would involve a gratuitous violation of faithfulness.

Directionality. This section presents an argument for directionality based on a class of derived cases involving medial nasal segments. Consider the data in (17). Nasality does not spread to the right, but it does spread to the left, confirming the need for directionally asymmetric constraints (see (18)).

(17) Derived medial nasality

a.	ũ-mã-sí	'having knowledge of an act'	< ù + mã + sí
b.	ũ-mṹ-ra	'preparedness'	< ù + mṹ + ara
c.	ũ-nĩ-ra	'difficulty'	< ù + nĩ + ara

(18) Directionality in harmony

/ù-mã-sí/	MaxNas	*Low/Nas	$*[O\ C_0\ N]_{Wd}$	*High/Nas
a. [ù-mã-sí]		*	*!	
b. [ù-mã-sĩ]		*	*!	*
☞ c. [ũ-mã-sí]		*		*
d. [ũ-mã-sĩ]		*		**!

Morpheme-internal and derived environments. A related class involves V_1NV_2 sequences derived by deletion (see Orie & Pulleyblank 2002). Morpheme concatenation and vowel deletion can result in a nasal-nonhigh vowel sequence. Though it is impossible within a morpheme for a nasal consonant to precede an oral vowel, such derived sequences are tolerated.[9]

---

[9] In a few cases, the initial vowel exceptionally fails to undergo nasalization even though followed by a nasal: [ùmoɟì] 'NAME OF A VILLAGE'; [ìmélé] 'laziness'; [ùmórù] 'PERSONAL NAME'.

(19) Derived V_1NV_2: V_1 = high; V_2 = nonhigh

    a. ù̩-m-ɛ̃rã   'instr. for/act of picking animals' < ù + mṹ + ɛrã

    b. ù̩-m-ɔ́kɔ́   'instr. for/act of picking hoes'   < ù + mṹ + ɔkɔ́

    c. ù̩-m-édé   'instr. for/act of picking shrimps' < ù + mṹ + edé

    d. ù̩-m-áɟá   'instr. for/act of picking dogs' < ù + mṹ + aɟá

The nonhigh vowel is unaffected by the consonant's nasality; the high vowel undergoes nasalization. In (20), we see flanking nonhigh vowels.

(20) Derived V_1NV_2: V_1 = nonhigh; V_2 = nonhigh

    a. a-m-ɛ̃rã   'person picking meat/animals' < a + mṹ + ɛrã

    b. a-m-ɔ́kɔ́   'person picking hoes'   < a + mṹ + ɔkɔ́

    c. a-m-édé   'person picking shrimps'   < a + mṹ + edé

    d. a-m-áɟá   'person catching/picking dogs' < a + mṹ + aɟá

Such cases are the motivation for restricting the *[N C₀ O]$_{Morph}$ constraint to the morpheme. As such, the constraint is not relevant for derived nasal-oral sequences. Tableaux for this kind of case would be comparable to (18).

The pattern is somewhat different when the postdeletion vowel following the nasal consonant is high. Consider the data in (21).

(21) Derived V_1NV_2: V_1 = high or nonhigh; V_2 = high

    a. ù̩-m-ĩwé   'instrument for taking book' < ù + mṹ + ìwé

    b. ù̩-m-ĩyɔ̀   'take/add salt (to)'   < ù + mṹ + iyɔ̀

    c. a-m-ĩlá   'person taking okra'   < a + mṹ + ilá

    d. a-m-ĩgò   'person taking bottle'   < a + mṹ + ìgò

As already seen, a high vowel prefix is nasalized while a nonhigh prefix remains oral (cf. (19) and (20)). Of interest here are the postnasal high vowels. So far, there is no constraint to drive the harmony in such cases, yet the postnasal high vowels are nasalized. We propose that Mo̩bà, like SY, exhibits an effect of *[Nas/son Oral/son]$_\sigma$ (3b)—the "Standard Yorùbá" syllable-delimited constraint. Since the effect is limited to high vowels, this means that *[Nas/son Oral/son]$_\sigma$ must be ranked below *Low/Nas but above *High/Nas. Consider the example of [a-m-ĩlá] 'person taking okra'.

(22) Syllable-internal nasalization of high vowels

/a-mṹ-ilá/	Max Nas	*Low /Nas	*[N O]$_\sigma$	*[O C₀ N]$_{Wd}$	*High /Nas
a. [a-m-ílá]			*!	*	
☞ b. [a-m-ĩlá]				*	*
c. [ã-m-ílá]		*!	*		

5 Phrasal Cases

Nasal harmony applies within syllables, but otherwise does not cross word boundaries. This can be seen in a "careful speech" form like [rí ũkũ] 'see squirrel' where [i] is unaffected by the following nasal vowel; if the vowel [i] deletes, however, the sonorant [r] undergoes nasalization: [r̃ũkũ]. It is not simply the fact of vowel deletion that allows or triggers nasal spreading. Examples like [yí ũkũ] ~ [yíkũ] 'roll squirrel' show that there is no derived nasal assimilation in cases where the spreading would not be motivated by syllable-internal harmony. In other words, word-level harmony is inapplicable; nasality in such a derived context is only possible syllable-internally.

A different type of case involves sequences where a nasal C_1 comes to precede an oral V_2, that is, cases of the type /m$\tilde{V}_1$ + V_2CV/ where $\tilde{V}_1$ deletes. The generalizations governing such cases are as follows: (i) deletion cannot result in a sequence of a nasal consonant followed by an oral high vowel, so either V_2 deletes in such a case ([mã ùkòkò] ~ [mãkòkò] 'mould pot') or the high vowel undergoes nasalization ([mũ igi] ~ [mĩgi] 'shake a tree'); (ii) unlike within morphemes, oral mid vowels may follow nasal consonants as a result of vowel deletion ([mũ olè] ~ [mólè] 'catch thief'); and (iii) there are no instances of derived nasalized low vowels—sequences of a nasal consonant and an oral low vowel are attested in vowel deletion contexts ([mũ aɟá] ~ [máɟá] 'catch dog', [mã adé] ~ [madé] 'know Ade'), and all instances of a nasal consonant followed by a nasalized low vowel are consistent with the nasalized low vowel being underlyingly present ([sã eó] ~ [sãó] 'pay money').

These cases can be derived by the slightly revised ranking of the constraints discussed in (22). Crucially, phrasal cases tolerate a nasal-oral sequence that the morpheme-internal cases do not (as seen in Section 3). The absence of morpheme-internal nasal-oral sequences results in the revised proposal by ranking *[N C_0 O]$_{Morph}$ (14) over MaxNas; *[N O]$_\sigma$ is ranked below both MaxNas and *Low/Nas. See (23) and (24).

(23) Possibility of phrasal nasal-oral sequences: high vowels

/mũ igi/	*[N C_0 O]$_{Morph}$	Max Nas	*Low /Nas	*[N O]$_\sigma$	*High /Nas
☞ a. [mĩgi]					*
b. [mígi]				*!	

(24) Possibility of phrasal nasal-oral sequences: nonhigh vowels

/mũ ajá/	*[N C$_0$ O]$_{Morph}$	Max Nas	*Low /Nas	*[N O]$_\sigma$	*High /Nas
a. [mãjá]			*!		
☞ b. [májá]				*	

6 Harmony and Locality

Pulleyblank (1996, 2002) and Hansson (2007) note that patterns of harmony such as in Mọ̀bà show a clear requirement for separating representational properties from constraint formulation. As shown here, harmony can result either in a multiply-linked nasal feature or in more than one singly-linked nasal feature. Hence the harmonic constraint must impose agreement for nasality without specifying a particular way of achieving such agreement. Even if the harmonic representations respect "strict locality" (Gafos 1999, Ní Chiosáin & Padgett 2001), it is clear for Mọ̀bà that the trigger and target of the harmonic constraint do not respect string adjacency.

Some relaxation of strict string adjacency is needed, and we propose to adopt the approach of Suzuki (1998). Consider two alternatives. According to Archangeli & Pulleyblank (1994), adjacency in a case like Mọ̀bà must be calculated at the root node level since both consonants and vowels are anchors for nasality. This would therefore rule out reference between vowels over a consonant and incorrectly predict Mọ̀bà to be impossible.

An alternative would be a proposal like that of Piggott (2003), an account that includes a treatment of certain aspects of Mọ̀bà. Piggott proposes that nasal harmony should be parametrized, with languages selecting either the segment or the syllable as the nasal-bearing unit. Selecting the segment results in nasalizing contiguous spans of segments, with any neutral segment interrupting the nasal sequence ("opacity"); selecting the syllable (like Mọ̀bà) results in nasalizing contiguous spans of syllables, with nasality percolating to all sonorants within the span. A neutral obstruent can therefore be "skipped" ("transparency") in the sense that a contiguous span of syllables is nasalized, without regard for any obstruents within the span.

A detailed examination of Mọ̀bà does not support the parametrization account. Piggott's proposal (2003: 389) is that in languages of the Mọ̀bà type, nasal syllables are governed by "Nasal Licensing/σ": "the nasal feature is licensed as a property of a syllable". He suggests that "in a nasal syllable, the feature must be associated with the nucleus and projected to all other sonorants". For Mọ̀bà, this requirement is satisfied within morphemes: [mũ] 'drink' vs. *[mu] or *[me] (see Section 3). A sequence of nasality and orality is only possible within a morpheme when a nasal vowel is preceded by a nonnasalizable consonant, as was seen in (2): [ỹã̀] 'choose' (*[yã]) vs. [tã̀] 'deceive'. In derived contexts, the nuclear requirement is problematic. For example, [a-m-áɟá] 'person catching/picking dogs' from (20) has a nasal consonant without a nasal nucleus, and [ũ̀-m-áɟá] 'instrument for/act of picking dogs' from (19) shows that the nasal consonant can initiate harmony though it is not a nucleus.

Overall, nasality is *not* a syllable-bound feature in any absolute sense. Though there is a strong tendency for all sonorant segments within a syllable to be either oral or nasal, this tendency is violable; nasality is not always licensed by linkage to a syllable nucleus. Piggott's (2003) parametric model succeeds only in accounting for a subset of the Mòbà data.

7   Constraints on Adjacent Moras

There is a systematic class of exceptions to the generalization that high vowels constitute targets of nasal harmony. Consider the data in (25), showing variant forms in careful and connected speech, respectively.

(25)   Mòbà: consonant deletion; vowel juxtaposition

a.	egbìgbò	eìgbò	'root'	d.	egĩgũ	eigũ	'bone'
b.	erírú	eírú	'ashes'	e.	àrĩrĩ́	àirĩ́	'middle'
c.	àkìkɔ	àikɔ	'fowl'	f.	ènĩnú̃	èínú̃	'mercy'

We would have expected regular nasal harmony to apply in cases like (25): a form like [eigũ] 'bone' (25d) would be expected to surface as *[eĩgũ].

The answer to this puzzle lies in a SY subpattern. Nasal harmony in SY holds within the syllable and does not (in general) spread either to the left or right. In one circumstance, however, nasality extends beyond the syllable. Where noun-noun sequences give rise to phrase-level assimilation (Orie & Pulleyblank 2002), nasality "piggybacks" on the vocalic assimilation to give forms like [èrĩ́ adé] ~ [èrĩ́ã̀ ãdé] 'Ade's laughter'. Such assimilation cannot result from simply generalizing the domain of *[Nas/son Oral/son]σ to include syllables to the right, since that would overgenerate in cases like [amã̀rí] 'somebody known (already)': *[amã̀rĩ́]. The correct generalization is that rightwards nasalization applies only between abutting vowels, not between a vowel and a following consonant. SY shows evidence of an additional constraint, related to but distinct from *[Nas/son Oral/son]σ (3b):[10]

---

[10] In Mòbà (Ajíbóyè 1999), there is no assimilation in this kind of phrase. Unlike in SY, phrases like [èrĩ́ adé] 'Ade's laughter' exhibit neither vocalic nor nasal assimilation.

(26) Agreement in a nasal vowel–oral vowel sequence (*[Nμ Oμ]$_{Phrase}$)

*[Nas/μ Oral/μ]$_{Phrase}$: an oral mora incurs a violation if immediately
following a nasal mora; domain = phrase

To solve the puzzle in (25), we propose a related MÒbà version of
*[Nμ Oμ]$_{Phrase}$, prohibiting adjacent oral-nasal vowel sequences within the
word:

(27) Agreement in an oral vowel–nasal vowel sequence (*[Oμ Nμ]$_{Wd}$)

*[Oral/μ Nasal/μ]$_{Wd}$: an oral mora incurs a violation if immediately pre-
ceding a nasal mora (i.e. vowel); domain = word

The effect of *[Oμ Nμ]$_{Wd}$ is to block harmony where its application
would result in an O-N vowel sequence; *Mid/Nas must outrank
*[Oμ Nμ]$_{Wd}$.

(28) MÒbà: nasal agreement between adjacent vowels

/egigũ/	*Mid/Nas	*[Oμ Nμ]$_{Wd}$	*[O C$_0$ N]$_{Wd}$	*High/Nas
☞ a. [eigũ]			*	*
b. [eĩgũ]		*!		**
c. [ẽĩgũ]	*!			**

Since the word-level harmony constraint and *[Oral/μ Nas/μ]$_{Wd}$ are in
direct conflict and *[Oral/μ Nas/μ]$_{Wd}$ wins, this means *[Oral/μ Nas/μ]$_{Wd}$
must outrank word-level harmony. Cases like [àídù̃] 'sweet thing' (*[àídù̃])
show that *[Oral/μ Nas/μ]$_{Wd}$ must also be ranked below *Low/Nas.

To summarize, both SY and MÒbà exhibit patterns where adjacent moras must agree in nasality. It is impossible for an oral vowel to either precede or follow a nasal vowel within the word. In SY, we find evidence for
the prohibition of nasal-oral sequences across word-boundaries; in MÒbà,
the prohibition on oral-nasal vowel sequences can be seen in cases of consonant deletion.[11] The prohibition against oral-nasal vowel sequences also
forms a subpart of the basic harmony pattern of MÒbà (see (5d)).

8   Sequential Prohibition

We adopt here Suzuki's (1998) proposal that constraints are subject to conditions on proximity and similarity. He proposes a proximity hierarchy: the

---

[11] These consonant-deletion cases are also seen in SY. The result is different, however, in that
the output exhibits agreement between both vowel quality and nasality, e.g. [egũgũ] ~ [eegũ]
'bone', [Òdúdú̃] ~ [ÒÒdú̃] 'KIND OF PLANT', [òkùkù̃] ~ [òòkù̃] 'darkness'. The SY pattern is
consistent with the predictions of *[Oμ Nμ]$_{Wd}$ but could independently be derived by postulat-
ing root node assimilation for such cases (Pulleyblank 1988, 2008).

closer two elements are to each other, the stronger their interaction.[12] Constraints subject to string adjacency (unmarked) are of the type at the left edge of the scale (*XX) while constraints holding over an unbounded string (marked) are of the right edge type (*X-∞-X), as presented in (29).

(29) $*XX \gg *X\text{-}C_0\text{-}X \gg *X\text{-}\mu\text{-}X \gg *X\text{-}\mu\mu\text{-}X \gg *X\text{-}\sigma\sigma\text{-}X \gg \dots \gg *X\text{-}\infty\text{-}X$

The full set of constraints discussed is summarized in (30), along with a reference to its location in the text and its relevance for SY and/or Mòbà.

(30) Assimilatory constraints on nasality in Standard Yorùbá and Mòbà

*[Oral/son Nas/son]$_\sigma$	(3a)	SY (& Mòbà)
*[Nas/son Oral/son]$_\sigma$	(3b)	SY & Mòbà
*[Oral/son C_0 Nas/son]$_{Wd}$	(8)	Mòbà
*[Nas/son C_0 Oral/son]$_{Morpheme}$	(14)	SY & Mòbà
*[Nas/μ Oral/μ]$_{Phrase}$	(26)	SY
*[Oral/μ Nasal/μ]$_{Wd}$	(27)	(SY &) Mòbà

The constraints observed in SY and Mòbà exhibit properties that are largely unsurprising. There is a tendency for constraints to hold of segments that are local, similar to each other, and in small domains (Yip 1989, Padgett 1991, Mohanan 1993, Pierrehumbert 1993, Archangeli & Pulleyblank 1994, 2002, Frisch 1997, Suzuki 1998, Hansson 2001, Pulleyblank 2002, 2006, Rose & Walker 2004). In SY, the only constraint not holding of strictly string-adjacent segments is the constraint holding of the smallest morphological domain, the morpheme. Mòbà shows evidence of the local constraints of SY, but has apparently innovated by allowing one constraint to apply over strings of segments—i.e. word-domain harmony. All constraints governing harmony apply to segments in the sonorant class, sometimes with the added requirement that the segments involved be moraic.

The proposal here differs in an important way from Rose & Walker (2004). Rose & Walker note the importance of similarity in long-distance harmony, building it into their formal account through the use of similarity-driven constraints on segment-to-segment correspondence. For local assimilation, they suggest that similarity is not a factor. They postulate two different types of constraints, one (similarity-based) to govern nonlocal assimilation and a second (not similarity-based) to govern local assimilation. This distinction between local and nonlocal types does not appear consistent with the nasality patterns of Mòbà, where the distinction between local and nonlocal constraints appears to be one of quantity, not quality. The same factors

---

[12] Nothing hinges on this scale being stipulated within the phonology. If it is possible to derive this scale, for example from phonetic facts, this would be completely consistent with the proposed analysis. Thanks to Jennifer Cole for discussion.

seem to be at play—similarity based on [sonorant] and moraic status—with the difference being that the local constraints require string adjacency while the nonlocal constraint of Mọ̀bà allows an intervening consonant. Whatever the precise mechanism for harmony, the patterns of Yorùbá suggest that it should be the same for both local and nonlocal effects.

9 Conclusion

This paper examined parallel processes of nasal harmony in Standard Yorùbá and Mọ̀bà. In the previously described pattern of Standard Yorùbá, sonorant segments agree for nasality within the syllable, and (sonorant) moras agree for nasality when adjacent to each other. Mọ̀bà exhibits these patterns, but extends the harmonic effects in one significant respect. Just as adjacent segments are required to agree in nasality in both dialects, in Mọ̀bà even vowels separated by a consonant exhibit harmony. Building an account of harmony based on sequential cooccurrence conditions, we have argued that the Mọ̀bà grammar involves a simple extension of the same constraint type responsible for the local effects of the standard language.

References

Ajíbóyè, Ọ. 1991. *Àtúnyẹ̀wò fonọ́lọ́jì Mọ̀bà*. Ilorin, Nigeria: University of Ilọrin MA thesis.

Ajíbóyè, Ọ. 1997. *Ní* in Mọ̀bà. Paper presented at the 9th Niger-Congo Syntax Workshop and Conference, University of Ghana, Legon.

Ajíbóyè, Ọ. 1999. A comparative study of vowel assimilation in Mọ̀bà and Standard Yorùbá. *Alóre: Ilọrin Journal of the Humanities* 10(1): 25–47.

Archangeli, D. & D. Pulleyblank. 1994. *Grounded phonology.* Cambridge, MA: MIT Press.

Archangeli, D. & D. Pulleyblank. 2002. Kinande vowel harmony: Domains, grounded conditions, and one-sided alignment. *Phonology* 19: 139–188.

Awóbùlúyì, Ọ. 1990. On the N~L alternation in Yorùbá. Unpublished manuscript, University of Ilọrin, Nigeria.

Awóbùlúyì, Ọ. 1992. Aspects of contemporary Standard Yorùbá in dialectological perspective. In A. Iṣọla (ed.), *New findings in Yorùbá studies*, 3–79. Lagos: J. F. Odunjọ Memorial Lectures Organising Committee.

Awóbùlúyì, Ọ. & F. Oyebade. 1995. Denasalization in Yorùbá: A non-linear approach. In K. Owólabí (ed.), *Language in Nigeria: Essays in honour of Ayọ̀ Bámgbóṣé*, 205–215. Ibadan: Group Publishers.

Bamisile, O. 1986. *Àgbéyẹ̀wò fonọ́lọ́jì Yorùbá-Mọ̀bà*. Ilọrin, Nigeria: University of Ilọrin MA thesis.

Clements, G. N. & R. Şonaiya. 1990. Underlying feature representation in Yoruba. *Studies in the Linguistic Sciences* 20: 89–103.

Cohn, A. C. 1990. *Phonetic and phonological rules of nasalization* (UCLA Working Papers in Phonetics 76). Los Angeles: UCLA Department of Linguistics.

Cole, J. & C. W. Kisseberth. 1994. *An Optimal Domains theory of harmony* (Cognitive Science Technical Report UIUC-BI-CS-94-02). Urbana, IL: The Beckman Institute.

Frisch, S. 1997. *Similarity and frequency in phonology.* Evanston, IL: Northwestern University dissertation.

Gafos, D. 1999. *The articulatory basis of locality in phonology.* New York: Garland.

Hansson, G. 2001. *Theoretical and typological issues in consonant harmony.* Berkeley: University of California dissertation.

Hansson, G. 2007. Blocking effects in agreement by correspondence. *Linguistic Inquiry* 38: 395–409.

Hyman, L. M. 1972. Nasals and nasalization in Kwa. *Studies in African Linguistics* 3: 167–205.

Itô, J., A. Mester & J. Padgett. 1995. Licensing and redundancy: Underspecification in Optimality Theory. *Linguistic Inquiry* 26: 571–613.

Keating, P. A. 1988. Underspecification in phonetics. *Phonology* 5: 275–292.

Kim, E.-S. & D. Pulleyblank. 2009. Glottalization and lenition in Nuu-chah-nulth. *Linguistic Inquiry* 40: 567–617.

Lombardi, L. 2001. Why place and voice are different: Constraint-specific alternations in Optimality Theory. In L. Lombardi (ed.), *Segmental phonology in Optimality Theory: Constraints and representations*, 12–45. Cambridge: Cambridge University Press.

Mohanan, K. P. 1993. Fields of attraction in phonology. In J. Goldsmith (ed.), *The last phonological rule: Reflections on constraints and derivations*, 61–116. Chicago: University of Chicago Press.

Ní Chiosáin, M. & J. Padgett. 2001. Markedness, segment realization, and locality in spreading. In L. Lombardi (ed.), *Segmental phonology in Optimality Theory: Constraints and representations*, 118–156. Cambridge: Cambridge University Press.

Ọla, Ọ. 1995. *Optimality in Benue-Congo prosodic phonology and morphology.* Vancouver, BC: University of British Columbia dissertation.

Orie, Ọ. Ọ. & D. Pulleyblank. 2002. Yoruba vowel elision: Minimality effects. *Natural Language & Linguistic Theory* 20: 101–156.

Owólabí, K. 1989. *Ìjìnlẹ̀ ìtúpalẹ̀ èdè Yorùbá (1): Fónẹ́tíìkì àti Fonólójì.* Ibadan, Nigeria: Onibonoje Press & Book Industries.

Oyebade, F. 1985. Oke-Akoko nasalization and denasalization and lexical phonology. *Journal of the Linguistic Association of Nigeria* 3: 13–21.

Padgett, J. 1991. *Stricture in feature geometry.* Amherst, MA: University of Massachusetts dissertation.

Perkins, J. 2005. *The RTR harmonic domain in two dialects of Yorùbá.* Vancouver, BC: University of British Columbia MA thesis.

Pierrehumbert, J. B. 1993. Dissimilarity in the Arabic verbal roots. In A. J. Schafer (ed.), *Proceedings of the North East Linguistic Society 23*, 367–381. Amherst, MA: GLSA, University of Massachusetts.

Piggott, G. 2003. Theoretical implications of segment neutrality in nasal harmony. *Phonology* 20: 375–424.

Prince, A. & P. Smolensky. 2004. *Optimality Theory: Constraint interaction in generative grammar.* Malden, MA: Blackwell.

Pulleyblank, D. 1988. Vocalic underspecification in Yoruba. *Linguistic Inquiry* 19: 233–270.

Pulleyblank, D. 1996. Neutral vowels in Optimality Theory: A comparison of Yoruba and Wolof. *Canadian Journal of Linguistics* 41: 295–347.

Pulleyblank, D. 2002. Harmony drivers: No disagreement allowed. In J. Larson & M. Paster (eds.), *Proceedings of the twenty-eighth annual meeting of the Berkeley Linguistics Society: General session and parasession on field linguistics*, 249–267. Berkeley: Berkeley Linguistics Society.

Pulleyblank, D. 2006. Mending your Ps & Qs. In J. Bunting, S. Desai, R. Peachey, C. Straughn & Z. Tomková (eds.), *Proceedings of the Chicago Linguistic Society 42-1: Main session*, 267–286. Chicago: Chicago Linguistic Society.

Pulleyblank, D. 2008. Yoruba vowel patterns: Asymmetries through phonological competition. In A. S. Bobda (ed.), *Explorations into language use in Africa*, 125–157. Frankfurt am Main: Peter Lang.

Rose, S. & R. Walker. 2004. A typology of consonant agreement as correspondence. *Language* 80: 475–531.

Ruhlen, M. 1975. Patterning of nasal vowels. In C. Ferguson, L. Hyman & J. Ohala (eds.), *Nasálfest: Papers from a symposium on nasals and nasalization*, 333–353. Stanford: Department of Linguistics, Stanford University.

Smolensky, P. 1993. Harmony, markedness, and phonological activity. Paper presented at Rutgers Optimality Workshop 1, Rutgers University.

Suzuki, K. 1998. *A typological investigation of dissimilation.* Tucson, AZ: University of Arizona dissertation.

Williamson, K. 1973. More on nasals and nasalization in Kwa. *Studies in African Linguistics* 4: 115–138.

Yip, M. 1989. Feature geometry and co-occurrence restrictions. *Phonology* 6: 349–374.

Zhang, J. 2000. Non-contrastive features and categorical patterning in Chinese diminutive affixation: MAX[F] or IDENT[F]? *Phonology* 17: 427–478.

3

Abstractness and Shingazidja Tonology: Evidence from French Loanwords

FARIDA CASSIMJEE & CHARLES W. KISSEBERTH

1 Introduction

This paper seeks to pay homage to Larry Hyman by returning to two themes that have been critical to the phonological enterprise ever since the rise of "generative" phonology: the validity of "abstract" representations in phonology (whatever "abstract" may be taken to actually mean) and the role of external evidence (e.g. borrowing) in motivating phonological analyses. These are, of course, themes that Larry pursued in his earliest publications (Hyman 1970a, 1970b), but they are themes of such critical importance that they can never be long out of view. The present paper, which looks at how French borrowings in Shingazidja help motivate an abstract (in anyone's definition of this word) analysis of the Shingazidja tone system, is intended as a contribution to these perennial themes. Due to space limitations, we will assume the reader's (general) familiarity with these themes and will not review the literature, preferring to concentrate on a presentation of the relevant material from Shingazidja.

2 Shingazidja Prosody

Shingazidja, a Bantu language spoken on Ngazidja (Grand Comore island), is closely related to Swahili, but differs from Swahili significantly at the prosodic level. In addition to Shingazidja, there are three other well-known dialects spoken in the Comoros Islands (Shindzwani, Shimwali and

Revealing structure.
Eugene Buckley, Thera Crane & Jeff Good (eds.).

Shimaore). In the recent literature on the prosody of the Comorien dialects, there have been both metrical and tonal analyses. Metrical analyses can be found in Philippson (1988) and Cassimjee & Kisseberth (1989, 1992); tonal analyses can be found in Cassimjee & Kisseberth (1998, 2010) and Patin (2007a, 2007b). In this paper, we will assume a tonal analysis of Shingazidja rather than a metrical one. However, this choice is in no way crucial to the point of the paper: one can make the same argument whether one is speaking about underlying tones or about some form of the lexical marking of metrical feet. Both analyses involve "marking" particular moras in a word: in a tonal analysis, these marked vowels are said to bear an underlying H tone; in a metrical analysis, these marked vowels are said to initiate an unbounded foot. What makes Shingazidja prosody abstract is that, in a phonological phrase there may be any number of marked vowels, but (counting from left to right) only the odd-numbered marked vowels find any physical manifestation of their marking (in the form of a raised pitch), and where the marking is manifested depends on the location of a following even-numbered marked vowel (specifically, the high pitch is heard on the mora preceding the even-numbered marked vowel). A more abstract analysis can hardly be imagined: a marked vowel does not necessarily get realized as high pitch, and when high pitch is manifested, it is not necessarily on a marked vowel!

If one surveys most of the literature on abstractness, one finds that it is primarily word-level phonology that is at issue. This is an important observation since when one is dealing with word-level phonology, one has the option of denying that the alternations observed are rule-governed, claiming that they are rather incorporated (somehow) as part of the mental lexicon. If, however, the alternations observed are governed by the location of the word in a sentence, the "listing" option is no longer available (there is no "lexicon" of sentences), and a rule-based analysis is required. What makes Shingazidja of particular interest in terms of the abstractness issue is that the tonal shape of a word is dependent both on its underlying representation and on its position in the sentence.

We will begin our discussion of Shingazidja prosody with nouns. Like many other Bantu languages, the morphological structure of a noun is fairly simple, consisting of a noun class prefix and a stem (in the examples below, we separate these two elements with a hyphen). Verb stems in Shingazidja exhibit a "reduced" ("restricted") tone system, but noun stems retain a considerable degree of tonal complexity. This complexity will be reviewed in some detail here.

We focus on noun stems that have the structure -(C)VCV or -(C)VCVCV. Stems with these structures represent the overwhelming majority of nouns. Restricting ourselves to the isolation form of the noun, most nouns of these structures have a H tone on either the final mora of the stem or the penult (though, in fact, there are two different phonetic shapes to penult H tones when they are at the end of an intonational phrase). There are also some trimoraic stems which have a H tone on the antepenult syllable. The penult syllable is somewhat lengthened when a word is pronounced in isolation (more generally, when it stands at the end of an intonational phrase). We do not indicate this lengthening in our transcriptions.

The first type of noun that we will discuss has a H tone on the final vowel. Examples are provided in (1).[1] In order to illustrate that the tone patterns observed in nouns can be found in other word classes, we add a few examples from outside the set of nouns, with bracketed numbers indicating noun class agreement. It should be emphasized that the pronunciation of these words may be rather flat in pitch: the final vowel is not always clearly raised in comparison to the preceding syllables.

(1) *nyumbá* 'house'   *godoró* 'mattress'   *m.-leví* 'drunkard'
     kapwá 'armpit'   *sutrú* 'spoon'   *mezá* 'table'
     hi-rí 'chair'   *n-kohó* 'dove'   *u-bú* 'porridge'
     u-só 'face'   *gadá* 'hole'   *i-tsawazí* 'kind of plate'
     teré 'drop'   *nangá* 'anchor'   *m.-tsuzí* kind of tree'
     m.-tsaná 'day'   *m-beré* 'finger ring' *m.-furiyapá* 'kind of tree'

     tsi-lindí 'I waited' *i-radjí* 'large [7]'   *tsi-hulú* 'I bought'
     djuú 'on'   *m-bilí* 'two [9/10]'   *tsi-hundrú* 'I found'
     tsi-tsahá 'I found' *tsi-lipví* 'I paid'

We indicate the final H tone in these words with an acute mark over the vowel. Notice that we also underline this vowel to indicate that the vowel in question is specified with a H tone in the underlying representation. In other words, we are suggesting that these words have an underlying H tone on the final vowel and this H tone is heard on the final vowel when the word is used in isolation. There is, of course, nothing abstract about such an analysis. We will label the words in (1) as F(inal)-words.

A second type of noun has, in its isolation pronunciation, a H tone on the (lengthened) penult syllable. Phonetically this H tone has a rising character to it, but given that this phonetic detail is predictable, we transcribe these words with an acute mark over the penult vowel. We also underline this vowel, thereby suggesting that this vowel is underlyingly specified as H. Since the H tone is in fact manifested on this very vowel, there is little

---

[1] In this paper, we indicate that a nasal is syllabic by putting a period after the nasal.

that is abstract about this analysis either. We label the words in (2) as P(enult)-words.

(2) *sh-onónde* 'knife'   *kalámu* 'pen'   *góra* 'hat'
     báo 'board'   *masikíni* 'poor person' *páha* 'cat'
     búku 'book'   *i-tránda* 'bed'   *kengéle* 'bell'
     falasíka 'bottle'   *almási* 'diamond'   *sabúni* 'soap'
     djuníya 'sack'   *i-fúba* 'chest'   *gungúno* 'knee'
     shishíyo 'ear'   *tího* 'roof'   *m.-sihíri* 'mosque'
     dzíwa 'lake'   *m.-dráya* 'quarter (city)'

     -kúu/-húu 'big'   *tsi-tsambúwa* 'I cleaned' *-ráru* 'three'
     tsi-wáha 'I built'   *háhe* 'his, hers, its'

Although there are additional types to be considered, we can begin to establish the core principles that govern Shingazidja tone by considering just F-words and P-words alone. It will be convenient, however, to introduce an additional aspect of nominal structure in Shingazidja at this time. A noun is rendered definite by means of a proclitic that precedes the noun. The shape of the definite proclitic is determined by the noun class to which the noun belongs. In (3) we provide a few representative examples.

(3) *ye m.-tshóro* 'the fugitive'   *wo wa-tshóro* 'the fugitives'
     le gári 'the car'   *ye ma-gári* 'the cars'
     she i-tambáa 'the cloth'   *ye zi-tambáa* 'the cloths'

Note that the definite proclitic has no tonal effect on an F-noun or P-noun following it. However, if the definite proclitic is preceded by the so-called "stabilizer" (which is also used to create clefts), it is quickly apparent that there is now a tonal effect. We provide only a few examples since many more will appear below.[2]

(4) *nd' e ḿ.-tshoro* '(it is) the fugitive' *ndo o wá-tshoro* 'the fugitives'
     nde lé gari '(it is) the car'   *nde e má-gari* 'the cars'
     nde she i-támbaa '(it is) the cloth'   *nde e zi-támbaa* 'the cloths'

It appears to be the case that when the definite proclitic is embedded in the stabilized construction, the proclitic bears an underlying H tone. The reason we do not consider the stabilizer element itself to have an underlying H tone derives from the fact that there are a few cases where it is *not* fol-

---

[2] Note that the proclitics *ye* and *wo* lack their onglide when preceded by a vowel. Also, the stabilizer is *nda/nde/ndo* depending on the proclitic. Finally, although the combination of stabilizer and proclitic *(y)e* or *(w)e* yields a sequence of two vowels in most cases, this sequence is contracted to a single mora when the noun class prefix is a syllabic nasal or a vowel.

lowed by a definite proclitic. In those cases, it has no effect on the following word (for example, *nda mí* '(it is) me'). In the following discussion, we will include this H-toned definite proclitic as an example of an F-word.

Having identified two prosodic types of nouns (F-words and P-words) and having seen that there are words of classes other than nouns that fall into these two types, we will begin to look at Shingazidja phrasal tonology. First of all, consider two-word sequences where both words are of the F type.

(5) *ma-soha ma-îli* 'two axes' *ma-bungu ma-îli* 'two bugs'
     biro m-bîli 'two offices, closets' *mi-ri mi-îli* 'two trees'
     mi-furiyapa mi-îli 'two of sp. of tree' *zi-tsawazi zi-îli* 'two plates'
     i-tsawazi i-râdji 'a large plate' *nde e nyûmba* 'the house'

What these data demonstrate is that in expressions consisting of two words, each of which have an underlying final H tone, neither of these vowels are realized with a raised pitch! There is just one raised pitch, and it is heard on the vowel in front of the second of the two final Hs. However, the raised pitch that appears on the (lengthened) penult vowel in these words is phonetically distinct from the rising pitch heard on P-words in isolation. We indicate this phonetic contrast by writing the symbol ^ above the penult vowel in these phrases. Descriptions of this pitch contrast have varied among different authors. Our impression from our consultant was that there is no rise in pitch on this syllable, but rather a raised pitch that is sustained through a large portion of the syllable but starts to descend before the onset of the next syllable. The rising pitch on a P-word in isolation does not descend at all on the penult syllable.

Let us now turn to a two-word sequence where an F-word is followed by a P-word.

(6) *ma-bungu má-raru* 'three bugs' *ye nyumba y-á hahe* 'his house'
     le kapwa l-á hahe 'his armpit' *nyumbá n-draru* 'three houses'
     nde e hayáwani 'the animal' *nde e kálamu* '(it is) the pen'

These data reveal the same generalization: only one H tone is realized, and it appears on the mora before the second underlying H tone (i.e. on the antepenult mora). Note that the mora that is realized with a raised pitch may in fact be the very mora that bears the first underlying H tone (e.g. *tsi-hundrú djembe* 'I found a hoe'), but if there is a mora that the first H tone can shift to, it does (e.g. *tsi-hundru shónonde* 'I found a knife').

Next, consider cases where a P-word is followed by an F-word.

(7) *i-trạnda djûu*   'on a bed'   *berạmu djûu*   'on a flag'
     tịho djûu   'on a roof'   *dzịwa djûu*   'on a lake'
     m-sihịri djûu   'on a mosque'   *sufurịya djûu*   'on a pan'
     tsi-wạha nyûmbạ   'I built a house'   *hirịzi m-bîlị*   'two amulets'

Again, these data reveal the same generalization: only one H tone is realized. This time, the H tone is realized on the penult vowel of the expression, that is, on the vowel preceding the final vowel of the F-word. This lengthened penult vowel has the same shape as in (5).

Finally, consider where a P-word is followed by a P-word.

(8) *z-ịba zí-rạru*   'three bones'   *sindạnú n-drạru* 'three needles'
     ma-katịli má-rạru   'three murderers'   *i-trạnda í-tịti* 'a small bed'
     ma-djunịya má-rạru   'three sacks'   *shạti í-tịti*   'a small shirt'
     w-ạna wá-tịti   'small children'   *bundụki n-tịnti* 'a small gun'
     tsi-komẹyá djẹmbe   'I touched a hoe'   *tsi-wọnó pạha*   'I saw a cat'

This time, the H tone is heard on the antepenult vowel in the phrase—that is, on the mora in front of the penult H in the P-word at the end.

We have provided a detailed analysis of these data in terms of Optimal Domains Theory (see Cassimjee & Kisseberth 1998). We provide a brief (partially modified) account below simply to give the reader a way to think about these complex data. Each underlying H tone specification in the representation of a phrase triggers the formation of what we refer to as a High Tone Domain (HTD). This principle is undominated. The mora bearing the H-tone specification (call this the "sponsor" of the H tone) stands at the left edge of the HTD. This principle is undominated. A HTD always extends as far as possible (call this principle Maximality). What does "as far as possible" mean? First of all, it means that if a domain is followed by another domain, the first HTD must stop at the mora in front of the next domain. Call this the No Overlapping principle. Second, the final mora in the intonational phrase (IP) is barred from being included in the domain. Call this the Nonfinality principle. (This paper does not look at phonological phrases that are not at the end of an IP, but it should be pointed out that there is no nonfinality effect at the end of such phrases—a HTD expands to include the final vowel; e.g. *mw-ána* is pronounced *mw-aná* in a sentence such as *mw-aná / ha-lindị* 'the child waited', where the slash separates two phonological phrases. It should be observed, however, that if the final mora of the intonational phrase sponsors a H tone, this mora must be in a HTD (since the principle that requires each H-sponsor to be in a domain dominates Nonfinality). Also note that Maximality cannot force a domain to expand leftwards due to the undominated principle that the sponsor is at the left edge of the HTD.

Give the preceding account of the organization of representations into domains, all that remains is to account for the pronunciation of H tone in these domains. There are two basic descriptive generalizations. First, a HTD manifests its H only on the last mora of the domain. We will refer to this phenomenon as High Tone Shift, though this process-based terminology does not mesh well with our actual constraint-based analysis in Cassimjee & Kisseberth (1998). The second generalization is that a HTD does not realize a H if it is preceded by a HTD. We call this Meeussen's Rule, a term widely used in the Bantu tonal literature (see Goldsmith 1984). We should note that Meeussen's Rule works in an alternating fashion, left-to-right in the phonological phrase. The Optimality-Theoretic account of this alternating pattern is beyond the scope of this paper.

Let us briefly illustrate how this analysis works. An F-word like *mezá* has the structure *me(zá)*, where a domain is enclosed in parentheses. The syllable *za* is specifed with a H tone underlyingly and initiates a domain. The H tone in the domain is realized on *za* since it is the last mora in the domain (in fact, the only mora in the domain). Nonfinality is violated since a mora specified as H-toned in the underlying representation must always initiate a domain. A P-word like *sh-onónde* has the structure *sh-o(nó)nde*. Here the mora *no* sponsors a H tone and initiates a HTD. The domain cannot include the final mora when the word is IP-final, due to Nonfinality. The last mora in the domain is pronounced with a H tone, but again, in this example, the last mora is in fact the only mora. Next take an example like *meza djúu*. This phrase has the structure *me(za djú)(u)*. In this example, both *za* and *u* initiate domains. The first domain expands due to Maximality, but cannot expand past *u*, due to No Overlapping. No H tone is realized in the second domain due to Meeussen's Rule. The H tone in the first domain is heard on *dju* due to High Tone Shift. Only one further point needs to be made: the H tone on *dju* in this example is distinct from the H tone on *no* in *sh-onónde*. We regard this as the consequence of phonetic implementation. A H tone on a lengthened penult vowel has the shape indicated by the symbol ˆ just in the event it precedes a toneless domain. In *sh-onónde*, the lengthened penult syllable is not followed by a toneless domain and thus is phonetically realized with a rising tone. This analysis assumes, of course, that domain structure is visible in the phonetic implementation component of the grammar.

Up until this point we have discussed only words that have either a final H or a penult H underlyingly. We will forego here any discussion of the issue whether there are toneless nouns in Shingazidja, since this is not a straightforward matter and does not bear on the central concerns of this paper. There *are* toneless adjectives and demonstratives, and it will be useful to look at phrases consisting of an F-word or a P-word when one of these toneless words follows, as in (9) and (10).

(9) F-word followed by a toneless word

ye ma-sutru̱ yánu	'these spoons'	*bungu̱ dzíma*	'one bug'
djwayi̱ dj-ángu	'soft egg'	*ma-djwayi̱ m-ángu*	'soft eggs'
m.-ri̱ mw-ángu	'light tree'	*mi-ri̱ m-ángu*	'light trees'
i-tsawazi̱ sh-éma	'a nice wooden plate'		

(10) P-word followed by a toneless word

ko̱li ny-ángu	'light package'	*mw-a̱na mw-ángu*	'light child'
w-a̱na w-ángu	'light children'	*u-pa̱nga mw-ángu*	'light sword'
ye si̱mba yínu	'this lion'	*ze si̱mba zínu*	'these lions'

What we see from these data is that the initial H tone in these phrases shifts to the penult vowel of the toneless word (in all cases, we are assuming that the phrase in question is IP-final). We are dealing here with structures like *ma-djwa(yi̱ m-á)ngu* and *u-(pa̱nga mw-á)ngu*. There is just one H-toned vowel in these representations, and it initiates a HTD. Maximality requires this domain to expand as far right as possible. Nonfinality prevents the domain from going further than the penult syllable when the phrase is at the end of an intonational phrase. High Tone Shift guarantees that only the final mora in the domain is pronounced with a H tone.

But now consider the case where the toneless word is preceded by two underlying H tones.

(11)   *nde lé̱ ga̱ri dzima*   '(it is) the one car'
      nde e̱ hírizi n-dzima   '(it is) the one amulet'
      nde e̱ m-bére̱ n-dzima '(it is) the one ring'

What these data show is that the first underlying H tone is realized on the mora in front of the second sponsor; the second H tone is not realized at all, and the toneless word is pronounced without any H tone. The structure involved here is shown in *nde (lé̱) (ga̱ri dzi)ma*. Note that even though the second domain initiated by *ga̱* expands, due to Maximality, to include the first syllable of the toneless word, there is no overt evidence of this since Meeussen's Rule prevents this domain from realizing its H tone.

Let us now return to the main point of this paper. There is no doubt that the analysis up to this point is abstract, in that the relationship between the surface form of the phrases and the underlying form is strikingly indirect. But it is also the case that when looked at from a different perspective, the analysis is not abstract at all. Specifically, the underlying representation of every word so far considered (setting aside the toneless adjectives and demonstratives, which in isolation realize a H tone on their penult vowel) is directly manifested on the surface when the word is pronounced in isolation. The underlying representation can be determined in a totally transparent fashion from the surface form of the word in isolation. It is only in joining words together in phrases that the determination of the pronunciation becomes opaque.

The underlying representation of words is not, however, as transparent as it has seemed up to this point. There are two more types of noun stems that we need to discuss. Look at the examples in (12).

(12) *m-hûngu* 'eel'   *n-kûde* 'beans'   *n-drôvi* 'banana(s)'
      i-kômbe 'cup'   *u-shâshi* 'scarcity' *u-nkôbe* 'spoon'
      u-hâdju 'tamarind'   *n-drôvi* 'banana'   *hidâya* 'gift'
      kapûka 'tin can'   *salûva* 'kind of garment worn by women'

      -êndji 'many'   *tsi-dûngu* 'I followed' *hângu* 'my'

These words are pronounced with a raised pitch on the penult, but this raised pitch is different in shape from the raised pitch on the penult of a P-type word. On the other hand, it is exactly the same as the raised pitch observed in (5) and (7) above, where an odd-numbered H tone shifted to the mora in front of a final H. As we will see below, the nouns in (12) are best treated as having two underlying H tones, one on the penult and one on the final vowel. We will refer to these as P+F-words.

There is another type of noun with a distinctive tone pattern—namely, an antepenult H tone. This is, of course, the same pattern that we observed when a word with a final H tone preceded a word with a penult H tone.

(13) *pútshari* 'knife type'   *báfuta* 'cloth type' *kúdume* 'rooster'
      dódoke 'sp. vegetable' *búdume* 'male goat'   *mákswada* 'aim'
      íliki 'spice type'   *bángili* 'bracelet'   *m.-fímatso* 'blind person'

      rí-piha 'we cooked'   *rí-lala* 'we slept'

We will see immediately below that these words must have two underlying H tones as well, one on the antepenult vowel and another on the penult. We will refer to these as A+P-words.

Let us now detail the evidence that P+F-nouns and A+P-nouns have an underlying representation where there are two vowels specified with a H tone. The evidence is straightforward. It involves showing that these words do not behave like either F-words or P-words, and that the way they *do* behave can be accounted for only by assuming two underlying H tones.

Let us take P+F-words first. The pronunciation of P+F-words when preceded by a H-toned word is shown in (14).

(14) *nde e hídayá* 'the gift'   *nde e bákwerá* 'the cane'
      nde le sáluvá 'the garment'   *nde le kápuká* the tin can'
      nde é n-droví 'the banana'

      tsi-wono mí-hungá 'I saw eels'   *tsi-li ú-hadjú* 'I ate a tamarind'
      tsi-hulu kápuká   'I bought a tin can'

What these examples show is that there are *two* surface H tones—one located on the antepenult mora, and the other located on the final mora. Obviously these pronunciations are entirely different from phrases where an F-word or a P-word is preceded by a H-toned word. In those cases, one hears only a single H tone, located on the mora preceding the location of the second underlying H tone. The fact that a H tone is heard on the last vowel of a word such as *hidaya* when preceded by a H-toned word clearly indicates that its last vowel is H-toned, even though in the isolation form *hidâya*, no H tone is heard on the last vowel. The fact that the first H tone in the phrase shifts to the mora in front of *da* indicates clearly that *da* must initiate a HTD, causing Maximality to block the first domain from expanding onto or past it.

The pronunciation of P+F-words before another word is shown in (15).

(15) *she i-kómbe shila* 'that cup'   *n-droví n-dzima* 'one banana'
      n-droví m-bili   'two bananas'   *ze n-káde zinu*   'these pages'
      kapúka l-a m-ádji 'a can of water'

The fact that the H tone associated with the penult vowel of these words does not shift can only be explained by there being a H tone on the final vowel; given such a H tone, the No Overlapping principle trumps Maximality and prevents shift. Since there are two underlying H tones in these words, Meeussen's Rule requires that the domain triggered by the second H tone be toneless. If there is a third H tone in the next word, that H tone will be realized. Thus the structure of 'two bananas' is *(n-dró)(vi m-bi)(lí)* while the structure of 'one banana' is *(n-dró)(vi n-dzi)ma*.

The pronunciation of A+P-words after H-toned elements is seen in (16).

(16) *nde é makswáda* 'the aim'   *nde é ilíki* 'the spice'
      tsi-hulú putshári 'I bought a knife'   *há putshári* 'with a knife'

From these examples we can see that the H tone on the antepenult syllable is no longer pronounced, an obvious effect of Meeussen's Rule. The first H tone in the phrase is realized on the syllable preceding the antepenult, an obvious effect of No Overlapping. But critically, we do find that there is another H tone, which in these examples surfaces on the penult vowel in the phrase. This H tone can only be explained by assuming that there is a *second* H tone in the underlying representation of these words, a H tone located on the penult.

The pronunciation of an A+P-word before another word is seen in (17).

(17) *ma-pútsh ̱a ̱ri ma-rá ̱ru*   'three knives'
      le kú ̱du ̱me linu   'this rooster'
      ma-pútsh ̱a ̱ri ma-yil ̱i   'two knives'

These data show that the H tone on the antepenult of A+P-words remains when another word follows. This is explicable of course by assuming that there is a H tone on both the antepenult and the penult: No Overlapping explains why the first H tone cannot shift. If the next word is toneless, no H tone is heard on it due to the effect of Meeussen's Rule: the structure of 'this rooster' is *le (kú ̱)(du ̱me li ̱)nu*. If the next word has a H tone in its structure, this H tone is heard, since it is an odd-numbered H tone, and Meeussen's Rule only deletes the even-numbered H tones. Thus the structure of 'two knives' is *ma-(pú ̱)(tsh ̱a ̱ri ma-yi)(li ̱)*.

So far we have restricted ourselves to two-word sequences (containing two or three underlying H tones). As indicated above, the tone principles of Shingazidja apply to phonological phrases (and the extent of these phrases must ultimately be determined, but that is not a topic we can go into here), and it turns out that phrases may consist of several words and thus there may be several underlying H tones. The account that we have already given accounts for the tone patterns observed in these phrases, except that it must be stressed that Meeussen's Rule affects *every* even-numbered High Tone Domain in a phrase and never affects an odd-numbered High Tone Domain. Also, we must remind the reader that due to Maximality, all High Tone Domains in a phonological phrase are adjacent to one another.

(18) a. A phrase with three underlying H tones
          ha-wo ̱no wa-lévi ̱ wa-(y)il ̱i   'he saw three drunkards'
          ye meza ̱ y-á hangú   'my table'
          tsi-wo ̱no ḿ.-hu ̱nga m.-dzíma   'I saw one eel'

      b. A phrase with four underlying H tones
          le kuvét ̱i l-a hângu   'my basin'
          wo u-nkó ̱be ̱ w-a hângu   'my spoon'
          tsi-wo ̱no ma-soróda ̱ m-êndji ̱   'I saw many soldiers'

      c. A phrase with five underlying H tones
          ye meza ̱ y-á hangu y-á sa ̱yá   'my other table'
          ze pútsh ̱a ̱ri m-bili ̱ z-á h-a ̱ngú   'my two knives'
          tsi-ni ̱ka dukúte ̱ra ̱ má-pe ̱sá   'I gave a doctor money'

    d.   A phrase with six underlying H tones

       ye ma-pútsha̱ri m-éndji̱ y-a há̱ngu̱   'my many knives'

       le kuvé̱ti̱ e mw-a̱na yá-ni̱ka dukuté̱ra̱ 'the basin that the child
                                                              gave a doctor'

The pronunciations above assume that the phrases in question are at the end of an intonational phrase.

These data illustrate all the primary observations that we have made about Shingazidja tone. When the last (underlying) H tone in these phrases is odd-numbered, it is realized on the surface on the final vowel (if that is where it is located in underlying structure), otherwise on the penult (Nonfinality prevents the H tone from shifting to the final vowel). Other odd-numbered H tones are realized on the mora preceding an even-numbered H tone. Even-numbered H tones are not realized.

With this much discussion of the Shingazidja tonal system, we can turn to the adaptation of French words into Shingazidja speech.

3   French Loanwords and Shingazija Tonology

In the course of our work on Shingazidja, we observed the presence of French loanwords in the speech of our consultants. Given the complex prosodic pattern that Shingazidja exhibits, the question naturally arises: how do French words, when adapted to Shingazidja, behave from a prosodic point of view? Specifically, how are they pronounced in isolation and how do they respond to being located in Shingazidja sentences?

Time did not permit us to attempt to identify which French words had actually been "institutionalized" (incorporated into the lexicon of monolingual speakers as well as bilingual speakers); since our primary consultant was bilingual in French and Shingazidja, we simply asked him to choose a significant number of French words and illustrate how he would pronounce these words when speaking Shingazidja. In particular, we asked him to pronounce the word in isolation, and (if the word was a noun) to pronounce it in the "stabilized" construction illustrated above. Our data is based entirely on our consultant's tape-recording of the words he selected. Some of the words are undoubtedly used generally in Shingazidja, but others perhaps represent on-the-fly adaptations. On occasion our consultant noted alternative pronunciations of an item.

A few remarks about the segmental phonology are in order before we turn to the prosody. Since all words in Shingazidja end in a vowel, every French word that ends in a consonant adds a final vowel when used in Shingazdija.

(19) **tôle**   [tol]   *tóli*   'sheet iron'
    stade   [stad]   *stádi*   'stadium'
    trésor   [trezɔr]   *trezóri*   'treasury department'

Of course, if the French word already ends in a vowel, that vowel is simply retained.

(20) **parapet**   [parapɛ]   *parapé*   'parapet'
    échafaud   [eʃafo]   *shafó*   'platform'
    tricot   [triko]   *tirikó*   'sweater'

Shingazidja does not permit coda consonants, and syllable-initial consonant clusters are restricted to consonant-glide sequences. As a consequence, the frequent consonant clusters found in French are contrary to the Shingazidja phonological pattern. As French loan words become institutionalized and fully integrated into the Shingazidja phonological pattern, it is very likely that all French consonant sequences would (eventually) be separated by vowels. But in the data on nonce borrowing from our consultant, there is variability in the treatment of consonant clusters. Sometimes clusters are allowed to remain, as seen in (21).

(21) a. Initial consonant cluster
         station   [stasjɔ̃]   *stasyó*   'station'
         plombier   [plɔ̃bje]   *plombiyé*   'plumber'

    b. Medial consonant cluster
         casquette [kaskɛt]   *kaskêti*   'cap'
         permis   [pɛrmi]   *permí*   'permit'

    c. Final consonant cluster
         vinaigre [vinɛgr]   *vinégre*   'vinegar'
         film   [film]   *fílmu*   'film'

However, very often a vowel is introduced between two successive consonants, as in (22).

(22) a. Initial consonant cluster
         sport   [spɔr]   *sipóri*   'sport'
         profit   [prɔfi]   *purofí*   'profit'
         gramme   [gram]   *girámu*   'gram'

    b. Medial consonant cluster
         charbon [ʃarbɔ̃]   *sharibó* 'charcoal'
         carton   [kartɔ̃]   *karitó*   'box, carton'
         patron   [patrɔ̃]   *patiró*   'boss, manager'

c. Final consonant cluster

chambre	[ʃãbr]	*shámbu̱ru*	'room'
ministre	[ministr]	*miní̱sti̱ri*	'minister'
mètre	[mɛtr]	*mé̱te̱ra*	'meter'

French nasalized vowels are denasalized in Shingazidja, and the vowel quality adapted to the Shingazidja vowel system. If the nasalized vowel is preconsonantal in the French word, while the nasality is lost from the vowel, it surfaces as the nasal component of a prenasalized consonant. If the nasalized vowel is word-final, however, then there is no retention of nasality (since a nasal consonant would be unacceptable in word-final position).

(23) ***parfum***   [parfœ̃]   *parfé̱*   'perfume'
    cément   [semã]   *simá̱*   'cement'
    volant   [vɔlã]   *volá̱*   'steering wheel'

A number of French words are adapted by including the definite article as well.

(24) ***cloche***   [klɔʃ]   *lakiló̱shi*   'bell'
    glace   [glas]   *lagilá̱si*   'ice'
    montre   [mõtr]   *lamó̱nti̱re*   'watch'

The French consonant system does not present many difficulties. The sound [ʒ] is not a phoneme in Shingazidja, but our consultant regularly retained this sound (contrasting it with the Shingazidja affricate *dj* [dʒ]). We use the symbol *j* in our Shingazidja orthography for the sound [ʒ]; for example, the French ***plage*** [plaʒ] is *pulá̱ji* 'beach' in Shingazidja.

The French vowel system is reduced to the five vowels of Shingazidja: *i e u o a*. We did not observe any cases where these vowel adjustments were not made. A few examples of the adjustments that are made can be seen in (25) and in other examples throughout the paper.

(25) ***veilleuse***   [vɛjøz]   *veyé̱zi*   'night light'
    pneu   [pnø]   *piné̱*   'tire'
    valeur   [valœr]   *valê̱ra*   'value'

Let us turn our attention now to the issue of prosody. French words are often said to have stress on the final syllable of a word when it is used in isolation, though the sentence stress is another matter. As we shall see, Shingazidja adaptations of French words clearly indicate that Shingazdija speakers hear word-final stress in French.

When a French word ends in a vowel, the Shingazidja adaptation retains that vowel and categorizes the word as being an F-word. A variety of examples of this type are given in (26).

(26) **échafaud** [eʃafo] *shafǒ* 'platform'
    parapet [parapɛ] *parapé̱* 'parapet'
    cément [semã] *simá̱* 'cement'

When French adaptations of this sort are located in an environment where they are preceded by an underlying H-toned vowel, they modify their pronunciation just as any F-word would.

(27) *nde le̱ parâpe̱* 'the parapet'   *nde e̱ tâpi* 'the carpet'
    nde e̱ shâfo̱ 'the platform'   *nde e̱ stâsyo* 'the station'
    nde e̱ purôfi̱ 'the profit'   *nde e̱ patîro̱* 'the boss'
    nde e̱ sîma̱ 'the cement'   *meza̱ y-a sîma̱* 'a cement table'

A French word that ends in a consonant has stress on the vowel preceding this consonant. However, in Shingazidja a vowel must be added after this consonant. This inserted vowel, however, does not bear a H tone (generally). Rather, it is the preceding vowel that is H-toned (in other words, the vowel that is stressed in French is H-toned in the Shingazidja adaptation). The resulting word thus falls into the P tonal category. Examples illustrating this pattern can be seen in (28).

(28) **cloche** [klɔʃ] *lakiló̱shi* 'bell'
    vote [vɔt] *vó̱ti* 'vote'
    vitre [vitr] *ví̱tri* 'windowpane'
    bocal [bɔkal] *boká̱li* 'druggist's bottle'

When words of this sort are preceded in a Shingazidja sentence by a H-toned element, then these words behave entirely analogous to native P-words in Shingazidja. Specifically, the first (underlying) H tone is heard on the vowel preceding the penult vowel.

(29) *nde e̱ lakílo̱shi* 'the bell'   *nde é̱ voti* 'the vote'
    nde é̱ vi̱tri 'the windowpane'   *nde e̱ vínegre* 'the vinegar'
    nde é̱ su̱pu 'the soup'   *nde é̱ stadi* 'the stadium'
    nde é̱ si̱nyi 'the sign'   *nde le̱ bóka̱li* 'the bottle'

The pitch on the (short) antepenult vowel is high, and the pitch falls in the course of the following (lengthened) penult syllable. The fall on the penult is a predictable aspect of pronunciation which we do not mark.

We can conclude from the preceding data that the Shingazidja speaker seeks to be faithful to the French word by assigning a H tone to the same vowel as bears stress in French. Of course, this faithfulness is with respect to the isolation pronunciation of the word. When placed in a sentential context, the underlying H tone is no longer (necessarily) realized on the vowel that is stressed in the corresponding French word. Rather, the general principles of Shingazidja determine whether the H tone that has been assigned to a vowel is realized and, if realized, where.

There is a complication, however, in this picture. Shingazidja words that have penult H tone in their isolation pronunciation are of two types: P-words (where the H tone has a rising quality) and P+F-words (where there is some dispute as to the phonetics, but which clearly start off with a higher pitch on the penult than do P-words). While this phonetic contrast is observable only on lengthened IP-penult vowels, its presence in this position raises the question of whether the stress on a consonant-final French word could be interpreted as similar to consonant-final words that are categorized as P+F-words rather than as P-words. The examples in (30) show that this is indeed possible.

(30) **la+colle** [kɔl] *lakôli* 'paste'
    cigarette [sigarɛt] *sigarêti* 'cigarette'
    cheval [ʃəval] *sheváli* or *shováli* 'horse'
    caramel [karamɛl] *karamêli* 'caramel'
    casserole [kasrɔl] *kasirôli* 'saucepan'

The question that we cannot answer at the present time is whether there is anything about the pronunciation of these French words that would lead the speaker of Shingazidja to equate them with P+F-words rather than P-words. It is certainly a matter that bears phonetic exploration.

When French adaptations of this sort are put into a sentence where there is a preceding H-toned element, we can see that in fact these words behave just like any other P+F-word.

(31) *nde e lákoli* 'the paste'   *nde e sigáreti* 'the cigarette'
    nde e shóvali 'the horse'   *nde e karámeli* 'the caramel'
    nde e kasíroli 'the saucepan' *nde e labíyerá* 'the beer'

There are also French words that are consonant-final that are put into the A+P category (characterized on the surface by an antepenult H tone in the isolation form of the word). Some of these words have no (obvious) explanation as to why their antepenult syllable should be treated as though it bears stress in French.

(32) **salade** [salad] *sáladi* 'salad'
    visite [vizit] *víziti* 'doctor's visit'

When words of this type are used in a sentence, they behave just like any native A+P-word.

(33) *nde lé saládi* 'the salad'   *nde é viziti* 'the doctor's visit'

There are, however, other A+P-words for which an explanation does exist for their pronunciation: their antepenult syllable is in fact the syllable that is stressed in French. These words represent cases where the French word ends in a consonant cluster. Such words always have a vowel added at the end. But in addition, they (sometimes) have a vowel added between the final consonants. When this happens, there are two epenthetic vowels after the vowel that is stressed in French.

(34) ***chambre***   [ʃãbr]   *shámburu*   'room'
                                       nde é shambúru   'the room'

    la+montre   [mɔ̃tr]   *lamóntire*   'watch'
                                       nde e lámontíre   'the watch'

    ministre   [ministr]   *minístiri*   'minister'
                                       nde e mínistíri   'the minister'

    mètre   [mɛtr]   *métera*   'meter'
                                       nde é metéra   'the meter'

    disque   [disk]   *dísiki*   'disk, plate' (or: *díski*)
                                       nde é disíki   'the disk' (or: *nde é diski*)

From the alternative pronunciation of *nde é diski* rather than *nde é disíki* shown above, we see that if the stressed vowel in the French word is followed by a single epenthetic vowel (at the end of the word), then there is no problem with categorizing it as a P-word. But when there are two epenthetic vowels, what underlying representation achieves the result that the French stressed vowel is H-toned in its isolation form in Shingazidja? For instance, given the monosyllabic word *chambre* in French, what underlying representation will yield a H-toned initial vowel in *shámburu*? Suppose that the Shingazidja speaker were to assign an underlying H tone to the initial syllable, and leave the two epenthetic vowels as toneless: /shamburu/. If this were the representation, then the pronunciation would have to be **shambúru* since the H tone would be realized as far right as possible (in the isolation form, Nonfinality would keep the H tone from reaching the final syllable). In order for a H tone to be pronounced on the antepenult syllable, the speaker *must* assign another H tone to the immediately following syllable. The representaion /shamburu/ explains both the isolation form *shámburu* (with an overt H tone on the very vowel that is stressed in the French source) and also a form like *nde é shambúru*, where the initial H tone in the noun is not realized, but the H tone on the second vowel is realized.

From these examples, we see clearly that the desire to be faithful to the French source word (by having the stressed vowel in French be specified with a H tone in Shingazidja and also having this H tone be realized on that vowel in the isolation pronunciation) forces the speaker to assign an abstract underlying representation where both the antepenult and the penult vowel is H-toned.

In summary, the overwhelming evidence from adaptations of French words in Shingazidja is that the general principle is this: assign an underlying H tone to the vowel that in the French source bears stress. However, there is a condition on the output: the vowel with an underlying H tone must also be pronounced with a H tone in the isolation form. Most of the time, this has no effect on the underlying representation selected. However, in the case of French words of the structure VCC# (when they are adapted as VCVCV#), the requirement that the antepenult vowel be realized as H in the isolation form requires another underlying H on the penult vowel. Two types of data still require explanation. Why do some CVC# words (adapted as CVCV#) assign an underlying H tone to the epenthetic final vowel as well as the penult? This richer representation is not required in order to guarantee that (in isolation) a H tone appears on the same vowel as in the French source; what it does do is cause the penult to have a different phonetic shape from that observed in P-words. And, why do a few CVCVC# words in French select an underlying representation (as A+P-words) that results in a H tone on the first syllable despite the fact that this syllable is not stressed in French (see (33) above)?

4 Conclusion

What do French adaptations tell us about Shingazidja tonology? Simply put, the adaptations reinforce exactly what the phrasal tonology tells us: the system of tonal principles and the underlying representation on which these principles depend are entirely productive. The adaptations show us that, given that a vowel is specified as H-toned, this tone is realized just in case the vowel is an odd-numbered H-toned element. Furthermore, the tone is realized on the specified mora just in the event that there is no available vowel to which it may shift (i.e. there is no following vowel, or there is only an IP-final vowel following, or the following vowel is itself specified as H). The H tone shifts as far to the right as possible.

But the phrasal data do not tell us *why* a particular vowel is underlyingly H-toned. The presence of a H tone is simply an arbitrary property of the lexical item which derives from proto-Bantu tone and possibly borrowing patterns from an earlier stage in the language's development. The present-day speaker simply must deduce the presence of this H tone from the (phrasal) behavior of the item. We have seen, however, that words adapted from French are different. There is a clear principle that guides the assignment of underlying H tones to these words. The speaker assigns an underlying representation which allows the isolation form to be pronounced with a H tone on the very vowel that corresponds to the stressed vowel in French.

In all the data we collected, there are no cases where an adapted French word is realized any differently from an indigenous word that shares the same underlying tonal representation. The abstract system of tone in Shingazidja is fully productive and exceptionless. Furthermore, at least in the case of French VCC# words, Shingazidja speakers assign an abstract underlying representation that is not reflected directly in the surface form: *shámburu* has only one H tone on the surface, but two H tones in underlying structure. It is hard to imagine any definition of abstractness that would not include this representation as an example. We conclude that on the basis of both the internal evidence derived from sentential tonology and the external evidence provided by French adaptations, abstract phonological analyses are not only insightful, but also necessary. This conclusion does not of course mean that *every* abstract analysis is justified. Naturally, it all depends on the evidence. But our conclusion is that abstract analyses are not to be rejected simply because they are abstract.

References

Cassimjee, F. & C. W. Kisseberth. 1989. Shingazidja nominal accent. *Studies in the Linguistic Sciences* 19(1): 33–61.

Cassimjee, F. & C. W. Kisseberth. 1992. Metrical structure in Shingazidja. In C. Canakis, J. M. Denton & G. P. Chan (eds.), *CLS 28: Papers from the 28th regional meeting of the Chicago Linguistic Society*, 72–93. Chicago: Chicago Linguistic Society.

Cassimjee, F. & C. W. Kisseberth. 1998. Optimal Domains Theory and Bantu tonology: A case study from Isixhosa and Shingazidja. In L. Hyman & C. W. Kisseberth (eds.), *Theoretical aspects of Bantu tone*, 33–132. Stanford: CSLI.

Cassimjee, F. & C. W. Kisseberth. 2010. The Shingazidja lexicon exemplified. Unpublished manuscript.

Goldsmith, J. 1984. Meeussen's rule. In M. Aronoff & R. T. Oehrle (eds.), *Language sound structure*, 245–259. Cambridge, MA: MIT Press.

Hyman, L. M. 1970a. How concrete is phonology? *Language* 46: 58–76.

Hyman, L. M. 1970b. The role of borrowing in the justification of phonological grammars. *Studies in African Linguistics* 1: 1–48.

Patin, C. 2007a. *La tonologie du shingazidja, langue bantu (G44a) de la Grande Comore: nature, formalisation, interfaces*. Paris: Université Paris 3 dissertation.

Patin, C. 2007b. Shingazidja focus hierarchy. *Nouveaux cahiers de linguistique française* 28: 147–154.

Philippson, G. 1988. L'accentuation du comorien: essai d'analyse métrique. *Études océan Indien* 9: 35–79.

4

On the Privileged Status of Boundary Tones: Evidence from Japanese, French, and Cantonese English

CARLOS GUSSENHOVEN

1 Introduction

In tonal phonology, a distinction is made between associated tones and nonassociated or floating tones. Whether or not a tone associates depends on the availability of tone bearing units (TBU) and the extent to which the phonology allows a tone to associate with a TBU. The fate of associated tones is unambiguous: they will be pronounced. The fate of floating tones is more precarious. In many cases, they are pronounced without fail, as in standard analyses of English and other European languages. In other cases, they are not themselves pronounced, but their presence is observable through the application or blocking of rules whose structural description is sensitive to them, as when a floating L causes downstep on a following H (Hyman 1975: 227, 2016). A third fate is, of course, deletion.

In this chapter, three cases are presented in which a tone that remains unassociated for lack of a TBU is deleted, while an intonational boundary tone that remains unassociated is preserved. The cases are seen as evidence that intonational boundary tones are more resistant to deletion than non-peripheral tones, whether lexical or intonational. The resistance to deletion is consistent with the finding that peripheral tones have been reported to be subject to truncation, the undershooting of the target of a final tone. Trunca-

Revealing Structure.
Eugene Buckley, Thera Crane & Jeff Good (eds.).
Copyright © 2018, CSLI Publications.

tion is a phonetic phenomenon, while deletion of unassociated tones is a phonological adjustment.

2 Japanese

My first case of a deleting floating tone where a boundary tone is pronounced in the same location is Tokyo Japanese. In order to appreciate the point to be made, I first argue for a representation of Japanese boundary tones which deviates from the classic analysis by Pierrehumbert & Beckman (1988). In particular, it is important to see that questions end in H%, not in LH%, as they argue (1988: 81).[1]

In the Pierrehumbert & Beckman analysis, the initial rise which marks the beginning of the accentual phrase in Japanese is analyzed as arising from a final boundary L-tone of the accentual phrase, notated Lα, which moves over to the next accentual phrase, so as to create a LαHα contour with the boundary H-tone that occurs at the beginning of each accentual phrase. This analysis in shown in (1). It necessarily assumes an initial boundary L-tone for the intonational phrase, notated Lι. More relevantly, it implies that the intonational phrase ends in a L-tone, Lα, the last tone of the last accentual phrase. The rival analysis is given in (2), from Gussenhoven (2004: 187). In (2), the last tone contributed by the accentual phrase to the intonational phrase is Hα, and any further pitch features will need to be provided by a boundary tone of the intonational phrase.

(1) { (   ) (   ) (   ) }
     Lι Hα   Lα Hα   Lα Hα   Lα (H%)

(2) { (   ) (   ) (   ) }
         LαHα   LαHα   LαHα   L% or H%

Data that can decide between (1) and (2) must be found among questions. Specifically, the prediction made by inserting H% after Lα differs from that made by inserting H% after Hα. In Figure 1, I give the declarative and interrogative intonations for an accented word, *omáwarisan* 'policeman', in which the acute indicates the accented syllable, and an unaccented

---

[1] The contours presented by Pierrehumbert & Beckman do show a falling trend before the rise on the last syllable, suggesting there is a low target there. There may be differences between varieties. Venditti (2005) has data without the falling trend. My speakers only had flat mid level stretches between the Hα of the accentual phrase and the interrogative H%, even when this stretch is very long, as in panel (b) of Figure 10.5 in Gussenhoven (2004: 203). I account for level stretches by assuming double-edged pronunciations of tones that fill up the space between the targets of other tones. A brief discussion is given in van de Ven & Gussenhoven (2011) and Gussenhoven (2018).

word, *garasudama* 'glass beads'. The declarative contours cannot tell us which analysis is correct. The weak fall in panel (a) can be attributed to a L% boundary tone of the declarative and the high, sharp fall in panel (b) is easily accounted for by the trailing L-tone of the pitch accent H*L, followed by an equally low realization of L%. However, the interrogative contour for *garasudama* (panel c) *can* tell us what we want to know. Observe that after the Hα of the initial rise, there is no fall. The final rise is evidently due to H%, just as it is in panel (d), where it occurs after the L-tone of the pitch accent H*L on *omáwarisan*.

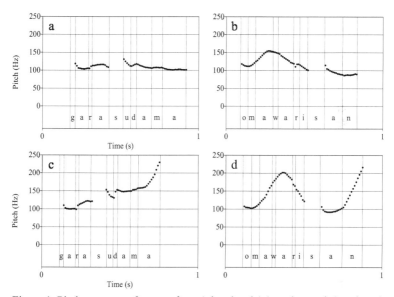

Figure 1. Pitch contours of *garasudama* 'glass beads' (panels a and c) and *omáwarisan* 'policeman' (panels b and d) in declarative (panels a and b) and interrogative (panels c and d) intonation; speaker SK

Tokyo Japanese thus has the grammar in (3). One or more accentual phrases, each of which may or may not be accented, will appear in an intonational phrase that ends either in L% or H%. (In (3), I leave out the intermediate phrase, which is a domain for downstep, and which Venditti (2005) argues can be collapsed with the intonational phrase.)

(3) (LαHα (H*L))₁ {L%,H%}

Given this grammar, there is one complication that remains unaccounted for. Consider the declarative and interrogative pronunciations of the monosyllabic words *hi* 'day, sun', *hí* 'fire', *san* 'three', and *sán* 'acid', shown in (4) and (5). The TBU being the sonorant mora, the first two words have one TBU, while the third and fourth have two. Also, the first and third words are unaccented, while the second and fourth are accented. Japanese associations are one-to-one, both spreading and contouring being disallowed. In cases of competition, the tones of the pitch accent associate prior to the accentual phrase tones, which in turn take priority over the intonational phrase tone; otherwise, within each tonal morpheme, H goes before L; and again otherwise, association is left-to-right (Pierrehumbert & Beckman 1988, Gussenhoven 2004: 190). The representations of the declarative contours are given in (4), those of the interrogative contours in (5). At issue is the fate of the trailing L-tone of the pitch accent in situations in which there is no TBU for it to associate with. Not much can be concluded from the data in (4), since all contours have a falling trend, and the final low target in (4d) could as readily be attributed to L% as to LL%. But this neutrality does not apply to the interrogative contours. The rise that is observed in (5b) corresponds to the fall-rise in (5d). Since the only difference between the two structures is the number of their TBUs, one in (5b) and two in (5d), the absence of a low target in (5b) must be due to the absence of a floating L-tone, circled in (5b). The absence of the L-tone is in turn attributable to the absence of a TBU. Now notice that while nonassociation of the L-tone in (5b), and by implication in (4b), leads to its deletion, a floating condition does not incur the same deletion penalty in the case of the intonational boundary tone, which remains unassociated in all forms except (4c) and (5c). A side issue here is that (4a) and (4b) and (5a) and (5b) neutralize in utterance-final position in the speech of some speakers (Vance 1995), but this has no bearing on the argument advanced here.

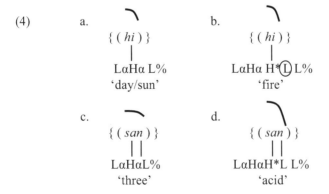

(4)　　a.　　⌐
　　　　{ (hi) }
　　　　　|
　　　　LαHα L%
　　　　'day/sun'

　　　　b.　　⌐
　　　　{ (hi) }
　　　　　|
　　　　LαHα H*ⓁL%
　　　　'fire'

　　　　c.　　⌐
　　　　{ (san) }
　　　　　||
　　　　LαHαL%
　　　　'three'

　　　　d.　　⌐
　　　　{ (san) }
　　　　　||
　　　　LαHαH*L L%
　　　　'acid'

(5)

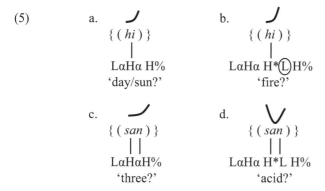

The deletion of L can profitably be extended to all nonperipheral floating tones, in particular to Hα before H*. In a one-word utterance like *kokóro* 'heart', Lα associates with the preaccentual syllable *ko*, leaving Hα floating between it and the H* on the accented syllable. The data in (4) and (5) suggest that the deletion of this Hα, while vacuous, is in keeping with the tone grammar of the language (Gussenhoven 2004: 195). The generalization for Tokyo Japanese therefore is that any nonperipheral tone that lacks an association is deleted.

3 French

Unlike Japanese, French lacks lexical tone, regardless of whether this is described as tone insertion in lexically marked accented syllables, as in Japanese, or as underlying tone in words (a distinction which Larry Hyman has repeatedly argued is not one of substance, but of analysis: see e.g. Hyman 2009), and unlike English, it lacks lexical stress. Yet the generalization we formulated for Tokyo Japanese in Section 2 applies equally to French. In the analysis of Post (2000: 154), the tonal grammar of French is as given in (6).

(6)   {%L,%H} (H*(L))$_0$ (H+)H* ({L%,H%})

According to (6), the grammar requires either a %L or %H at the beginning of the intonational phrase, allows any number of prenuclear pitch accents which are either H* or H*L, allows a leading H for the obligatory pitch accent H*, and is closed by H%, L%, or no tone. What is at issue here is the fate of the optional trailing L-tone of the prenuclear pitch accent. In Gussenhoven (2004: 272), I argued that tones in French associate with syllables on the basis of the fact, noted in Mertens (1992), that the trailing L is optional if there are one or more syllables between the prenuclear accent and the nuclear accent, but disallowed when these syllables are adjacent. In

(7), I give examples of the situation where the prenuclear and nuclear accents are nonadjacent, while in (8), I show the one form for the adjacent case. If we assume that French has obligatory downstep of H* after a H-tone (Post 2000: 156, Gussenhoven 2004: 268), the facts are straightforwardly explained by the absence of a L-tone in (8). That is, in French a nonperipheral tone which is not associated is deleted, quite as in Japanese. The new aspect the French case brings is that the tone is an intonational tone, not a lexical tone.

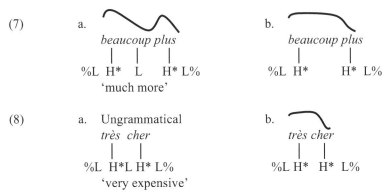

(7) a.
beaucoup plus
| | |
%L H* L H* L%
'much more'

b.
beaucoup plus
| |
%L H* H* L%

(8) a. Ungrammatical
très cher
| |
%L H*L H* L%
'very expensive'

b.
très cher
| |
%L H* H* L%

Again, the deletion of the nonperipheral L occurs in a system that allows a boundary tone like L% in (7) and (8) to remain in the representation. The question that remains is whether the Japanese and French peripheral tones are favored because they are peripheral, or because they are intonational boundary tones. To answer this question, we turn to the third case of discriminatory floating tone deletion, Cantonese English (Gussenhoven 2017).

4   Cantonese English

A Cantonese English word is H-toned if it is monosyllabic, like *tea*, or if the first syllable has secondary stress and the final has main stress, like the words *Chinese* and *Japanese*. Any syllable after the main stress has L; any syllable before the main stress, or before the secondary stress if there is one, is M. These observations are illustrated in (9). In (9a) and (9b), only H-toned syllables occur, because there is neither a syllable before the (primary or secondary) stress nor any syllable after the (primary) stress. In (9c) the L appears, while in (9d), we observe both the M and the L. Finally, (9e) illustrates a M-toned function word. The pitch contours of examples (9a), (9b), (9c), and (9d) are shown in Figure 2.

(9) a. *tea*   b. *Chinese*   c. *character*   d. *consideration*   e. *into*

      | | | | | | | | | | | | |

      H   H H   H L L   M H H H L   M M

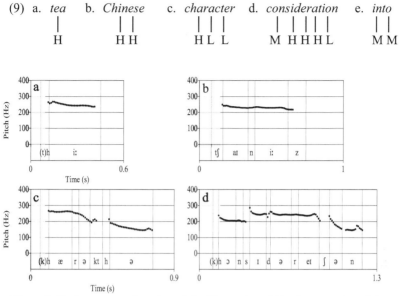

Figure 2. Pitch contours of *tea* (panel a), *Chinese* (panel b), *character* (panel c), and *consideration* (panel d); speaker CK

Luke (2000) analyzed the relation between British English and the tonal structure of Cantonese English as in (10). Observe that while he presented the description as if it applied to words that have stress and whose stressed syllables are provided with a pitch accent, his description was intended as an account of the historical development from British English to Cantonese English, and there was no implication that tones are "assigned" to Cantonese words. Rather, these tone patterns form part of the lexical representations of words (again, regardless of whether these are described as such or through the mediation of accents). Below, I have found it convenient to continue his metaphor of "tone assignment" for "historical origin of the word tones".

(10) a. Place MH*L on the main stress of the word.
    b. Place MH*L on any secondary stress preceding the main stress.
    c. Place M on any function word.
    d. Raise L to H if followed by either H or M.
    e. Delete M after any other tone in the word.

The description of the pronunciation of function words in (10c) leaves apparent regularities out of account, like the H-tone on subject pronouns or the treatment of *about* as a lexical word.

First, I simplify Luke's account somewhat. Rule (10b) appears to apply across word boundaries. Thus in a sentence like (11), from Luke (2000), there is in fact no L-tone.

(11) *You should stop thinking about it*

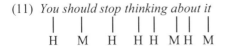

    H   M   H   H H M H M

In effect, L only shows up on any IP-final word-internal post–main stress syllables. It makes sense therefore to generate L only in that location. Second, apart from function words, the M-tone of the pitch accent only shows up in any word-initial syllable that is unstressed in British English. Since it also appears on function words, we can remove it from the pitch accent and assign it by default. This leaves us with H* as the prenuclear pitch accent and H*L as the nuclear pitch accent. The H* and L spread to any following syllables in the word, as does M in polysyllabic function words, like *into*. In return, we lose (10d) and (10e), resulting in the simplification seen in (12).

(12) a. Place H*L on the last main stress in the intonational phrase.
    b. Place H* on any preceding stresses.
    c. Place M on word-initial syllables without tone.
    d. Spread right.

The representations of (9) therefore now look like (13), where the spreading of H* and M has been indicated where applicable.

(13) a. *tea* b. *Chinese*   c. *character* d. *consideration* e. *into*

    HL   H HL   H L   M H H L   M

Luke's description ignored the data that make Cantonese English interesting for our topic. Without making this explicit, he in fact gave only declarative forms. On the basis of scripted speech by one speaker, I found three intonation patterns for words like *tea* and *Chinese*: a rise, a level tone, and a fall. Curiously, however, for a word like *apple*, there appeared to be only two patterns, a fall-rise and a fall. These forms are shown in Figure 3, where panels (a), (b), and (c) respectively show a level, a fall, and a rise for *tea*, panel (f) shows the fall-rise for *apple*, while panels (d) and (e) show two instances of the fall for *apple*.

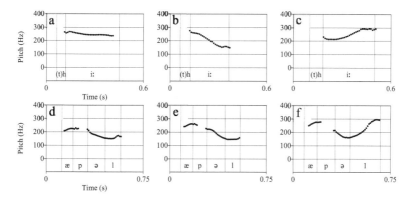

Figure 3. Declarative (panels a and d), emphatic declarative (panels b and e), and interrogative (panels c and f) intonation contours for *tea* (panels a, b, and c) and *apple* (panels d, e, and f); speaker CK

It is unexpected for intonation contours to be nonorthogonal with word-prosodic structures. That is, a given intonation contour in a language, like the high fall (H*L L%) in English, would be expected to be usable on any word that has a syllable with main stress, regardless of the position of that syllable in the word or the number of syllables. The cases of non-orthogonality that have been reported either concern avoidance of contours that involve excessive tone crowding or avoidance of contours that would form a precarious contrast with another contour. The first case is exemplified by the avoidance of the English rise-fall-rise on monosyllables (Leben 1975). This is the only case in which four tones with opposite values appear in one syllable, L*HL H%. Leben points out that this contour can be used in answer to a question like *What forms of industrial action could we possibly take?* But while it can be used in *We could demonstrate!*, where the nuclear syllable is antepenultimate in the intonational phrase and the tones approximately divide as L*, H, and LH% over the three available syllables, it is not readily used on *We could strike!*, where the nuclear syllable is IP-final and all four tones would need to be realized on it. The second motivation for avoidance has been found in the poor discriminability of the avoided contour with some other contour. This happens in some of the tonal dialects of Limburgish. The first case was the avoidance of the fall-rise on an IP-final syllable when used in combination with the lexical tone known as Accent 1 (Gussenhoven & van der Vliet 1999). For less complex intonation contours of the dialect, like the level contour or the rise, the phonetic cue to the lexical tone contrast between Accent 1 and Accent 2 is largely durational. For the fall-rise, a durational distinction is not salient enough for the lexical tone contrast to be comfortably signaled to the listener. The fall-rise intonation in the Venlo dialect is an interrogative contour by the side of the interrogative rise. Not much is lost communicatively by having a single interrogative contour for final-stressed words with Accent 1 in IP-final position, the rise, but two for otherwise equivalent syllables with Accent 2, the rise and the fall-rise.[2]

Could Leben's tone crowding or Gussenhoven & van der Vliet's low contrast perceivability explain the nonorthogonality of the Cantonese intonation system? It is easy to see that the answer must be "no". First, of the six potential forms obtained by combining a fall, a rise, and a level intonation with *tea* and *apple*, the missing contour is by far the easiest to produce, a level tone over two syllables. Second, if there were a concern over the maintenance of the phonological contrast between M and H, both of which are level tones, it would be as problematic on monosyllables as on disyllables. In fact, there is such a contrast, by virtue of the fact that function words have M and lexical words have H. As a result, *can* 'tin' and the auxiliary *can* 'be able' form a tonal minimal pair, as do *inn* and *in*, and *wood* and *would*, and so on. An example is given in (14). There is no case to be made, therefore, for contour avoidance motivated by a concern for the low perceivability of a contrast.

(14) a. *The workers can fish*   b. *The workers can fish*

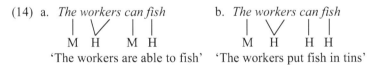

        M H   M H   M H   H H
    'The workers are able to fish' 'The workers put fish in tins'

A solution to the conundrum shown in Figure 3 can be found in the deletion of floating tones, combined with the intonational system of the language. A fairly common intonation system relies on an optional boundary tone which can be L% or H%, in effect giving three endings. This has been claimed to be the case in Dutch (Gussenhoven 2005), English (Grabe 1998, Gussenhoven 2004), French (Post 2000), and German (Grabe 1998, Peters 2006). The level tone for an IP-final syllable is a neutral declarative, the fall is an emphatic declarative, and the rise an interrogative. The tonal analysis is given in (15). The emphatic declarative was elicited by means of an exclamation mark in the script.[3]

---

[2] A nonorthogonal intonation system has meanwhile been reported in Gussenhoven (2012).

[3] Wee (2016) reports *only* falls on word-final stressed syllables and accordingly reanalyzes the lexical L as a boundary tone, L%. Wee's suggestion that level tones are not in fact declaratives but instances of listing intonation is contradicted by Luke (2000), who only reported level tones in isolated declaratives, while my speaker pronounced numbers before every item, preventing list intonation. Moreover, the results of perception data in Gussenhoven (2017) show that a level tone is perceived as a declarative, though a less emphatic one than a fall. Wee's

(15)   Declarative: Ø
        Emphatic declarative: L%
        Interrogative: H%

The second element in the solution is that, just as in Japanese and French, unassociated tones are deleted. Thus, the assignment of nuclear H*L to a word like *tea* will lead to a deletion of L, because there is no syllable after *tea* which can serve as its TBU. The representations of the contours in Figure 3 are given in (16a), (16b), and (16c) for the contours in panels (a), (b), and (c), respectively, and in (17a), (17b), and (17c) for the contours in panels (d), (e), and (f), respectively. The explanation for the absence of the level tone for *apple* is provided by the fact that the word has a L-tone on its last syllable, giving a fall, regardless of whether a boundary L% is added. And the absence of this L-tone in (16) explains why three contours show up for the IP-final H-toned syllable.

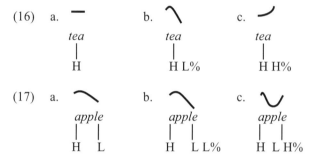

Observe that form (16a) suggests that the peripheral status of a floating tone is by itself not enough to save it from deletion. In (16a), there is no floating L after the H, which we may have expected on the basis of the H*L assignment in the descriptions in (10) and (12). That is, the floating tones that are preserved in Japanese, French, and Cantonese English are all intonational boundary tones. A second observation is that the L tone that appears in syllables after the last main stress in the IP is not the declarative L%, as we might think given that it only shows up finally in the IP. If it was, we would be unable to explain the low pitch in (17c), which is an interrogative form, and neither would it be clear how (17a) and (17b) can have the same contour, while (16a) and (16b) have different contours.

---

suggestion is also inconsistent with the fact that level pitch in IP-final words that have penultimate stress in British English, like *apple*, is unacceptable. The fact that I found both level tones and falls, Wee only falls, and Luke only level tones rather suggests language change or the existence of different lects.

The phonology of Cantonese English shows that it is not a good idea to leave intonation out of a tonal analysis. Typologically interesting interactions frequently occur between the lexical and postlexical tones of a language. My initial characterization of the intonation contours of Cantonese English as "fall-rise", "rise", "level", and "fall", as if they were in any way comparable to similarly termed intonation contours of British English, was of course misleading, and can only be forgiven on the grounds that the switch in perspective provided by the representations in (16) and (17) makes the misleading nature of those characterizations so clear. In reality, Cantonese English has a "zero" declarative intonation, a L% emphatic declarative, and a H% interrogative.

5 Conclusion

Unassociated intonational boundary tones may be preserved in situations in which other tones are deleted, as was shown to be the case in Tokyo Japanese, French, and Cantonese English. This suggests that these boundary tones have a privileged status compared to other tones, which must be a consequence of their morphemic status. Frequently, intonational boundary tones carry discourse meanings. The truncation of final boundary tones that has been reported for a number of languages cannot therefore be attributed to the fact that they are unassociated, but must be due to articulatory convenience in situations in which the identity of the boundary tone is not jeopardized by the truncation.

References

Grabe, E. 1998. *Comparative intonational phonology: English and German.* Nijmegen: Max Planck Institute.

Gussenhoven, C. 2004. *The phonology of tone and intonation.* Cambridge: Cambridge University Press.

Gussenhoven, C. 2005. The transcription of Dutch intonation. In S. A. Jun (ed.), *Prosodic typology: The phonology of intonation and phrasing*, 118–145. Oxford: Oxford University Press.

Gussenhoven, C. 2012. Asymmetries in the intonation system of the tonal dialect of Maastricht Limburgish. *Phonology* 29: 39–79.

Gussenhoven, C. 2017. On the intonation of tonal varieties of English. In M. Filppula, J. Klemola & D. Sharma (eds.), *The Oxford handbook of World Englishes*, 569–598. Oxford: Oxford University Press.

Gussenhoven, C. 2018. Prosodic typology meets phonological representations. In L. M. Hyman & F. Plank (eds.), *Phonological typology*, 389–418. Berlin: Mouton de Gruyter.

Gussenhoven, C. & P. van der Vliet. 1999. The tone and intonation of the Dutch dialect of Venlo. *Journal of Linguistics* 35: 99–135.

Hyman, L. M. 1975. *Phonology: Theory and analysis.* New York: Holt, Rinehart and Winston.

Hyman, L. M. 2009. How not to do phonological typology: The case of pitch accent. *Language Sciences* 31: 213–238.

Hyman, L. M. 2016. Amazonia and the typology of tone systems. In H. Avelino, M. Coler & W. L. Wetzels (eds.), *The phonetics and phonology of laryngeal features in Native American languages*, 235–257. Leiden: Brill.

Leben, W. R. 1975. The tones of English intonation. *Linguistic Analysis* 2: 69–107.

Luke, K. K. 2000. Phonological re-interpretation: The assignment of Cantonese tones to English words. Paper presented at the 9th International Conference on Chinese Linguistics, National University of Singapore, June.

Mertens, P. 1992. L'accentuation de syllabes contiguës. *ITL Review of Applied Linguistics* 95/96: 145–165.

Peters, J. 2006. *Intonation deutscher Regionalsprachen.* Berlin: De Gruyter.

Pierrehumbert, J. B. & M. E. Beckman. 1988. *Japanese tone structure.* Cambridge, MA: MIT Press.

Post, B. 2000. *Tonal and phrasal structures in French intonation.* The Hague: Thesus.

Vance, J. T. 1995. Final accent vs. no accent: Utterance-final neutralization in Tokyo Japanese. *Journal of Phonetics* 23: 487–499.

Ven, M. van de & Gussenhoven, C. 2011. The timing of the final rise in falling-rising intonation contours in Dutch. *Journal of Phonetics* 39: 225–236.

Venditti, J. J. 2005. The J_ToBI model of Japanese intonation. In S. A. Jun (ed.), *Prosodic typology: The phonology of intonation and phrasing*, 172–200. Oxford: Oxford University Press.

Wee, L.-H. 2016. Tone assignment in Hong Kong English. *Language* 98: e67–e87.

5

The Foot as a Phonotactic Domain: *aw* and *wa* in English

JOHN HARRIS

1 Introduction

Of all the constituents of the prosodic hierarchy, it is surely the syllable that
has been called on to do the most work in phonological and phonetic analysis. For all that, there have always been questions about whether the syllable's place in phonology is just quite as central as is often thought. Some of
the most searching of these questions have been raised by the work of Larry
Hyman. The one that I wish to take up here concerns the extent to which the
syllable can be said to act as a domain for segmental phonology.

Many of the West African languages described and analyzed by Hyman, particularly those spoken in the border region of Nigeria and Cameroon, exhibit segmental distributions and processes that are best stated in
terms of the stem rather than the syllable (see e.g. Hyman 1982, 1983,
1990). These stems typically conform to prosodically delimited canonical
shapes which, although we are dealing here with tone languages, bear a
strong resemblance to trochaic feet in stress languages. It is a matter of debate whether this means that the stems actually are metrical feet or not.
What is clear, however, is that in these languages some domain larger than
the syllable and smaller than the word plays a pivotal role in conditioning
segmental phonology. Some of the segmental patterns involved are strikingly similar to patterns that have been analyzed in syllabic terms in stress languages. The West African precedent is one reason to consider if these patterns might be better analyzed in terms of the foot in stress languages too.

Revealing Structure.
Eugene Buckley, Thera Crane & Jeff Good (eds.).
Copyright © 2018, CSLI Publications.

It has been argued elsewhere that this is certainly true of a set of segmental phenomena in English that are standardly analyzed in syllabic terms. Examples include tapping and glottalling of **t**, deletion of **h**, prefortis vowel clipping, and (in certain nonrhotic dialects) deletion of **r** (see e.g. Harris 1994, Davis & Cho 2003). One context that recurs in these patterns is intervocalic position, which is typically accommodated in syllabic analyses through ambisyllabicity. There are many reasons to reject this device, some of which I review below. Not the least of these is the point that stating the patterns in terms of the foot provides a much simpler analysis.

In this paper, I will further push the case for a foot-based approach to segmental phonology by presenting evidence from two more segmental patterns in English. Both involve phonotactic restrictions between a vowel and a following consonant. One of the patterns is well enough known to have made it into the Halle & Clements (1983) workbook: the diphthong **aw** cannot be followed by any consonant other than a coronal. This explains why we have words such as *shout*, *crown*, etc. but none along the lines of **awk, *awm*, etc. It has been claimed that the domain within which this restriction holds—call it the awT pattern—is the syllable rime (see Section 2).

The other pattern is rather less well studied. It has to do with the sound change that caused historical short **ă** to merge with short **ŏ** after **w**, which explains why *swat* rhymes with *hot* rather than *hat* (as the *a*-spelling might have suggested). The change was blocked when a dorsal consonant followed, which explains why *wax* rhymes with *lacks* rather than *locks*. As we will see, the dorsal blocking effect—call it the waK pattern—occurs under essentially the same prosodic conditions as awT. So if the syllabic analysis is valid for awT it should also be valid for waK. The extent to which the awT and waK patterns can be considered phonologically regular and synchronically live is revealed by word counts that I have extracted for this paper from the CELEX2 lexical database (Baayen, Piepenbrock & Gulikers 1995).

Available descriptions of awT fail to note that it also holds before an unstressed vowel; hence *powder*, *thousand*, etc., but nothing along the lines of **awgɚ, *awvi*, etc. The same detail is observable with waK: it holds not only when the blocking dorsal occurs word-finally or in a final cluster (as in *wax*) but also when it occurs before an unstressed vowel (as in *wagon*). This environment can only be accommodated within a syllabic analysis by allowing the intervocalic consonant to affiliate with the syllable to its left—most usually by assuming it to be ambisyllabic. However, I will argue here that the grounds for rejecting ambisyllabicity in general also apply in particular to these two phonotactic patterns. In any event, there is an alternative analysis that is much simpler: to say that the domain within which the patterns operate is the foot.

The evidence for treating awT and waK as foot-centered patterns is presented in Sections 2 and 3 respectively. Weight-related reasons for preferring the particular foot analysis proposed here over possible alternatives are given in Section 4. The main conclusions are summarized in Section 5.

2 *aw*

In English, the vowel in the MOUTH class of words (*mouth, loud, cow,* etc.) can vary considerably in quality from one dialect to another. For present purposes, we can abstract away from these differences and symbolize it as the diphthong **aw** that occurs in standard and many other varieties.

Under the awT restriction, the only kind of consonant that can follow **aw** is a coronal. This can be a single stop (1a), a fricative (1b), an affricate (1c), a nasal (1d), or some cluster of these (1e).

(1) a. *shout, pout, crowd, loud*
     b. *mouse, louse, browse, carouse, mouth* (n.), *south, mouth* (v.)
     c. *couch, slouch, gouge*
     d. *town, brown*
     e. *mount, fount, mound, ground, lounge, scrounge, pounce, flounce, joust*
     f. *howl, owl*
     g. *sour, power*

Depending on the dialect, the coronal can also be a liquid (see (1f) and (1g)). It can be a lateral in those varieties that do not show a historically excrescent schwa in this context (and thus have **fawl**, for example, rather than **fawəl**). The same can be said of *r* in those rhotic varieties that lack excrescent **ə** (and thus have **sawr** rather than **sawər**). Noncoronals cannot follow **aw**; hence the absence of words along the lines of **lawp, *lawk, *lawf, *lawm,* or **lawŋk*.

The majority of awT examples are monosyllabic words, like those in (1).[1] It is apparently on the basis of examples such as these that the awT restriction has been claimed to hold within the syllable rime (Selkirk 1982, Anderson & Ewen 1987, Spencer 1996, Hammond 1999, Kubozono 2001).

As would be expected under the rime analysis, awT is also in force in words where the consonant forms a word-internal coda. The examples in CELEX2 are not many, but in all cases the coda is either **n** or **s**, as in (2).

---

[1] The Halle & Clements (1983) workbook only asks students to list monosyllables.

(2) a.   *bounty, fountain, mountain,*
          founder, foundry, scoundrel,
          council, counsel
     b.   *frowsty*

The relative paucity of examples with word-internal closed rimes containing **aw** is understandable, given the tight constraints on the type of consonant that can follow any long vowel in this context in English. The coda here is pretty much restricted to the coronals **l**, **n** or **s**, as in *shoulder, dainty,* and *oyster* (Selkirk 1982, Harris 1994).[2]

The rime-based studies of awT just cited overlook a third context where the effect is to be observed. It occurs where a post-**aw** consonant is followed by an unstressed vowel (symbolized below as **v̆**), as in the following examples:

(3) *chowder, doughty, dowdy, powder, rowdy, blowzy, frowsy,*
     thousand, tousle, trouser

These are the only monomorphemic examples of **awCv̆** to be found in CELEX2. The numbers may be relatively small, but the pattern is clear: here too the consonant following **aw** must be a coronal. There are no examples of **awCv̆** morphemes where the consonant is a labial or dorsal; there is nothing along the lines of **lawbi, *lawkl,* or ** lawmpɚ*.

It is not difficult to think of further examples of **awCv̆** sequences if we include forms where the unstressed vowel belongs to a word-level affix, as in *louder, browser,* and *crowning*. Data such as these cannot be considered phonotactically "clean", however. We need to bear in mind that, in English, word-level (level-2) morphology can create segment sequences that ride roughshod over phonological restrictions that are systematically enforced within morphemes or within forms created by root-level (level-1) morphology (see Bermúdez-Otero & McMahon 2006 for discussion and references). Since one of the contexts where awT holds is at the end of a word, it is hardly surprising that **awCv̆** examples derived at word level also only contain coronals. These examples would be consistent with the assumption that awT holds as a rime-based restriction within the inner word domain.

A similar point can be made in respect of **awCv̆** words where the unstressed vowel belongs to a root-level affix; here too the consonant is always coronal. CELEX2 includes the examples *carousal, espousal,* and *outage*. Since root-level morphology is phonotactically conforming, these might have counted as evidence of a systematic awT effect before un-

---

[2] The lack of words containing internal **awl** rimes is due to a now-defunct sound change that merged historical **awl** with **oːl** in *shoulder, poultry*, etc.

stressed vowels. However, it could be argued that the semantics and morphology of these examples are so transparent as to suggest they behave like word-derived forms in containing two phonotactically independent domains.

To summarize: The awT restriction holds not just (i) word-finally (*loud*) and (ii) preconsonantally (*fountain*), but also (iii) before an unstressed vowel (*powder*). The only way a rime-based analysis of this pattern can be generalized over all three of these contexts is to allow the intervocalic consonant in words of the *powder* type to syllabify into the coda of the syllable containing **aw**.

There is, however, a much simpler alternative. The reference to stress alerts us to the fact that the foot is involved here. We can generalize over the three contexts by saying that the awT restriction operates within the foot. The foot can be monosyllabic, as in {*loud*} (feet in curly brackets), or disyllabic, as in {*powder*} and {*bounty*}.

The ban on noncoronals is inoperative when a consonant is separated from a preceding **aw** by a foot boundary; hence the possibility of having noncoronals following **aw** in examples such as {*cow*}{*girl*} and {*cow*}{*boy*}. Because of the close relation between feet and words in English, examples of this structure will almost always be morphological compounds. (In principle, we might have expected monomorphemic examples, but CELEX2 does not contain any.)

Note that this analysis is based on a rather traditional view of the English foot, in which the first syllable of a disyllabic trochee can be light (as in {*city*}), heavy (as in {*powder*}), or superheavy (as in {*bounty*}). Below we will consider whether the analysis is compatible with other models of English foot structure.

3 *wa*

Going purely on the *a*-spelling, we might have expected *want* to rhyme with *pant*. Originally it did, a state of affairs that is preserved in Scots and some regional dialects in England. The reason *want* now rhymes instead with *font* has to do with a sound change that caused historical short **ă** to merge with short **ŏ** after a labial-velar (see e.g. Jespersen 1909, Lass 1999). At least initially, the change was phonologically regular, affecting inherited Germanic words (generally spelt with *w*, as in (4a)) as well as established Romance loans (mostly spelt with *qu*, as in (4b)).

(4) a.   *swan, swap, want, wash*
     b.   *quality, quantity, quarrel, squad*

For the purposes of the present paper, I will refer to these as the "wa" words. The change also affected historically voiceless *wh*, which accounts for why *what* rhymes with *hot* rather than *hat* (at least in some dialects, including those that retain the contrast between **w** and **ʍ** (*witch* ≠ *which*)).

At the time the change was in progress (roughly from the late fifteenth century to the mid eighteenth), short **ă** was a front unround vowel, while short **ŏ** was back and round (Lass 1999). The change can thus be seen as assimilatory: **ă** underwent rounding and backing under the influence of a preceding consonant that is itself round/labial and back/velar. The change, which I will refer to as "wa"-darkening, has left its mark on most present-day dialects of English (but not on Scots).

There is a fair amount of present-day variation in the developments of short **ă** and **ŏ**, a reflection of the fact that both vowels have undergone certain dialect-specific changes in particular phonological contexts. Short **ă** has been subject to various combinations of tensing/lengthening, front-raising, and retraction (the last resulting in merger with broad **a** in *calm*, etc.). Short **ŏ** has undergone various combinations of unrounding, fronting, and tensing/lengthening (the last resulting in merger with historical **au** in *caught*, etc.).[3]

Words with "wa" have been caught up in these changes no less than other words with historical **ă** and **ŏ**. However, for the purposes of studying the current phonology of "wa", we can abstract away from the resulting dialect differences and speak of two generic vowel categories which I will label "A" and "O". In the past, all "wa" words had A. As a result of "wa"-darkening, most of these words, including those in (4), now have O. Depending on the dialect, O in these words can show up as unround central **a** or back **ɑ**, or as round low **ɒ** or mid **ɔ**. For example, in one dialect we might find **ɑ** in *what* and **ɔə** in *warm* (New York City, for example), while in another we find **ɒ** in *what* and **ɔ:** *warm* (London, for example); all of these variants count as O.[4]

Just how regular is "wa"-darkening? The total number of "wa" words in CELEX2 is 148 (excluding morphological derivatives). The O vowel occurs in 117 of these, A in 40. Included in these subtotals are nine words listed as varying between the two vowels. At first sight, this looks pretty irregular. On closer inspection, however, a significant proportion of the 40 words that appear to be exceptions to "wa"-darkening display a striking subregularity.

---

[3] For an overview of the dialect differences that result from these various developments, see for example Schneider et al. (2004).

[4] Another context where historical **ă** has dark-merged with **ŏ/au** is before **l**, especially when this is word-final or preconsonantal; hence O in *tall*, *fall*, *salt*, etc. There are a few words where the two sources of darkening converge, e.g. *wall* and *squall*.

Going by the *wa*-spelling alone, we might have expected *wax* to rhyme with *locks*. The reason it rhymes instead with *lacks* is that darkening was blocked when "wa" was followed by a dorsal consonant (Jespersen 1909). The resulting waK pattern is almost completely regular. Of the 24 words in CELEX2 containing "wa" plus **k**, **g** or **ŋ**, 23 have A, listed here:

(5) a.   *quack, Sarawak, thwack, WAC, wack, wax, whack*
  b.   *scallywag, swag, wag, quagga, swagger, waggery, waggle, wagon, wagonette*
  c.   *quango, swank, twang, wangle, wank, whang*

The remaining word is only partly exceptional: CELEX2 records *quagmire* as having both A and O variants.

To the list of waK examples given in (5) we can add words that failed to make it into CELEX2 (either because they are too new or were perhaps deemed too colloquial). At www.urbandictionary.com, for example, we find scores of words beginning with **wæk**, many of which are disyllables, e.g. *wackard, wackal, wackle, wacko*. (The morphology and etymology of many of these words are obscure.)

The waK blocking effect is quite specific to dorsals. Palatoalveolars, the consonants closest to them in place, failed to block retraction; hence the appearance of O in *squash, wash, watch*, etc.

To underline just how phonologically regular the waK pattern is, let us compare its effects with the remaining "wa" words that unexpectedly have A—those where the vowel is not followed by a dorsal consonant. The behavior of these words really is irregular. Of the 18 such words listed in (6), 17 appear in CELEX2 (I have added *WAP* 'wireless application protocol'). Some of the words are recorded in CELEX2 as having the regular O variant in addition to exceptional A (I've added the O variant of *aquatic*).

(6) A   a.   *swam, loquacity*
       b.   *palsy-walsy, WAP*
       c.   *wigwam, wham*
  A ~ O   d.   *aquatic, twat*
       e.   *kumquat, kwashiorkor, loquat, quatercentenary, swastika, wadi, wassail*
  A ~ O   f.   *Guatemala, suave, Taiwan*

The A variant in (6f) is entered in CELEX2 as broad **a** (in those dialects where this vowel occurs in, for example, *calm* and stands in contrast with both **æ** (*hat*) and **ɒ/ɔ** (*hot, caught*)).

In the case of the words in (6a) and (6b), we can appeal to analogy, one of the best acknowledged sources of exceptionality in sound change. The words in (6a) all exhibit root-level morphology. The past-tense form *swam* evidently retains A under pressure from a strong-verb prototype in æ; compare *sang*, *began*, and *ran*. We could speculate that A in *loquacity* and *aquatic* represents the æ of the **æ ~ ey** component of Vowel Shift (*vanity ~ vain*, *volcanic ~ volcano*, etc.); compare *loquacious* and *aquaceous*. In the reduplicative form *palsy-walsy* ((6b), presumably a word-level compound), *-walsy* retains the A of its base. Likewise, *WAP* retains the A of its base *application*.

The A variant of *twat* in (6d) is almost certainly borrowed from one of the regional British dialects where "wa"-darkening never took off. As for the other words, those in (6c), (6e), and (6f), I have no sensible explanations to offer for the unexpected occurrence of A—other than to note that they are relatively recent loans, or non-English proper names, or possibly onomatopoeic.

To summarize: There are two distinct ways in which "wa" words can deviate from the basic darkening pattern. We first have the words in (6) that are true exceptions, lacking any kind of systematic phonological motivation. We then have the words in (5), which exhibit a robust phonological regularity: "wa"-darkening is blocked when a dorsal consonant follows.

What is the domain within which the waK restriction holds? The dorsal must immediately follow "wa" in one of the following contexts: in absolute word-final position (7a), in a final cluster (7b), in an internal coda (7c), or before an unstressed vowel (7d).[5]

(7) a. *quack, Sarawak, scallywag, swag, twang, thwack, WAC, wack, wag, wax, whack, whang*
   b. *swank, wank, wax*
   c. *quango, wangle*
   d. *quagga, swagger, wacko, waggery, waggle, wagon, wagonette*

As with awT, these contexts can be subsumed under the foot, whether monosyllabic (e.g. {*wag*}, {*wax*}) or disyllabic (e.g. {*wangle*}, {*wagon*}).

4 Vowel-Consonant Phonotactics and Weight

Let me now explain why the particular foot-based analysis of the awT and waK patterns proposed here is preferable to two other prosodically-based accounts, one based on ambisyllabicity and one on maximally bimoraic feet.

---

[5] The sequence "wa" can also appear pretonically before a dorsal, e.g. *Waukegan, Wakashan* (Jeff Good, p.c.). Unless unstressed and thus reduced, the "wa" syllable here bears secondary stress and thus forms its own foot. The O in these forms follows the expected pattern: the waK restriction is inapplicable since the dorsal occurs in a separate foot.

Recall the conjunction of linearly expressed environments where awT and waK operate: (i) word-finally, (ii) before a consonant, and (iii) before an unstressed vowel. Syllable-based approaches to English segmental phonology have been confronted with this conjunction before. It is essentially the same combination of contexts where we find, for example, t-tapping, t-glottalling and **h**-deletion. According to a syllabic analysis, the positions are unified under the coda. The word-final consonant is assumed to occupy a coda in basic syllabification, while the prevocalic consonant affiliates with the coda of the preceding syllable (in violation of the otherwise basic onset-only syllabification of VCV sequences). In the most widely adopted version of this approach, the intervocalic consonant is ambisyllabic (see e.g. Kahn 1976, Borowsky 1986, Hammond 1999).

For the sake of argument, let us consider whether ambisyllabicity provides a viable treatment of awT and waK. According to this approach, both restrictions are stated over the rime: "any consonant following **aw** within the same rime must be coronal"; "a dorsal consonant following 'wa' within the same rime blocks darkening". In both cases, the coda consonant is either word-final (as in *loud* or *what*) or ambisyllabic (as in *powder* or *wagon*).

There are numerous reasons for rejecting the whole notion of ambisyllabicity. These have been set out in detail elsewhere (see e.g. Harris 1994, 2004, Jensen 2000, Bermúdez-Otero 2011). I will limit myself here to a brief consideration of two arguments that are most relevant to awT and waK.

One fairly straightforward argument against ambisyllabicity should be stated right away: why enrich prosodic theory in this way when there is a simpler analysis based on an independently motivated entity, the foot?

The other argument centers around the interaction between phonotactics and weight. For ambisyllabic analyses of processes such as tapping, glottalling and **h**-deletion to get off the ground, it is necessary to allow an intervocalic consonant to become affiliated with any kind of preceding open syllable, regardless of its weight. This is because these processes are blind to weight: tapping occurs in *meter* (where the relevant syllable is heavy) no less than in *city* (with a light syllable, at least in basic syllabification). The upshot is the creation of novel internal superheavy rimes (such as the **miːt** of *meter*). This turns out to have certain undesirable consequences.

The weight issue does not arise when an ambisyllabic analysis is applied to waK. The relevant vowel is historically short, so ambisyllabicity in a word such as *wagon* will create no more than a heavy rime (**æg**). (This is essentially the thinking behind the traditional description of short vowels as 'checked' in English.) In contrast, weight is very much an issue with an ambisyllabic treatment of awT. Because **aw** is inherently heavy, any newly closed rime it appears in will inevitably be superheavy (indeed maybe even extra-superheavy, as in the **awnt** of *bounty*).

Using ambisyllabicity to create internal superheavy rimes in disyllables such as *powder*, in an attempt to unify them with final awT in words such as *loud*, is founded on the assumption that the final sequence itself forms a superheavy rime. In both contexts, the consonant is assumed to be a coda. The immediate problem with this analysis is that a final consonant in English acts extrametrically (cf. Hayes 1982); in failing to contribute to the weight of the preceding rime, it does not behave like a coda at all. Since this undermines that case for saying that final awT forms a rime (let alone a superheavy one), there is little reason to suppose internal awT should form one either.

Quite apart from this weight evidence, there are also phonotactic reasons to be suspicious of the ambisyllabic analysis. Genuine internal codas in English (i.e. those followed by an onset, as in *bounty*) are subject to the severe phonotactic restrictions mentioned earlier, being largely limited to **n, l, s**. This is in stark contrast to the novel codas created by ambisyllabicity, which are free to contain any kind of coronal consonant (including for example **t, d, z**, in awT examples such as *doughty*, *powder*, and *trouser*).

The weight and phonotactic anomalies thrown up by ambisyllabicity simply do not arise with the foot-based treatment of awT and waK presented above. As noted earlier, the analysis proposed here assumes an inventory of foot shapes in English that includes uneven syllabic trochees. With awT, this allows us to define adjacency between **aw** and a following coronal in trochees with an initial heavy syllable (as in {*powder*}) as well as in those with an initial superheavy (as in {*bounty*}).[6] This account is clearly incompatible with an analysis of the English foot as maximally bimoraic (proposed for example by Hayes 1995).

Maximal foot bimoraicity predicts that, where phonotactic restrictions on vowel-consonant sequences are prosodically conditioned, they can only involve short vowels. With waK, for instance, the monomoraicity of the short vowel **æ** leaves room for the following dorsal consonant to fall within the same foot, in monosyllables (as in {*wag*}, where the consonant itself occupies the second mora) and in disyllables (as in {*wagon*}, where the consonant occupies the onset of the syllable containing the second mora).

With awT, the situation is quite different, because of the length of the diphthong. Being bimoraic, **aw** will saturate any foot it finds itself in, under this analysis. The diphthong thus could never occupy the same foot as a following consonant. Any such consonant would either remain unfooted, as

---

[6] The bimoraicity of **aw** means that light-light trochees do not figure in the awT restriction.

in {*lou*}*d* or {*pow*}*der*, or belong to a separate foot, as in the compound examples such as {*cow*} {*boy*} mentioned above.

In fact, maximal foot bimoraicity also rules out a syllable-based treatment of any phonotactic restriction that holds between a long vowel and a following consonant. In particular, it forestalls any attempt to salvage a syllabic analysis of awT by resorting to ambisyllabicity. The intervocalic consonant in a form such as *powder* could not be captured into the syllable containing **aw** without violating maximal foot bimoraicity: *{*powd*}*er*.

As our case study of awT demonstrates, the prediction that prosodically conditioned VC phonotactics can only ever involve short vowels is incorrect. There is as much of a phonotactic interaction between the **aw** and **d** of *powder* as there is between the **wæ** and **g** of *wagon*.

The difficulty maximal foot binarity faces in dealing simultaneously with the facts of weight and vowel-consonant phonotactics is just one of several reasons to stick with the traditional view that English allows syllabic trochees larger than two moras (see also Hammond 2006).

5   Conclusion

Although the awT and waK patterns are phonologically regular, neither of them looks particularly natural, at least as first sight. Behind each pattern lies a familiar historical scenario where an accumulation of individually natural sound changes arrives at an end point that is phonetically arbitrary.

The main historical source of **aw** in present-day English is long **ū** via Vowel Shift. The absence of noncoronals following **aw** is mainly due to two factors that were in place before Vowel Shift got under way. Firstly, some noncoronals were missing from the relevant context, either because there was simply no source for them in Old English or because they had been removed from the system through weakening or deletion (see Lass 1999). Secondly, **ū** had been subject to selective shortening, with the result that shortened reflexes were diverted out of the path of Vowel Shift, which only targeted long vowels (Jespersen 1909).

As to why following dorsals should prevent "wa"-darkening, the historical and comparative dialect evidence supports the reconstruction of these consonants as palatal at the time the change was in progress (see Harris 1987). This explains the blocking effect: being front, the dorsals were able to exert an assimilatory influence on **ǎ** that restrained it from backing.

Although now phonetically arbitrary, neither of the synchronic patterns bequeathed by these historical developments could be described as dramatically unnatural in the way that we sometimes find with patterns involving abstract underlying representations or derivational opacity. Nevertheless, both illustrate a point that has been one of the recurring themes of Larry

Hyman's work: phonological grammars are full of systematic patterns that lack any synchronic phonetic motivation (e.g. Hyman 1970, 1988).

The domain within which the awT and waK restrictions hold is the foot. They can be added to the growing data-bank of foot-based segmental patterns that we find not just in English (e.g. t-allophony and h-deletion) but also in other languages (see Hyman 2011). Many of these effects show a clear leftward bias in the way they are distributed within feet, reflecting the left-headedness of trochees. It is true that the phonotactic patterns associated with awT and waK do not show this sort of leftward asymmetry (beyond the more general fact that a full vowel must occur in the head syllable of the foot). Nevertheless, they still show how the foot can act as a vehicle that carries phonological segments to phonetic expression.

References

Anderson, J. M. & C. J. Ewen. 1987. *Principles of dependency phonology.* Cambridge: Cambridge University Press.

Baayen, R. H., R. Piepenbrock & L. Gulikers. 1995. *CELEX2.* Philadelphia, PA: Linguistic Data Consortium, University of Pennsylvania.

Bermúdez-Otero, R. 2011. Cyclicity. In M. van Oostendorp, C. Ewen, E. Hume & K. Rice (eds.), *The Blackwell companion to phonology, vol. 4*, 2019–2048. Oxford: Wiley-Blackwell.

Bermúdez-Otero, R & A. McMahon. 2006. English phonology and morphology. In B. Aarts & A. McMahon (eds.), *The handbook of English linguistics*, 382–410. Oxford: Blackwell.

Borowsky, T. J. 1986. *Topics in the lexical phonology of English.* Cambridge, MA: MIT dissertation.

Davis, S. & M.-H. Cho. 2003. The distribution of /h/ and aspirated stops in American English and Korean: An alignment approach with typological implications. *Linguistics* 41: 607–652.

Halle, M. & G. N. Clements. 1983. *Problem book in phonology.* Cambridge, MA: MIT Press.

Hammond, M. 1999. *The phonology of English: A prosodic optimality-theoretic approach.* Oxford: Oxford University Press.

Hammond, M. 2006. Prosodic phonology. In B. Aarts & A. McMahon (eds.), *The handbook of English linguistics*, 411–432. Oxford: Blackwell.

Harris, J. 1987. On doing comparative reconstruction with genetically unrelated languages. In A. G. Ramat, O. Carruba & G. Bernini (eds.), *Papers from the 7th International Conference on Historical Linguistics*, 267–282. Amsterdam: Benjamins.

Harris, J. 1994. *English sound structure.* Oxford: Blackwell.

Harris, J. 2004. Release the captive coda: The foot as a domain of phonetic interpretation. In J. Local, R. Ogden & R. Temple (eds.), *Phonetic interpretation* (Papers in Laboratory Phonology 6), 103–129. Cambridge: Cambridge University Press.

Hayes, B. 1982. Extrametricality and English stress. *Linguistic Inquiry* 13: 227–276.

Hayes, B. 1995. *Metrical stress theory*. Chicago: University of Chicago Press.

Hyman, L. M. 1970. How concrete is phonology? *Language* 46: 58–76.

Hyman, L. M. 1982. The representation of nasality in Gokana. In H. van der Hulst & N. Smith (eds.), *The structure of phonological representations, part I*, 111–130. Dordrecht: Foris.

Hyman, L. M. 1983. Are there syllables in Gokana? In J. Kaye, H. Koopman, D. Sportiche & A. Dugaset (eds.), *Current approaches to African linguistics, vol. 2*, 171–179. Dordrecht: Foris.

Hyman, L. M. 1988. Underspecification and vowel height transfer in Esimbi. *Phonology* 5: 255–273.

Hyman, L. M. 1990. Non-exhaustive syllabification: Evidence from Nigeria and Cameroon. In M. Ziolowski, M. Noske & K. Deaton (eds.), *Papers from the 26th regional meeting of the Chicago Linguistic Society: The parasession on the syllable in phonetics and phonology*, 175–195. Chicago: Chicago Linguistic Society.

Hyman, L. M. 2011. Does Gokana really have no syllables? Or: What's so great about being universal? *Phonology* 28: 55–85.

Jensen, J. T. 2000. Against ambisyllabicity. *Phonology* 17: 187–235.

Jespersen, O. 1909. *A Modern English grammar on historical principles, part I: Sounds and spellings*. London: Allen & Unwin.

Kahn, D. 1976. *Syllable-based generalizations in English phonology*. Cambridge, MA: MIT dissertation.

Kubozono, H. 2001. On the markedness of diphthongs. *Kobe Papers in Linguistics* 3: 60–73.

Lass, R. 1999. Phonology and morphology. In R. Lass (ed.) *The Cambridge history of the English language, vol. 3*, 56–186. Cambridge: Cambridge University Press.

Schneider, E. W., K. Burridge, B. Kortmann, R. Mesthrie & C. Upton (eds.). 2004. *A handbook of varieties of English, vol. 1: Phonology*. Berlin: Mouton de Gruyter.

Selkirk, E. O. 1982. The syllable. In H. van der Hulst & N. Smith (eds.), *The structure of phonological representations, part II*, 337–384. Dordrecht: Foris.

Spencer, A. 1996. *Phonology: Theory and description*. Oxford: Blackwell.

6

Phylogenetic Classification of Grassfields Languages

JEAN-MARIE HOMBERT & REBECCA GROLLEMUND

1 Introduction

In the foreword of a book on noun classes in Grassfields languages (Hyman & Voorhoeve 1980), Greenberg mentions that

> the questions raised by these languages have a broad significance not only for African historical linguistics and general linguistic theory, but beyond this to the whole panoply of historical disciplines which are concerned with the problem of how and when the vast areas of East, Central and Southern Africa came to be settled by their present Bantu-speaking inhabitants. (Greenberg 1980: 39)

The complex relationship between Grassfields languages and their neighboring Bantu and non-Bantu languages has been explored in the last fifty years with the aim of understanding both the great linguistic diversity found in this geographical area—one language covers on average less than twenty square kilometers (Stallcup 1980)—and its role in the emergence of Bantu languages.

In order to better understand these two problems, we will review the position of the Grassfields languages in recent linguistic classifications and propose a new classification based on a phylogenetic approach from data collected by the Grassfields Bantu Working Group (GBWG) in the 1970s. With the appearance of new methods borrowed from biology, linguists have at their disposal new tools to classify languages with more accuracy. Indeed, the analogies observed between biological evolution and language

Revealing Structure.
Eugene Buckley, Thera Crane & Jeff Good (eds.).
Copyright © 2018, CSLI Publications.

evolution (Pagel 2000, 2009, Atkinson & Gray 2005) have shown that phylogenetic tools used to reconstruct evolutionary relationships among species can also be applied to languages.

2   Grassfields Languages

Grassfields languages are situated in the West and the North-West Regions of Cameroon. As can be observed in Figure 1, Grassfields languages are surrounded by languages belonging to various linguistic subgroups that are more or less closely related to them: Narrow Bantu, other less well-known South Bantoid language groups (Beboid, Tivoid, Nyang, Ekoid), North Bantoid languages (Mambiloid), and Jukunoid languages.

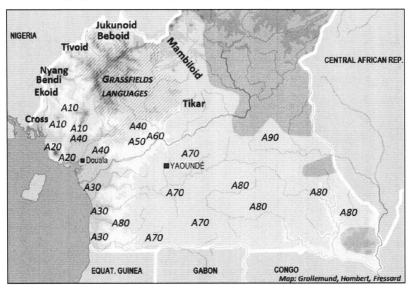

Figure 1. Location of Grassfields languages (hatched area) in Cameroon

3   Grassfields Bantu Working Group

In the 1970s, the Grassfields Bantu Working Group under the direction of Larry Hyman and Jan Voorhoeve collected data from these languages. Results from this fieldwork have been published by the different participants (in particular by Boum, Elias, Hombert, Hyman, Leroy, Voorhoeve, and Watters). A synthesis of these results can be found in Hyman & Voorhoeve (1980), in the Grassfields chapter of ALCAM (Dieu & Renaud 1983), in

Watters (2003), and in books published both on Bantu and Grassfields languages in the Southern California Occasional Papers in Linguistics series.[1]

4 Previous Classifications

4.1 External Classifications

Since the early 1960s, several classifications have been established in order to understand the position of the Bantoid languages within the Niger-Congo family. The first proposal comes from Greenberg (1963), who gave a genetic classification of African languages using the mass comparison method. Within the Niger-Kordofanian phylum, one of the four phyla he proposed, he distinguished a Bantoid subgroup, which was treated as a coordinate subgroup of Benue-Congo, together with Plateau, Jukunoid and Cross River. This classification is represented in Figure 2.

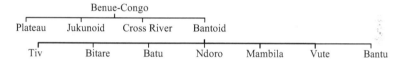

Figure 2. Classification of Benue-Congo languages (Greenberg 1963)

Greenberg (1974) proposed a refined classification (see Figure 3). Based on lexical and grammatical innovations, he divided the Bantoid group into two subgroups: Bantoid 1 (composed of Mambiloid and Tivoid) and Bantoid 2 (composed of Bane and Bantu). In order to distinguish Bantu and Bane, he used lexical innovations such as *-du* 'bee' for Bane vs. *-joke* for Bantu or *-nyuŋ* 'hair' for Bane vs. *-júede* for Bantu.

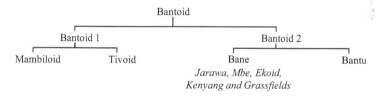

Figure 3. Classification of Bantoid (adapted from Greenberg 1974: 118)

---

[1] See http://gsil.sc-ling.org/list.html#SCOPIL:_Southern_California_Occasional_ for a list of the publications in this series.

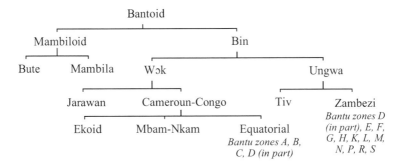

Figure 4. Classification of Bantoid languages (Bennett & Sterk 1977: 272)

Bennett & Sterk (1977) presented a classification of Niger-Congo languages based on lexicostatistical methods and shared lexical innovations (see Figure 4). They divided Bantoid into two branches: Mambiloid and Bin. Bin was further subdivided, with one of its subgroups (Wɔk) comprised of Jarawan, on the one hand, and a grouping of Ekoid, Mbam-Nkam (later called Eastern Grassfields) and Bantu languages belonging to zones A, B, C, and part of D, on the other.[2]

In the *Atlas Linguistique du Cameroun* (ALCAM), Dieu & Renaud (1983) presented a classification of languages spoken specifically in Cameroon, including Bantoid languages. In this classification (see Figure 5), Bantoid is divided into two subgroups: Mambiloid and Bantu. In the Bantu group, they classified the following groups at the same level: Jarawan, Tivoid, Ekoid, Nyang, Beboid, Grassfields, Mbam languages (i.e. A40 and A60 languages), Tikar and Ndemli, Equatorial languages (composed of Northwestern Bantu languages from zones B and C and parts of A and D), and Zambesi which corresponded to the remaining Bantu languages (parts of D and E, E/J, F, G, H, K, L, M, N, P, R, and S).

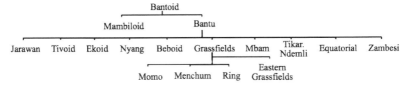

Figure 5. Classification of Bantoid (adapted from Dieu & Renaud 1983: 360)

---

[2] The Bantu-speaking area was divided into 15 referential zones by Guthrie (1967–1971), who assigned a letter to each of them: A, B, C, D, E, E/J, F, G, H, K, L, M, N, P, R, and S. Roughly speaking, languages in zones A, B, C, and D occupy the northwestern part of the Bantu area.

The currently employed division of the Bantoid subgroup into Northern versus Southern was first established by Blench & Williamson (1987), but has been further refined by others.

Watters & Leroy (1989) divided the Southern Bantoid group into eleven subgroups: Tivoid, Jarawan, Mbe, Ekoid, Nyang, Beboid, Wide Grassfields, Tikar, Ndemli, Mbam and Narrow Bantu (see Figure 6). In this classification, Wide Grassfields languages include Menchum, Western Momo and Narrow Grassfields. Watters & Leroy found that Menchum was difficult to classify because its position within the tree shifted depending on the lexico-statistical method used. The Narrow Grassfields group was specifically divided into three subgroups: Momo, Ring (West, Center, East), and Mbam-Nkam. The Mbam-Nkam languages were further divided into the North, Nun, Ngemba, and Bamileke groups.

I. Northern Bantoid			
II. Southern Bantoid			
A. Tivoid			
B. Jarawan			
C. Mbe			
D. Ekoid			
E. Nyang			
F. Beboid	1. West		
	2. East		
G. Wide Grassfields	1. Menchum		
	2. Western Momo		
	3. Narrow Grassfields	a. Momo	
		b. Ring	West
			Center
			East
		c. Mbam-Nkam	North
			Nun
			Ngemba
			Bamileke
H. Tikar			
J. Ndemli			
K. Mbam	1. West		
	2. Yambasa		
	3. Sanaga		
L. (Narrow) Bantu			

Figure 6. Classification of Southern Bantoid (Watters & Leroy 1989: 433)

Using different lexicostatistical methods, Bastin & Piron (1999) showed that Mbam languages held a pivotal position with respect to the connection between Bantu and other Southern Bantoid languages.

Williamson & Blench (2000) suggested a more detailed classification of the Bantoid languages (see Figure 7). They divided South Bantoid into Tivoid, Beboid, Wide Grassfields (divided into Narrow Grassfields against Menchum and Momo), Ekoid with Mbe and Nyang, Jarawan, and, finally, Narrow Bantu. Narrow Bantu was in turn divided into two subgroups: Northwestern ("North-West") versus other Bantu. In this classification, Bantu languages were presented as a first division of Southern Bantoid. In more recent presentations (Blench 2004: 12, 2011), there are slightly different representations for Northern Bantoid and the position of Narrow Bantu.

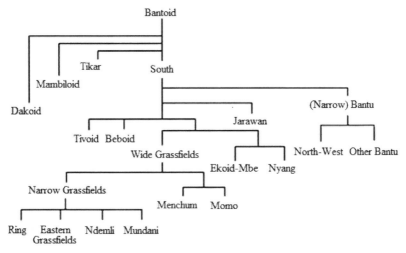

Figure 7. Classification of Bantoid (Williamson & Blench 2000: 35)

From the previous classifications it seems clear that the internal classification of Southern Bantoid needs further investigation. Furthermore, as mentioned by Watters (1989), many questions concerning the relationship of Northern and Southern Bantoid to Narrow Bantu are also not resolved.

4.2 Internal Classification

On the basis of the data collected by the Grassfields Bantu Working Group (GBWG) between 1974 and 1976, Stallcup (1980: 53) proposed a division of the Grassfields languages into two subgroups: Western Grassfields, composed of the subgroups Lower Mundani-Njen, Widikum, Menchum, and Ring, and Mbam-Nkam (Eastern Grassfields), composed of the four subgroups Nun, Bamileke, Ngemba, and Nkambe.

Based on supplementary data collected by the GBWG, Dieu & Renaud (1983) proposed an internal classification of Grassfields languages into four subgroups: Momo, Menchum, Ring, and Eastern Grassfields. In Figure 8, language names are included in addition to subgroups.

Grassfields

Momo	Menchum	Ring	Eastern Grassfields			
			Ngemba	Bamileke	Nun	North
Ngwɔ, Ngishe, Ngie, Meta', Moghamo, Busa, Menka, Atoŋ, Ambele, Mundani, Ngamambo	*Modele, Befang*	-West: *Aghem* -Center: *Mmɛm, Kom, Bum, Babanki, Kuɔ* -East: *Lamnsɔ'* -South: *Vəŋo, Kənswei nsei, Bamunka, Wushi*	*Bafut, Mundum, Mankon, Bambili, Nkwen, Awing, Pinyin*	*Ngombale, Məgaka, Ngomba, Ngyɛmbɔɔŋ, Yemba, Ɗwe, Ghɔmala', Fe'fe', Nda'nda', Kwa'*	*Mungaka, Shʉ pamɔm, Medʉmba, Mamənyan*	*Limbum, Dzodinka, Mfumte, Yamba, Mbə'*

Figure 8. Classification of Grassfields (adapted from Dieu & Renaud 1983: 362)

The classification established by Watters (2003) provides a detailed internal classification of Grassfields languages, similar to that established by Dieu & Renaud (1983). A distinction is made between a Narrow Grassfields subgroup consisting of Momo, Ring (further subdivided), Ndemli, and Eastern Grassfields (also further subdivided), and other Grassfields languages, as in Figure 9. Individual language names in Figure 9 are italicized.

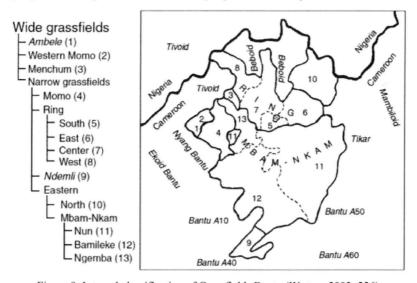

Wide grassfields
- *Ambele* (1)
- Western Momo (2)
- Menchum (3)
- Narrow grassfields
  - Momo (4)
  - Ring
    - South (5)
    - East (6)
    - Center (7)
    - West (8)
  - *Ndemli* (9)
  - Eastern
    - North (10)
    - Mbam-Nkam
      - Nun (11)
      - Bamileke (12)
      - Ngemba (13)

Figure 9. Internal classification of Grassfields Bantu (Watters 2003: 226)

In summary, the various classifications indicate that Narrow Grass-fields should be divided into three groups: Eastern Grassfields, Momo, and Ring, though there remain languages of unclear status, such as Ndem-li. Several other languages should be included in a larger Wide Grass-fields unit; they include Ambele and those languages of the Menchum group, and Western Momo, which has recently been renamed Southwest Grassfields (Blench 2010).

5 Phylogenetic Classification: Data and Method

5.1 Languages

In order to establish our phylogenetic classification, we have selected a basic vocabulary wordlist of 96 words from 96 languages.[3] These data were extracted from a larger database collected by the Grassfields Bantu Working Group between 1973 and 1978. It includes data from Grassfields languages as well as other South Bantoid languages, namely Beboid, Tivoid (Esimbi), Mamfe (Kenyang), and Ekoid (Keake and Ejagham), and one non-Bantoid language, Mbembe (Jukunoid). When using phylogenetic methods, it is important to include a language which does not belong to the language group under investigation in order to be able to root the general representa-tion of these languages, which is the role of Mbembe here.

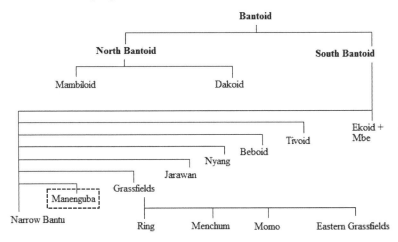

Figure 10. Position of Manenguba in South Bantoid (Blench 1993: 155)

To further elaborate the classification, we added languages generally classified as Bantu located near the Grassfields area, specifically belonging

---

[3] A list of these languages is presented in the Appendix.

to zones A10 (also known as the Manenguba group, Hedinger 1987) and A20 groups (specifically the A24 language Duala). Manenguba languages have, in fact, been suggested as occupying an intermediate position between Narrow Bantu and Grassfields languages (Blench 1993, 2004), making their value for this study clear (see Figure 10).

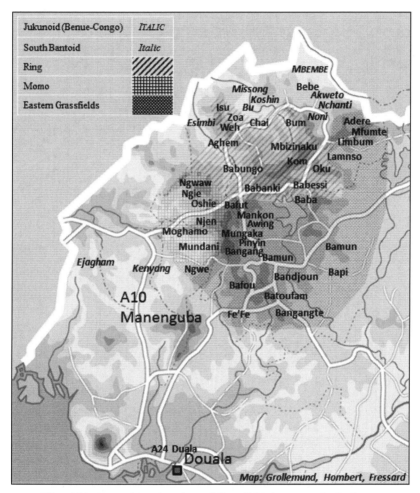

Figure 11. Approximate locations of Grassfields languages in database

Our classification is based on cognacy judgements. For each word list term, decisions were made regarding apparent cognate groupings. These judgments were established by means of regular sound correspondences when such data were available (using in particular reconstructions proposed by Hyman 1979 and Elias, Leroy & Voorhoeve 1984).

Items	mouth		eye		head		tooth	
P-G (Hyman)	*cùl`		*ft`		*tú`		*sòŋ´	
Bakossi_A15C	ǹnsôl	1	dī(t)/mī(t)	1	nlū	1	á'sóŋ	1
Fefe_EG	?	?	zāh/nāh	2	thū	1	sèʔ°	1
Bandjoun_EG	swə̀	1	tsə́/m̀ɲə́	2	thə́	1	sùŋ°	1
Bambu_EG	ǹtsò	1	ìlí/m̀mí	3	àtú/ìtú	1	nīsɔ̄ŋ	1
Mankon_EG	ǹtsùə̀	1	nǐdɨγə̀	3	àtúə̀/ìtúə̀	1	nǐ-sɔ̀ŋə́	1
Mundum_EG	ǹcpùə̀	1	nǐnɨγə̀	3	àtpúə̀/ìtpúə̀	1	nǐ-sɔ̀ŋə́	1
Bandeng_EG	nc̆ù	1	jə́ʔ/mɨ́ʔ	3	ə́'c̆ú	1	sɔ	1
Njen_Momo	ìcû/mìcû	1	ìγɨ́/àγɨ́	4	àtú/ìtú	1	ììsóŋ/ààsóŋ	1
Oshie_Momo	òtsɔ̂k/ètsɔ̂k	1	ìγɨ́/àγɨ́	4	àtɔ́k/òtɔ́k	1	ísɔ̄ŋ/ásɔ̄ŋ	1
Ngie_Momo	ùcéû̃/ìcéû̃	1	ìγɨ́/àγɨ́	4	àtéu̯/ùtéu̯	1	ísɔ̄ŋ/ásɔ̄ŋ	1
Babungo_Ring	ʃû:	1	jìsɨ́	1	tɔ́ˆ	1	èγɨ̂ʔ/jìγɨ̂ʔ	2
Babessi_Ring	tʃý	1	vɛ̌sə́	1	túkə̄	1	gu̯ə̄ʔ	2
Kom_Ring	ə̀cv̀ʉ̀/àcv̀ʉ̀	1	ìsɨ̂/asɨ̂	1	àtú`/ə̀tú`	1	ísɔ̃'ŋ́/ásɔ̃'ŋ́	1
Babanki_Ring	ə̀tʃỳ	1	ə̄ʃʉ̀`	1	kə̀thŷ`	1	ə̀sóŋ`	1
Aghem_Ring	édzúγó	1	ísɨ̀	1	kɨ́tú	1	ísɔ́ŋ	1
Weh_Ring	dzú/àdzú	1	ísɨ́/tísɨ́	1	kɨ́tíu̯/útíu̯	1	īsɔ̄ŋ/āsɔ̄ŋ	1
Bum_Ring	ə̄tʃû	1	īʃʉ̀	1	āthû	1	īʃɔ́ŋ̄	1

Figure 12. Sample of the Grassfields database

After judgments regarding cognacy were made, the next step concerned data encoding. There are two ways to encode data of this kind when it is to be analyzed phylogenetically: binary coding (presence or the absence of a feature) and multistate coding. The multistate coding chosen in this analysis requires that each putative cognate set receive a different code. Such an encoding will provide a more accurate tree than binary encoding. In Figure 12, a sample of our database is presented. A selection of seventeen languages is given in column 1 with a selection of four lexical items (with meanings 'mouth', 'eye', 'head', and 'tooth'). The Proto-Grassfields reconstructions established by Hyman (1979) are presented in the second row and greyscale coding is used to delineate cognate sets (with white serving as one of the colors here). The multistate coding which is used as input to phylogenetic algorithms discussed below is represented as an integer next to each form. For example, for 'mouth', all of the languages share the same cognate and consequently receive the same color-code and the same number (i.e. 1).

The phylogenetic method used here is the network-building method Neighbor-Net (Bryant & Moulton 2004), a "distance-based method", producing visual representations of relatedness among languages. This method produces a network representation that is different from a "classical" tree where the data are "forced" to fit into a more restricted representation.

6 Results

Figure 13 presents the network obtained from our 96-language sample.

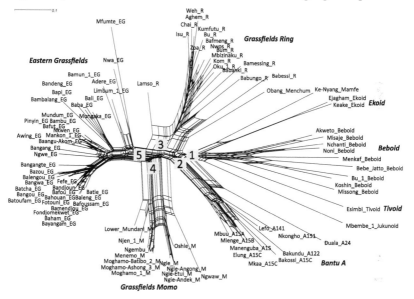

Figure 13. Neighbor-Net network of the sampled languages

The analysis of the network shows five major groupings. The first branch (1) is composed of a non-Bantoid language, Mbembe (Jukunoid), and South Bantoid languages excluding Wide Grassfields. In this subgroup, we distinguish Esimbi (Tivoid) and Beboid languages (divided into two subgroups, Missong, Koshin, Bu, Bebe Jatto, and Menkaf versus Noni, Nchanti, Akweto, and Misaje). Close to the Beboid languages, we find Ejagham and Keake (Ekoid), followed by Kenyang (Mamfe).

The second branch (2) is composed of Bantu languages belonging to zone A. This grouping splits into two subgroups. The first one is composed of Manenguba languages from zone A10 (Mbuu A15A, Mienge A15B, Elung A15C, Mkaa A15C, Manenguba A15, Bakossi A15C, Bakundu

A122, Lefo A141, and Nkongho A151), whereas the second one is composed of only Duala (A24).

The third branch (3) contains all Ring languages, organized in several groupings. The network shows first a subgroup of very closely related languages composed of Zoa, Kumfutu, Aghem, Isu, Chai, Weh, and Bu (West Ring); and another composed of Bum, Mbizinaku, Kom, Oku, and Babanki (Center Ring). South Ring languages (Bamessing, Babungo, Babessi, and Obang) are slightly more diversified. It should be noticed that Obang (Menchum) is located on the side of this branch and that the position of Lamnso (East Ring) is situated between Ring and Eastern Grassfields languages.

The fourth branch (4) is composed of Momo languages, where a subgroup composed of Ngie, Ngie-Angong, Ngie-Andek, Ngie-Etui, and Oshie is distinguishable. The position of Ngwaw, however, is somewhat distant. A second subgroup is composed of Moghamo, Ngembu, Menemo, Moghamo-Ashong, Moghamo-Batibo, Njen, and Lower Mundani. (Njen and Lower Mundani are slightly separated from this second subgroup.)

The last subgroup (5) is composed of Eastern Grassfields languages which split into several subgroups: Bamileke, Ngemba, Nun, and North. Bamileke languages divided into two subbranches, with Bafoussam, Batie, Bahouan, Bamendjou, Baleng, Bandjoun, Bafou, Fefe, Fotouni, Baham, Fondjomekwet, and Bayangam versus a second division composed of Bangante, Balengou, Bazou, Batoufam, Bangwa, Bangou, and Batcha. The second subgroup is composed of Ngemba languages: Ngwe, Bangang, Awing, Pinyin, Mankon, Mundum, Bambu, Bafut, Baangu Akom, and Nken. The third subgroup is composed of Nun languages: Bali, Mungaka, Baba, Bandeng, Bamun, Bapi, and Bambalang. And the last distinguishable subdivision is composed of North languages of this Eastern Grassfields branch: Adere and Limbum (closely related) versus Nwa and Mfumte.

The webbing observed in this type of network representation allows us to visualize the "noise" within the data, probably due to borrowings (Fitch 1997). Another way to visualize the same data is to build a phylogenetic tree (rooted). In Figure 14, we apply the neighbor-joining algorithm (Saitou & Nei 1987) in order to draw a tree-like representation.

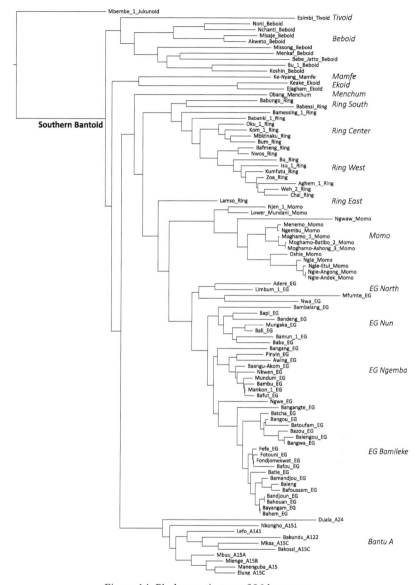

Figure 14. Phylogenetic tree of 96 languages

In Figure 14, the first groups to diverge are Tivoid and Beboid followed by Kenyang and Ekoid languages. There is a clear separation of Narrow Grassfields into three groups: Ring, Momo, and Eastern Grassfields. The subdivisions within these three groups are also very apparent, and correspond to the ones observed in the network. We should notice that this tree does not suggest that Momo and Ring should be regrouped into one "Western Grassfields" unit. As in the previous network representation, Lamnso has a relatively isolated position. The distinction between Narrow and Wide Grassfields is, in this database, limited to one Menchum language. Finally, the last group to split off is composed of Bantu (A10 and A24).

7   Conclusion

As mentioned at the beginning of this paper, our intention was to use a new method of classification using lexical data, mostly unpublished, collected by the Grassfields Bantu Working Group in the 1970s. Our results support earlier proposals, but they provide a clearer structure for the internal and external classifications of Grassfields languages. They support the internal classification of Narrow Grassfields into three groups: Ring, Momo, and Eastern, and they also indicate the position of Bantu groups (A10 and A20) within the South Bantoid classification. This study could be improved by taking into account languages not covered by the Grassfields Bantu Working Group in the northern part of the Grassfields area (Beboid languages in particular) and also by including a larger sample of Bantu languages spoken south of the Grassfields area (especially A40, A50, and A60).

References

Atkinson, Q. D. & R. D. Gray. 2005. Curious parallels and curious connections—Phylogenetic thinking in biology and historical linguistics. *Systematic Biology* 54(4): 513–526.

Bastin, Y. & P. Piron. 1999. Classifications lexicostatistiques: bantou, bantou et bantoïde. De l'intérêt des 'groupes flottants'. In J.-M. Hombert & L. M. Hyman (eds.), *Bantu historical linguistics: Theoretical and empirical perspectives*, 149–163. Stanford, CA: CSLI.

Bennett, P. R. & J. P. Sterk. 1977. South Central Niger-Congo: A reclassification. *Studies in African Linguistics* 8(3): 241–273.

Blench, R. 1993. New developments in the classification of Bantu languages and their historical implications. In D. Barreteau & C. von Graffenried (eds.), *Datation et chronologie dans le bassin du lac Tchad/Dating and chronology in the Lake Chad basin.* Paris: Éditions de l'ORSTOM.

Blench, R. 2004. The Benue-Congo languages: A proposed internal classification. http://www.rogerblench.info/Language/Niger-Congo/BC/General/Benue-Congo%20classification%20latest.pdf.

Blench, R. 2010. The Momo and "Western Momo" languages: Branches of Grassfields. http://www.rogerblench.info/Language/Niger-Congo/Bantoid/Grassfields/Momo/Classification%20of%20Momo%20and%20West%20Momo.pdf.

Blench, R. 2011. The membership and internal structure of Bantoid and the border with Bantu. http://www.rogerblench.info/Language/Niger-Congo/Bantoid/General/Blench%20Bantu%20IV%20Berlin%20Bantoid%202011.pdf.

Blench, R. & K. Williamson. 1987. A new classification of Bantoid languages. Paper presented at the 17th Colloquium on African Languages and Linguistics, Leiden.

Bryant, D. & V. Moulton. 2004. Neighbor-Net: An agglomerative method for the construction of phylogenetic networks. *Molecular Biology and Evolution* 21(2): 255–265.

Dieu, M. & P. Renaud (eds.). 1983. *Situation linguistique en Afrique centrale. Inventaire préliminaire: Le Cameroun.* Paris-Yaoundé: ACCT–DGRST–CERDOTOLA.

Elias, P., J. Leroy & J. Voorhoeve. 1984. Mbam-Nkam or Eastern Grassfields. *Afrika und Übersee* 67(1): 31–107.

Fitch, W. M. 1997. Networks and viral evolution. *Journal of Molecular Evolution* 44: 65–75.

Greenberg, J. H. 1963. *The languages of Africa.* The Hague: Mouton.

Greenberg, J. H. 1974. Bantu and its closest relatives. *Studies in African Linguistics* Supplement 5: 115–124.

Greenberg, J. H. 1980. Foreword. In L. M. Hyman & J. Voorhoeve (eds.), *L'expansion bantoue: Actes du colloque international du CNRS, Viviers (France), 4–16 avril 1977, vol. 1: Les classes nominales dans le bantou des Grassfields*, 39–42. Paris: SELAF.

Guthrie, M. 1967–1971. *Comparative Bantu: An introduction to the comparative linguistics and prehistory of the Bantu languages.* Farnborough, Hampshire: Gregg.

Hedinger, R. 1987. *The Manenguba languages (Bantu A. 15, Mbo cluster) of Cameroon.* London: School of Oriental and African Studies.

Hyman, L. M. 1979. List of Proto-Grassfields reconstructions. Unpublished manuscript.

Hyman, L. M. & J. Voorhoeve (eds.). 1980. *L'expansion bantoue: Actes du colloque international du CNRS, Viviers (France), 4–16 avril 1977, vol. 1: Les classes nominales dans le bantou des Grassfields.* Paris: SELAF.

Pagel, M. 2000. The history, rate and pattern of world linguistic evolution. In C. Knight, M. Studdert-Kennedy & J. R. Hurford (eds.), *The evolutionary emergence of language: Social function and the origins of linguistic form*, 391–416. Cambridge: Cambridge University Press.

Pagel, M. 2009. Human language as a culturally transmitted replicator. *Nature Reviews Genetics* 10: 405–415.

Saitou, N. & M. Nei. 1987. The neighbor-joining method: A new method for reconstructing phylogenetic trees. *Molecular Biology and Evolution* 4(4): 406–425.

Stallcup, K. 1980. La géographie linguistique des Grassfields. In L. M. Hyman & J. Voorhoeve (eds.), *L'expansion bantoue: Actes du colloque international du CNRS, Viviers (France), 4–16 avril 1977, vol. 1: Les classes nominales dans le bantou des Grassfields*, 43–57. Paris: SELAF.

Watters, J. R. 1989. Bantoid overview. In J. Bendor-Samuel (ed.), *The Niger-Congo languages: A classification and description of Africa's largest language family*, 401–420. Lanham, MD: University Press of America.

Watters, J. R. 2003. Grassfields Bantu. In D. Nurse & G. Philippson (eds.), *The Bantu languages*, 225–256. London: Routledge.

Watters, J. R. & J. Leroy. 1989. Southern Bantoid. In J. Bendor-Samuel (ed.), *The Niger-Congo languages: A classification and description of Africa's largest language family*, 430–449. Lanham, MD: University Press of America.

Williamson, K. & R. Blench. 2000. Niger-Congo. In B. Heine & D. Nurse (eds.), *African languages: An introduction*, 11–42. Cambridge: Cambridge University Press.

Appendix

List of 96 languages selected in our database, with their names, ISO 639-3 code, and their classification.[4]

Languages	ISO	Classification
Mbembe	nza	Jukunoid/Central
Noni	nhu	Beboid /Eastern
Nchanti	ncr	Beboid/Eastern
Misaje		Beboid/Eastern
Akweto	asj	Beboid/Eastern
Menkaf	mff	Beboid/Eastern
Bebe Jatto	bzv	Beboid/Eastern
Bu	boe	Beboid/Western
Koshin	kid	Beboid/Western
Missong	mij	Beboid/Western
Keake	etu	Ekoid
Ejagham	etu	Ekoid
Esimbi	ags	Tivoid
Kenyang	ken	Mamfe
Adere	add	Eastern Grassfields/North
Limbum	lmp	Eastern Grassfields/North
Mfumte	nfu	Eastern Grassfields/North
Ba'angu Akom		Eastern Grassfields/Mbam-Nkam/Bamileke
Bafou	ybb	Eastern Grassfields/Mbam-Nkam/Bamileke
Bafoussam		Eastern Grassfields/Mbam-Nkam/Bamileke
Baham	xmg	Eastern Grassfields/Mbam-Nkam/Bamileke
Bahouan		Eastern Grassfields/Mbam-Nkam/Bamileke
Baleng		Eastern Grassfields/Mbam-Nkam/Bamileke
Balengou		Eastern Grassfields/Mbam-Nkam/Bamileke
Bamendjou		Eastern Grassfields/Mbam-Nkam/Bamileke
Bandjoun		Eastern Grassfields/Mbam-Nkam/Bamileke
Bangang	nnh	Eastern Grassfields/Mbam-Nkam/Bamileke
Bangangte		Eastern Grassfields/Mbam-Nkam/Bamileke
Bangou		Eastern Grassfields/Mbam-Nkam/Bamileke
Batcha	nnh	Eastern Grassfields/Mbam-Nkam/Bamileke
Batie		Eastern Grassfields/Mbam-Nkam/Bamileke
Batoufam	nnz	Eastern Grassfields/Mbam-Nkam/Bamileke
Bayangam		Eastern Grassfields/Mbam-Nkam/Bamileke

---

[4] If the ISO 639-3 code is missing, this means that we could not determine which code is associated with the language, if any.

Languages	ISO	Classification
Bazou		Eastern Grassfields/Mbam-Nkam/Bamileke
Fe'fe'	fmp	Eastern Grassfields/Mbam-Nkam/Bamileke
Fondjomekwet	fmp	Eastern Grassfields/Mbam-Nkam/Bamileke
Fotouni	fmp	Eastern Grassfields/Mbam-Nkam/Bamileke
Ngwe	nwe	Eastern Grassfields/Mbam-Nkam/Bamileke
Nwa		Eastern Grassfields/Mbam-Nkam/Bamileke
Awing	azo	Eastern Grassfields/Mbam-Nkam/Ngemba
Bafut	bfd	Eastern Grassfields/Mbam-Nkam/Ngemba
Bambu		Eastern Grassfields/Mbam-Nkam/Ngemba
Bangwa		Eastern Grassfields/Mbam-Nkam/Ngemba
Mankon	nge	Eastern Grassfields/Mbam-Nkam/Ngemba
Mundum I		Eastern Grassfields/Mbam-Nkam/Ngemba
Nkwen	mfd	Eastern Grassfields/Mbam-Nkam/Ngemba
Pinyin	pny	Eastern Grassfields/Mbam-Nkam/Ngemba
Baba	bbw	Eastern Grassfields/Mbam-Nkam/Nun
Bali	mhk	Eastern Grassfields/Mbam-Nkam/Nun
Bambalang	bmo	Eastern Grassfields/Mbam-Nkam/Nun
Bamun	bax	Eastern Grassfields/Mbam-Nkam/Nun
Bandeng		Eastern Grassfields/Mbam-Nkam/Nun
Bapi		Eastern Grassfields/Mbam-Nkam/Nun
Mungaka	mhk	Eastern Grassfields/Mbam-Nkam/Nun
Obang	bby	Menchum
Lower Mundani	mnf	Narrow Grassfields/Momo
Menemo	mgo	Narrow Grassfields/Momo
Moghamo	mgo	Narrow Grassfields/Momo
Moghamo-Ashong	mgo	Narrow Grassfields/Momo
Moghamo-Batibo	mgo	Narrow Grassfields/Momo
Ngembu	nbv	Narrow Grassfields/Momo
Ngie	ngj	Narrow Grassfields/Momo
Ngie-Andek	ngj	Narrow Grassfields/Momo
Ngie-Angong	ngj	Narrow Grassfields/Momo
Ngie-Etui	ngj	Narrow Grassfields/Momo
Ngwaw	ngn	Narrow Grassfields/Momo
Njen	njj	Narrow Grassfields/Momo
Oshie	nsh	Narrow Grassfields/Momo
Lamnso	lns	Ring/East
Babessi	nsh	Ring/South
Babungo	bav	Ring/South
Bamessing	ndb	Ring/South
Babanki	bbk	Ring/Center

Languages	ISO	Classification
Bafmeng	bfm	Ring/Center
Bum	bmv	Ring/Center
Kom	bkm	Ring/Center
Mbizinaku	bkm	Ring/Center
Oku	oku	Ring/Center
Aghem	agq	Ring/West
Bu	lmx	Ring/West
Chai		Ring/West
Isu	isu	Ring/West
Kumfutu		Ring/West
Nwos		Ring/West
Weh	weh	Ring/West
Zoa	zhw	Ring/West
Bakundu	bdu	Bantu/A122
Lefo	bwt	Bantu/A141
Manenguba	mbo	Bantu/A15
Mbuu		Bantu/A15A
Mienge	bsi	Bantu/A15B
Elung	bqz	Bantu/A15C
Mkaa	mcp	Bantu/A15C
Bakossi	bss	Bantu/A15C
Nkongho	nkc	Bantu/A151
Duala	dua	Bantu/A24

7

Overexponence and Underexponence in Morphology

SHARON INKELAS

1 Introduction

Larry Hyman's research into the detailed morphological workings of Bantu
languages has uncovered two departures from the ideal structuralist morphological system: overexponence (as in affix doubling in Chichewa) and
underexponence (as in H tone merger in Chichewa). Any theory of morphology must account for these effects. This paper applies Optimal Construction Morphology (Caballero & Inkelas 2013) to these problems.

2 The Basic Model: Optimal Construction Morphology

Optimal Construction Morphology (OCM; Caballero & Inkelas 2013) is a
target-driven cyclic approach to word formation in which, on each cycle of
word formation, all morphological constructions in the language compete to
combine with a given stem. OCM has elements in common with rule-based
realizational approaches (Anderson 1992, Stump 2001), and with constraint-based approaches in Optimality Theory (Xu & Aronoff 2011).

OCM is target-driven in the sense that for a given morphosyntactic target (e.g. 'plural noun meaning BOOK'), all possible words that the grammar
can create are compared to see which one is optimal for that target. Candidates are evaluated cyclically. On the first cycle of evaluation, a root is selected from the lexicon. On the next cycle, all individual morphological
constructions (affixation, reduplication, truncation, etc.) that could combine

Revealing Structure.
Eugene Buckley, Thera Crane & Jeff Good (eds.).
Copyright © 2018, CSLI Publications.

with that root are compared to see which one's output is optimal, given the meaning target. Each winning output becomes an input to the next cycle of evaluation. Cycles continue until an output is produced which is of the category of Word and matches the meaning target perfectly. The derivation is then complete. A simplified example from English is provided in (1), which presents competing morphological constructions that attach to noun roots.

(1)　PLURAL construction:　　[[　]Noun.root]Noun.word.plural

　　　ISH construction:　　　　[[　]Noun.root]Adjective.word."Xish"

　　　WORD construction:　　　[[　]Noun.root]Noun.word

The first two entries in (1) are suffixation constructions which add morphosyntactic information and promote the input Root to the category of Word. The third is a conversion construction which simply promotes an input root to the category Word, enabling it to be used in the syntax. Each construction comes with its own cophonology (see e.g. Orgun 1996, Anttila 1997, 2002, Inkelas 1998, Inkelas & Zoll 2005). The ranked phonological constraints in that cophonology determine the phonological output form for the candidate produced by the corresponding morphological construction.

Competition among constructions is mediated, for any given word being generated, by two types of constraints: faithfulness and well-formedness (or markedness). Faithfulness constraints evaluate how well a given output (stem + single morphological construction) matches the morphosyntactic target for the word in question. Well-formedness constraints assess the form of the output. The nature and ranking of well-formedness constraints may differ across the cophonologies of different morphological constructions. We will give examples of well-formedness constraints in Section 3.

The tableau in (2) shows how faithfulness constraints determine the outcome of the second cycle of derivation for the word *books*. The root BOOK is the input to the tableau, which compares the results of combining each (compatible) construction in the language.

(2)		Target meaning: BOOK, NOUN, PLURAL Input meaning: BOOK Input form: *book*	FAITH-MEANING
☞	a.	BOOK, NOUN, PLURAL Relevant construction: PLURAL *books*	
	b.	BOOK, ADJECTIVE, "ISH" Relevant construction: ISH *book-ish*	*! (PLURAL, "ISH")
	c.	BOOK, NOUN Relevant construction: WORD *book*	*! (PLURAL)

3 XY Constraints

Numerous well-formedness constraints can affect word formation (Caballero & Inkelas 2013). This paper focuses on a basic member of this category, namely the set of XY constraints. These constraints accomplish affixation (and other types of morphological exponence) by specifying the phonological form (Y) that a stem with morphosyntactic properties X must assume. XY constraints are similar to the realizational rules of Anderson (1992) or Stump (1991, 2001), and to the exponence constraints of Xu & Aronoff (2011), which also explores issues of multiple versus single exponence.

(3) *Construction*   *Cophonology*
     PLURAL construction: XY constraint requires final /z/
     ISH construction: XY constraint requires final /ɪʃ/
     WORD construction: no XY constraint; default stress assignment

This paper explores the various effects of an XY constraint on morphological exponence, focusing on whether it is present in one construction's cophonology, or in many cophonologies. A taxonomy of possible effects is sketched in (4), and each is discussed in turn in the following sections.

(4) *Canonical exponence*: an XY constraint with a unique Y exists in the cophonology of exactly one construction, the one which introduces property X

    Underexponence: multiple constructions have XY constraints where X varies by construction but Y is the same; the same Y formative satisfies multiple XY constraints simultaneously

    Overexponence: multiple cophonologies have an XY constraint with the same X, causing the corresponding Y formative(s) to be introduced more than once

4 Canonical Exponence

Canonical exponence is the situation in which Y unambiguously and exceptionlessly expones X. (This clean situation is possibly more common in introductory linguistics textbooks than in real language.) For example, English regular noun pluralization can be modeled using the XY constraint [NOUN.PLURAL, ALIGN-R-z], or PL-z for short, which is present in the cophonology of the pluralizing construction.

(5) PLURAL construction: input noun stem unmarked for number; output noun stem marked [plural]; cophonology enforces PL-z

The tableau in (6) shows that XY constraints are only relevant to candidates employing the construction whose cophonology contains the XY constraint. Candidates (6a) and (6c) are both formed by the noun plural construction and subject to PL-z. Candidate (6b) is not formed by this construction and is not subject to it; the construction is simply not applicable. Candidate (6b) does worse than (6a,c) in terms of matching the meaning target. Candidate (6a) does better than (6c) in terms of satisfying PL-z.[1]

(6)

		Target: BOOK, NOUN, PLURAL Input: BOOK *(book)*	FAITH-MEANING	PL-z
☞	a.	BOOK, NOUN, PLURAL Construction: PLURAL *books*		✓
	b.	BOOK, ADJECTIVE, "ISH" Construction: ISH *book-ish*	*!	N/A
	c.	BOOK, NOUN, PLURAL Construction: PLURAL *book*		*!

The XY constraint in (6) is not, of course, completely "canonical", in the sense that not all plural nouns end in the regular plural /-z/, and there are other suffixes (or enclitics) in English which also take the form /z/. However, the example suffices to illustrate XY constraints.

In the next sections we see how the basic technology of FAITH-MEANING and XY constraints produces not only canonical exponence but also underexponence and overexponence.

5 Underexponence: Multiple Sources, One Form

An example of underexponence that Larry Hyman has often used in his classes on phonology and morphology is the verb *hit* in English, which fails to combine with the regular past tense suffix -*t*/-*d* to produce **hitted*. Hyman has frequently observed (p.c.) that many verbs exhibiting this behavior end in *t* or *d*. Of 174 English irregular verbs, 38% of them end in -*t*/-*d* (and

---

[1] Note that while PL-z is irrelevant to candidate (6b), hence the 'N/A' mark, candidate (6b) does satisify the XY constraint for the ISH construction, requiring the presence of final [ɪʃ]. That constraint is not shown in this tableau but would be ranked below FAITH-MEANING. The expected situation is for all XY constraints to rank below FAITH-MEANING; if an XY constraint were ranked higher than FAITH-MEANING, the result would be that all words would be compelled to combine with a construction supplying meaning X, and to have form Y, regardless of the target meaning for any individual word.

55% end in coronals of some kind).[2] Hyman's interpretation of this skewing is that a verb-final -*t*/-*d* tends to be interpreted as past tense -*t*/-*d*, obviating the need for redundant suffixation of the regular past tense ending. English has only a statistical tendency to underexpone past tense. But in other cases the pattern is regular, as will be seen in the next sections.

5.1 Nitinaht Reduplication (Two Reduplicative Exponents Merge)

Stonham (1994: 40) writes, of Nitinaht reduplication, that

> [a] certain subset of the lexical suffixes in this language require that certain effects on the shape of the root be manifested, either length on the root vowel, reduplication of some portion of the root, or some combination of the above.

Some affixes induce reduplication of the first CV of the root, copying vowel length if any ("NR" reduplication, in Stonham's terms). Others copy the first CV and lengthen the reduplicant vowel ("CV:R"). The relevant aspect of Nitinaht reduplication is that when more than one reduplication-triggering affix occurs in the same word, reduplication occurs only once. Stonham provides the following illustrative examples (p. 49):

(7)   a. $\lambda'u{:}\lambda'uq^w + a{:}\Omega d\mathit{l}_{NR} + a{:}p_{CV:R}$ ($*\lambda'u{:}\text{-}\lambda'u\text{-}\lambda'uq^w$)
        'X's legs are really big'
     b. $sa{:}sa{:}tq + 'aqsi\mathit{l}_{NR} + a{:}p_{CV:R}$ ($*sa{:}\text{-}sa{:}\text{-}sa{:}tq$)
        'X's eyes were really itchy'
     c. $ba{:}ba\mathit{l} + aski + yab\mathit{l}_{NR} + a{:}p_{CV:R}$ ($*ba{:}\text{-}ba\text{-}ba\mathit{l}$)
        'X is really cold on the shoulders'

     Stonham proposes an analysis in which each suffix can require a root to assume a particular shape; the competing demands of multiple suffixes "unify", in his terms. This insight is readily modeled using XY constraints in OCM. All of the suffixes in (7) are associated with a cophonology requiring the root to be reduplicated. The cophonologies of the CV:R suffixes, in addition, require the reduplicant vowel to be long. Setting aside lengthening, the XY constraint in question requires that the root be reduplicated. In (8), X stands for all constructions triggering reduplication, including the -*a:ʔdl*, -*a:p*, -*'aqsil* and -*yabl* suffixation constructions in (7).

---

[2] Data compiled by Susan Jones; https://web.archive.org/web/20110402060443/http://www2.gsu.edu/~wwwesl/egw/jones.htm.

(8)   X-REDUP: The input root must surface with CV reduplication

The XY constraint in (8) will be satisified as long as a reduplicated root is present, as shown in (9).[3] For notational simplicity, the meaning elements of the tableau are suppressed here. The point of these tableaux is to show that multiple affixation does not trigger multiple reduplication.[4]

(9)   Multiple reduplicating suffixes: one reduplicant satisfies each X-REDUP

1. Cycle of -a:ʔdɫ suffixation:

	Input: λ'uqʷ	X-REDUP	*STRUC
☞ a.	λ'u-λ'uqʷ-a:ʔdɫ		
b.	λ'uqʷ-a:ʔdɫ	*!	

2. Cycle of -a:p suffixation:

	Input: λ'u-λ'uqʷ-a:ʔdɫ	X-REDUP	*STRUC
a.	λ'u-λ'u-λ'uqʷ-a:ʔdɫ-a:p		*! (λ'u)
☞ b.	λ'u-λ'uqʷ-a:ʔdɫ-a:p		

Multiple instances of reduplication (e.g. λ'u-λ'u-λ'uqʷ-a:ʔdɫ-a:p) produce extra structure, violating *STRUC without improving well-formedness.

5.2   H tone assignment in Chichewa (two tonal exponents merge)

Hyman & Mtenje (1999) demonstrate that when multiple morphological constructions in the Chichewa verb call for a H tone on the verb stem, only one H is added. The H tones contributed by the constructions merge rather than accumulating. For example, Hyman & Mtenje (1999) observe several verbal constructions requiring penultimate tone. Three of these (negative infinitive, aspectual *ka-*, reflexive *dzi-*) are illustrated in (10b)–(10d). The forms in (10e) contain all three sources of a penultimate H; only one H surfaces.

(10)   a.   Imperative: toneless roots, no penultimate H insertion
             meny-a   'hit!'
             thandiz-a   'help!'
             vundikir-a   'cover!'
             fotokoz-a   'explain!'

---

[3] The *STRUC constraint in (9) penalizes excess phonological structure (see Zoll 1996).

[4] As Stonham observes (1994: 48), the ability of an outer affix (such as -*a:p* in (9)) to determine whether the root is reduplicated violates strong versions of the Bracket Erasure principle, in which the internal morphological structure of a stem is invisible to the phonology applying on an outer cycle of affixation (see e.g. Siegel 1974, Allen 1978, Pesetsky 1979, Kiparsky 1982, Orgun & Inkelas 2002, Shaw 2009). However, weaker versions of Bracket Erasure which permit internal access within a particular stratum of morphology would be consistent with this analysis.

b. Negative infinitive: adds penultimate H
   ku-sa-mény-a   'to not hit'
   ku-sa-thandíz-a   'to not help'
   ku-sa-vundikír-a   'to not cover'
   ku-sa-fotokoz-ér-a   'to not explain to'

c. Reflexive *dzí-*: is itself H, but also adds penultimate H
   ku-dzí-vúndikír-a   'to cover self'
   ku-dzí-fótokoz-ér-a   'to explain to self'

d. Aspectual *ká-*: is itself H, but also adds penultimate H
   ku-ká-vúndikír-a   'to go & cover'
   ku-ká-fótokoz-ér-a   'to go & explain'

e. Negative infinitive + *ká-* + *dzí-*: penultimate Hs unify
   ku-sa-ka-dzí-ph-a   'to not go & kill self'
   ku-sa-ka-dzi-mény-a   'to not go & hit self'
   ku-sa-ka-dzi-thandíz-a   'to not go & help self'
   ku-sa-ka-dzi-vundikír-a   'to not go & cover self'
   ku-sa-ka-dzi-fotokoz-ér-a 'to not go & explain to self'

A similar pattern is exhibited by verbal constructions requiring final tone. For example, the verb in (11) contains a H-toned verb root, intensive suffix, passive suffix, and subjunctive suffix, all of which assign H to the final vowel of the verb stem. Only one H tone is observed, rather than four:

(11) [*ti-* [[[[*pez*] -*etsets*] -*edw*] -*e*]] → *ti-pez-etsets-edw-é*
              H   H   H   H   'let's be found a lot'
       1P   find   INT   PASS SUBJ

We can model the tonal differences between the affixation constructions in (10) and (11) by assigning them different cophonologies. The constructions in (10) have cophonologies enforcing an XY constraint requiring a *penultimate* H-toned vowel. The constructions in (11) instead are affiliated with cophonologies enforcing an XY constraint requiring an H-toned *final* vowel. Each cophonology ranks PENULT-H and FINAL-H differently:

(12)

X	Y
Negative infinitive	PENULT-H » FINAL-H
Aspectual -*ka*	
Reflexive	
Intensive	FINAL-H » PENULT-H
Passive	
Subjunctive	

By modeling the two tonal patterns with XY constraints, rather than with floating Hs and linking rules, we predict that, rather than *adding* a H tone, the constructions just require a H to be present in a particular location. This requirement can result in the addition of H if none is present in the input; it will result in no change if H is already present in the desired location. It can also result in the shifting of an input H to a different location.

Because it is cyclic, OCM makes clear predictions in the case of complex candidates built by constructions associated with distinct cophonologies. The cophonology associated with the outermost construction is the one which applies. This can be illustrated using the Chichewa constructions seen so far. Hyman & Mtenje (1999) show that when a final-H-assigning suffix (subjunctive *-e* in (13a)) is attached outside of a penultimate-H-assigning suffix (reflexive *dzi-* in (13b)), H ends up on the final syllable (13c).[5]

(13) a. *ti-vundikir-é*   'let us cover'   Subjunctive assigns
                                                          final H

      b. *ku-dzí-vúndíkír-a*   'to cover self'   Reflexive assigns
                                                          penult H

      c. *ti-dzi-vúndíkir-its-é* 'let us cover our-   Subjunctive and
                                    selves'   reflexive compete;
                                                          subjunctive wins,
                                                          assigns final H

5.3 Underexponence versus antihomophony

Since the underexponence of penultimate H in Chichewa is so easy to model, the question naturally arises as to how OCM would model the opposite situation, in which all four constructions add a new H tone, and the four Hs accumulate in the verb stem. Or, similarly, how might one model a language which differs from Nitinaht in that each reduplication-triggering affix induces a new reduplicative copy, or for that matter any language in which homophonous segmentally fixed affixes are allowed to occur in sequences? The answer lies in antihomophony constraints which prevent two words with different meanings from assuming the same phonological form.

Even in real Nitinaht, antihomophony constraints are required to ensure that inflectional reduplicative prefixes do not "unify" their reduplicative demands with those of derivational suffixes of the kind seen earlier in (7). For example, the distributive construction induces prefixing CV reduplica-

---

[5] Note that Hyman & Mtenje (1999) motivate the layering of subjunctive *-e* outside of reflexive *dzi-* on the grounds that the subjunctive takes wider semantic scope than the reflexive.

tion. Stonham (1994: 57) notes that the distributive can combine with an already reduplicated stem, producing two instances of reduplication, for example *ka-ka-kawad-ataχ* 'DIST$_{RED}$-RED-killer.whale-hunt = hunting killer whales here and there'. (The lexical 'hunt' suffix in this verb requires the first instance of reduplication.) Since the distributive is not itself associated with a segmentally overt affix, deriving the insistence of its reduplicative behavior with an antihomophony constraint is an intuitively straightforward solution. The tableau in (14) assumes that the input *ka-kawad-ataχ* 'hunting killer whales' combines in both output candidates with the distributive morphological construction, which is associated with the same X-REDUP constraint seen earlier in (8). The cophonology of the distributive contains the constraints shown in the tableau.[6]

(14)   Cycle of distributive affixation:
         X-REDUP and ANTIHOMOPHONY force repeat of reduplication

		Target meaning: distributive of 'hunting killer whales' Input meaning: 'hunting killer whales' *ka-kawad-ataχ*	X-REDUP	ANTIHOM	*STRUC
	a.	*ka-kawad-ataχ* Construction: DISTRIBUTIVE	✓	*!	
☞	b.	*ka-ka-kawad-ataχ* Construction: DISTRIBUTIVE	✓		*

In conclusion, the difference between underexponence and "normal" exponence is governed not only by the distribution of XY constraints in the cophonologies of the language but also by the ranking of antihomophony constraints. Underexponence of the kind discussed in this section corresponds to haplology, the phenomenon to which Menn & MacWhinney (1984) draw attention in their well-known paper on the Repeated Morph Constraint (RMC). The RMC bans sequences of homophonous affixes. One response to situations in which the morphology of a language might be inspired to create such sequences is haplology, in which one affix appears but does the work of two. This is precisely the situation illustrated in Chichewa affixes that contribute H tones, and Nitinaht derivational affixes that trigger reduplication, seen earlier. However, as Menn & MacWhinney observe for

---

[6] Stonham's own account of these facts differs; he suggests that inflectional affixes are blind to the internal structure of derivational stems. For this reason, their reduplicative demands cannot be satisifed by reduplication on the derivational stratum. On Stonham's account it is coincidence that the inflectional distributive is marked only by reduplication, not (also) by a segmentally fixed affix. By contrast, an antihomophony account predicts that double reduplication should be allowed just in case it would be the only mark of a morphological category.

other languages, and as illustrated here with Nitinaht inflectional reduplication, the RMC also admits numerous exceptions. Modeling haplology effects with violable and rerankable constraints provides an appropriately flexible means of modeling both regular exponence and underexponence.

6   Overexponence: One source, Multiple Forms

We have seen how XY constraints can contribute to regular exponence and underexponence. The third logical possibility, overexponence, can result when the same XY constraint is present in two different cophonologies—one for the individual morphological construction adding meaning X, and one for another construction to which stems with property X are input.

Overexponence is discussed (as "extended exponence" or "multiple exponence") by numerous authors (Matthews 1974, Anderson 2001, Stump 2001, Blevins 2003, Xu & Aronoff 2011, Caballero & Inkelas 2013, Harris 2017). A familiar example comes from Breton (Stump 1991: 678, 696). Breton nouns pluralize either through stem suppletion (15a) or through the addition of the regular plural suffix -où (15b). Singular nouns diminutivize through the addition of -ig. Plural diminutives show overexponence of plural. The root forms a plural in the usual way (suppletion or -où suffixation). The diminutive -ig attaches to the plural stem, and then the regular plural suffix -où is added outside the diminutive, as seen in (15).

(15)		Gloss	SG	SG DIM	PL	PL DIM
	a.	'bone'	*maen*	*maen-ig*	*mein*	*mein-ig-où*
		'stone'	*askorn*	*askorn-ig*	*eskern*	*eskern-ig-où*
	b.	'boat'	*bag*	*bag-ig*	*bag-où*	*bag-où-ig-où*
		'prayer'	*pedenn*	*pedenn-ig*	*pedenn-où*	*pedenn-où-ig-où*
		'thing'	*tra*	*tra-ig*	*tra-où*	*tra-où-ig-où*

Perhaps the most compelling example of overexponence in the literature comes from work on Bantu affix doubling, by Hyman. As documented in Hyman (2003), Bantu languages can exhibit suffix doubling in response to what Hyman characterizes as a tension between the logical syntactic/semantic ("scope-based") order in which derivational suffixes should appear versus the strict linear templatic requirements imposed by the language.[7] Hyman provides evidence for a pan-Bantu affix ordering template, CARP (root-Causative-Applicative-Reciprocal-Passive). CARP represents the preferred linear order in which these four valence-changing affixes ap-

---

[7] See also Downing (2005) for an account of Jita causative doubling based on paradigm uniformity.

pear when any of them cooccurs with the others. The Chichewa instantiation of the template is given in (16).

(16)   CARP template (Hyman 2003), instantiated in Chichewa
        Root > *-its-* > *-il-* > *-an-* > *-idw-*
                  CAUS   APP   REC   PASS

In Chichewa words where semantic considerations motivate an order of affixation which is inconsistent with CARP, Hyman shows that an inner affix can be added again as an outer affix so that its second instantiation appears in the correct (CARP-based) order with respect to neighboring affixes. This is illustrated in (17), in which the applicative and reciprocal suffixes combine with the root *mang-* 'tie'. According to Hyman, the two different possible logical orders of attachment of these suffixes should produce two different meanings.

(17)   a. [[*mang-*] APP] REC] 'tie [X] for each other'
        b. [[*mang-*] REC] APP] 'tie each other for [Y]/at [Y]'

The first of these two logical orders, in (17a), is consistent with the CARP template, and the corresponding verb is generated unproblematically:

(18)   [[*mang*] APP] REC] *mang-il-an-* 'tie [something] for each other'

The second of these two orders, (17b), however, conflicts with CARP. In this case, Hyman shows, two "repairs" for the conflict between scope-based and templatic ordering are possible. Either the linear order in (17a) is used instead, producing homophony, or affix doubling occurs:

(19)   [[*mang*] REC] APP] **mang-an-il-*   'tie each other for/at'
                                  mang-il-an-   (homophonous with 18)
                                  mang-an-il-an- (affix doubling)

The affix doubling examples resemble Breton diminutives; the same affix is added twice, if and only if another affix intervenes, and without adding any apparent meaning.

Affix doubling of this kind can be modeled using XY constraints. The key insight is that the attachment of one affix prevents an inner affix from satisfying a high-ranked XY constraint; hence the inner affix must be added again. Where the Breton and Chichewa XY constraints cause a departure from canonical exponence is in their distribution. In Chichewa, the XY constraints instantiating the CARP affixes occur in two places: in the cophonology associated with the specific morphological construction in question, and again in a general stem-level cophonology to which all derived stems in the language are subject. It is this latter stem-level construction, and its associated cophonology, which gives the Chichewa verb stem its templatic character.

The following constructions and constraints can model the Chichewa reciprocal doubling illustrated in (19). First are the individual affixation constructions, whose cophonologies feature the constraints in (20). The RECIPROCAL construction takes a stem as input and outputs a stem in which the agent and patient are coindexed and associated with the subject. Its cophonology, via the constraint RECIP-an, requires the output to end in -*an*. The APPLICATIVE construction takes a stem as input and outputs a stem with an additional object argument, associated with locative, instrumental, or beneficiary semantics. Its cophonology, via the constraint APPLIC-il, requires the output to end in -*il*.

(20) RECIP-an: a stem with reciprocal argument structure must end in -*an.*
       APPLIC-il: a stem with applicative argument structure must end in -*il*.

What makes Chichewa templatic is the requirement that the output of each suffixation construction is input to the DSTEM construction, which enforces well-formedness. "Dstem" (derivational stem) is the term given by Downing (1997) to the verbal subconstituent which contains the root and any derivational suffixes, and which itself is the input to inflectional suffixation and prefixation. In the case of Chichewa, the Dstem cophonology enforces the CARP template. Each individual XY constraint, from the individual derivational affixation cophonologies, is also present in the Dstem cophonology, ranked according to CARP:

(21) Dstem cophonology: CARP
       ALIGN-R-*idw*- » ALIGN-R-*an*- » ALIGN-R-*il*- » ALIGN-R-*its*-

We will assume for purposes of this analysis that each derivational suffix combines with a root (Rstem) or Dstem and produces an output of category Rstem. The reason for this assumption is to force the output of derivational suffixation to be converted back to a Dstem by means of the DSTEM construction, which enforces the CARP template. Only Dstems are capable of being inflected (forming Istems) and passing on as complete words to the syntax.

The Dstem cophonology, and the obligatoriness of the construction associated with it, is what makes the system templatic. This analysis imports directly into OCM the insight of Hyman & Mchombo (1992), in which morphological features are spelled out cyclically by ordered rules.

To see how the analysis works, consider, as an example, the verb 'tie each other, for the benefit of someone else or at a location', which is an applicativized reciprocal. On the first cycle, the root *mang*- 'tie' is selected from the lexicon. The tableaux below start with the second cycle, in which all of the morphological constructions of Chichewa are considered to see which does the best job of bringing *mang-* 'tie' closer to the meaning target of 'tie each other for/at'.

To simplify matters, the tableaux are limited to transparent candidates whose only differences are those forced by satisfaction of XY constraints.

(22)   Suffixes and DSTEM construction compete for root *mang-* 'tie'

	Target: '[[tie each other] for /at]' Input: 'tie' (*mang-*) Category: Dstem	FAITH	RECIP-an	APPLIC-il
☞ a.	*mang-an-* Construction: RECIPROCAL Category: Rstem	*	✓	N/A
☞ b.	*mang-il-* Construction: APPLICATIVE Category: Rstem	*	N/A	✓
c.	*mang-a* Construction: (inflection) Category: Istem	**!	N/A	N/A

Tableau (22) produces two winners: (22a) and (22b). Candidate (22c) loses because it does not possess either of the constructions that bring candidates (22a) and (22b) closer in meaning to the target. The XY constraints in this tableau are inapplicable to it. Below, we track each successful candidate through the next cycle of affixation. First, in (23), both submit to the DSTEM construction, which is satisfied by the existing stem and imposes no overt changes. No other constructions compete for these inputs; the DSTEM construction is the only one that can combine with stems of the category Rstem.

(23)   DSTEM construction licenses *mang-an-* and *mang-il-* from (22)

	Target: '[[tie each other] for /at]' Input: 'tie each other' (*mangan-*) Category: Rstem	FAITH	RECIP-an	APPLIC-il
☞ a.	*mang-an-* Construction: DSTEM Category: Dstem	* (Appl)	✓	N/A
☞ b.	*mang-il-* Construction: DSTEM Category: Dstem	* (Recip)	N/A	✓

Now, both *mang-an-* and *mang-il-* are ready for further affixation. We track them in turn, starting with *mang-an-* 'tie each other':

(24) Applicative and inflectional suffixation compete for input *mang-an-*

	Target: '[[tie each other] for/at]' Input: 'tie each other' (*mangan-*) Category: Dstem	FAITH	RECIP-an	APPLIC-il
☞ a.	*mang-an-il-* Construction: APPLICATIVE Category: Rstem		*	✓
b.	*mang-an-a* Construction: (inflection) Category: Istem	*! (Appl)	N/A	N/A

The winning output in (24) is *mang-an-il-* 'tie each other for/at', which is perfect except that it is only an Rstem and cannot exit the lexicon without being converted to a Dstem, the precursor to inflectability and wordhood. The DSTEM construction forces another iteration of *-an-* suffixation, in (25).

(25) *mang-an-il-* converted to Dstem cophonology

	Target: '[[tie each other] for /at]' Input: 'tie each other' (*manganil-*) Category: Rstem	FAITH	RECIP-an	APPLIC-il
☞ a.	*mang-an-il-an-* Construction: DSTEM Category: Dstem		✓	*
b.	*mang-an-il-* Construction: DSTEM Category: Dstem		*!	✓

Thus, *mang-an-il-an-* is the best output when *mang-an-* is chosen on the first cycle of affixation.

When *mang-il-* is chosen on the first cycle of affixation, a different result obtains. The tableaux in (26) and (27) track the progress of the Dstem *mang-il-* on its path to wordhood. First, *mang-il-* is input to two competing constructions: further derivation (reciprocal) and inflection.

(26) Reciprocal and inflectional suffixes compete for *mang-il-*

	Target: '[[tie each other] for/at]' Input: 'tie for/at' (*mang-il-*) Category: Dstem	FAITH	RECIP-an	APPLIC-il
☞ a.	*mang-il-an-* Construction: RECIPROCAL Category: Rstem	(✓)	✓	*
b.	*mang-il-a* Construction: (inflection) Category: Istem	*!	N/A	N/A

Candidate (26a) clearly outperforms candidate (26b) on FAITH; a reciprocalized applicative (26a) is closer than a plain applicative (26b) to the target meaning of an applicativized reciprocal. However, (26a) is not completely identical in scope to the target meaning. This partial faithfulness is indicated by the parenthesized check mark.

The tableau in (27) tracks *mang-il-an-*, whose only viable option is to be converted to a Dstem, subject to the Dstem cophonology.

(27)   *mang-il-an-* converted to Dstem

	Target: '[[tie each other] for /at]' Input: 'tie for e. o.' (*mang-il-an-*) Category: Rstem	FAITH	RECIP-an	APPLIC-il
☞ a.	*mang-il-an-* Construction: DSTEM Category: Dstem	?	✓	*
b.	*mang-il-an-il-* Construction: DSTEM Category: Dstem	?	*!	✓

In this case, double affixation is no improvement. The faithful *mang-il-an-* (27a) outperforms *mang-il-an-il-* (27b). The ranking of RECIP-an » APPLIC-il in the Dstem cophonology is what creates the asymmetry between *mang-an-il-an-* (the winner of tableau (25)) and **mang-il-an-il-* (the loser of tableau (27)).

One question remains, namely why *mang-il-an-* can mean either 'tie each other for/at' or 'tie (something) for each other', while *mang-an-il-an-* can only mean 'tie each other for/at'. This follows, on the OCM analysis, from cyclicity. It is assumed that after the first cycle of suffixation, a simple reciprocal (e.g. *mang-an-*) is syntactically monovalent, though its single subject argument is linked to two semantic roles (e.g. agent and patient in the case of 'tie each other'). Applicativizing such a stem results in the addition of an object argument bearing a different thematic role—instrumental, locative, and so on—producing a meaning like 'tie each other for a reason/at a place/with an instrument'. This is the correct prediction for *mang-an-il-*, which we have seen must surface as *mang-an-il-an-* for templatic reasons. By contrast, a simple applicativized verb like *mang-il-* has three arguments: the syntactic subject is associated with agentive semantics; the original object is associated with patient thematic role; and the object added by the APPLICATIVE construction is associated with benefactive, locative, or instrumental thematic roles. Reciprocalizing such an input (*mang-il-an-*) coindexes the subject with either the original object (the patient) or the added object (the benefactive, location, or instrument). This is what provides for the morphosyntactic ambiguity of *mang-il-an-*.

Hyman (2003) provides a different, very interesting account in which affix doubling *and* the semantics of *mang-il-an-* and *mang-an-il-an-* follow from the free ranking of two constraints. One is the CARP constraint, termed "Template" or "T" in Hyman's analysis. The other is a SCOPE constraint (termed "Mirror" or "M"), which compels affixes to appear in a linear order reflecting scope relations. In Chichewa, Hyman proposes, the key interaction is between T and a conjunction of M and T. Tableau (28), adapted slightly from Hyman (2003: 256), illustrates the analysis of a reciprocalized applicative (28i) and applicativized reciprocal (28ii). Hyman interprets the T and M&T constraints as licensers. If all of the affixes in a given candidate are fully licensed by a constraint, the candidate satisfies that constraint:

(28)		Logical input: [[[*mang-*] APP] REC]	T	M & T
	i.			
	a.	*mang-an-il-*		
☞	b.	*mang-il-an-*	*il-an*	
	c.	*mang-an-il-an-*	*il-an*	
	d.	*mang-il-an-il-*		
	ii.	Logical input: [[[*mang-*] REC] APP]	T	M & T
	d.	*mang-an-il-*		
☞	f.	*mang-il-an-*	*il-an*	
☞	g.	*mang-an-il-an-*	*il-an*	*an-il-an*
◗	h.	*mang-il-an-il-*	*il-an*	*il-an-il*

On Hyman's analysis, none of the winners (*mang-il-an-* (28b, 28f), *mang-an-il-an-* (28g)) are perfect. The form *mang-il-an-* violates M&T, in that the *-il-an-* sequence is not licensed by M&T; *mang-an-il-an-* violates T (the *-an-il-* sequence is not licensed by T). However, each is optimal in context. Hyman does note one problem with his analysis: it predicts *mang-il-an-il-* (28h) to be as good a "repair" as *mang-an-il-an-* (28g) for the Scope/CARP problem posed by applicativized reciprocals, yet (28h) is ungrammatical. Hyman speculates that a cyclic analysis could explain this, noting that for input [[[*mang-*] REC] APP], *mang-an-il-an-* is an improvement over **mang-an-il-* in terms of scope, while for input [[[*mang-*] APP] REC], *mang-il-an-il-* is *not* scopally superior to *mang-il-an-*. Hyman (2003: 256–257) writes:

> Cyclicity seems to be crucial here... A cyclic spell-out is allowed to override TEMPLATE, but only if it is repaired by a templatic sequence. A templatic sequence [like *mang-il-an-*, SI] would have no reason to be "repaired" ... and hence *-il-an-il-* is not an appropriate output for [an applicativized reciprocal, SI].

The cyclic analysis offered here in the OCM framework exploits this insight of Hyman's.

7 Conclusion

In conclusion, Larry Hyman's insightful work on Bantu languages has uncovered problems of morphological exponence which pose challenges to any model of morphology. This paper has suggested that Optimal Construction Morphology is a suitable framework for handling these problems.

References

Allen, M. 1978. *Morphological investigations*. Cambridge, MA: MIT dissertation.

Anderson, S. R. 1992. *A-morphous morphology*. Cambridge: Cambridge University Press.

Anderson, S. R. 2001. On some issues in morphological exponence. In G. Booij & J. van Marle (eds.), *Yearbook of morphology 2000*, 1–17. Dordrecht: Springer.

Anttila, A. 1997. Deriving variation from grammar. In F. Hinskens, R. van Hout & W. L. Wetzels (eds.), *Variation, change and phonological theory*, 35–68. Amsterdam: Benjamins.

Anttila, A. 2002. Morphologically conditioned phonological alternations. *Natural Language & Linguistic Theory* 20: 1–42.

Blevins, J. 2003. Stems and paradigms. *Language* 79: 737–767.

Caballero, G. & S. Inkelas. 2013. Word construction: Tracing an optimal path through the lexicon. *Morphology* 23: 103–143.

Downing, L. 1997. Correspondence effects in Siswati reduplication. *Studies in the Linguistic Sciences* 25: 17–35.

Downing, L. 2005. Jita causative doubling provides optimal paradigms. In L. Downing, T. Hall & R. Raffelsiefen (eds.), *Paradigms in phonological theory*, 122–144. Oxford: Oxford University Press.

Harris, A. 2017. *Multiple exponence*. Cambridge: Cambridge University Press.

Hyman, L. M. 2003. Suffix ordering in Bantu: A morphocentric approach. In G. Booij & J. van Marle (eds.), *Yearbook of morphology 2002*, 245–281. Dordrecht: Kluwer.

Hyman, L. M. & S. A. Mchombo. 1992. Morphotactic constraints in the Chichewa verb stem. In L. Buszard-Welcher, L. Wee & W. Weigel (eds.), *Proceedings of the eighteenth annual meeting of the Berkeley Linguistics Society: General session and parasession*, 350–363. Berkeley: Berkeley Linguistics Society.

Hyman, L. M. & A. Mtenje. 1999. Prosodic morphology and tone: The case of Chichewa. In R. Kager, H. van der Hulst & W. Zonneveld (eds.), *The prosody-morphology interface*, 90–133. Cambridge: Cambridge University Press.

Inkelas, S. 1998. The theoretical status of morphologically conditioned phonology: A case study from dominance. In G. Booij & J. van Marle (eds.), *Yearbook of morphology 1997*, 121–155. Dordrecht: Kluwer.

Inkelas, S. & C. Zoll. 2005. *Reduplication: Doubling in morphology*. Cambridge: Cambridge University Press.

Kiparsky, P. 1982. Lexical morphology and phonology. In I. S. Yang (ed.), *Linguistics in the morning calm*, 3–91. Seoul: Hanshin.

Matthews, P. H. 1974. *Morphology*. Cambridge: Cambridge University Press.

Menn, L. & B. MacWhinney. 1984. The repeated morph constraint: Toward an explanation. *Language* 60: 519–541.

Orgun, C. O. 1996. *Sign-based morphology and phonology: With special attention to Optimality Theory*. Berkeley: University of California dissertation.

Orgun, C. O. & S. Inkelas. 2002. Reconsidering bracket erasure. In G. Booij & J. van Marle (eds.), *Yearbook of morphology 2001*, 115–146. Dordrecht: Kluwer.

Pesetsky, D. 1979. *Russian morphology and lexical theory*. Cambridge, MA: MIT dissertation.

Shaw, P. 2009. Inside access. In K. Hanson & S. Inkelas (eds.), *The nature of the word: Essays in honor of Paul Kiparsky*, 241–272. Cambridge, MA: MIT Press.

Siegel, D. 1974. *Topics in English morphology*. Cambridge, MA: MIT dissertation.

Stonham, J. 1994. *Combinatorial morphology*. Amsterdam: Benjamins.

Stump, G. 1991. A paradigm-based theory of morphosemantic mismatches. *Language* 67: 675–725.

Stump, G. 2001. *Inflectional morphology: A theory of paradigm structure*. Cambridge: Cambridge University Press.

Xu, Z. & M. Aronoff. 2011. A Realization Optimality Theory approach to blocking and extended morphological exponence. *Journal of Linguistics* 47: 673–707.

Zoll, C. 1996. *Parsing below the segment in a constraint-based framework*. Berkeley: University of California dissertation.

Abbreviations

1P	First person plural
APP	Applicative
CAUS	Causative
DIM	Diminutive
DIST	Distributive
INT	Intensive
PASS	Passive
PL	Plural
REC	Reciprocal
RED	Reduplication
SG	Singular
SUBJ	Subjunctive

8

The Phonetics of Downstep in Abron and Adioukrou

WILLIAM R. LEBEN & FIRMIN AHOUA

1   Background

In several languages of West Africa, the interval between a High tone and a following downstepped High has been found to be nearly constant.[1] Dolphyne's (1994) Akan measurements, based on data from five speakers, found a relatively constant pitch interval between downstepped High tone and the preceding High tone, while the interval between two High tones triggered by downdrift in the sequence High Low High was more variable.

Constant musical intervals were also found for downstep by Rialland & Somé (2011) in Dagara-Wulé, a dialect of Dagaare, a Gur language, with a new twist: the size of the interval was consistent for each of four subjects, but across subjects the interval size varied considerably, depending on each speaker's overall pitch range. As with Akan, the authors noticed a marked difference in Dagara-Wulé between the behavior of downstep and downdrift.[2]

---

[1] We thank Salomon Kouakou, linguistics doctoral student at the Université Félix Houphouët-Boigny, Abidjan, for long hours of measurements under our supervision and for help in producing the paper. We also express our gratitude to Larry Hyman for his comments on an earlier version of this paper. The largest debt of all is to Annie Rialland, who gave her time freely to help us formulate a research strategy and interpret our findings.
[2] Several other smaller instrumental studies deserve mention here as well. Liberman et al. (1993: 158), working with one speaker, found an appreciably larger interval for downdrift than for downstep in Igbo, an Igboid language of the Benue Congo group. Bird & Stegen's (1993)

Revealing Structure.
Eugene Buckley, Thera Crane & Jeff Good (eds.).
Copyright © 2018, CSLI Publications.

Another factor in downstep interval size is utterance length. Rialland & Somé (2011: 119) found anticipatory raising at the start of longer Dagara-Wulé utterances, which they interpret as "a global adjustment in pitch range in order to accommodate a larger number of intervals". A similar adjustment has been discussed regarding downdrift, for Yoruba (Laniran & Clements 2003).

If it is normal in tone languages to equalize steps, as found in the above languages, should we expect similar behavior among intonational steps in non-tone languages? Ladd (2008: 78–79) summarizes relevant results from Liberman & Pierrehumbert (1984) and Beckman & Pierrehumbert (1986):

> The steps in a downstep sequence … are of equal size. More precisely, the value of each accent peak in a downstep series is a constant proportion (in terms of the model's parameters) of the previous peak. Similar results have been obtained for other languages (e.g. Dutch: van den Berg, Gussenhoven, and Rietveld 1992).

This represents a third way in which downsteps can exhibit equal intervals: calculated as a fixed fraction of the F_0 value of a preceding High.

Our goal here is to report on Abron and Adioukrou, two Kwa languages of Côte d'Ivoire, and to determine whether downstep and downdrift affect High tones in phonetically similar ways and whether there is a regular way of characterizing the step interval for downstep.

2   Methodology

For this study we chose two Kwa languages of Côte d'Ivoire, Abron and Adioukrou. Abron, with more speakers in Ghana, is particularly closely related to Akan. We recorded three male speakers of Abron and three male speakers of Adioukrou using a DAT Edirol recorder at 44.1 kHz with high quality headset professional microphones.[3] A set of test utterances, given in the Appendix, were used with a carrier phrase in order to minimize the final

---

tonal study of Dschang, a Grassfields Bantu language, includes downstep, with a passing comment about a constant interval but no actual discussion. Hogan & Manyeh (1996) report on downstep in Kono, which they identify as a Northern Mande language. This is the first published case we are aware of that finds downstep to target a constant musical interval, but it is based on data from a single speaker. Snider (2007) is explicitly directed at downstep in Chumburung, which is closely related to Akan and spoken nearby. The study collected ten tokens each from two sentences, spoken by two subjects, and found very similar F_0 profiles for downstep and downdrift.

[3] We would like to thank our Abron informants, three male speakers from the villages of Assueffry and Priti, where the Abron variety is called Western Brong; it is called Ivory Coast Brong in the dialect survey of Dolphyne (1976: 45). We also express gratitude to our informants for Adioukrou, three male speakers from the village of Tiaha, Sous-préfecture of Dabou.

lowering and sentence vocal initiation effects. For Abron, utterances were elicited in the carrier phrase *mí kà X nné bíó* 'I say X today again'. For Adioukrou, the carrier phrase was *mè sé X èmɛ́* 'I say X again'.

Speakers pronounced each utterance set in randomized order three times in three rounds. Thus, there were nine tokens of each test utterance for each speaker. There were seven test utterances in Abron (four downstep and three downdrift). A total of 189 tokens were measured for Abron. In Adioukrou, there were 324 tokens in all from twelve utterances (five downstep and seven downdrift). Test items were constructed to vary utterance length and number and placement of downstepped and downdrifted High tone. The data were processed with the software package Praat, and calculations were made using Microsoft Excel.

3   Abron

3.1   Overview of Tone System

Abron has downstep from three distinct sources (Timyan-Ravenhill 1982, Diabah & Osam 2004). The realization of downstep is the same, regardless of its source, as is the case with downstep in general (Clements 1979). The three sources are:

a. *Lexical downstep*: For example, proper nouns like *á⁺má* 'name for woman born on Saturday' and *fó⁺dió* 'name for man born on Friday' contain lexical downstep.

b. *Associative marker*: This marker typically expresses possession of the second noun by the first. It consists of a downstep inserted between two nouns. All of the downsteps in our data below come from this associative marker.

c. *Phonological downstep*: This downstep is triggered by the delinking of a Low tone. Timyan-Ravenhill (1982: 115) provides a good illustrative example from Abron, given in (1).

(1)   *dɔ̀ŋgɔ́   á-⁺warí   hínɪ́   bá   kí*
      Dongo   PRF-marry   chief   child   SPEC
      'Dongo married the chief's daughter.'

The perfective aspect marker *à* whose underlying tone is uncontroversially Low, here carries a High tone that is spread from the subject on the left. Spreading in turn displaces the aspect marker's underlying Low, which floats between the aspect marker and the verb. The delinked Low of the aspect marker is heard as a downstep between the flanking High tones.

3.2 Data and Measurements in Abron

To minimize consonant influences, measurements were taken at the mid-point of vowels, located by listening to the signal as it was displayed on the screen. The values were converted into semitones to normalize for differences in speakers' pitch ranges. For the baseline (where the value is zero semitones), we followed Rialland & Somé (2011) in choosing 127.09 Hz in order to accommodate a wide range of normal speaker pitch heights. The formula we used for converting F_0 from Hertz into semitones was:

(2) Frequency $= 12 \times \log_2 \left(\frac{\text{Frequency (Hz)}}{127.09} \right)$

Data for each utterance in the corpus were plotted and tabulated. Due to space limitations, we combined the results for the entire corpus into the composite charts for downstep and downdrift in Figures 1 and 2.[4]

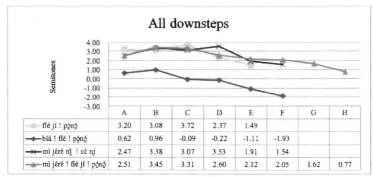

	A	B	C	D	E	F	G	H
fíé jí ! pɔ́nɔ́	3.20	3.08	3.72	2.37	1.49			
bíá ! fíé ! pɔ́nɔ́	0.62	0.96	-0.09	-0.22	-1.11	-1.93		
mí jéré ní ! cé ní	2.47	3.38	3.07	3.53	1.91	1.54		
mí jéré ! fíé jí ! pɔ́nɔ́	2.51	3.45	3.31	2.60	2.12	2.05	1.62	0.77

Figure 1. Abron downstep

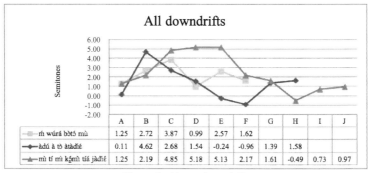

	A	B	C	D	E	F	G	H	I	J
ḿ wúrá bɔ̀tɔ́ mù	1.25	2.72	3.87	0.99	2.57	1.62				
àdú à tɔ̀ àtàdíé	0.11	4.62	2.68	1.54	-0.24	-0.96	1.39	1.58		
mù tí mì kɔ́mì tíá jàdíé	1.25	2.19	4.85	5.18	5.13	2.17	1.61	-0.49	0.73	0.97

Figure 2. Abron downdrift

---

[4] In the downstep figures, the last line seems to have a lower reference line than the two other graphs. The reason is that one speaker, who had a higher voice, was removed for this example.

3.3 Discussion

Each line in the figure plots combined semitone averages for the syllables of an utterance across subjects. Visual comparison of Figures 1 and 2 shows how similarly the downstep utterances behave in relation to each other compared with the downdrift ones. For example, the last and longest downstep utterance, eight syllables long, undergoes a fairly smooth descent. By comparison, the eight-syllable downdrift utterance undergoes register resetting after the sixth syllable.

Figure 1 shows that for downstep the general shape of the curves is the same, no matter how many downsteps. Also, the size of downstep interval is reduced in proportion to the number of downsteps. The further the downstep is from the beginning of the utterance, the smaller the interval. The data are in semitones, meaning that the size of the musical interval signaling downstep is not constant but decreases during the utterance.

4 Adioukrou

4.1 Overview of Tone System

Adioukrou has High and Low tones, which can combine to form falls and rises. Some nouns are followed by a floating tone which affects a following TBU (tone bearing unit). If no TBU follows, the floating tone is dropped. In our data below, the nouns *gbàŋkɔ́* 'horse', *ɔ́cń* 'fish', and *álú* 'kola nut' end with a floating Low tone, which downsteps a following High tone.

4.2 Data and Measurements in Adioukrou

As with Abron, F_0 values were converted into semitones to normalize for speakers' pitch ranges. The baseline, zero semitones, was set at 127.09 Hz. Composite charts for downstep and downdrift are given in Figures 3 and 4.

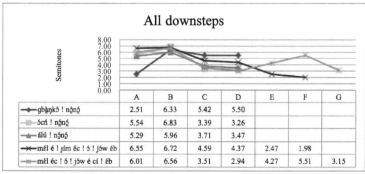

	A	B	C	D	E	F	G
gbàŋkɔ́ ! nɔ̀nɔ́	2.51	6.33	5.42	5.50			
ɔ́cń ! nɔ̀nɔ́	5.54	6.83	3.39	3.26			
álú ! nɔ̀nɔ́	5.29	5.96	3.71	3.47			
mɛ́l é ! ɟím 6c ! ɔ́ ! jɔ́w ɛ́b	6.55	6.72	4.59	4.37	2.47	1.98	
mɛ́l 6c ! ɔ́ ! jɔ́w é cí ! ɛ́b	6.01	6.56	3.51	2.94	4.27	5.51	3.15

Figure 3. Adioukrou downstep

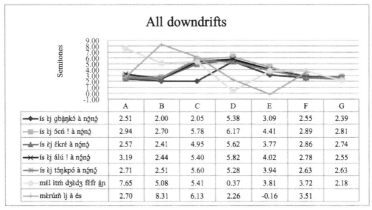

	A	B	C	D	E	F	G
ís èj gbànkɔ́ à nɔ́nɔ́	2.51	2.00	2.05	5.38	3.09	2.55	2.39
ís èj ɔ́cń ! à nɔ́nɔ́	2.94	2.70	5.78	6.17	4.41	2.89	2.81
ís èj ékrɛ́ à nɔ́nɔ́	2.57	2.41	4.95	5.62	3.77	2.86	2.74
ís èj álú ! à nɔ́nɔ́	3.19	2.44	5.40	5.82	4.02	2.78	2.55
ís èj tɔ́ŋkpó à nɔ́nɔ́	2.71	2.51	5.60	5.28	3.94	2.63	2.63
mɛ́l ìtń dʒèdʒ fɛ̀fr ɑ́ɲ	7.65	5.08	5.41	0.37	3.81	3.72	2.18
mèrúḿ lj à és	2.70	8.31	6.13	2.26	-0.16	3.51	

Figure 4. Adioukrou downdrift

5 Results and discussion

5.1 Research Questions

We examined our results in search of answers to the following questions:[5]

a. Is the size of the downstep interval constant in a given phrase?

b. Do utterances all tend to start at the same level, regardless of length or number of downsteps, or do longer utterances or those with many downsteps tend to start higher? The answer would tell us something about preplanning.

c. Does utterance-final High tone tend to end on the same pitch irrespective of length or the number of downsteps? The answer would reveal whether interval size was manipulated in order to fit into a fixed pitch range, independently of the length of the utterance.

5.2 Qualitative Observations

The studies of Akan, Yoruba, and Dagara-Wulé cited above all found evidence of anticipatory raising, the tendency to begin a longer utterance on a higher pitch in order to make room for a greater number of tonal intervals. Our results for Abron and Adioukrou do not show this effect. For example, in Figure 1, the shortest Abron utterance is actually the one that began on the highest pitch. The pitch of the first syllable thus can vary from utterance to utterance, but without any evident correlation to length of utterance.

---

[5] We are most grateful to Annie Rialland for contributing to this list of questions.

The pitch of the final High tends to be higher in short utterances (with fewer downsteps) than in longer utterances (with more). That finding seems consistent with the hypothesis that the downstep interval is constant, yet we also observe that the size of the downstep interval, measured in semitones, shrinks as the utterance progresses. If backed up by quantitative measures, this result goes against the constant interval hypothesis.

5.3   Quantitative Observations: Downstep versus Downdrift

Do downstep and downdrift occasion similar drops in register between the affected High tones? The data, as seen above, show considerable variability across speakers and across utterances for both downstep and downdrift. To quantify the overall degree of variation in downstep and in downdrift, we defined a Variability Index, a quantitative measure of the variations in interval size in a given set of data, which could weigh the overall tendency toward constant intervals for downstep against those for downdrift.[6]

Our Variability Index captures the average size of pitch intervals in the data for each sequence H⁺H in the downstep data. We applied the same measure to each set of High tones separated only by one or more (nonfloating) Low tones in the downdrift data. The formula used is given in (3).

(3) $\Delta x_{ji} = (x_{j+1i} - x_{ji})/x_{ji}$

> where
> j: position of tone; $j = 1, 2, ..., n$
> i: speaker number; $i = 1, 2, ..., n$
> x_{ji}: pitch of tone j (speaker i)
> x_{j+1i}: pitch of tone $j+1$ (speaker i)
> Δx_{ji}: change in pitch in relation to pitch of tone j and $j+1$ (speaker i)

For downstep, Table 1 charts the values of $\bar{Y}$ (arithmetic average of variations) for H⁺H sequences in the corpora for Abron and Adioukrou.[7] The formulas we used to calculate $\bar{Y}$ values are given in (4).

---

[6] Our deepest thanks to Kouadio Jean-Marc and Ibrahim Ouattara, statisticians at the Université Alassane Ouattara, Bouaké, for advising us on how to define and formulate this measure and on how to map and interpret the results.

[7] Results for both languages are combined for brevity. This may seem odd, but we separate results for the two languages below and show that they are comparable. An average variation of 35.72 semitones, an outlier, was left out of our calculations in Table 1.

(4) $\bar{Y} = \frac{1}{n}\sum_{j=1}^{n} \bar{Y}'_j$

  n = total number of H$^+$H sequences observations
  $\bar{Y}'_j$ = marginal arithmetic average of jth H$^+$H sequences
  j = 1, 2, ..., n

with

  $\forall j; j$ = 1, 2, ..., n, $\bar{Y}'_j = \frac{1}{n}\sum_{i=1}^{n} \Delta X_{ij}$

where

  j: number of H$^+$H sequence; j = 1, 2, ..., n
  i: number of speaker; i = 1, 2, ..., n

Speaker (i) → *H$^+$H sequences (j) ↓*	*1*	*2*	*3*	*4*	*5*	*6*	*Average* *$\bar{Y}'_j$*
nị$^+$ and cɛ́	-0.17	-4.49	-1.15	-	-	-	-1.93
á$^+$ and fí	-1.91	-0.90	-	-	-	-	-1.41
rɛ́$^+$ and fí	-1.04	-1.14	0.02	-	-	-	-0.72
cń$^+$ and nɔ̣	-0.82	-0.31	-0.57	-	-	-	-0.57
cí$^+$ and ɛ́b	-0.59	-0.34	-0.46	-	-	-	-0.46
é$^+$ and ɟím	-0.44	-0.19	-0.43	-	-	-	-0.35
lú$^+$ and nɔ̣	-0.15	0.07	-0.31	-0.56	-	-	-0.24
ŋkɔ́$^+$ and nɔ̣	-0.17	-0.17	-	-	-	-	-0.17
ɟí$^+$ and pɔ̣	0.97	1.07	-0.03	-1.35	-1.07	-0.16	-0.09
ɔ́$^+$ and ɟɔ́w	1.32	-0.05	-0.21	-0.88	-0.07	-0.15	-0.01

Table 1. Distribution of variations in downstep intervals

The Variability Index for downstep, computed on the arithmetic average in Table 1, is $\bar{Y}$=-0.42. This means that the average amount of variation among all the downstep intervals in our data is 42%.

For downdrift, we do not include a table comparing across-speaker percentages for each downdrifted High tone in the corpus. There are so many instances in the corpus, and the values for different subjects are so scattered, from a low of 1.1% to a high of 170.8%, as to make an average meaningless. Instead, Table 2 separately lists the arithmetic averages for each speaker. L$_1$ in the expression HL$_1$H in the left-hand column designates a sequence of one or more Low tones.

Speaker	1	2	3	4	5	6	*Average*
Variation HL₁H	-0.37	-1.71	-1.59	-0.01	-0.02	0.99	-0.45

Table 2. Distribution of variations in downdrift

In Figures 5 and 6 we plot the averages of the variation amounts from Tables 1 and 2.

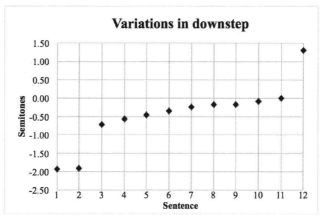

Figure 5. Scatter plot of average variation in downstep

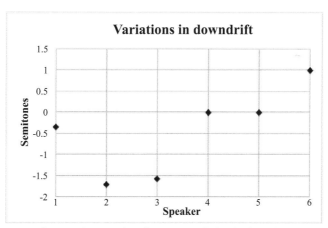

Figure 6. Scatter plot of average variation in downdrift

The standard deviation is 0.82 for downstep and 1.03 for downdrift. For downstep, the values fall within the range [-2.06, 1.22], while for downdrift the spread is greater, [-2.51, 1.61]. Thus, the variability is less for downstep than for downdrift, though the figure for downstep is more variable than one might expect, given the findings cited above from Dagara-Wulé and from Akan.

Looked at separately, the Abron and Adioukrou results confirm what is seen above while also showing differences. Compare Tables 3 and 4.

Abron	á ⁺fî	é ⁺pɔ̰	jí ⁺pɔ̰	ré ⁺fî	nị̱ ⁺cé	Average
Variation	-1.41	1.29	0.39	-1.09	-1.93	-0.55

Table 3. Abron downstep

Adioukrou	ŋkɔ́ ⁺nɔ̰	cń ⁺nɔ̰	lú ⁺nɔ̰	é ⁺ɟím	ɔ́ ⁺jɔ́w	cí ⁺éb	Average
Variation	-0.17	-0.57	-0.34	-0.35	-0.01	-0.46	-0.32

Table 4. Adioukrou downstep

The same tendencies are observed in both languages, with a slightly less rapid drop in pitch in Adioukrou (32%). For Adioukrou, the standard deviation is also less, 0.20 as compared with 1.34 for Abron, showing that downstep is more stable in the Adioukrou data. Downdrift is highly variable in Abron, less so in Adioukrou. For Abron the standard deviation is 3.46, and for Adioukrou, it is 1.70. See Tables 5 and 6.

Speaker	1	2	3	4	5	6	7	8	9	Average
Variation HL_1H	6.50	-1.18	-1.16	5.49	0.00	0.00	7.28	-0.16	0.39	1.91

Table 5. Abron downdrift

Speaker	3	16	19	21	Average
Variation HL_1H	0.37	-2.39	1.44	0.85	0.07

Table 6. Adioukrou downdrift

5.4 Discussion

Let us try to make sense of these results. The greater degree of variability for downdrift than for downstep is hardly surprising because, as described in section 3.1, all instances of downstep in our study are contrastive lexically, morphologically, or phonologically. Downdrift, of course, is not contrastive in Abron or Adioukrou, nor in other languages. That simple fact allows certain variations in downdrift to occur without affecting contrast, and indeed that is what we find. For example, in Yoruba, Laniran's (1992) measurements of downdrift turned up considerable interspeaker variation among her four subjects.[8] Her result is especially revealing because Yoruba has three level phonological tones, which reduces the amount of potential space for pitch variation, as compared with two-tone languages like Abron and Adioukrou.

Regardless of the number of phonological tone levels, a degree of variability in downdrift is to be expected in any downdrifting language, given the many factors that combine to form a downdrift contour. These include utterance length and speed, phrasing, possible intonational highlighting of specific elements, and—as Ladd (2008: 158–159) notes—modulation of pitch range for paralinguistic purposes such as denoting emotion. Yet another source of variation is the resetting of register in mid-utterance. Laniran & Clements (2003: 216) found that Yoruba speakers reset the High tone ceiling at least once in longer utterances, but with little consistency from speaker to speaker and not necessarily at overt pauses.

Other influences on downdrift contours include local and long-distance effects beyond the lowering effect of Low tones on subsequent High tones. A frequent phenomenon is the raising of High tones when Low tones follow, as documented for Hausa by Meyers (1976). But of potentially greater interest is the finding of Laniran & Clements (2003: 218) for Yoruba that the first High tone is elevated in an utterance of mixed High-Low sequences, as compared with an all-High utterance, where no raising is evident. They attribute this effect to the interaction of High Raising with downdrift and offer preliminary calculations (Laniran & Clements 2003: 232–243) to back up their proposal. But another possibility is that the elevation of the initial High tone anticipates the need for more tonal space to accommodate the effects of downdrift in an utterance of mixed Highs and Lows.

Overall, studies to date have not really been designed to tease out the separate factors influencing the course of downdrift. Still, what is known suggests that, as Laniran & Clements (2003: 203) put it, "competing factors culminate on individual tones to produce functionally motivated 'compromise' f0 patterns".

6 Conclusion

Our data on downstep and downdrift in Abron and Adioukrou show greater phonetic variability in downdrift than in downstep. This is not surprising, because downstep is contrastive, while downdrift is not. We believe that any intonational contour is a result of a complex set of calculations and adjustments, with downdrift more readily available for variation than down-

---

[8] Laniran (1992) refers to downdrift as "downstep", as do Laniran & Clements (1993) in an article pursuing Laniran's findings. Yoruba lacks downstep in the sense of the term used here.

step because the latter carries a phonologically important functional load.[9] We hope that our findings from Abron and Adioukrou will contribute to a typology of downstep and downdrift systems that uses instrumental phonetic data to complement and validate the groundbreaking phonological work of Hyman (1979), Clements (1979), and others.

References

Beckman, M. E. & J. B. Pierrehumbert. 1986. Intonational structure in Japanese and English. *Phonology Yearbook* 3: 255–309.

Berg, R. van den, C. Gussenhoven & T. Rietveld. 1992. Downstep in Dutch: Implications for a model. In G. J. Docherty & D. R. Ladd (eds.), *Papers in laboratory phonology II: Gesture, segment, prosody*, 335–359. Cambridge: Cambridge University Press.

Bird, S. & O. Stegen. 1993. Principles of F_0 measurement: A case study of tone and register in Bamileke-Dschang. Poster paper presented at the Fourth International Conference on Laboratory Phonology, Oxford.

Clements, G. N. 1979. The description of terraced-level tone languages. *Language* 55: 536–558.

Diabah, G. & E. K. Osam. 2004. Aspects of some phonological processes in Bono. In M. E. K. Dakubu & E. K. Osam (eds.), *Studies in the languages of the Volta Basin, vol. 2*, 228–238. Accra: Combert Impressions.

Dolphyne, F. 1976. Delafosse's Abron wordlist in the light of a Brong dialect survey. In H. M. J. Trutenau (ed.), *Languages of the Akan area*, 35–46. Basel: Basler Afrika Bibliographien.

Dolphyne, F. 1994. A phonetic and phonological study of downdrift and downstep in Akan. Paper presented at the 25th Annual Conference on African Linguistics, Rutgers University.

Hogan, J. T. & M. Manyeh. 1996. A study of Kono tone spacing. *Phonetica* 53(4): 221–229.

Hyman, L. M. 1979. A reanalysis of tonal downstep. *Journal of African Languages and Linguistics* 1: 9–29.

Ladd, D. R. 2008. *Intonational phonology*, 2nd edn. Cambridge: Cambridge University Press.

Laniran, Y. 1992. *Intonation in a tone language: The phonetic implementation of tone in Yoruba*. Ithaca, NY: Cornell University dissertation.

Laniran, Y. & G. N. Clements. 2003. Downstep and high tone raising: Interacting factors in Yoruba tone production. *Journal of Phonetics* 31(2): 203–250.

---

[9] It is also worth noting that downstep's contrastive function does not exempt it from phonological changes. In the related Kwa language Baule, Leben & Ahoua (2006) describe emphatic particles that neutralize the contrast between Low and High tone. Among the High tones neutralized are downstepped Highs.

Leben, W. R. & F. Ahoua. 2006. Phonological reflexes of emphasis in Kwa languages of Côte d'Ivoire. *Studies in African Linguistics* Supplement 11: 145–158.

Liberman, M. & J. B. Pierrehumbert. 1984. Intonational invariance under changes in pitch range and length. In M. Aronoff & R. T. Oehrle (eds.), *Language and sound structure*, 157–233. Cambridge, MA: MIT Press.

Liberman, M., J. M. Schultz, S. Hong & V. Okeke. 1993. The phonetic interpretation of tone in Igbo. *Phonetica* 50: 147–160.

Meyers, L. F. 1976. *Aspects of Hausa tone* (UCLA Working Papers in Phonetics 32). Los Angeles: UCLA Department of Linguistics.

Rialland, A. & A. P. Somé. 2011. Downstep and linguistic scaling in Dagara-Wulé. In J. A. Goldsmith, E. Hume & W. L. Wetzels (eds.), *Tones and features: Phonetic and phonological perspectives*, 108–136. Berlin: De Gruyter.

Snider, K. L. 2007. Automatic and non-automatic downstep in Chumburung: An instrumental comparison. *Journal of West African Languages* 34(1): 105–115.

Timyan-Ravenhill, J. 1982. L'Abron. In G. Hérault (ed.), *Atlas des langues Kwa de Côte d'Ivoire, vol. 1*, 83–128. Abidjan: Institut de Linguistique Appliquée.

Abbreviations

AUX	Auxiliary
CONN	Connective
DEF	Definite
IDENT	Identificational
PRF	Perfective
SPEC	Specifier
VB.EXT	Verbal extension

Appendix

Abron

1	Tones	HH	H	L	H H		
	Phonetic	fíé	jí	!	pɔ̰́nɔ̰́		
	Gloss	house	this		door		
	Translation	'The door of this house'					

2	Tones	HH	L HH		L	H H	
	Phonetic	bíá	! fíé		!	pɔ̰́nɔ̰́	
	Gloss	woman	house			door	
	Translation	'The door of the woman's house'					

3	Tones	H	H H	H	L	H	H
	Phonetic	mí	jéré	nɪ̰́	!	cé	nɪ̰́
	Gloss	my	wife	this		hat	IDENT
	Translation	'This is my wife's hat'					

4	Tones	H	H H	L	HH	H	L	H H
	Phonetic	mí	jéré	!	fíé	jí	!	pɔ̰́nɔ̰́
	Gloss	my	wife		house	this		door
	Translation	'That door of my wife's house'					

5	Tones	H	H L	H H	L	
	Phonetic	ḿ	wúrà	bɔ́tɔ́	mù	
	Gloss	I	enter	bag	inside	
	Translation	'I swept into the bag'				

6	Tones	L H	L	L	LL HH	
	Phonetic	àdú	à	tɔ̀	àtàdíé	
	Gloss	adou	AUX	buy	clothes	
	Translation	'Adou bought clothes'				

7	Tones	L	H L	H L	HH	L HH
	Phonetic	mì	tímì	kɔ̰̀mì	tíá	ɟàdíé
	Gloss	I	can	struggle	against	disease
	Translation	'I can struggle against the disease'				

Adioukrou

	Tones	H H		L	H H					
1	Phonetic	gbàŋkɔ́	!		nɔ̰́nɔ̰́					
	Gloss	horse			many					
	Translation	'Many horses'								

	Tones	H H		L	H H					
2	Phonetic	ɔ́cń	!		nɔ̰́nɔ̰́					
	Gloss	fish			many					
	Translation	'Many fish'								

	Tones	H H		L	H H					
3	Phonetic	álú	!		nɔ̰́nɔ̰́					
	Gloss	kola.nut			many					
	Translation	'Many kola nuts'								

	Tones	H	H	L H	H		L H L H			
4	Phonetic	mɛ́l	é	! ɟím	éc	!	ɔ́ ! jɔ́w			
	Gloss	Mel	CONN	son	CONN		women			
	Translation	'The wives of Mel's son'								

	Tones	H	H	L H L H	HH		L H			
5	Phonetic	mɛ́l	éc	! ɔ́ ! jɔ́w	écí	!	éb			
	Gloss	Mel	CONN	women	CONN		village			
	Translation	'The village of Mel's wives'								

	Tones	H	L	L H	L	H H				
6	Phonetic	ís	ɛ̀j	gbàŋkɔ́	à	nɔ̰́nɔ̰́				
	Gloss	bring	us	horse	DEF	many				
	Translation	'Bring us many horses'								

	Tones	H	L	H H L	L	H H				
7	Phonetic	ís	ɛ̀j	ɔ́cń!	à	nɔ̰́nɔ̰́				
	Gloss	bring	us	fish	DEF	many				
	Translation	'Bring us many fish'								

	Tones	H	L	H H	L	H H				
8	Phonetic	ís	ɛ̀j	ékrɛ́	à	nɔ̰́nɔ̰́				
	Gloss	bring	us	fox	DEF	many				
	Translation	'Bring us many foxes'								

9	Tones	H	L	H H L	L		H H
	Phonetic	ís	ɛ̀j	álú !	à		nɔ̰́nɔ̰́
	Gloss	bring	us	kola nuts	DEF		many
	Translation	'Bring us many kola nuts'					

10	Tones	H	L	H H	L		H H
	Phonetic	ís	ɛ̀j	tóŋkpó	à		nɔ̰́nɔ̰́
	Gloss	bring	us	hoe	DEF		many
	Translation	'Bring us many hoes'					

11	Tones	H	L H	L	H L	H
	Phonetic	mέl	ìtm̀	dʒɛ̀dʒ	féfr̀	án
	Gloss	Mel	mark.PRF	Djèdj	kaolin	face
	Translation	'Mel marked Djedj's face with kaolin'				

12	Tones		L H	L	L	L	H
	Phonetic	m	ɛ̀rú	m̀	ìj	à	és
	Gloss	me	lay.PRF	VB.EXT	child	DEF	down
	Translation	'I laid the children down'					

9

Penultimate Shortening in NPs:
The Case of Símákonde

SOPHIE MANUS

1 Introduction

The goals of this paper are to present an overview of penultimate shortening processes in Símákonde noun phrases (NPs) and their consequences for noun tone patterns.[1] I will therefore give an account of prosodic domain formation in NPs, depending on the quality and the number of modifiers involved, with a special focus on demonstratives which have the ability to shorten every preceding penult of an NP in Símákonde.

In Section 2, I first provide some general preliminaries about Símákonde prosody. In Section 3, I present noun phrases which consist of a noun and one modifier. In Section 4, I present noun phrases made up of a noun and more than one modifier. I then give special consideration to nonfinal demonstratives in Section 5. Having documented the various phrasing possibilities in noun phrases in Símákonde, I conclude in Section 6 by summarizing all the phrasing possibilities in NPs.[2]

---

[1] I would like to thank Larry Hyman for his enthusiasm about Símákonde in general and its noun phrases in particular. His questions and comments about what might make a demonstrative vowel shorten have expanded my analysis about Símákonde NPs. I am of course solely responsible for any mistakes in this paper.

[2] Relative clauses will not be addressed here. For a detailed description of relative clause morphology and prosody, see Manus (2003, 2010).

Revealing Structure.
Eugene Buckley, Thera Crane & Jeff Good (eds.).
Copyright © 2018, CSLI Publications.

2   Símákonde Prosody

Símákonde is a dialect of Makonde (Eastern Bantu, P23, according to Guthrie (1948) and Maho (2003)), spoken by immigrant Mozambican communities in Tanzania, both in Zanzibar (Unguja island) and on the mainland (in the areas of Tanga, Dar es Salaam, and Bagamoyo). Makonde tone has been studied in various dialects by the following authors: Devos (2008), Kraal (2005), Leach (2010), Liphola (2001), Manus (2003, 2010, 2014, 2017), and Odden (1990a, 1990b).

As in other languages which have lost the historical Proto-Bantu vowel length contrast (Hyman 2013), Símákonde has a regular phrase-final rule which lengthens the penultimate syllable of every phonological phrase.

The examples in (1) illustrate penultimate lengthening in Símákonde.[3]

(1)   a.   *kúlúúma*   'to bite'
      b.   *kúlúmúúla*   'to cut'
      c.   *kúlúmúláánga*   'to cut into small pieces'
      d.   *kúlúmúlángííla*   'to cut into small pieces for someone'

Prosodic analysis requires the presence of the long penult observed in these transcriptions. The prominent phrase-final lengthened penult can bear all five tone patterns of the system (level tones H and L and contours LH, HL, and LHL). Light syllables can only bear level tones (H or L). The final syllable of a phonological phrase almost never bears a high tone, due to a nonfinality constraint that bars H tones from being anchored to phrase-final syllables.[4]

There are five tone patterns or melodies on the penultimate syllables of disyllabic nouns, corresponding to the five tone patterns of the system: H, HL, L, LH, LHL.[5] These are exemplified in (2).

(2)   a.   H   *sí-lóólo*   'mirror'
      b.   HL   *sí-júulu*   'hat'
      c.   L   *i-pooso*   'present'
      d.   LH   *li-jeémbe*   'hoe'
      e.   LHL   *si-loôngo*   'pot'

---

[3] All data presented in this paper were elicited and recorded by the author in Tanzania between 2000 and 2010.
[4] The only phrase-final Highs in the language are in the remote demonstrative (e.g. in class 7, *asiilá* 'that one'), in the discourse deictic (e.g. in class 7, *nasanaasó* 'with it'), in the word for 'egg' (singular *liií*), and in one relative verb form (Subject Relative, Positive Near Past; e.g. *álotiilé* 'the one who just wanted).
[5] There are only four penultimate melodies on verbs, as shown in Manus (2003, 2014, 2017).

These five melodies link directly to the penult. The noun prefixes are almost always toneless and take a mere copy of the first penultimate tone.[6] The final syllable takes a default low tone.

As mentioned above, phonological phrase boundaries are systematically marked by penultimate lengthening in Makonde. Símákonde has very strict rules defining which constituents must be grouped into a single phonological phrase within noun phrases and which cannot be. Tonal alternations are conditioned by the presence or absence of the heavy penult. Phonological phrases made up of a noun and one or more modifiers shorten those penults not found in phrase-final position, thus partially or fully neutralizing the five tone alternations.

3 Noun Phrases Made Up of a Noun and One Modifier

Noun phrases which consist of a noun and one modifier can either form a single phonological phrase (henceforth, PhPhrase) or two distinct PhPhrases. Depending on the nature of the modifier, three different phrasing possibilities are observed: some modifiers are required to phrase with the head noun, others are required to phrase separately, while still others can either form a single PhPhrase or two PhPhrases with the head noun.

For example, in (3), consisting of noun + adjective + verb, the three occurrences of penultimate length indicate that each word constitutes a separate PhPhrase, as marked by the parentheses.

(3) (noun)   (adjective)   (verb)
     (sílóólo)   (síkúmeêne)   (sindiîgwa)
     7.mirror   7.big   7.PAST.fall
     '(a) big mirror fell'

In the rest of this section, we will look at the effects of modifiers on length. The modifiers we will consider are adjectives, demonstratives, numerals, genitives, possessives, and intensifiers.

3.1 Noun + One Modifier: One PhPhrase

If the modifier is a demonstrative (proximal, distal, or anaphoric), it has to phrase together with the head noun, as shown in (4a). It can never phrase separately, as shown in (4b).

---

[6] Some prefixes exceptionally contribute a High tone (Manus 2003).

(4) a. (noun   demonstrative)
       (*sílóló*   *asiilá*)
       7.mirror DEM.7
       'that mirror'

     b. *(noun)   (demonstrative)
        *(*siloolo*) (*asiila*)

The shortening of the noun's long penult dissociates the penultimate tonal melodies H, HL, L, LH, and LHL. An initial floating high tone on the noun results in a tonal high plateau, neutralizing all five noun tone patterns, as summarized in Table 1 and shown in examples (4a) and (5a)–(5d).

Noun	Melody		Shortened form
sílóólo	(H)	>	*sílóló*
sijúulu	(HL)	>	*sijúlú*
ipooso	(L)	>	*ipósó*
lijeémbe	(LH)	>	*lijémbé*
siloôngo	(LHL)	>	*sílóngó*

Table 1. Tone patterns on NPs in demonstrative constructions

The initial floating high triggered by the demonstrative is probably a trace of the augment (Bantu preprefix) which no longer exists in Símákonde.

(5) a. (noun   demonstrative)
       (*sijúlú*   *asiilá*)
       7.hat   DEM.7
       'that hat'

     b. (noun   demonstrative)
        (*ipósó*   *aiilá*)
        9.present DEM.9
        'that present'

     c. (noun   demonstrative)
        (*lijémbé*   *aliilá*)
        5.hoe   DEM.5
        'that hoe'

     d. (noun   demonstrative)
        (*sílóngó*   *asiilá*)
        7.pot   DEM.7
        'that pot'

3.2 Noun + One Modifier: Two PhPhrases

If the modifier is an adjective, a numeral, or a genitive, it has to phrase separately in NPs made up of a noun and one modifier only, and it can never phrase with the head noun, as shown in (6), (7), and (8).[7]

(6) a. (noun)   (adjective)
        (*lingéela*)   (*líkúmeêne*)
        5.mango   5.big
        '(a) big mango'

     b. *(noun   adjective)
        *(*lingela   likumeene*)

(7) a. (noun)   (numeral)
        (*lingéela*)   (*liímo*)
        5.mango   5.one
        'one mango'

     b. *(noun   numeral)
        *(*lingela   liimo*)

(8) a. (noun)   (genitive)
        (*lingéela*)   (*lyá   nkoôngwe*)
        5.mango   5.CO   1.woman
        'the woman's mango'

     b. *(noun   genitive)
        *(*lingela   lya nkoongwe*)

As can be seen, when the noun phrases separately from the modifier, it keeps its heavy penult and its full tone pattern.

3.3 Noun + One Modifier: One or Two PhPhrases

If the modifier is a possessive or an intensifier (meaning 'himself', 'herself', or 'itself'), it can either phrase with the head noun and constitute a single phonological phrase with it, as shown in (9a) and (10a), or not phrase with the head noun and be parsed into an independent phonological phrase, as shown in (9b) and (10b).

According to Hyman (2013: 321), "a number of Bantu languages treat noun + possessive as a single domain". Símákonde does treat a noun followed by a possessive as a single domain when the possessive ('my') forms

---

[7] This is true only in an NP made of a noun and one modifier *only*. In an NP made of a noun and two modifiers with the last modifier being a demonstrative, the NP would constitute a single PhPhrase, as will be seen in Section 4.5.

one PhPhrase with its head noun and is then almost cliticized, as in (9a). In (9b), the possessive ('mine') is appositional and takes the same form one would get for 'mine' with a zero head, as in (9c); note the difference in tone in *yáangu* compared with *yaángu*.[8]

(9) a. (noun   possessive)
         (*iposó*   *yaángu*)
         9.present 9.POSS.SG1
         'my present'

     b. (noun)   (possessive)
         (*ipooso*)   (*yáangu*)
         9.present 9.POSS.SG1
         'my present (present [of] mine)'

     c. (possessive)
         (*yáangu*)
         9.POSS.SG1
         'mine'

(10) a. (noun   intensifier)
         (*ípósó*   *yeene*)
         9.present 9.INT
         'the present itself'

     b. (noun)   (intensifier)
         (*ipooso*)   (*yéene*)
         9.present 9.INT
         'the present itself'

As seen, when the noun phrases separately from the modifier, it maintains its long penult and associated tone pattern. However, when the noun is parsed into a single PhPhrase with its modifier, its penult is shortened and loses its melody.

When the modifier is a possessive, the five tone patterns H, HL, L, LH, and LHL are partially neutralized into two distinct tone patterns, as shown in (9a) and (11a)–(11d). Nouns with a penultimate melody starting with a H (H and HL) become H, whereas nouns with a penultimate melody starting with a L (L, LH, and LHL) become L. The possessive also contributes a floating High tone that links to the final syllable(s) of the nouns.[9] These patterns are summarized in Table 2.

---

[8] Note that a conjugated verb can be added after both (9a) and (9b); it will always phrase separately.
[9] See Manus (2003) for a detailed autosegmental analysis.

Noun	Melody		Possessed form
sílóólo	(H)	>	*sílóló*
síjúulu	(HL)	>	*síjúlú*
ipooso	(L)	>	*iposó*
lijeémbe	(LH)	>	*lijembé*
siloóngo	(LHL)	>	*silongó*

Table 2. Tone patterns on NPs in possessive constructions

(11) a. (noun   possessive)
        (*sílóló*   *saángu*)
        7.mirror 7.POSS.SG1
        'my mirror'

    b. (noun   possessive)
        (*síjúlú*   *saángu*)
        7.hat   7.POSS.SG1
        'my hat'

    c. (noun   possessive)
        (*lijembé*   *lyaángu*)
        5.hoe   5.POSS.SG1
        'my hoe'

    d. (noun   possessive)
        (*silongó*   *saángu*)
        7.pot   7.POSS.SG1
        'my pot'

When the modifier is an intensifier, the five tone patterns H, HL, L, LH, and LHL are all neutralized and become completely high (comparable to what is seen in (5) when the modifier is a demonstrative). This is shown in (10a) and (12a)–(12d).

(12) a. (noun   intensifier)
        (*sílóló*   *seene*)
        7.mirror 7.INT
        'the mirror itself'

    b. (noun   intensifier)
        (*síjúlú*   *seene*)
        7.hat   7.INT
        'the hat itself'

    c. (noun   intensifier)
        (*líjémbé*   *lyeene*)
        5.hoe   5.INT
        'the hoe itself'

d. (noun   intensifier)
   (*sílóngó* *seene*)
   7.pot   7.INT
   'the pot itself'

To summarize, noun phrases made of a noun and one modifier can either form a single phonological phrase (if the modifier is a demonstrative) or be parsed into two distinct phonological phrases (if the modifier is an adjective, a numeral, or a genitive), or constitute either a single phonological phrase or two phonological phrases (if the modifier is a possessive or an intensifier). The five tone melodies (H, HL, L, LH, and LHL) surface on the penults only when the penults are not shortened.

Table 3 summarizes the various tone patterns of nouns in NPs depending on the modifiers involved and on the shortening which is or is not triggered by the various modifiers.[10]

N / _ ADJ, NUM, GEN, # N / _ POSS, INT	N / _ DEM, INT	N / _ POSS
sílóólo (H)	*sílóló*	*sílóló*
sijúulu (HL)	*sijúlú*	*sijúlú*
ipooso (L)	*ipósó*	*iposó*
lijeémbe (LH)	*lijémbé*	*lijembé*
siloôngo (LHL)	*sílóngó*	*silongó*

Table 3. Tone patterns in NPs made up of a noun and one modifier

4   Noun Phrases with a Noun and More than One Modifier

Noun phrases made up of a noun and more than one modifier can either be parsed into more than one phonological phrase in a number of different ways (in Sections 4.1–4.4), or the NP may form a single phonological phrase (Section 4.5). This is in many ways parallel with what was seen in Section 3: adjectives, numerals, and genitives modifiers form separate PhPhrases, while possessives and intensives may be separate from the noun or form a single PhPhrase with the noun. However, there are certain additional complexities.

4.1   Noun + Two Modifiers: Three PhPhrases

An NP which consists of a noun and two modifiers may be parsed into three PhPhrases. For example, in (13), a noun is followed by an adjective and a numeral. As would be expected from Section 3, the noun and its two modi-

---

[10] The tone patterns in the first column are also the ones that nouns have before a pause.

fiers have to phrase separately, as shown in (13a), and none of the elements can phrase together in any combination, as shown in (13b)–(13d).

(13) a. (noun)   (adjective)   (numeral)
       (*viloôngo*) (*víkúmeêne*) (*viviíli*)
       8.pot   8.big   8.two
       'two big pots'

   b. *(noun   adjective   numeral)
      *(*vilongo* *vikumene*   *viviili*)

   c. *(noun   adjective)   (numeral)
   d. *(noun)   (adjective   numeral)

4.2   Noun + Three Modifiers: Four PhPhrases

In (14) we see a similar example with three modifiers following a noun. The noun and its three modifiers have to phrase separately as shown in (14a) and cannot constitute a single PhPhrase as in (14b), nor phrase together as shown in (14c)–(14e).

(14) a. (noun)   (adjective)   (genitive)   (numeral)
       (*viloôngo*) (*víkúmeêne*) (*vyá   naáswe*) (*viviíli*)
       8.pot   8.big   8.CO white   8.two
       'two big white pots'

   b. *(noun   adjective   genitive   numeral)
      *(*vilongo* *vikumene*   *vya naswe*   *viviili*)

   c. *(noun   adjective)   (genitive   numeral)
   d. *(noun)   (adjective   genitive   numeral)
   e. *(noun   adjective   genitive)   (numeral)

4.3   Noun + Two Modifiers: Two PhPhrases

Noun phrases made of a noun and more than one modifier can also be parsed into fewer PhPhrases, if some of the elements can phrase together. Let us look in (15) at an example of a noun and two modifiers which form two PhPhrases only, with the noun phrasing together with the first modifier. As might be expected given Section 3, this is possible because the first modifier here is a possessive.

(15) (noun   possessive)   (adjective)
     (*lijembé* *lyaáko*)   (*lídíkídiîki*)
     5.hoe   5.POSS.SG2   5.small
     'your small hoe'

4.4 Noun + Three Modifiers: Three PhPhrases

In (16), a noun and three modifiers constitute three PhPhrases only, with the noun phrasing together with its first modifier, a possessive.

(16) (noun   possessive)   (adjective)   (adverb)
     (*lijembé*   *lyaáko*)   (*lídíkídiîki*)   (*nameêne*)
     5.hoe   5.POSS.SG2   5.small   very
     'your very small hoe'

4.5 Noun + More Than One Modifier: One PhPhrase

Noun phrases made of a noun and more than one modifier can also form a single phonological phrase, but this only occurs if the last modifier is a demonstrative.

In Section 3.1, it was seen that a demonstrative and its head noun always have to constitute a single PhPhrase. In fact, every noun phrase that ends with a demonstrative (proximal, distal, or anaphoric), whether it is made of a noun and one, two, three, or even four modifiers, must be parsed into a single phonological phrase as shown in (17), (18), and (19).

(17) (noun   adjective   demonstrative)
     (*vílóngó*   *víkúméné*   *aviilá*)
     8.pot   8.big   DEM8
     'those big pots'

(18) (noun   adjective   numeral   demonstrative)
     (*vílóngó*   *víkúméné*   *vívílí*   *aviilá*)
     8.pot   8.big   8.two   DEM8
     'those two big pots'

(19) (noun   adjective   genitive   numeral   demonstrative)
     (*vílóngó*   *víkúméné*   *vyá*   *náswé*   *vívílí*   *aviilá*)
     8.pot   8.big   8.CO   white   8.two   DEM8
     'those two big white pots'

The final demonstrative triggers an initial floating High tone on the noun (a potential trace of the augment as mentioned in Section 3.1) that causes a high plateau to surface on each syllable preceding the demonstrative in the NP.

There may be a functional explanation to this, in that it is probably useful for hearers to receive information early on that they are dealing with a modifier structure (parsed into a single phonological phrase and announced by the high plateau) and not a predicate structure.[11]

To summarize, NPs made of a noun and more than one modifier are parsed into more than one PhPhrase in Símákonde except if the last modifier is a demonstrative.

5 Nonfinal Demonstratives

It was Larry Hyman who asked me whether there was anything that could make a demonstrative vowel shorten in Símákonde. I then extensively documented nonfinal demonstratives in NPs, and here are the results.

One modifier that can actually make a demonstrative vowel shorten is the possessive. Noun phrases made of a noun, a demonstrative, and a possessive can either constitute two PhPhrases with the demonstrative phrasing with the head noun and the possessive phrasing separately, as shown in (20) and (21), or be parsed into a single PhPhrase, with the demonstrative vowel being then shortened, as shown in (22) and (23).

(20) (noun   demonstrative)   (possessive)
      (*ipósó*   *aiilá*)   (*yáangu*)
      9.present   DEM9   9.POSS.SG1
      'that present of mine'

(21) (noun   demonstrative)   (possessive)
      (*sílóngó*   *asiilá*)   (*sáangu*)
      7.pot   DEM7   7.POSS.SG1
      'that pot of mine'

(22) (noun   demonstrative   possessive)
      (*ipósó*   *ailá*   *yáangu*)
      9.present   DEM9   9.POSS.SG1
      'that present of mine'

(23) (noun   demonstrative   possessive)
      (*sílóngó*   *asilá*   *sáangu*)
      7.pot   DEM7   7.POSS.SG1
      'that pot of mine'

The five tone patterns of disyllabic nouns H, HL, L, LH, and LHL are all neutralized in front of a demonstrative as seen earlier in Section 3, and an initial floating High tone on the noun causes plateauing. However, the tone pattern of the demonstrative is preserved, despite the very clear short-

---

[11] I am grateful to Lutz Marten for discussion of this point.

ening of its penult. For instance, the class 9 distal demonstrative *aiilá* becomes *ailá* (compare (20) and (22)), the class 9 anaphoric *aayó* would become *ayó*, and the class 9 proximal *ááí* would become *áí* in this context.

6   Conclusion

I have presented an overview of penultimate shortening processes in Símákonde noun phrases and their consequences for noun tone patterns, with a special focus on final demonstratives, which have the power to shorten every penultimate vowel preceding them in an NP.

NPs made up of a noun and one modifier can either form a single phonological phrase or two distinct PhPhrases, depending on the nature of the modifier. If the modifier is a demonstrative (proximal, distal, or anaphoric), it is required to phrase with the head noun. If the modifier is an adjective, a numeral, or a genitive, it has to phrase separately, and the NP is consequently made up of two distinct PhPhrases. If the modifier is a possessive or an intensifier ('himself', 'herself', or 'itself'), it can either phrase with the head noun and constitute a single PhPhrase with it or not phrase with the head noun and be parsed in an independent PhPhrase.

Finally, NPs made of a noun and more than one modifier are parsed into more than one PhPhrase in Símákonde unless the last modifier is a demonstrative.

References

Devos, M. 2008. *A grammar of Makwe.* Munich: LINCOM.

Guthrie, M. 1948. *The classification of the Bantu languages.* Oxford: Oxford University Press.

Hyman, L. M. 2013. Penultimate lengthening in Bantu: Analysis and spread. In B. Bickel, L. Grenoble, D. Peterson & A. Timberlake (eds.), *Language typology and historical contingency: In honor of Johanna Nichols*, 309–330. Amsterdam: Benjamins.

Kraal, P. 2005. *A grammar of Makonde (Chinnima, Tanzania).* Leiden: Leiden University dissertation.

Leach, M. B. 2010. *Things hold together: Foundations for a systemic treatment of verbal and nominal tone in Plateau Shimakonde.* Leiden: Leiden University dissertation.

Liphola, M. M. 2001. *Aspects of phonology and morphology of Shimakonde.* Columbus, OH: The Ohio State University dissertation.

Maho, J. 2003. A classification of the Bantu languages: An update of Guthrie's referential system. In D. Nurse & G. Philippson (eds.), *The Bantu languages*, 639–651. London: Routledge.

Manus, S. 2003. *Morphologie et tonologie du Símákonde, parlé par les communautés d'origine mozambicaine de Zanzibar et de Tanga (Tanzanie)*. Paris: Institut National des Langues et Civilisations Orientales dissertation.

Manus, S. 2010. The prosody of Símákonde relative clauses. In L. Downing, A. Rialland, J. M. Beltzung, S. Manus, C. Patin & K. Riedel (eds.), *Papers from the workshop on Bantu relative clauses* (ZAS Papers in Linguistics 53), 159–185. Berlin: ZAS.

Manus, S. 2014. Melodic patterns in Símákonde. *Africana Linguistica* 20: 263–276. (Special issue: D. Odden & L. Bickmore (eds.), *Melodic tone patterns in Bantu*.)

Manus, S. 2017. The conjoint/disjoint alternation in Símákonde. In J. van der Wal & L. M. Hyman (eds.), *The conjoint-disjoint alternation in Bantu*, 239–257. Berlin: De Gruyter Mouton.

Odden, D. 1990a. Tone in the Makonde dialects: Chimaraba. *Studies in African Linguistics* 21: 61–105.

Odden, D. 1990b. Tone in the Makonde dialects: Chimahuta. *Studies in African Linguistics* 21: 149–187.

Abbreviations

1, 5, 7, 9	Noun classes
ADJ	Adjective
CO	Connective
DEM	Demonstrative
GEN	Genitive
INT	Intensifier
NUM	Numeral
PAST	Past
PhPhrase	Phonological phrase
POSS	Possessive
SG1	First person singular
SG2	Second person singular

10

On Tones in Chisubiya (Chiikuhane)

JOYCE T. MATHANGWANE

1   Introduction

Chisubiya (Chiikuhane) is a Bantu language spoken in the northwestern part of Botswana, mainly in the Chobe district and the surrounding areas.[1] Chisubiya is classified by Guthrie (1967–1971) as K42 in Botswana. Chisubiya speakers are also found in the Caprivi Strip in Namibia and further north in Zambia (see Andersson & Janson 1997: 101, www.ethnologue.com). This explains why scholars such as Ohanessian & Kashoki (1978) consider the language as belonging to the Tonga group of languages spoken in western and southern Zambia and along the Zambezi river east of Victoria Falls. According to Ohanessian & Kashoki (1978), the other languages found in this group include Ila, Tonga, and Totela.

Speakers refer to their language as Chiikuhane and to themselves as Veekuhane. The exact number of speakers of this language in Botswana is not known; however, several works have estimated the number of speakers to be about 7,000 (e.g. Andersson & Janson 1997, Batibo, Mathangwane & Mosaka 1997, Hasselbring 2000), and the 2001 Botswana National Census estimated 6,477 speakers across three districts (see Central Statistics Office 2003, Chebanne & Nyati-Ramahobo 2003, Batibo, Mathangwane & Tsonope 2003).[2]

---

[1] I would like to thank my colleague Dr. Ndana Ndana who is a native speaker of Chisubiya for providing me with the Chisubiya data. My gratitude also goes to Mr. E. S. Mukono, my second informant, from whom I got some of this data.

[2] The population census in Botswana is not by ethnic group, but the 2001 population and housing census solicited data on the language used in the home. The question did not ask about

Revealing Structure.
Eugene Buckley, Thera Crane & Jeff Good (eds.).
Copyright © 2018, CSLI Publications.

This paper is a preliminary study of the tonology of the Chisubiya language as spoken in Botswana. The study highlights the tonal patterns in the nominal and verbal systems as well as in reduplicated forms. The paper first demonstrates that Chisubiya has contrastive vowel length, but that vowels occurring before both voiced and voiceless prenasalized segments are always long. The paper then shows that Chisubiya has a two-tone system in which underlying tones are unpredictable and marked lexically on all the tone bearing units. Unlike in many Bantu languages, High tones in Chisubiya do not spread to neighboring vowels. The tense system has a role to play in the assignment of grammatical High tones within verbal phrases. As in many other Bantu languages, the process of reduplication is very productive in Chisubiya, thus making it imperative to consider the behavior of tones in these forms as well. This paper demonstrates that Chisubiya is one of the rare Bantu languages in which the reduplication process copies both the segmental and the tonal material.

2   Some Facts on Chisubiya Phonology

Like many other Bantu languages, Chisubiya has a ten vowel system, where all short vowels have long counterparts. Example (1) gives some minimal pairs, showing that vowel length in Chisubiya is contrastive.

(1)   Minimal pairs of short and long vowels

/i/	siká	'arrive'	/ii/	siiká	'kindle (a fire)'
/e/	seka	'laugh'	/ee/	seeka	'hide'
/a/	zalá	'make (bed)'	/aa/	záalá	'beget'
/u/	vúsa	'rule'	/uu/	vúusá	'wake-up'

Thus, a large number of Chisubiya words have underlying long vowels which are not conditioned by phonological factors. As such, long vowels are common in the environment of different segment types such as stops, fricatives, laterals, affricates, and so on. However, there are some cases where phonological factors influence vowel length, as demonstrated in (2).

(2)   a.   Class 5 prefix *i-* before polysyllabic roots

i-téénde	'claw/foot'
i-kopé	'cloud'
i-chakala	'porcupine'
i-súúnsuuní	'owl'

---

one's ethnicity, and in a country such as Botswana, the language one uses in the home may not necessarily be one's ethnic language.

b. Class 5 prefix *i-* before monosyllabic roots

íí-vwé	'stone'	cf.	*má-vwé*	'stones'
íí-wá	'field'	cf.	*má-wá*	'fields'
íí-yí	'egg'	cf.	*má-yí*	'eggs'
íí-zwí	'knee'	cf.	*má-zwí*	'knees'

In (2a) above, we see the class 5 prefix *i-* preceding polysyllabic roots. In (2b), on the other hand, we observe mora doubling in the class 5 prefix *i-* before monosyllabic roots; this doubling does not occur with a CV class prefix, such as when these noun roots take the class 6 prefix *ma-* in the plural.

In (3) below, we can see another case of vowel length, where it occurs across a morpheme boundary when a noun root begins with a vowel identical to that of the preceding class prefix.

(3) Similar vowels juxtaposed at morpheme boundary

cí-ira	>	*cíira*	'virgin land'
cí-iná	>	*cííná*	'that' (class 7 demonstrative singular)
zí-iná	>	*zííná*	'those' (class 8 demonstrative plural)
ló-oza	>	*lóoza*	'feather'

Vowel length is predictable before prenasalized segments in Chisubiya. The language has both a set of voiceless and a set of voiced prenasalized consonants, and these include both stops and fricatives, as seen in (4).[3]

(4) Chisubiya prenasalized consonants

Stops	*mp*	*mb*	*nt*	*nd*	*nk*	*ng*
	mbw					
Fricatives			*ns*	*nz*		

In (5) below are examples of lexical items in which we observe vowel lengthening before these prenasalized segments irrespective of whether the vowel occurs word-initially, in a noun class prefix, or medially within the root.

(5) Sequences of vowel + prenasalized consonant

/mp/	*íímpene*	'goat'	/mb/	*káng'oombe*	'thumb piano'
/nt/	*múúntu*	'person'	/nd/	*íhaande*	'bark (of tree)'
/nk/	*káankafwá*	'bat'	/ng/	*zííngi*	'many'
/ns/	*múúnsi*	'pestle'	/nz/	*íyáanza*	'hand'
/mbw/	*ípóómbwe*	'baboon'			

---

[3] The presence of voiceless prenasalized stops in Chisubiya is an indication that the markedness constraint *NÇ, which prohibits nasal plus voiceless obstruent sequences (Kager 1999), is ranked low in this language.

Some studies in Bantu languages have described the behavior exemplified in (5) above in terms of compensatory lengthening rules (see e.g. Hyman & Katamba 1993 on Luganda and the references therein, or Ngunga 2001 on Ciyao). These studies have argued that such variation in vowel duration in the Bantu languages provides evidence for moraic structure in the phonology and morphology of these languages. On the other hand, others such as Maddieson (1993) and Hubbard (1993, 1994) have claimed that long vowels resulting from compensatory lengthening in languages such as Sukuma and Ruyambo are not as long as underlying long vowels. In the absence of phonetic evidence, this paper does not claim either way for the Chisubiya language. However, tone appears to be assigned at the level of the mora.

3 Basic Tones of Chisubiya

3.1 Underlying Tones and Tone Patterns on Nouns and Verbs

Like many Bantu languages, Chisubiya has an underlying two-tone system, with a High (H) tone and a Low (L) tone. Because tone is assigned to moras, long vowels can have HH, LL, LH, and HL tone, depending on the context. For some Chisubiya words, the only contrasting element is tone, making tone phonemic, as illustrated in the minimal pairs in (6).

(6) Tonal minimal pairs

vúlye	H-L	'length'	*vulyé*	L-H	'how is it'
kulye	L-L	'far'	*kulyé*	L-H	'sweep'
luungá	L-H	'it's nice'	*lúúnga*	H-L	'add (spice/salt)'
váánda	H-L	'open forcefully'	*vaánda*	LH-L	'praise'

From the data, Chisubiya is one of those Bantu languages in which underlying tones are unpredictable; as such, they are marked lexically on all the tone bearing units. As a result, High and Low tones in both verbals and nominals can occur on any vowel. Such languages have been referred to as "pure tone systems" (Kisseberth & Odden 2003).

The range of possible tonal patterns in Chisubiya verb stems, based on the data collected, are shown in (7).

(7) Tonal patterns in verb stems

Monosyllabic			Disyllabic		
H	*lyá*	'eat'	L-L	*kuma*	'touch'
L	*twa*	'pound'	L-H	*volá*	'rot'
			H-L	*hwéza*	'poke/pierce/stab'
			H-H	*válá*	'read'

Polysyllabic

L-L-L	*savaanga*	'dismantle'
L-L-H	*ihiká*	'cook'
H-L-H	*bhákulá*	'grab/catch suddenly'
H-H-L	*búkúla*	'make fire'
H-L-H	*chévoká*	'look around'
L-L-L-L	*saandumuna*	'turn over'
H-L-L-H	*fútatirá*	'turn one's back'

We observe that verb stems in Chisubiya have a maximum of two High tones. These H tones can appear on any vowel within the stem.

In (8) are illustrations of the tonal patterns of Chisubiya nominal stems which, unlike verb stems, have a maximum of three High tones. This is a result of the H tone found on the noun class prefixes in Chisubiya, which leads to nominal tonal patterns beginning with a High tone.[4] Nouns with zero prefixes beginning with a Low tone on the first vowel have not been found in the data, at least as yet.

(8)   Tonal patterns in noun stems

Disyllabic

H-H	*íi-vwé*	'stone'
	mú-nwé	'finger'
	mú-zí	'village'
H-L	*kú-twi*	'ear'
	mú-twi	'head'
	ká-swa	'trap'

Polysyllabic

H-L-H	*lú-vumú*	'tripe'
H-H-L	*chí-vúna*	'plant'
H-L-L	*má-sasa*	'papyrus mats'
H-L-H	*zí-muní*	'lamps'
H-H-L-H	*í-wóngoló*	'millipede'
H-L-L-H	*ká-ankafwá*	'bat'
H-L-L-L	*í-hemere*	'bucket'

In many Bantu languages, noun class prefixes are typically toneless (Kisseberth & Odden 2003). Furthermore, in Proto-Bantu the preprefix is said to have had a High tone. However, Chisubiya appears to be one of those Bantu languages which have lost the preprefix. I am therefore assuming that when the H-toned preprefix was lost in Chisubiya, its H tone was retained and reassigned to the class prefix, resulting in the language having H-toned noun class prefixes except in the case of the locative prefixes of classes 16, 17, and 18, illustrated in (9).

(9)   Nouns with prefixes of classes 16 *ha-*, 17 *ku-*, and 18 *mu-*
   ha-chí-húna   'on the chair'   (class 16)
   ku-mú-lyáángo   'at the doorway'   (class 17)
   mu-ká-háámbwe 'in the water-pot' (class 18)

---

[4] The exceptions to this rule are the prefixes for classes 16, 17, and 18, which carry a Low tone; see the example in (9).

3.2 Absence of Tone Spreading in Chisubiya

From the data, it is evident that there is no tonal spreading in Chisubiya, unlike what is typical for many other Bantu languages. In (10) we can see examples of nominal phrases where possessives or adjectival modifiers are added to nouns with H tones and these H tones fail to spread to the adjacent vowels even when the adjacent vowel carries a Low tone. This data demonstrates the lack of H tone spreading in Chisubiya noun and verb phrases.

(10) a. No H tone spreading in noun phrases

Underlying forms		Surface forms	
lú-vumú + lu-a-ngú	>	*lúvumú lwaangú*	'my tripe'
chí-vúna + chi-a-ngú	>	*chívúna chaangú*	'my plant'
ká-ankafwá + ka-a-ngú	>	*káankafwá kaangú*	'my bat'
ká-vumwé + ka-kándo	>	*kávumwé kakáándo*	'big scorpion'

b. No H tone spreading in verb phrases
kú-suumpa hápe	'to call again'
kú-duunka hápe	'to swim again'
kú-ihiká hápe	'to cook again'
kú-kúmbulusá hápe	'to remind again'

3.3 Tonal Domains in Verb Stems

The structure of the verb stem in Chisubiya, as in other Bantu languages, is morphologically complex, with an elaborate number of affixes. The minimal verb stem consists of a root and a final vowel, as in *-suump-a* 'call', while the maximal verb stem consists of a sequence of prefixes, the root, a sequence of suffixes, and the final vowel, as in *ni-mu-súump-ir-á* 'I am calling him/her for'. The tonal pattern in the verb stem is equally complex, as illustrated in (11). The verb stem (including the final vowel) is included in parentheses after each verb form in (11a) for ease of comparison.

(11) Present tense
(*keté-* = present progressive tense marker; *ni-* = I; *u* = you; *u* = s/he)

a. First person singular

L tone stems
keté-ni-zw-á	'I am coming out' (*-zwa*)
keté-ni-súump-a	'I am calling' (*-suumpa*)
keté-ni-dúunk-a	'I am swimming' (*-duunka*)

H tone stems
keté-ni-ly-á	'I am eating' (*-lyá*)
keté-ni-vééz-a	'I am carving' (*-vééza*)
keté-ni-tus-á	'I am helping' (*-tusá*)

b. Second person singular

L tone stems

keté-u-zw-á	'you are coming out'
keté-u-súump-a	'you are calling'
keté-u-dúunk-a	'you are swimming'

H tone stems

keté-u-ly-á	'you are eating'
keté-u-veez-á	'you are carving'
keté-u-tus-á	'you are helping'

c. Third person singular

L tone stems

keté-u-zw-á	's/he is coming out'
keté-u-suump-á	's/he is calling'
keté-u-duunk-á	's/he is swimming'

H tone stems

keté-u-ly-á	's/he is eating'
keté-u-veez-á	's/he is carving'
keté-u-tus-á	's/he is helping'

We observe in (11a) and (11b) that in addition to the H tone in the second vowel of the present progressive tense inflectional prefix *keté-*, a High tone is assigned to the first mora of a Low tone verb stem in the first and second person; in monosyllabic L tone verb stems, the H tone is assigned to the final vowel. Verb stems with underlying High tones retain their lexical Hs in the first person, while in the second and third persons, a H tone is assigned to the final vowel as seen in *keté-u-veezá* 's/he is carving' (< *kú-vééza* 'to carve'); this is also the case on L tone verb stems in the third person. I am assuming that the lexical H of the H tone verb stems is lost in the third person and replaced by a grammatical H tone on the final vowel. I therefore propose that in Chisubiya, a grammatical High is assigned to the first mora or the final vowel of the verb stem, depending on its tense or person. I am assuming that the underlying H of High tone verbs gets deleted through a constraint given in (12).

(12) *HH: No H should be placed adjacent to a grammatical High within a verb stem (cf. Mathangwane & Mtenje 2010)

The assignment of a grammatical H tone is much more transparent in the immediate past tense, in which it is always placed on the final vowel of the verb stem. Examples to exemplify this are given in (13), with the verb stems for the verb forms indicated in parentheses in (13a).

(13) Immediate past tense
   (*a-* = immediate past tense marker)

    a. First person singular

L tone stems		H tone stems	
na-zwá	'I came out' (*-zwa*)	*na-lyá*	'I ate' (*-lyá*)
na-suumpá	'I called' (*-suumpa*)	*na-veezá*	'I carved' (*-vééza*)
na-duunká	'I swam' (*-duunka*)	*na-tusá*	'I helped' (*-tusá*)

    b. Second person singular

wa-zwá	'you came out'	*wa-lyá*	'you ate'
wa-suumpá	'you called'	*wa-veezá*	'you carved'
wa-duunká	'you swam'	*wa-tusá*	'you helped'

    c. Third person singular

waa-zwá	's/he went out'	*waa-lyá*	's/he ate'
waa-suumpá	's/he called'	*waa-veezá*	's/he carved'
waa-duunká	's/he swam'	*waa-tusá*	's/he helped'

The forms for the distant past tense are given in (14). We observe that not only is a grammatical H assigned to the first vowel in L tone verb stems, the final vowel of the verb stem also changes in quality to a close front vowel -*i*. However, the H tone verbs have retained their H tones, but with a change in final vowel quality identical to that in Low tone verb stems.

(14) Distant past tense (*va-* = distant past tense marker)

    a. First person singular

L tone stems		H tone stems	
ni-va-zwí	'I came out'	*ni-va-lyí*	'I ate'
ni-va-súumpi	'I called'	*ni-va-véézi*	'I carved'
ni-va-dúunki	'I swam'	*ni-va-tusí*	'I helped'

    b. Second person singular

u-va-zwí	'you came out'	*u-va-lyí*	'you ate'
u-va-súumpi	'you called'	*u-va-véézi*	'you carved'
u-va-dúunki	'you swam'	*u-va-tusí*	'you helped'

    c. Third person singular

a-vaa-zwí	's/he came out'	*a-vaa-lyí*	's/he ate'
a-vaa-súumpi	's/he called'	*a-vaa-véézi*	's/he carved'
a-vaa-dúunki	's/he swam'	*a-vaa-tusí*	's/he helped'

Thus, the grammatical H tone on the different tenses is best demonstrated on L tone verb stems which, in the case of the immediate past tense in (13), is realized on the final vowel, while in the distant past tense (14) it is realized on the first vowel of the verb stem.

Examples of immediate/near future and distant future verbs are given in (15) and (16) respectively. The grammatical H tone is assigned to the final vowel of the verb stem, which also changes in quality to a mid vowel -*e*.

(15) Immediate/near future (*mú-* = immediate future tense marker)

   a. First person singular

L tone stems		H tone stems	
mú-ni-zwé	'I will come out'	*mú-ni-lyé*	'I will eat'
mú-ni-suumpé	'I will call'	*mú-ni-véezé*	'I will carve'
mú-ni-duunké	'I will swim'	*mú-ni-tusé*	'I will help'

   b. Second person singular

   L tone stems

Surface form		Underlying form	
móo-zwé	<	mú-u-zwé	'you will come out'
móo-suumpé	<	mú-u-suumpé	'you will call'
móo-duunké	<	mú-u-duunké	'you will swim'

   H tone stems

móo-lyé	<	mú-u-lyé	'you will eat'
móo-véezé	<	mú-u-véezé	'you will carve'
móo-tusé	<	mú-u-tusé	'you will help'

   c. Third person singular

   L tone stems

mwá-zwé	<	mú-a-zwé	'you will come out'
mwá-suumpé	<	mú-a-suumpé	'you will call'
mwá-duunké	<	mú-a-duunké	'you will swim'

   H tone stems

mwá-lyé	<	mú-a-lyé	'you will eat'
mwá-véezé	<	mú-a-véezé	'you will carve'
mwá-tusé	<	mú-a-tusé	'you will help'

(16) Distant Future (*ká-* =distant future tense marker)

    a. First person singular

L tone stems		H tone stems	
ká-ni-zwé	'I will come out'	*ká-ni-lyé*	'I will eat'
ká-ni-suumpé	'I will call'	*ká-ni-véezé*	'I will carve'
ká-ni-duunké	'I will swim'	*ká-ni-tusé*	'I will help'

    b. Second person singular

L tone stems

Surface form		Underlying form	
kóo-zwé	<	ká-u-zwé	'you will come out'
kóo-suumpé	<	ká-u-suumpé	'you will call'
kóo-duunké	<	ká-u-duunké	'you will swim'

H tone stems

kóo-lyé	<	ká-u-lyé	'you will eat'
kóo-véezé	<	ká-u-véezé	'you will carve'
kóo-tusé	<	ká-u-tusé	'you will help

    c. Third person singular

L tone stems		H tone stems	
ká-a-zwé	'you will come out'	*ká-a-lyé*	'you will eat'
ká-a-suumpé	'you will call'	*ká-a-véezé*	'you will carve'
ká-a-duunké	'you will swim'	*ká-a-tusé*	'you will help'

Note that in cases where some phonological processes apply, such as vowel lowering and glide formation in (15), as well as vowel coalescence (a+u=*oo*) in (16), both the underlying and the surface forms are given to illustrate. The verb *véeza* 'carve' is an interesting case also worth noting in (16), in that its lexical High tone is realized only on the first mora of the first syllable, which surfaces as HL, when a grammatical H is assigned to the final vowel, in order not to violate the *HH constraint given in (12).

From the above examples (13)–(16) we observe the important role played by the morphology in the assignment of tones in Chisubiya. Within the mini grammars of each of these tenses, there is a constraint which assigns a grammatical High tone to either the first vowel/mora or the final vowel of the verb stem. The constraint in (17) works with other constraints such as *HH given in (12) to derive the optimal output.

(17) Grammatical H[stem]: Place a grammatical High tone on either the first mora or the final vowel of the stem

3.4 Tones in Derivational Suffixes

As in many Bantu languages, in addition to the verb root and final vowel
which are obligatory, the Chisubiya verb stem may also combine with derivational suffixes. Chisubiya verbal extensions include the passive suffix -w-, applicative suffix -er-, reciprocal suffix -an-, and causative suffix -is-, all of which are toneless, as is common across Bantu languages (see
Schadeberg 2003).[5] The four derivational suffixes common to Chisubiya are
illustrated in the infinitive forms given (18)–(21).

(18) Applicative form with -er-

kú-wóónda	'to arrest'	kú-wóónd-er-á	'to arrest for'
kú-ihiká	'to cook'	kú-ihik-ir-á	'to cook for'
kú-suumpa	'to call'	kú-suump-ir-á	'to call for'

(19) Causative form with -is-

kú-chóola	'to break'	kú-chóol-es-á	'to cause to break'
kú-wúúnga	'to bury'	kú-wúúng-is-á	'to cause to bury'
kú-vúva	'to lie low'	kú-vúv-is-á	'to cause to lie low'

(20) Reciprocal form with -an-

kú-tóya	'to hate'	kú-tóy-an-á	'to hate each other'
kú-kuma	'to touch'	kú-kum-an-á	'to touch each other'
kú-kómoká	'to surprise'	kú-kómok-an-á	'to surprise each other'

(21) Passive form with -w-

kú-tusá	'to help'	kú-tus-w-á	'to be helped'
kú-chéesá	'to catch/trap'	kú-chées-w-á	'to be caught'
kú-núúngirá	'to connect'	kú-núúngir-w-á	'to be connected'

We further observe that a grammatical High tone is always assigned to
the final vowel of the verb stems (18)–(21) by the Grammatical $H_{[stem]}$ constraint. In all the examples which have an underlying final High tone, we
are assuming the deletion of this H tone when these affixes are attached
e.g. kú-ihik-ir-á 'to cook for' (< kú-ihiká) or kú-kómok-an-á 'to surprise
each other' (< kú-kómoká) in order to not violate the high ranking *HH constraint when the grammatical H is assigned. Furthermore, we observe the
occurrence of vowel harmony in the applicative and causative stems in (18)
and (19) respectively.

---

[5] Very few examples with the intensive suffix -isiz- could be found, and I am assuming that
these may have come into Chisubiya from other neighboring Bantu languages; an example is
vúuzá 'ask' > vúuz-ísiz-á 'ask a lot'.

4 Reduplication and Tone in Chisubiya

4.1 Overview of Chisubiya Reduplicatives

In Chisubiya, like in many Bantu languages, reduplication is a productive word formation process. This is primarily complete reduplication, where the whole stem becomes the reduplicant. As exemplified in (22), reduplication occurs in three grammatical classes: verbs, nouns, and adjectives.

(22) a. Verbal reduplication

suumpa	'call'	*suumpasuumpa*	'call continuously'
seka	'laugh'	*sekaseka*	'giggle/laugh continuously'
zíma	'walk'	*zímazíma*	'walk aimlessly about'
chévoká	'look'	*chévokáchévoká*	'look around repeatedly'

b. Nominal reduplication

má-wá	'fields'	*má-wáwá*	'many fields'
chí-vata	'scar'	*chí-vatavata*	'many scars'
mú-vála	'color'	*mú-válavála*	'multi-colored' (sg.)
má-vála	'colors'	*má-válavála*	'multi-colored' (pl.)
ménzí	'water'	*ménzíménzí*	'water all over'

c. Adjectival reduplication

kalyé	'long ago'	*kalyékalyé*	'long long ago'
zííngi	'many'	*zííngizííngi*	'very many'
kulye	'far away'	*kulyekulye*	'far far away'
káándo	'big'	*káándokáándo*	'very big'
fwihi	'short'	*fwihifwihi*	'very short'

The reduplicant in all examples in (22) is the entire stem, irrespective of whether that stem is monosyllabic or polysyllabic. Stems with long vowels are also reduplicated without change to the vowel quantity. We therefore conclude that the reduplication process in Chisubiya is faithful to word minimality constraints (see (29)).

Semantically, the process of reduplication in Chisubiya has different functions depending on the grammatical class of the reduplicated form. These include repetition, intensity, size, and continuance, all semantics expressed through reduplication in a variety of other languages (see e.g. Katamba (1993) on Papago, Sundanese, and Tzeltal, Mathangwane (2002) on Ikalanga, Mtenje (2003) on Ciyao, and Mtenje (1988) on Chichewa).

In addition to complete reduplication as demonstrated above, evidence of partial reduplication is found in Chisubiya in the quantitative formative 'only/alone'. The concordial consonant plus the particle *-e-/-o-* is reduplicated before the root *-ná* whenever this quantitative occurs with nouns in exclamatory expressions, as seen in (23). Note that vowels are lengthened before quantitative -ná in these contexts; the conditioning of this lengthening requires further investigation.

(23) Partial reduplication in quantitative formatives

Underlying form	Surface form	Gloss
yó+yóoná ímpene	> *yóyóoné mpene*	'only a goat!'
yé+yéená úndávu	> *yéyéenó ndávu*	'only a lion!'
mé+méená imé	> *méméené-me*	'I alone!'
só+swéená uswé	> *sóswéenó-swe*	'we alone!'
wó+wéená uwé	> *wówéenó-we*	'you (sg.) alone!'
nó+nwéená unwé	> *nónwéenó-nwe*	'you (pl.) alone!'
yé+yéená múswisú	> *yéyéená múswisú*	'only a boy!'
vó+vóoná vámbwa	> *vóvóoná váámbwá*	'only dogs!'

The reduplicant is highlighted at the beginning of each quantifier. Two observations can be made from the above data. First, there is a vowel coalescence rule which comes into play when the quantifier precedes a vowel initial noun or pronominal. Secondly, the final High tone of the pronominals *imé* 'I', *uswé* 'we', *uwé* 'you' (singular), and *unwé* 'you' (plural) is lost after the application of the coalescence rule. From the way in which partial reduplication works here, we conclude that the reduplication process in Chisubiya is prefixal.

Further evidence for prefixal reduplication in Chisubiya is derived from a set of lexicalized verbs illustrated in (24).

(24) Prefixal reduplication in verbs
lyolyoteká	'ululate'
chochoteká	'talk in harsh tones'
bwabwatiká	'talkative'
gwegweta	'run around/jog'
mwemweta	'smiling/grinning'
hohosha	'stammering'

Note that this process is not productive in the language and none of these words has a nonreduplicative form. Morphologically, some of these verbs appear to have the stative formative -*ik*-, which seems to have fossilized to become part of the verb stem. Semantically, these verbs have onomatopoeic meanings signifying something continuous or persistent.

4.2 Tones in Reduplicated Forms

As indicated above, most productive reduplication in Chisubiya is complete reduplication, whereby the whole stem, including long vowels, becomes the reduplicant. The process is common to both Low tone and High tone stems. In (25) below, with Low tone verbs, we observe that all the segmental material is copied, irrespective of whether the stem is monosyllabic or polysyllabic (the infinitive prefix is not reduplicated).

(25) Reduplication of L tone verbs in the infinitive

kú-twa	'to pound'	*kú-twatwa*	'to pound continuously'
kú-seka	'to laugh'	*kú-sekaseka*	'to laugh continuously'
kú-nuunka	'to smell'	*kú-nuunkanuunka*	'to smell about'
kú-sooha	'to gossip'	*kú-soohasooha*	'to gossip a lot'
kú-juma	'to graze'	*kú-jumajuma*	'to graze about'

In stems with underlying High tones, both the segmental and tonal materials are copied in the reduplicant, as exemplified in (26)–(28).

(26) Reduplication of H tone verbs

kú-lyá	'to eat'	*kú-lyályá*	'to eat continuously'
kú-voóza	'to spread'	*kú-voózavoóza*	'to spread continuously'
kú-wáámba	'to talk'	*kú-wáámbawáámba*	'to talk continuously'

(27) Reduplication of H tone nouns

íí-vwé	'stone'	*lú-vwévwé*	'gravel/pebbles'
má-wá	'fields'	*má-wáwá*	'many fields'
mú-vála	'color'	*mu-válavála*	'multi-colored' (sing.)
ménzí	'water'	*ménzíménzí*	'water all over'

(28) Reduplication of H tone adjectives

zííngi	'many'	*zííngizííngi*	'very many'
káándo	'big'	*káándokáándo*	'very big'
kalyé	'long ago'	*kalyékalyé*	'long long ago'

We observe that with verbs (26) and adjectives (28), both the segments and tones are copied. However, in the case of nouns with class prefixes (27), just like in many other Bantu languages, only the root is copied, not the class prefix (see also Mtenje 1988, Mathangwane 2002). In nouns without a class prefix such as *ménzí* 'water', all the segmental and tonal material is copied. This is evidence of Chisubiya being very faithful to word minimality constraints, given in (29).

(29) Stem minimality: Reduplicate the whole stem regardless of length (see Mathangwane & Mtenje 2010, among others)

In a parallel way, when verbs with derivational suffixes are reduplicated, the stem is reduplicated (leaving out the infinitive prefix), as in examples such as *kú-sekaná* 'to laugh at each other' > *kú-sekanásekaná* 'to laugh at each other continuously' or *kú-kumaná* 'to touch each other' > *kú-kumanákumaná* 'to touch each other continuously'.

The copying of both segmental and tonal materials is also observed in fossilized nouns, an indication that the reduplication process must have occurred before the lexicalization process took place. Examples of these can be seen in (30).

(30) Reduplicated fossilized nouns with H tones
    ń-sékwasékwa   'type of wild fruit'
    ń-cholyícholyí   'type of grass' (found in rivers)
    lú-mééngaméénga 'very sharp blade' (as of knife)
    mú-chíingachíinga 'type of fruit'
    ún-fúkefúke   'an insect/creature'
    ká-fúmbifúmbi   'grudge'

In (31), we observe reduplication of deadjectival nouns with the class 14 prefix *bu-*. The class prefix does not form part of the reduplicant in this case either. Once again, tone is faithfully reduplicated.

(31) Reduplication of deadjectival nouns of class 14

bú-káándo	'bigness'	*bú-káándokáándo*	'very big'
bú-siha	'blackness'	*bú-sihasiha*	'pitch black'
bú-tuva	'whiteness'	*bú-tuvatuva*	'very white'
bú-fwihi	'shortness'	*bú-fwihifwihi*	'very short'
bú-hubá	'lightness'	*bú-hubáhubá*	'very light'

The copying of both segments and tones is considered to be a rare occurrence in Bantu (see Hyman & Mtenje 1999, Downing 2001); other Bantu languages where this occurs are Chichewa (see Mtenje 1988, Hyman & Mtenje 1999) and Cinamwanga (see Mtenje 2006b).

5   Conclusion

This paper presents Chisubiya, a Bantu language with a two-tone system, a High tone and a Low tone. Like in many other Bantu languages, tones in Chisubiya are unpredictable in stems and as such are marked lexically on all tone bearing units, putting this language in the category of those languages considered to have pure tone systems. High tones in Chisubiya do not spread to neighboring vowels, an observation also made by Mtenje (2006a) for Cindali, a Bantu language spoken in Malawi. The paper has shown Chisubiya to be a language in which the morphology plays a role in the assignment of H tones: for instance, within the mini grammars of different tenses, there are constraints relating to the grammatical High tone that is assigned to either the initial or final vowel of the verb stem. This grammatical H is also observed in the final vowel of derivatives such as applicatives, reciprocals, causatives, and passives, and is seen in both Low and High tone verb stems. Finally, Chisubiya is one of those rare Bantu languages in which the reduplication process copies both the segmental and the tonal material, putting it in a category with languages such as Chichewa (Mtenje 1988, Hyman & Mtenje 1999) and Cinamwanga (Mtenje 2006b). In Chisubiya, however, the reduplicant is prefixal, with evidence derived from the quantifier 'only/alone' as well as from some fossilized verbs.

References

Andersson, L.-G. & T. Janson. 1997. *Languages in Botswana: Language ecology in southern Africa*. Gaborone: Longman Botswana.

Batibo, H. M., J. T. Mathangwane & N. Mosaka. 1997. Prospects for sociolinguistic research undertakings in Botswana: Priorities and strategies. In R. Dirven (ed.), *Proceedings of the Regional Seminar on Sociolinguistic Research in Africa: Priorities and Methodologies*, 123–143. Duisburg: LICCA Publications.

Batibo, H. M., J. T. Mathangwane & J. Tsonope. 2003. *A study of the third language teaching in Botswana* (consultancy report). Gaborone: Department of Curriculum Development, Ministry of Education.

Central Statistics Office. 2003. *Republic of Botswana 2001 population and housing census*. Gaborone: Ministry of Finance and Development Planning.

Chebanne, A. & L. Nyati-Ramahobo. 2003. Language knowledge and language use in Botswana. In *Proceedings of the CSO: 2001 Population and Housing Census Dissemination Seminar, September 8–11, 2003*, 284–297. Gaborone: Central Statistics Office, Ministry of Finance and Development Planning.

Downing, L. J. 2001. Tone (non-)transfer in Bantu verbal reduplication. In U. Gut & D. Gibbon (eds.), *Typology of African prosodic systems* (Bielefeld Occasional Papers in Typology 1). Bielefeld: University of Bielefeld.

Guthrie, M. 1967–1971. *Comparative Bantu: An introduction to the comparative linguistics and prehistory of the Bantu languages*. Farnborough, Hampshire: Gregg.

Hasselbring, S. 2000. *A sociolinguistic survey of the languages of Botswana, vol. 2*. Gaborone: Basarwa Languages Project, University of Botswana.

Hubbard, K. 1993. The manifestation of vowel quality in Bantu: A comparative study. Paper presented at the 24th Annual Conference on African Linguistics, The Ohio State University, Columbus, Ohio, July 23–25.

Hubbard, K. 1994. *Duration in moraic theory*. Berkeley: University of California dissertation.

Hyman, L. M. & F. X. Katamba. 1993. A new approach to tone in Luganda. *Language* 69: 34–67.

Hyman, L. M. & A. Mtenje. 1999. Prosodic morphology and tone: The case of Chichewa. In R. Kager, H. van der Hulst & W. Zonneveld (eds.), *The prosody-morphology interface,* 90–133. Cambridge: Cambridge University Press.

Kager, R. 1999. *Optimality Theory.* Cambridge: Cambridge University Press.

Katamba, F. 1993. *Morphology.* New York: St. Martin's Press.

Kisseberth, C. & D. Odden. 2003. Tone. In D. Nurse & G. Philippson (eds.), *The Bantu languages,* 59–70. London: Routledge.

Maddieson, I. 1993. Splitting the mora. *UCLA Working Papers in Phonetics* 83: 9–18.

Mathangwane, J. T. 2002. Reduplicatives and their tonology in Ikalanga. In *LASU: Journal of the Linguistics Association of SADC Universities* 1: 50–61.

Mathangwane, J. T. & A. Mtenje. 2010. Tone and reduplication in Wandya and Subiya. In K. Legere & C. Thornel (eds.), *Bantu languages: Analyses, description and theory,* 175–189. Cologne: Rüdiger Köppe.

Mtenje, A. 1988. On tone and transfer in Chichewa reduplication. *Linguistics* 26: 125–155.

Mtenje, A. 2003. An optimality theoretic account of Ciyao verbal reduplication. In J. M. Mugane (ed.), *Lingistic typology and representation of African languages* (Trends in African Linguistics 5), 43–68. Trenton, NJ: African World Press.

Mtenje, A. 2006a. Tone in Cindali. *Lingua* 116: 1495–1506.

Mtenje, A. 2006b. Tone transfer and reduplication in Bantu: The case of Cinamwanga. Paper presented at the 5th World Congress of African Linguistics, Addis Ababa University, August 7–11.

Ngunga, A. S. A. 2001. The verb stem reduplication in Ciyao. *Afrikanistische Arbeitspapiere* 66: 147–165.

Ohanessian, S. & M. E. Kashoki (eds.). 1978. *Language in Zambia.* London: Oxford University Press for the International African Institute.

Schadeberg, T. 2003. Derivation. In D. Nurse & G. Philippson (eds.), *The Bantu languages,* 71–89. London: Routledge.

11

The Phonology of Tone in the Imperative in Kinande

NGESSIMO M. MUTAKA

1 Introduction

It has been shown for several of the Interlacustrine Bantu languages that predicting the morphological tones on verbs is extremely complex, where there is often a need for a /H/ vs. /L/ vs. /Ø/ distinction, as well as morpheme-specific and boundary tones which come in at both the lexical and postlexical levels. Among the languages studied, Kinande, a language of the Democratic Republic of Congo, is perhaps the most complex. Previous work has revealed the unusual properties of Kinande, which notably include: a three-way opposition in /H/ vs. /Ø/ verb roots, and a suffixal L tone assigned, for example, in the remote past tense, as in /tu-a-mu-túm-a L/ [twamutuma] 'we sent him'; the need for multiple strata; a causative (and passive) "spurious" H in the recent and remote past tenses; complex rules for assigning lexical tones (Mutaka 1994); and boundary tones which are sensitive to the /L/ vs. /Ø/ distinction (Hyman 1990).

The complexity of the assignment of tones in Kinande is particularly revealed in the imperative, as predicted in Meeussen (1962), who rightly noted that imperative tones can be complex or irregular in Bantu languages (see also Meeussen 1961). In this paper I discuss some complexities that have been overlooked in previous accounts to show that there is a need to distinguish the hortative from the imperative with respect to the assignment of the suffixal H, the imperative L, the causative H, the boundary H tone, and the domains in which these tones apply.

Revealing Structure.
Eugene Buckley, Thera Crane & Jeff Good (eds.).
Copyright © 2018, CSLI Publications.

The paper will be organized as follows. In the first section, I will account for the imperative in verbs in isolation so as to show, firstly, how the imperatives behave differently from hortatives and, secondly, how H tone verbs differ in significant ways from toneless verbs with respect to the assignment of the suffixal H and the spurious H. In the second section, I will argue that the domain of the imperative is the intonational domain, that an imperative intonational L is associated to the final vowel of this intonational domain, and that, between the verb in the imperative and the last word in the intonational domain, phrasal domains function as expected with the usual across-the-board rules and phrasal H assignment.

2   The Imperative and the Hortative Forms in Isolation

Consider first the following forms in the imperative in (1); note that this includes one form, *uta* 'you bury', with imperative function that appears with a second person subject marker due to minimality constraints.

(1) | Imperative | | | Infinitive | |
|---|---|---|---|---|
| *tuma* | /túm-aC-a/ | 'send!' | *erí-túm-a* | 'to send' |
| *bula* | /búl-aC-a/ | 'wonder!' | *erí-búl-a* | 'to wonder' |
| *korogota* | /kórogot-aC-a/ | 'scratch!' | *erí-korogót-a* | 'to scratch' |
| *uma* | /úm-aC-a/ | 'dry up!' | *ery-ûm-â* | 'to dry' |
| *oga* | /óg-aC-a/ | 'purge!' | *ery-ôg-â* | 'to purge' |
| *uta* | /tá-aC-a/ | 'bury!' | *erí-t-â* | 'to bury' |

These are H tone verbs. They all surface with a Low tone that is the result of a suffixal L on the last vowel. I have put their underlying representations between slashes and have also indicated their infinitive forms, where the reader can notice that the infinitive prefix -*ri*- surfaces with a H tone, which is the result of the lexical H on the root vowel, as argued in Mutaka (1994) and Hyman & Valinande (1985). The -C- in the underlying representation is a phantom consonant whose presence is argued for in Mutaka (1994). Following a previous analysis of tone in Kinande (Mutaka 1994), the failure of the lexical H to surface on the root is the result of a General Delinking rule that applies in the language; its application is seen here as the fact that the H tone that will have associated on the first root vowel at stratum one does not surface on its sponsor. Let us also examine the forms of toneless verb roots, seen in (2); like in (1), the final verb here appears with a second person subject marker due to minimality constraints.

(2) Imperative   Infinitive
     huma   /hum-aC-a/   'hit!'   *eri-húma*   'to hit'
     gula   /gul-aC-a/   'buy!'   *eri-gúl-a*   'to buy'
     sangana   /sangan-aC-a/   'meet!'   *eri-sangán-a* 'to meet'
     esa   /es-aC-a/   'play!'   *ery-es-â*   'to play'
     uswa   /so-aC-a/   'grind!'   *eri-sw-â*   'to grind'

The forms here also surface with a L, which is the result of a suffixal L assigned by the imperative. Unlike with the H tone verbs in (1), the infinitive marker *-ri-* surfaces with a Low tone in (2). The suffixal L assigned by the imperative is responsible for blocking the phrasal H that would surface on the penultimate vowel; this phrasal H can be seen in the infinitival forms in both (1) and (2).

Note that forms with the causative *-į-* do not introduce any additional H, the so-called spurious H, as would be the case in a recent past tense or remote past tenses as observed in Mutaka (1994) and as shown in (3).

(3) Imperative   Infinitive
     bųlaya   /búl-aC-į-a/   'ask!'   *erį-bųl-į-a*   'to ask'
     gųlaya   /gul-aC-į-a/   'sell!'   *erį-gųl-į-a*   'to sell'

So far, we have dealt with the imperative. Let us now contrast it with the hortative, whose structure consists of a subject marker (SM) plus the stem, as seen in (4).

(4) *tu-túmê*   /tu-túm-aC-e/   'let us send'
     tu-tum-irírê   /tu-túm-irir-aC-e/   'let us send on purpose'
     tu-mê   /tu-úm-aC-e/   'let us dry up'
     tu-tê   /tu-tá-aC-e/   'let us bury'
     tw-ogê   /tu-óg-aC-e/   'let us purge'

As shown in the underlying representations in (4), these are H tone verb roots. In these forms, a suffixal HL must be posited, as it surfaces in the way it applies in the recent past tense (as argued in Mutaka 1994). This tone assignment is obvious on a long stem, where a H surfaces on the penultimate (first part of the falling tone) and the final vowel. Let us now examine the forms of toneless verb roots, seen in (5)—here, I have indicated the suffixal HL in the underlying representation.

(5) *tú-húme*   /tu-hum-aC-e HL/   'let us hit'
     tú-húmirire   /tu-hum-irir-aC-e HL/   'let us hit on purpose'
     twése   /tu-es-aC-e HL/   'let us play'
     túswe   /tu-so-aC-e HL/   'let us grind'

In a toneless verb root, the assignment of the suffixal HL is obvious. The H surfaces on the root and preroot vowel, as is the case in the recent past tense where the same HL is assigned, and the L associates to the final vowel, where it prevents the assignment of the phrasal H.

Consider now the forms in (6), where an object marker (OM) is introduced in the hortative form of H tone verb roots. (The infinitive form of the verb 'refuse', given in (6), is *er-ị̂m-â*.)

(6) *tú-mú-tume*   /tu-mu-túm-aC-e HL/   'let us send him'
     tú-mú-tum-irire /tu-mu-túm-irir-aC-e HL/ 'let us send him on purpose'
     túmúte   /tu-mu-tá-aC-e HL/   'let us bury him'
     túmwoge   /tu-mu-óg-aC-e HL/   'let us purge him'
     tụ́mwịme   /tu-mu-ị́m-aC-e HL/   'let us refuse to give him'

As shown in these forms, a H tone verb root with an OM surfaces with a H on the OM and the pre-OM. What is curious is that the H does not surface in the stem. If we assume that the same HL was assigned in these forms as with the forms without an OM, we must conclude that there is a rule that deletes the H from the stem of a H tone verb in the hortative.

(7) *tu-mú-húme*   /tu-mu-hum-aC-e HL/   'let us hit him'
     tu-mú-húmirire /tu-mu-hum-irir-aC-e HL/ 'let us hit him on purpose'
     tumwése   /tu-mu-es-aC-e HL/   'let us play him'
     tumúswe   /tu-mu-so-aC-e HL/   'let us grind him'

In the hortative of toneless verb forms with an OM, as seen in (7), the suffixal HL behaves as expected, that is, the H surfaces on the root and pre-root vowel, and the Low assigned to the final vowel blocks the phrasal H.

Consider now the forms in (8), which consist of an OM followed by the stem.

(8) *tú-tume*   /tu-túm-aC-e/   'send us'
     tú-tum-irire /tu-túm-irir-aC-e/   'send us on purpose'
     túte   /tu-tá-aC-e/   'bury us'
     twoge   /tu-óg-aC-e/   'purge us'

I will label forms whose structure is OM + stem as hortative. Another term that fits them is "mild imperative", as I will mention later in this paper. As observed earlier, the H does not surface in the stem of a H tone verb. The OM here surfaces with a H that originates from the root vowel on which the underlying H of a H tone verb is associated at the first stratum.

The forms in (9) consist of an OM and the stem of a toneless verb root. These show no peculiarities with respect to the suffixal HL—these tones surface as expected, that is, the H surfaces on the root and preroot vowel, and the L associates to the final vowel.

(9) *tú-húme*   /tu-hum-aC-e HL/   'hit us'
    tú-húmirire /tu-hum-irir-aC-e HL/   'hit us on purpose'
    twése   /tu-es-aC-e HL/   'play us'
    túswe   /tu-so-aC-e HL/   'grind us'

Consider now the forms in (10), which consist of SM + stem. In this case, the stems contain the causative -*ị*-.

(10) *tú-gúláye*   /tu-gul-aC-ị-e HL/   'let us sell'
     tú-gúlịrịráye   /tu-gul-irir-aC-ị-e HL/   'let us sell on purpose'
     tụ-bụláyê   /tu-búl-aC-ị-e HL/   'let us ask'
     tụ-bụlịrịráyê   /tu-búl-irir-aC-ị-e HL/   'let us ask on purpose'

In hortatives whose stem contains the causative -*ị*- and whose structure is SM + stem, both the toneless verb and the H tone verb surface with a spurious H.[1] Notice also the absence of this spurious H in the structure OM + stem, as shown in the forms in (11).

(11) *tú-bụlịranaye*   /tu-búliran-aC-ị-a/   'make us disappear'
     (from *erị-bụlịran-ị-a*)

     tú-bụlịraye   /tu-búl-ir-aC-ị-e/   'ask for us'
     (from *erị-bụl-ịr-ị-a* 'to ask for')

     tú-bụlaye   /tu-búl-aC-ị-e/   'ask us'
     (from *erị-bụly-â* 'to ask')

     tú-bụlịrịraye   /tu-búl-irir-aC-ị-e/   'ask for us on purpose'

     twụmaye   /tu-um-aC-ị-e/   'dry us'
     (from *ery-ụ̂my-â* 'to dry')

As shown in forms in (11) with an OM, there is no spurious H in a H tone verb that contains the causative -*ị*-. Let us also examine the forms of a toneless verb with this causative -*ị*- in the OM + stem structure.

(12) *tú-gúláye*   /tu-gul-aC-ị-e/   'sell us'
     túgúlịráye   /tu-gul-ir-aC-ị-e/   'sell for us'
     túgúlịrịráye   /tu-gul-irir-aC-ị-e/   'sell for us on purpose'

For the toneless verb root, notice that, in addition to the suffixal HL that surfaces as expected, the causative -*ị*- triggers the so-called spurious

---

[1] For the naming of the spurious H, see Hyman & Katamba (1990) and also Meeussen (1967: 92), who previously observed the presence of a H that is curiously assigned in the presence of the causative -*ị*-.

H that surfaces here on the penultimate vowel, after the causative -į- has devocalized.

For the sake of completeness, note that the passive -u- behaves like the causative -į-, as illustrated in the examples in (13), where the passive morpheme -u- occupies the same position as the causative morpheme -į- in the verb structure.

(13) Forms with causative -į-   Forms with passive -u-

  sųbalaya /-subal-aC-į-a/ *gulawa* /-gul-aC-u-a/
  'cause someone to pee'   'be bought'

  lengekanaya /-lengekan-aC-į-a/ *humawa* /-hum-aC-u-a/
  'think'   'be hit'

  bųlaya /-búl-aC-į-a/   *tumawa* /-túm-aC-u-a/
  'ask'   'be sent'

  lenderaya /-lénder-aC-į-a/ *korogotawa* /-kórogot-aC-u-a/
  'cause someone to walk'   'be scratched'

(14) *tutumáwê* /tu-túm-aC-ú-e/ 'let us be sent'
  túgúláwê /tu-gul-aC-ú-e/ 'let us be bought'

Just as the causative -į- triggers the spurious H, the passive -u- triggers it as well in the SM + stem hortative. This can be seen in (14), where the spurious H surfaces on the vowel that precedes the devocalized -u- and also as the H that is the first part of the falling tone on the final vowel.

3 The Imperative and the Hortative Forms Used in a Phrasal Construction

This section looks at the use of imperative and hortative in larger phrases. In (15), we can see examples of nouns used after an imperative in the first column, together with the underlying forms (UR) of the nouns and their surface forms in isolation. Unlike verb forms, where the underlying tone distinction is H vs. Ø, in certain nouns a Low tone (indicated here as a grave accent) also appears on the final vowel, and no phrasal H surfaces as a result. A Low tone is also grammatically assigned to the final vowel of the verb in certain tenses; we saw this for the imperative in Section 2, and it is also the case with the remote past tense, whose penultimate vowel never surfaces with a phrasal H. Note that many of the nouns in (15) are used as names, and so written with a capital letter; however, the names are formed from common nouns.

(15) Noun after imperative   UR of noun   Word in isolation
      huma Magu:lu 'hit Magulu'   /a-ma-gulu/   *a-ma-gú:lu* 'legs'
      humá Mábo:ko 'hit Maboko'   /a-ma-bóko/   *a-má-bó:ko* 'arms'
      huma Mugó:ngo 'hit Mugongo'   /o-mu-gongó/   *o-mu-gó:ngo* 'back'
      huma Káhú:ka 'hit Kahuka'   /a-ka-húká/   *a-ká-hú:ka* 'insect'
      huma abáka:lį 'hit the women' /a-ba-kálį̀/   *a-bá-ka:li* 'women'
      huma Kihe:ka 'hit Kiheka'   /e-ki-hekà/   *e-ki-he:kà* 'lorry'

As shown in the forms in the first row in (15), when the imperative is followed by a noun whose final and penultimate vowels are toneless, both the imperative verb and the noun surface with a Low tone. This is unusual and is specific to phrasal constructions where the imperative is used, and it can be compared with the forms in the table in (16). In (16) we see that, when the noun *Magulu*, with its final two toneless vowels, follows the infinitive or the remote past tense (which, as mentioned above, ends with a Low tone), the noun surfaces with a phrasal H on the penultimate vowel, even though the final vowel of the remote past tense is associated with a Low tone. The behavior following the imperative is distinctive.

(16) After infinitive   After future   After remote past
      erihuma Magú:lu   *tukándihuma Magú:lu*   *twahuma Magú:lu*
      'to hit Magulu'   'we will hit Magulu'   'we hit Magulu'

      erihumá Mábó:ko   *tukándihumá Mábó:ko*   *twahuma Mábo:ko*
      erihuma Mugó:ngo   *tukándihuma Mugó:ngo*   *twahuma Mugó:ngo*
      erihuma Káhú:ka   *tukándihuma Káhú:ka*   *twahuma káhú:ka*
      erihuma abáka:lį   *tukándihuma abáka:lį*   *twahuma abáka:lį*
                            tukándihumá báka:lį
      erihuma Kihe:ka   *tukándihuma Kihe:ka*   *twahuma Kihe:ka*

The forms exemplified in (15) and (16), which have been the subject of previous analysis (Hyman 1990, Mutaka 1994), are given here to illustrate three assumptions about the phonology of Kinande: (i) the imperative assigns a suffixal L that prevents the assignment of a phrasal H; (ii) the phrasal H surfaces on the penultimate vowel when the last two vowels are not associated with a lexical tone (L or H); and (iii) vowel lengthening in penultimate position indicates the end of an intonational domain on the last vowel it precedes.

The tones that occur on a noun that follows a verb in the imperative are obviously of interest for this paper. Notice that neither the spurious H (in the case of a verb with a causative -*į*-) nor the lexical H surfaces on the verb in the imperative, as illustrated in the forms in (17).

(17) *bula Magu:lu*   /búl-aC-a Magulu/   'miss Magulu'
      (from -*búl*- [erí-bú:la] 'to miss, to wonder')
      bụlaya Magu:lu   /búl-aC-ị-a Magulu/   'ask Magulu'
      gula Magu:lu   /gul-aC-a Magulu/   'buy Magulu'
      (from -*gul*- [eri-gú:la] 'to buy')
      gụlaya Magu:lu   /gul-aC-ị-a Magulu/   'sell Magulu'

As pointed out earlier, the General Delinking rule proposed in Mutaka (1994) delinks the H from the root of a H tone verb. The suffixal L assigned by the imperative surfaces on the final vowel of the stem. The question now is: Should this imperative L be assigned on the final vowel of the verb, or at the end of the intonational domain, that is, on the final vowel of the noun that ends the intonational domain of the imperative?

My proposal is that the imperative does assign a suffixal L to the final vowel of the verb, as proposed in Mutaka (1994). However, this is supplemented by an additional rule, the imperative intonational L, where a L is inserted at the end of the intonational domain and applies postlexically, just as phrasal H assignment also applies postlexically.

Consider the forms in (18), which consist of the OM + stem followed by a noun.

(18) *túgụ́lịráye Magu:lu* /tu-gul-ir-aC-ị-e HL Magulu/ 'sell Magulu for us'
      túbụlịraye Magu:lu /tu-búl-ir-aC-ị-e HL Magulu/ 'ask Magulu for us'

This OM + stem structure was discussed in Section 2. As can be seen in the forms in (18), this form with the structure OM + stem assigns imperative intonational L. To a certain extent, this form with the OM is not a full-fledged imperative. It stands between the imperative and the hortative. For this reason, we can also call it "mild imperative." The difference between the mild imperative and the imperative is mostly apparent in toneless verbs. Whereas the imperative stem surfaces with a L (cf. *gụlaya Magulu* 'sell Magulu'), a suffixal HL assigned in the mild imperative surfaces, as expected, in the toneless verb root, notably with a H on the root and preroot vowel. The spurious H surfaces on the penultimate vowel. In H tone verbs, the imperative differs from the mild imperative in that the mild imperative surfaces with a H on the OM vowel. Everything else is just like the imperative in that the stem surfaces with a L. Importantly, an imperative intonational L is assigned to the final vowel of the noun in the imperative intonational domain.

(19) *ụtụgụlịráye Magú:lu*   /u-tu-gul-ir-aC-ị-e HL magulu/
      '(please) sell Magulu for us'
      ụtụbụlịraye Magú:lu   /u-tu-búl-ir-aC-ị-e magulu/
      '(please) ask Magulu for us'

As shown in these forms, presenting another kind of hortative that is associated with a construction making use of *kúmbeé* 'please', the assignment
of a phrasal H on the noun in a phrasal construction is what differentiates a
hortative from an imperative form. As pointed out earlier, the stem of a H
tone verb in the hortative surfaces with a L, as is illustrated in the second
example above.

Consider also the forms in (20), in which more material separates the
verb in the imperative from the noun at the end of what may be termed an
imperative intonational phrase.

(20) *gend' úmbwiriry'   abálumé | ng' okó námáhụtalya Magu:lu ||*
     go   you.tell.for.me men   that on I.have.hurt Magulu
     'go and tell the men that I have just hurt Magulu'

Assuming the analysis of Hyman (1990), this sentence can be analyzed
as consisting of two phrasal domains, which I have separated with a vertical
bar. They jointly constitute one intonational phrase, the end of which is
marked by a double vertical bar. In this sentence, the first verb followed by
the noun constitutes a phrasal domain. We know that the H tone on the last
vowel of *abálumé* is a phrasal H, that is, a boundary tone, because, underlyingly, the form is /a-ba-lúme/. After H spreading followed by delinking,
which occurs lexically, the form would end with two toneless vowels. In
such a case, a phrasal H targets the final vowel at the end of the phrasal domain. As for the second phrasal domain, notice that the noun *Magulu*,
whose last two vowels are toneless at the output of the lexical stratum,
should have ended with a phrasal H and an intonational Low. But it ends in
L. This L can only be caused by the imperative at the beginning of the example. For that reason, I have termed this an imperative intonational domain. The question now is to decide whether this L is the L that was directly assigned by the imperative, which has been assumed in previous work
(Mutaka 1994, Hyman 1990) to associate to the final vowel of the verb in
the imperative, or is this a different L? Before answering this question, let
us examine the utterances in (21), which were produced at various paces.
While the sentences in (21a) were spoken rapidly, those in (21b) were ut-
tered with a very slow pace.

(21) a. *gendá* |*ụnyịléberáy'*   *abálumé* |*ng' abanámágula amagu:lu* ||
go   you.look.for.me men   that they.buy   legs
'go and check for me whether the men are buying legs'
sịgalá | *ukálindirira   Magu:lu* ||
stay   you.wait.for Magulu   (cf. *erị-sịgal-a* 'to stay')
'stay and wait for Magulu'

b. *gendá* |*ụnyịléberáy'*   *abálu:mé* || *ng' abanámágula amagu:lu* ||
go   you.look.for.me men   that they.buy   legs
'go and check for me whether the men are buying legs'
sịgal' enyụ:má || *úlíndirire   Magu:lu* ||
stay behind   you.wait.for Magulu
'stay behind and wait for Magulu'

In the two sentences in (21a), the imperative verbs end with a H tone. I
have marked the end of these verbs with a vertical line to show the boundary of a phrasal domain. This shows that the H on the final vowel of the imperative verb in these sentences is a phrasal H. In the sentences in (21b), I
have put double vertical lines to indicate where, in a slow rhythm, one can
put a pause. In other words, the phrasal domain now reads as an intonational
domain, much like list intonation. The problem is this: If the end of the sentences in (21b) is marked with an intonational domain boundary, why does
the phrasal H not appear on the penultimate vowels? My proposal is that the
end of an imperative form is associated with an imperative L that was assigned lexically. If it was not associated with a lexical Low, one could expect the phrasal H to surface on the penultimate vowel, as shown in the following examples, where I use a verb that ends with two toneless vowels.

(22) a. *ukándibyá   wamagendá* | *ịwatwalánịa   Magú:lu* ||
if.you.be you.go   that.you.bring.with Magulu
'if ever you leave, take Magulu with you'

b. *ukándibyá wamagenda eBúte:mbó* || *ịwatwalánịa   Magú:lu* ||
if.you.be you.go   to.Butembo that.you.bring.with Magulu
'if ever you go to Butembo, take Magulu with you'

c. *ukándibyá wamagenda eBụnyụ́:ká* || *ịwatwalánịa   Magú:lu* ||
if.you.be you.go   to.Bunyuka that.you.bring.with Magulu
'if ever you go to Bunyuka, take Magulu with you'

d. *ukándibyá wamagenda eKísú:ngá* || *ịwatwalánịa   Magú:lu* ||
if.you.be you.go   to.Kisunga that.you.bring.with Magulu
'if ever you go to Kisunga, take Magulu with you'

e. *ukándibyá wamagé:ndá* || *ịwatwalánịa   Magú:lu* ||
if.you.be you.go   that.you.bring.with Magulu
'if ever you leave, take Magulu with you'

As shown in (22a), when a toneless verb ends the phrasal domain, it is associated with a H tone. If this phrasal domain is turned into an intonational domain, by putting a pause after the verb, the phrasal H appears on the penultimate vowel and the intonational H on the final vowel before the pause, as seen in (22a). The names of three villages with underlying representations of /e-Butémbò/, /e-Bụnyụka/, and /e-Kisúngá/ are found in (22b), (22c), and (22d). A H tone in them will spread backward lexically, and the right branch of a multiply linked H will delink. Thus, prior to the assignment of the phrasal H and intonational H, they appear as *Bútembò*, *Bụnyụka*, and *Kísúnga*, as opposed to what is found in the examples.

Of great interest for us is the form of *Butembo* that ends with a lexical L. As shown in (22b), the phrasal H, or the intonational H, does surface on its final vowel. This is exactly what happens with the verb *genda* in the earlier examples. It, too, ends in a phrasal H because the lexical Low that was assigned by the imperative is knocked out by the boundary tones (phrasal H or intonational H). In (23), I indicate a phrasal boundary after the verb in the imperative and show that, when the last vowel is deleted to avoid a vowel hiatus, the phrasal H can be realized on the following vowel as the first half of a falling tone, as shown in the examples in (23b).

(23) a. *gendá | úmbirikirire Magu:lu ||*   'go and call Magulu for me'
          gendá | únyítumire Magu:lu || 'go and send Magulu for me'
          gendá | ubirikíré Magu:lu || 'go and call Magulu'
          gendá | utúmé Magu:lu || 'go and send Magulu'

      b. *gend' | úmbirikirire Magu:lu ||*
          gend' | únyítumire Magu:lu ||
          gend' | úbirikíré Magu:lu ||
          gend' | útúmé Magu:lu ||

In (24), I show that the end of the imperative intonational domain is marked with an imperative intonational Low regardless of the number of phrasal domains that separate the final noun with the verb in the imperative.

(24) a. *gendá | ụ́mbụlịráy'   âbálumé | ng'   abanámágul' amagu:lu ||*
          go   you.ask.for.me men   if   they.buy   legs
          'go and ask the men if they are buying legs'

      b. *gendá | ụ́mbụlịráy'   âbálumé | ng'   abanámundísalá*
          go   you.ask.for.me men   if   they.will.vomit
          bịmy'   oko magu:lu ||
          they.take on   legs
          'go and ask the men if they have finally taken a decision on taking
          some legs'

In (25), I show that, for a long sentence, if a speaker turns his utterance into a hortative construction, although it starts with an imperative form, he is then likely to end the intonational phrase with the phrasal H on the penultimate vowel and the intonational L on the last vowel.

(25) *gend' úmbųlįráy'*   *âbálumé|* *ųbábųlayé |*
       go   you.ask.for.me men   you.ask.them
       ng' abanámundísalá   bįmy'   oko magú:lu
       if   they.will.vomit they.take on   legs
       'go and ask the men, ask them if they have finally taken a decision on taking some legs'

The end of the sentence gives the feeling that it is a hortative construction. If the intention is to convey an order, *magu:lu* with low tones would sound better.

Consider also the following examples that start with the imperative of a H tone verb. In (26b) I have made the second part of the sentence hortative and the first part an intonational domain with the lengthening of the penultimate vowel of the noun.

(26) a. *tumira   oko mųkonį |*   *uty'*   *alété*   *amagu:lu ||*
          tumir'   oko mųkonį | *uty'*   *aléty'* *ámagu:lu ||*

      b. *tumira   oko mųko:nį ||*   *uty'*   *alété*   *amagú:lu ||*
          send.for on   patient   you.say he.brings legs
          'send for the patient, tell him to bring the legs'

As shown in (26), the observations made about the toneless verb root in the imperative, notably that the verb in the imperative bears an imperative L tone and that the noun at the end of the imperative intonational domain also surfaces with an imperative intonational L, fully apply to the H tone verb. The third example is of interest in that the noun at the end of the intonational domain may surface with a phrasal H and an intonational L if the speaker decides to end an imperative sentence as a hortative. In order for such a sentence to be acceptable, I have turned the end of the first phrasal domain, the one that ends with *mųkó:nį*, into an intonational domain.[2]

The question now is why the imperative intonational domain is not assigned to the final vowel of that word (*mųkó:nį*). The answer is that this H must be an intonational H like the one that was assigned on the word *Butembo* that was discussed earlier. The imperative intonational L only appears at the very end of the imperative intonational domain at the end of the utterance.

---

[2] Notice also that I am marking the phrasal H and the intonational H on the word *muko:ní* in this preceding sentence as a Nande speaker would have read it inside the English sentence.

Consider now the forms in (27) where the structure consists of a verb in the imperative followed by a conjoined noun. In these examples, *Kambale* is /kambálè/ underlyingly. That is, it ends in a lexical L at the output of the lexical strata, just like the word *Butembo*, discussed earlier.

(27) *birikira Kámbalé* | *bana Magu:lu* ‖ 'call Kambale and Magulu'
      birikira Magulú | *bana Kámba:le* ‖ 'call Magulu and Kambale'
      birikira Kámbalé | *bán' omụko:nị* ‖ 'call Kambale and the patient'
      birikira omụkonị | *bana Magu:lu* ‖ 'call the patient and Magulu'
      birikira Magulú | *bán' omụko:nị* ‖ 'call Magulu and the patient'
      birikir' omụkonị | *n' omụhụ:mị* ‖ 'call the patient and the hitter'
     *birikira omụkonị | *n' omụhụ́:mị* ‖ 'call the patient and the hitter'
      birikira omụko:nị ‖ *n' omụhụ:mị* ‖ 'call the patient and the hitter'

      birikira omụko:nị ‖ *na Magu:lú* ‖ *n'omụhụ:mị* ‖
      'call the patient, Magulu, and the hitter'

The now familiar observation is that the end of the imperative intonational domain ends in a L, specifically the imperative intonational L. The noun that appears just before the particle *na* 'and' or *bana* 'with' marks the end of the phrasal domain, and its final vowel is thus marked with a phrasal H. If the speaker chooses to turn this phrasal domain into an intonational domain, that is, by making a pause, the penultimate vowel of that noun is lengthened and the final vowel is marked with a H tone. This H can only be the intonational H, and the reason the preceding lengthened vowel does not bear a phrasal H is because the imperative H must have been assigned on the final vowel of that noun. When it is subsequently knocked off by the intonational H in utterance nonfinal position, the form surfaces as is shown in those examples.

As also observed earlier, if the speaker chooses to turn the end of an imperative into a hortative, the noun at the end of the imperative intonational domain will bear a phrasal H on the penultimate vowel followed by an intonational L on the final vowel, as shown in (28). As I have indicated with a question mark at the beginning of these utterances, the sentence is not preferred. The preferred sentence is the one that ends with an imperative intonational L.

(28) *?birikira omụko:nị* | *n' omụhụ́:mị* ‖
      'call the patient and the hitter'

      ?birikira omụko:nị ‖ *na Magu:lú* ‖ *n' omụhụ́:mị* ‖
      'call the patient, Magulu, and the hitter'

The examples that have been discussed above have been with a H tone verb. Forms with the toneless verb in the imperative produce similar effects, as seen in (29). That is, we see a phrasal H on the final vowel of the noun that precedes the conjunction *na* and an imperative intonational L at the end of the imperative intonational domain.

(29) *huma Kámbalé | bana Magu:lu ||*   'hit Kambale and Magulu'
     huma Magulú | n' omuko:ni || 'hit Magulu and the patient'
     hum' omukoní | n' omuhu:mi || 'hit the patient and the hitter'

The hortative examples in (30) show that, unlike the imperative, the hortative does not assign a L at the end of the intonational domain. That is why the noun in these examples surfaces with the expected phrasal H on the penultimate vowel and an intonational L on the final vowel.

(30) a. *ubirikíré Kámbalé | bana Magú:lu ||* 'call Kambale and Magulu'
       ubirikíré Magulú | n' omukó:ni || 'call Magulu and the patient'
       ubirikíry' ômukoní | n' omuhú:mi || 'call the patient and the hitter'
       (cf. /u-bírikir-aC-e/ [ubirikírê])

       ubuláyé Kámbalé | bana Magú:lu || 'ask Kambale and Magulu'
       (cf. u-búl-aC-i-e [ubuláyê])

    b. *úhúme Kámbalé | bana Magú:lu ||* 'hit Kambale and Magulu'
       úhúme Magulú | n' omukó:ni || 'hit Magalu and the patient'
       úhúmy' omukoní | n' omuhú:mi || 'hit the patient and the hitter'
       úgúláye Kámbalé | bana Magú:lu || 'sell Kambale and Magulu'
       úgúláyé Kátwiró | bana Magú:lu || 'sell Katwiro and Magulu'

The final vowel in both the H tone verbs in (30a) and the toneless verbs in (30b) ends with a lexical L at the output of the lexical stratum. There are postlexical rules such as vowel deletion and phantom consonant -C- deletion that I ignore in this paper (see Mutaka (1994) for a discussion of these). The end result is that in a H tone verb, the form ends in a H tone, while in a toneless verb, the form ends in a lexical L. Between the verb and the noun, H tone spreading will occur as in the last example (*úgúláyé*), and if the noun has a floating L that precedes the noun, the final vowel of a toneless verb ends with a L, as in the next to last example (*úgúláye*).

4   Conclusion

As has been shown here, there are major differences between the imperative and the hortative with respect to the behavior of the suffixal tones in these moods. These differences are best illustrated by the data in (31) and (32).[3]

---

[3] The tone on the first word in (32a) is somewhat unusual. One would expect a form like *úgé-nde* 'go' as would be the case for *úhúme* 'hit'. The form *úgénde* would be correct before a

(31) Imperative

    a. *gendá | ụnyíléberáyé   Mábokó | ng'anámundigul' oko*
       go   you.look.for.me Maboko if he.will.buy   on
       magu:lu ‖
       legs
       'go and check for me whether Maboko will buy legs'

    b. *sịgal' enyụ:má* ‖ *ụlébáyé   Mábo:kó ‖ ng'*
       stay   behind   you.look   Maboko   if
       anámundigul' oko magu:lu ‖
       he.will.buy   on   legs
       'stay behind and see whether Maboko will buy legs'

(32) Hortative

    a. *ugéndeé | ụkándịnyịleberyá   Mábó:kó* ‖
       you.go   you.will.look.for.me Maboko
       ng' anámundigul' oko magú:lu ‖
       if   he.will.buy   on   legs
       'please go and see (for me) whether Maboko will buy legs'

    b. *ụsịgály' ênyụ:má* ‖ *ụkándịlebyá Mábó:kó* ‖
       you.stay behind   you.will.look Maboko
       ng' anámundigul' oko magú:lu ‖
       if   he.will.buy   on   legs
       'please stay behind and see whether Maboko will buy legs'

The most glaring difference is seen in the tones that the last noun in each utterance bears. The imperative ends with an imperative intonational L that prevents the assignment of a phrasal H, whereas the hortative bears the phrasal H and the intonational L as expected. A second difference is seen in the tones of a noun such as *Mábóko* at the end of a phrasal domain in mid position. In an imperative, only the intonational H appears on the last vowel, whereas for the hortative, the phrasal H appears on the penultimate vowel and the intonational H on the last vowel. We know that this is the end of an intonational phrase because of the pause that is marked by the lengthening of the penultimate vowel. The same difference can be observed in the word *enyụ́ma* 'behind': in the imperative, the word bears an intonational H on the last vowel whereas, in the hortative, the phrasal H on the penultimate vowel and the intonational H on the final vowel are both clearly exhibited.

---

pause, and in such a case, a form like *úgéndeé* would not sound correct. The reader may also wonder why the penultimate vowel in *gendá* or *ugénde* is not long. This is due to the structure of the verb, which has an *-aC-*, that is, it is *gend-aC-e* or *u-gend-aC-e*. It is argued in Mutaka (2000) that such forms are immune to penultimate lengthening.

As has been argued in the paper, the verb in the imperative ends with an imperative L, and at the end of an intonational phrase in which there is a verb in the imperative, the last noun bears an imperative intonational L. This L, which is a boundary tone, prevents the assignment of the phrasal H. However, as has also been shown in the paper, the imperative L is easily knocked out by an intonational H, such as the list intonation H that *gendá* bears in (31a), or the H on *enyu̜:má* in (31b).

That the H on the final vowel in *Mábo:kó* in (31b) is intonational rather than phrasal can be deduced from examples with list intonation, as in (33).

(33) a. *enyú̜:má, n' amábó:kó n' amagú:lu*
'the back, and the arms, and the legs'

b. *kanganay' enyu̜:má, n' amábo:kó, n' amagu:lu*
'show the back and the arms and the legs'

The nouns in the phrase in (33a) have both a phrasal H on the penultimate vowel and an intonational H or L on the last vowel. Those in the sentence in (33b) lack a phrasal tone on the penultimate vowel and surface with list intonation, while the last word surfaces with the imperative intonational L, as argued for in this paper, because of the imperative form of the verb.

References

Hyman, L. M. 1990. Boundary tonology and the prosodic hierarchy. In S. Inkelas & D. Zec (eds.), *The phonology-syntax connection*, 109–125. Chicago: University of Chicago Press.

Hyman, L. M. & F. Katamba. 1990. Spurious high-tone extensions in Luganda. *South African Journal of Linguistics* 10: 142–158.

Hyman, L. M. & N. Valinande. 1985. Globality in the Kinande tone system. In D. L. Goyvaerts (ed.), *African linguistics: Essays in memory of M. W. K. Semikenke*, 239–260. Amsterdam: Benjamins.

Meeussen, A. E. 1961. Le ton des extensions verbales en bantou. *Orbis* 10: 424–427.

Meeussen, A. E. 1962. De tonen van subjunktief en imperatief in het Bantoe. *Africana Linguistica* 1: 57–74.

Meeussen, A. E. 1967. Bantu grammatical reconstructions. *Africana Linguistica* 3: 79–121.

Mutaka, N. M. 1994. *The lexical tonology of Kinande*. Munich: LINCOM.

Mutaka, N. M. 2000. Penultimate lengthening and stress in Kinande. In F. Remotti (ed.), *Ambienti, lingue, culture: Contributi della Missione Etnologica Italiana in Africa Equatoriale*, 103–117. Alessandria: Edizioni dell'Orso.

12

A Direct/Inverse Subsystem in Ingush Deictic Prefixes

JOHANNA NICHOLS

1 Introduction

The single greatest catalyst that pushed my work on Ingush (of the Nakh branch of Nakh-Daghestanian, spoken in the central north Caucasus at the far south of Russia) to full-scale documentation was Larry Hyman. As chair of Berkeley's Linguistics Department when violence first began to be visited on the Caucasus, he recognized the opportunity to increase world awareness of the Ingush and Chechen people, give graduate students a rare opportunity, and make the most of national funding priorities. Together we planned a field methods course and successful grant proposals. Administrative and logistical obstacles that had halted me before melted away. His organizational know-how, boundless enthusiasm and optimism, and scholarly judgment, more than my expertise and more than the inherent interest of the language, got the project off to a sound start and in particular made it possible to create the electronic and organizational groundwork for a grammar, dictionary, and text collection, all three now realities.

Larry does most of his work with elicitation rather than corpora, and this paper is intended to demonstrate the positive contribution that elicitation can have, not only in explicitly recovering patterns of such low frequency that they show up only in a corpus larger than a documentation project is likely to produce, but also in revealing semantic and pragmatic phenomena that are not evident in a corpus but are readily accessible to native or native-like intuitions and show up clearly when an investigator

Revealing Structure.
Eugene Buckley, Thera Crane & Jeff Good (eds.).
Copyright © 2018, CSLI Publications.

asks the right questions (see Hyman 2007). Thus this paper first analyzes the system as it emerges from a text survey (Section 4) and then as it appears in elicitation (Section 5).

This paper ties into my recent work on ditransitives and their alignment, which has its roots in the eye-opening experience of reading Hyman & Duranti (1982). That paper helped me realize that head and dependent marking can respond to different referential hierarchies but code the same argument relations, that indirect objects and other second objects should be included in a typology of argument marking, and that both their referential hierarchies and the clause morphosyntax are interesting in themselves.

2 Deictic prefixes in Ingush

Ingush has a set of four verbal deictic prefixes—*dwa-* 'away from speaker', *hwa-* 'toward speaker', *hwal-* 'up', and *wa-* 'down'—of which only the first two concern us here.[1] They can have literal deictic function, as in (1) and (2).

(1) *Muusaa* **hwa**-*qeachar.*
    Musa   DX-arrive.WP
    'Musa has arrived (here).' (in speaker's location)

(2) *Muusaa* **dwa**-*qeachar=ii?*
    Musa   DX-arrive.WP=Q
    'Has Musa arrived (there)?' (interlocutor addressed via telephone)

In word formation they have various conventionalized functions. For instance, proximal *hwa-* appears in a number of verbs indicating entry into a normal, desirable, or fully aware state and distal *dwa-* can indicate entry into a nonnormal, undesirable, or nonaware state: *hwa-soma-d.oal* (DX-wake-D.VZ:INCP) 'wake up', *dwa-twous* (DX-fall asleep) 'fall asleep, go to sleep'.[2] It is the more or less literal functions that are of interest here.

---

[1] In the all-lower-ASCII, diacritic-free Latin practical spelling used in Nichols (2011), Nichols & Sprouse (2004), the Berkeley Ingush corpus, and elsewhere, *w* spells pharyngeal and pharyngealization. (It is used because it is the only letter not otherwise needed and it resembles the letter used for the same purpose in the extended Georgian alphabet used for transliteration in Georgian publications.) The marker *dwa-* consists of /d/ plus a pharyngealized vowel; *hwa-* has an initial voiceless pharyngeal fricative plus an automatically pharyngealized vowel.

[2] For a fuller treatment of deixis, see Nichols (2011: 346–358).

3 The Direct/Inverse System

As it turns out, the more or less literal functions of the deictic prefixes are not simply motion toward speaker versus away from speaker. What is relevant is not just any motion but specifically motion (or transfer) between subject (A/S) and indirect object or goal (G).[3] Thus few monotransitives have literal deictic prefixes, but nearly all tokens of ditransitives and motion verbs have them. Monotransitives such as 'scare', 'feed', 'catch', and 'push over' rarely or never have deictic prefixes, while ditransitives such as 'send', 'give', 'tell (story)', and 'introduce' generally do have them. Motion verbs such as 'go', 'come', and 'arrive', transitive motion verbs such as 'bring (a person to a place)' and 'take (a person to a place)', and verbs of communication such as 'say, tell', 'inform', and 'introduce' almost always have deictic prefixes.

Languages of the Kartvelian family (southern Caucasus) also have deictic prefixes that make what appears to be a similar distinction to Ingush *dwa-/hwa-*. Lacroix (2011a, 2011b) shows that in Laz (Kartvelian, spoken in southwestern Georgia and northeastern Turkey) the verb 'give' takes the deictic prefixes in a direct/inverse system indexing the relative statuses of T (the more theme-like argument) and G: *mo-* is used when G is higher than T, *me-* otherwise.[4] (Outside of this ditransitive system, *mo-* indicates proximal, and *me-* distal, deixis.) The relevant referential hierarchy is person: $1 > 2/3$.[5] Figure 1 gives my diagram of the facts described by Lacroix. The verb agrees with whichever of T and G is higher on the person hierarchy, and the deictic prefix disambiguates the role (T or G) of the agreement prefix.

	T	G
me-	1	2/3
mo-	2/3	1

Figure 1. Deictic prefix choice and T/G person categories in Laz

Upon reading Lacroix (2011a), I tested several Ingush ditransitives in elicitation and surveyed several in the Berkeley Ingush Corpus[6] to see whether their deictic prefixes behave like those of Laz. They do not; in Ingush the person of the T is entirely irrelevant to the choice of prefix, as seen in (3)–(6).

---

[3] See Abbreviations for a fuller statement of the argument types A, S, O, T, and G.

[4] Lacroix uses R rather than G to label the more goal-like argument.

[5] For referential hierarchies, see Bickel (2011: 410); for person in direct/inverse systems, see Siewierska (2011).

[6] Some 300,000 words of transcribed text, about half interlinearized, representing about 30 hours of speech. This represents about 10% of the recording done so far in the corpus project.

						Person:	T	G
(3)	a.	*Cuo*	**hwa**-*j.ouziitagjy*	*hwo*	*suoga.*		2	1
		3s.ERG	DX-J.introduce.J.FUT	2s.NOM	1s.ALL			
		'He'll introduce you to me.'[7]						
	b.	*Cuo*	**hwa**-*j.ouziitagjy*	*yz*	*suoga.*		3	1
		3s.ERG	DX-J.introduce.J.FUT	3s.NOM	1s.ALL			
		'He'll introduce her to me.'						
(4)	a.	*Cuo*	**hwa**-*j.ouziitagjy*	*so*	*hwuoga.*		1	2
		3s.ERG	DX-J.introduce.J.FUT	1s.NOM	2s.ALL			
		'He'll introduce me to you.'						
	b.	*Cuo*	**hwa**-*j.ouziitagjy*	*yz*	*hwuoga.*		3	2
		3s.ERG	DX-J.introduce.J.FUT	3s.NOM	2s.ALL			
		'He'll introduce her to you.'						
(5)	a.	*Aaz*	**dwa**-*j.ouziitagjy*	*hwo*	*cynga.*		2	3
		1s.ERG	DX-J.introduce.J.FUT	2s.NOM	3s.ALL			
		'I'll introduce you to him.'						
	b.	*Aaz*	**dwa**-*j.ouziitagjy*	*yz*	*cynga.*		3	3
		1s.ERG	DX-J.introduce.J.FUT	3s.NOM	3s.ALL			
		'I'll introduce her to him.'						
(6)	a.	*Wa*	**dwa**-*j.ouziitagj*=*ii*	*so*	*cynga?*		1	3
		2s.ERG	DX-J.introduce.J.FUT=Q	1s.NOM	3s.ALL			
		'Will you introduce me to him?'						
	b.	*Wa*	**dwa**-*j.ouziitagj*=*ii*	*yz*	*cynga?*		3	3
		2s.ERG	DX-J.introduce.J.FUT=Q	3s.NOM	3s.ALL			
		'Will you introduce her to him?'						

Rather, as shown by (3) and (4) vs. (5) and (6), it is the person of A vis-à-vis G that is relevant. The combination of third person A and either first or second person G triggers the prefix *hwa-*; first or second person A and third person G triggers *dwa-*. It is the same for the S and G of an intransitive motion verb. Thus *dwa-* is used when S/A outranks G and *hwa-* when G outranks S/A. See Figure 2 and Table 1.

---

[7] The verb means not so much 'introduce' as 'familiarize, tell about, acquaint', but I gloss it as 'introduce' because that English verb is most similar in alignment, treating the T as direct object and the G as indirect object. So, in these examples, *ergative* introduces *nominative* to *allative*. (The verb is an indirect causative of 'know (kennen)'.)

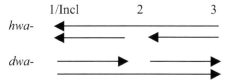

Figure 2. Ingush deictic prefixes and S/A (arrow base) and G (arrow point)

3 > 2 only *hwa-*
2 > 1 only *hwa-*
3 > 1 only *hwa-*

1 > 2 chiefly *dwa-*; *hwa-* if 1 and 2 in same place or similar special interpretation
2 > 3 only *dwa-* for most verbs; occasionally *hwa-* with special interpretation
1 > 3 only *dwa-* for most verbs; occasionally *hwa-* with special interpretation

Table 1. S/A > G person combinations and deictic prefixes

The use of *hwa-* when G outranks A is almost without exception. The use of *dwa-* when A outranks G is the default and the most frequent, but various special interpretations allow *hwa-* to be used in this context as well. When both A and G are third person, either *dwa-* or *hwa-* can be used depending on speaker perspective and other factors.

4   Text Survey

A text survey of the Berkeley Ingush corpus gives a cleaner picture than Table 1: all of the side clauses about special interpretations can be removed, as no evidence of them shows up in the corpus. The verbs *oal-* 'say' and *d.uuc-* 'tell' have high text frequency and can be used to illustrate the various combinations and further details. The corpus has a good number of examples of these verbs with prefixes where fieldworker and recordee discuss the recording procedure. While in English it is probably most natural to speak of the speaking itself without indirect objects ('OK, go ahead and start talking.' 'Here's what I can say about cheesemaking.'), in Ingush it is usually phrased in terms of the recordee speaking to the fieldworker ('Go ahead and speak to me/us.' 'Here's what I can tell you about cheesemaking.'). The indirect objects are not often overt, but they are easily restored by consultants. *Hwa-* is used in all examples where the fieldworker asks the recordee to speak. (Here and below, example numbers are followed by a schematic indication of the person of A and G: A>G.)

(7)   2>1 **Hwa-*duucal,*   *naanii.*
       DX-D.tell.IMPVmild   grandma
       (Turning on the recorder) 'OK, go ahead.' (using the polite mild imperative and a polite form of address to an older woman)

(8) 2>1 *Hwa-duuca,*   *hwa-duuca.*
         DX-D.tell.IMPV   DX-D.tell.IMPV
         'OK, go ahead.'

(9) 2>1 *Yz myshta ju*   *hwa-duucalahw.*
         3s how   J.make   DX-D.tell.IMPVmild
         (After mentioning recipe) '(Could) you tell me how it's made?'

Dwa- is used if the recordee discusses talking or what to talk about:

(10) 1>2 *Dolccha_bessa* **dwa-duuc**   *aaz*   *hwuona.*
          properly   DX-D.tell   1s.ERG   2s.DAT
          'I'll tell you all about it.'

(11) 1>2 *Handz* **dwa-duucazh**   *joall*   *so.*
          now   DX-D.tell.CVsim   J.PROG   1s
          'I'm coming to that. (I'm (in the process of) telling (you) now.)'
          (fieldworker has asked about something recordee is about to get to)

The same usage is found in examples not about the recording situation:

(12) 2>1 *Hwa-duucal,*   *boqq'ala.*
          DX-D.tell.IMPV   really:EMPH
          'Tell me, I pray you.'[8]

Hwa- is used in all examples with third person A and first person G:

(13) 3>1 *belxa='a*   *belxazh*   **hwa-duucar**   *cy*
          RED=&   B.cry.CVsim   DX-D.tell.IMPF   DEM.OBL
          shin   *voaqqa* *sagaz*   *yz*
          two.OBL   V.old   man.ERG   3s
          'The two old men cried when they told me that.'
          (men were at speaker's house talking about speaker's mother)

(14) 3>1 [__   *yz* **hwa-duuca**]   *sag*
          (ERG)   3s DX-D.tell.PPL   person
          'someone to tell me about it, a person who could tell me about it'[9]

Dwa- is used in all corpus examples with a third person G:

(15) 1>3 *Aaz*   *shiedar*   **dwa-duucaddy**   *cynna*   *hwogh.*
          1s.ERG   everything   DX-D.tell.FUT.D   3s.DAT   2s.LAT
          'I'll tell her everything about you.'

---

[8] From the text: I. Kodzoev. *Pacchahw Lir* [King Lear]. Undated manuscript.

[9] Example (14) is a relative construction. The relative clause is bracketed. Ingush uses relativization by deletion. In (14) the nonovert argument is indicated by an underscore, and the case it would have if overt is parenthesized in the interlinear gloss.

(16) 2>3 *wa*   ***dwa**-duucie* ...
      2s.ERG   DX-D.tell.CVseq
      'If you tell him …'

(17) 3>3 *Txy*   *deasiesaguo*   *cynna*   *q'eilagh*   ***dwa**-duucazh*
      our.EXCL   stepmother.ERG   3s.DAT   secretly   DX-D.tell.CVsim
      xannad   *shiina*   *bwarjg+deina*   *hamaazh.*
      PROG.NARP   3s.DAT   eye+seen   thing.PL
      'Our stepmother told her in confidence what she had seen.'

(18) 3>3 *Yz shiiga*   ***dwa**-diicacha* ...
      3s 3s.RFL.ALL   DX-D.tell.CVtemp
      'When they told him about it …'

In all cases of situations of reciprocation, the first verb has *dwa-* and the second one *hwa-*, as in (19). No literal deixis is evident; this is a back-and-forth transfer that would have deictic value only for the two third person parties.[10]

(19) 1>1 *Vai*   *mella='a*   ***dwa**-duucie,*   ***hwa**-duucie* ...
      1pINCL.ERG   how_much   DX-D.say.CVseq   DX-D.say.CVseq
      'No matter what we say (how much we talk back and forth) …'

The word 'give' is another high-frequency verb well attested enough to illustrate the operation of the hierarchy. Again, *dwa-* is used for 1>2, 2>3, and 1>3, and *hwa-* for 2>1 and 3>1. Examples for 3>2 are also attested (see (23)).

(20) 1>2 *Kopezh hwa='a beaxaa*   *juxa*   ***dwa**-lugjy*
      copy.PL DX=& B.take:PL.CVant   back   DX-give.FUT.J
      vai.
      1pINCL.ERG
      'We'll make copies and return them.'

(21) a. 2>1 *Vow var*   *sy*   *jer,*   ***hwa**-vaa*   *suona*   *jer.*
      son V.was   my   3s   DX-V.give.IMPV   1s.DAT   3s
      'This is my son. Give him to me.'

     b. 1>2 *Dynien=t'y*   *mal_dolazh_doa hama daragh*
      world=on   all   thing   for
      lugvaac,   ***dwa**-lugvaac.*
      give-V.FUT.NEG   DX-give-V.FUT.NEG
      'Not for anything on earth will I give him over to you.' [11]

---

[10] I found no 3>2 examples in the corpus.

[11] Example (21) is a fragment of a dialog between a father and orphanage director.

(22) 3>1 *Diitt shu   dealacha   **hwa**-luzh   my   dii*
D.14 year D.pass.CVtemp DX-give.CVsim EMPH   D.PROG
yzh   paaspartazh.
DEM.PL   passport.PL
'At age 14 they give (us) passports, don't they?'

(23) 3>2 *Hwuona   boaghar   ealar   uq   kuoragh*
2s.DAT   B.come.NZ   say.WP   DEM.OBL   window.LAT
***hwa**-lubby   hwuona ealar.*
DX-give.FUT.B   2s.DAT say.WP
'What you're entitled to will be given to you through that window, he said.' (translated as passive; active grammatically)

(24) 1>3 *Ruzq'a   mexkarazhta   **dwa**-lugdar.*
wealth   daughter.PL.DAT   DX-give.FUT.D.COND
'I'd give the wealth to my daughters.'[12]

In text examples, all 3>3 scenarios use *dwa*-:

(25) 3>3 *Hwa-hwii Wumaar, uqanna   zhop   dahwiitalahw,*
hey   Umar   this-DAT   answer   D.send.IMPVmild
*ealie,   cynga   **dwa**-luora   cuo   keaxat.*
say.CVseq   3s.ALL   DX-give.IMPF   3s.ERG   letter
'Here, Umar, answer this, he would say and give him the letter.'

(26) 3>3 *biezachoa   **dwa**-luora*
B.need.PPL.NZ.DAT   DX-give.IMPF
'They would give (it) away to those who needed it.'

Again, when there is a back-and-forth or reciprocal transfer, one verb
takes *dwa*- and the other *hwa*-, whether or not there is any clear deixis involved. Example (27) is from a Pear Film narrative (Chafe 1975) describing
a scene in which two boys give each other things. The first boy comes from
closer to the camera and the second from farther away, but when they exchange the objects they are basically side by side.

(27) 3>3 *Yz   furaazhka **dwa** my   jelinjgehw   vuoquo*
DEM   cap   DX   EMPH   J.give.CVjust   other.ERG
*qo   qor   **hwa**-lu*
three pear   DX-give.
'As soon as (he) gives him the cap, the other boy gives (him)
three pears.'[13]

---

[12] From the text: I. Kodzoev. *Pacchahw Lir* [King Lear]. Undated manuscript.

[13] Example (27) illustrates a pattern which occurs elsewhere, where certain particles are allowed to intervene between the deictic prefixes and their host verb.

5 Elicitation

For the verbs discussed in Section 4 and for others, elicitation generally confirms the picture outlined above. For example, there is complete ungrammaticality of *hwa-* in some 1>2 and 3>3 scenarios:

(28) 1>2 *Aaz   hwa   axcha qoana   dwa-luddy/*hwa-luddy.*
       1s.ERG 2s.GEN money tomorrow DX-give.FUT.D
       'I'll give your money back tomorrow.'

(29) 3>3 *Cuo   dwa-lugjy/*hwa-lugjy so mearie   Muusaaiga.*
       3s.ERG DX-give.FUT.J   1s in.marriage Musa.ALL
       'He's going to marry me to Musa.' (i.e. 'give me in marriage')

But elicitation also reveals further flexibility. In the following examples using 'give in marriage', both prefixes are possible for several scenarios. In particular, *hwa-* is possible for most scenarios that show only *dwa-* in the texts. The choice depends on who is where and/or who is whose relative.

(30) 1>2 *Aaz   hwa-lugjy/dwa-lugjy yz hwuoga mearie.*
       1s.ERG DX-give.FUT.J   3s 2s.ALL in.marriage
       'I'll give her to you in marriage.' (father to suitor or suitor's relative; *hwa-* is possible, atypically for 1>2 scenarios, because both men are in the same place and the bride-to-be is elsewhere; it may also serve as a solidarity enhancer)

(31) 3>3 *Cuo   hwa-lugjy/dwa-lugjy yz mearie   Muusaaiga.*
       3s.ERG DX-give.FUT.J   3s in.marriage Musa.ALL
       'He's going to give her in marriage to Musa.' (*hwa-* if Musa's relatives speaking; *dwa-* if bride's relatives, or any other party)

(32) 3>3 *Hwo dwa-lugj=ii/hwa-lugj=ii   cuo   Muusaaiga?*
       2s   DX-give.FUT.J=Q   3s.ERG Musa.ALL
       'Is he going to give you to Musa?' (*hwa-* possible if Musa's relatives speaking to the prospective bride; otherwise, only *dwa*)

For 3>2 examples—none of these are attested for 'say', but there are two for 'give', both with *hwa*—consultants volunteer both prefixes, with the choice depending on the deictic value of the A:

(33) 3>2 *Uquo   dwa-diicaad=ii   hwuoga?*
       this.ERG DX-D.tell.NW=Q   2s.ALL
       'Did he (this person) tell you?'

(34) 3>2 *Cuo   hwa-diicaad=ii   hwuona?*
       that.ERG DX-D.tell.NW=Q   2s.DAT
       'Did he (that person) tell you?'

Example (33) has proximal deictic *uquo* 's/he, this one', whose referent is understood to be close to the speaker. So, this 3>2 scenario is deictically similar to a 1>2 scenario and uses the prefix that would occur in that scenario. Example (34), with distal/neutral deictic *cuo* 's/he, that one', is an ordinary 3>2 scenario. This suggests that what operates in such pairs is the actual spatial deictic situation and not a strict calculation of person categories, or at least that speakers have recourse to spatial deixis in cases where the person categories allow some leeway. What is important here is that a 3>2 scenario can use either *dwa-* or *hwa-*, depending on the location of the third person A relative to the second person G and the speaker.

Similar patterns can easily be elicited for other verbs as well (and in fact are often volunteered by all consultants):

(35) 3>2 *Muusaa **hwa**-qeachar=ii   hwo volcha?*
        Musa   DX-arrive.WP=Q   2s   V.be.PPL.OBL
        'Did Musa get to your place?' (speaker and hearer are together; at issue is whether Musa arrived at the hearer's place on some previous occasion, coming from elsewhere)

(36) 3>2 *Muusaa **dwa**-qeachar=ii   hwo volcha?*
        Musa   DX-arrive.WP=Q   2s   V.be.PPL.OBL
        'Has Musa arrived at your place?' (over the telephone; speaker and hearer are in different places, and Musa has just left the speaker's house to go to hearer's house)

The only 3>2 examples found in the survey for 'give', (23) above and a nearby similar sentence describing the same scene, are consistent with this opposition. There, the speaker and hearer are together in a room and something for the hearer is to be pushed through a window into the room. That is, speaker and hearer are together and the T comes from elsewhere.

Additional details show up when a consultant comments on examples that fit the typical corpus picture. Recall that (27) above had the sequence *dwa-* ... *hwa-* representing back-and-forth transfer without any particular spatial deixis. The reactions of consultants (when I ask about the prefix without showing the film) assume literal deixis, which is in fact supported by the context. In this scene from a Pear Film narrative, a boy on foot walks from near the camera to farther away where a boy on a bicycle is standing. The boy on foot returns a dropped hat to the boy on the bicycle, who gives him three pears in return. The boy on foot comes back toward the camera and the boy on the bicycle rides off away from the camera. Though during the exchange the boy on foot is only slightly closer to the camera than the other boy, he comes from and returns to the space closer to the viewer, so when he gives the hat the verb has *dwa-* and when he is given pears it has *hwa-*.

These various elicited examples indicate that it is not strict person categories but location, literal or metaphorical, that determines prefix choice. *Hwa-* is always used if the G is first person, and it can be used (overriding the regular rule) if the G is in the same place or the same family as the first person, whether that first person is A as in (30) or a speaker of a clause that contains no first person argument as in (31) and (32).

6   Typological Perspective

The behavior of the Ingush deictic prefixes raises several typological questions. First, can the direct/inverse schema be simplified by collapsing the first and second person categories into a single speech act participant (SAP) category? No, because 1>2 and 2>1 scenarios behave differently. In text examples, 1>2 has *dwa-* and 2>1 has *hwa-*. In elicited examples, 2>1 is inflexibly *hwa-* while 1>2 ordinarily has *dwa-* but can easily have *hwa-* where the first and second person are in the same place. This difference shows that 1 and 2 do not form an unstructured single category, but 1 and 2 occupy different positions in the hierarchy. Therefore the deictic prefixes constitute a three-step hierarchy and a true direct/inverse system, not just an SAP vs. other system opposition.

Could the schema be simplified by collapsing second and third person so as to yield a simple opposition of 1 to 2/3? This appears more likely. In all scenarios where G is first person, *hwa-* is required. In scenarios where G is second person, in elicitation either *dwa-* or *hwa-* is often possible: *hwa-* is possible where the first and second person are in the same place or in the same family or are in some other sense together, but *dwa-* is required wherever they are not together. This suggests that second person is not an independent position in the hierarchy but belongs deictically with either first or third, depending on the location or affiliation of the second person. If the system is simplified in this way, it looks much like the 1 > 2/3 system of Laz. It can still be described as a direct/inverse system, but it could also be described as a simple contrast in first vs. nonfirst person G.

Is this a person-based system at all? Text material shows three clear person categories, but in the elicited material whenever more than one prefix is possible for a given scenario it is not the person categories but the locations, affinities, etc. of the arguments that are indexed by the deictic prefixes: first and second person are or are not in the same place, the S or T comes from the the speaker's side vs. a third party's side, etc. The text-based examples were described above in terms of person categories, but they too could perfectly well be described in terms of location. Therefore it may be more accurate to describe the prefixes as based on spatial deixis rather than the person hierarchy. This is in fact what one might expect, as Ingush has virtually no inflectional category of person: verbs agree only in gender, and there are no pronominal affixes. A category of person might well not be available at all in such a language.

Finally, how does the deictic prefix system fit into the typology of ditransitive argument realization? In all other respects Ingush is an un-swervingly direct/indirect object language (in the terms of Dryer 1986), with the T surfacing as the direct object and the G surfacing as indirect ob-ject. The deictic prefixes, however, index the G and not the T, thereby con-stituting a primary/secondary object subsystem. Since deictic prefixes ap-pear on nearly every token of a ditransitive verb and most tokens of motion verbs, this primary/secondary object subsystem is not a marginal corner of the language but a robust and high-frequency part of the grammar.

Both direct/inverse systems and primary/secondary object systems are quite unusual in western Eurasia, but attested in languages of the Caucasus (for the primary/secondary nature of object agreement in Kartvelian, see Lacroix 2011b and Tuite 2009), and the Ingush material I have presented here adds to the evidence that they are not merely attested but well attested and well installed in the Caucasus. Both of these systems have to do with letting referential hierarchies outweigh argument roles in determining ac-cess to objecthood, which brings us back to Hyman & Duranti (1982).[14]

References

Bickel, B. 2011. Grammatical relations typology. In J. J. Song (ed.), *The Oxford handbook of linguistic typology*, 399–444. Oxford: Oxford University Press.

Chafe, W. L. 1975. *The pear film*. http://pearstories.org.

Dryer, M. S. 1986. Primary objects, secondary objects, and antidative. *Language* 62: 808–845.

---

[14] IREX provided funding and logistics for field work on Ingush chiefly in Tbilisi in 1979, 1981, and 1984, and in Grozny in 1989. The Oriental Institute of the Georgian Academy of Science in Tbilisi provided facilities and administrative support and valuable professional contacts. NSF BCS 96-16448 made possible the field methods course and other efforts men-tioned in the text. The Linguistics Department of the Max Planck Institute for Evolutionary Anthropology provided facilities and administrative and technical support, and an excellent research environment, for descriptive and documentational work from 2002 to 2014. UC Berkeley's Committee on Research and Institute for Slavic, Eurasian, and East European Stud-ies have provided some further funding. Ronald Sprouse, technical director of the Berkeley Ingush project, has provided invaluable technical support, created most of the project's elec-tronic infrastructure, and also contributed as linguist to the analytic work of the project.

Hyman, L. M. 2007. Elicitation as experimental phonology: Thlantlang Lai tonology. In M.-J. Solé, P. S. Beddor & M. Ohala (eds.), *Experimental approaches to phonology*, 7–24. Oxford: Oxford University Press.

Hyman, L. M. & A. Duranti. 1982. On the object relation in Bantu. In P. J. Hopper & S. A. Thompson (eds.), *Studies in transitivity*, 217–239. New York: Academic Press.

Lacroix, R. 2011a. Person hierarchy and direct/inverse marking in the Laz verb 'give'. Paper presented at the Workshop on Referential Hierarchies in Three-Participant Constructions, Lancaster, May 20–21.

Lacroix, R. 2011b. Ditransitive constructions in Laz. *Linguistic Discovery* 9(2): 78–103.

Nichols, J. 2011. *Ingush grammar* (UCPL 143). Berkeley: University of California Press.

Nichols, J. with R. L. Sprouse. 2004. *Ingush-English and English-Ingush dictionary.* London: Routledge/Curzon.

Siewierska, A. 2011. Person marking. In J. J. Song (ed.), *The Oxford handbook of linguistic typology*, 322–345. Oxford: Oxford University Press.

Tuite, K. 2009. Agentless transitive verbs in Georgian. *Anthropological Linguistics* 51(3/4): 269–295.

Abbreviations

Argument types

A	Subject of two- or three-argument verb
S	Subject of one-argument verb
O	Object of monotransitive
T	More theme-like object of ditransitive
G	More goal- or recipient-like object of ditransitive; I use G for the goal of an intransitive motion verb without implying that this is the same syntactic or semantic role as the G of a ditransitive

Other abbreviations

&	Coordinating/chaining clitic
1s, 2s, 3s,1p	First, second, third person singular, first plural (exclusive)
ALL	Allative (case)
B	Gender agreement marker
COND	Conditional
CV	Converb
D	Gender agreement marker
DAT	Dative
DEM	Demonstrative
DX	Deictic prefix
EMPH	Emphatic
ERG	Ergative
EXCL	Exclusive
FUT	Future
GEN	Genitive
IMPF	Imperfect
IMPV	Imperative
INCL	Inclusive
INCP	Inceptive
J	Gender agreement marker
LAT	Lative (case)
NARP	Narrative past
NEG	Negative
NOM	Nominative (citation form, S/O; not glossed for nouns)
NW	Nonwitnessed
NZ	Nominalizer
OBL	Oblique
PL	Plural
PPL	Participle
PROG	Progressive auxiliary
Q	Interrogative
RED	Reduplicant
RFL	Reflexive
V	Gender agreement marker
VZ	Verbalizing derivational suffix
WP	Witnessed past

13

The Aerodynamic Voicing Constraint and its Phonological Implications

JOHN J. OHALA

1   Introduction

The "Aerodynamic Voicing Constraint" (AVC) has long been recognized in phonetics-phonology (Passy 1890, Chao 1936, Ohala 1983): voicing requires a sufficient airflow through the adducted vocal cords. The airflow requires a sufficient pressure difference (ΔP) between subglottal pressure (P_s) and oral pressure (P_o). During an obstruent, air accumulates in the oral cavity, thus increasing P_o. When the P_o approaches P_s, the airflow falls below that needed for vocal cord vibration and thus voicing is extinguished.[1]

2   Adapting to the AVC

There are two basic ways that speakers adapt to the AVC: (i) let the AVC prevail, and (ii) circumvent the AVC.

2.1 Do Nothing: Let the AVC Prevail

Consequences of letting the AVC prevail include those given below.

---

[1] My thanks to Larry Hyman and Maria-Josep Solé for advice and discussions useful in the preparation of this paper. This is a revised version of a paper that appeared in the Proceedings of the 17th International Congress of the Phonetic Sciences, Hong Kong, 2011.

Revealing Structure.
Eugene Buckley, Thera Crane & Jeff Good (eds.).
Copyright © 2018, CSLI Publications.

2.1.1. Obstruents will be voiceless. Many languages have only voiceless obstruents; these include Cantonese, Hawaiian, Zuni, Ainu, and Quechua.[2] This pattern is especially evident with voiced geminate stops, where the longer duration of the stop closure aggravates the AVC.

2.1.2. Fricatives and the AVC. Among obstruents, there will be a greater tendency for fricatives than stops to be voiceless. This asymmetry arises because optimal voicing requires that P_o be substantially below P_s but optimal frication requires P_o be substantially higher than atmospheric pressure. Languages that have voiced and voiceless stops but only voiceless fricatives include Malayalam, Welsh (Cymraeg), and Thai.

2.1.3. [-Anterior] stops and the AVC. Voicing may be present only on anterior stops, because more forward articulations expose a greater amount of compliant surface to the impinging P_o and so more glottal airflow can be accommodated before ΔP falls below the level needed to support voicing. Languages which manifest voicing on anterior stops but not nonanterior consonants (primarily velars)—excluding loanwords—include Thai, Dutch, Czech, and some dialects of Arabic.

2.1.4. VOT variations due to vowels. Voiceless stops will have VOT proportional to the degree of constriction of the following vowel or glide (Ohala 1981a). A close constriction attenuates the rate of airflow exiting the vocal tract after a stop and thus delays the time when P_o is low enough to initiate voicing. Occasionally this longer VOT before close vowels leads to a sound change where aspiration becomes distinctive.

(1) | Proto-Bantu | Ikalanga | |
|---|---|---|
| *tɪma | tima | 'heart' |
| *tima | t͡sʰima | 'well' |
| *tʊma | tuma | 'sew' |
| *tuma | tʰuma | 'send' |

For example, as documented by Mathangwane (1996), the Bantu language Ikalanga merged the proto-language's "superclose" high vowels */i/ and */u/ and the lower vowels */ɪ/ and */ʊ/ respectively into the /i/ and /u/ vowels, but in the process gave rise to distinctive aspiration (and affrication, due to the high airflow) in the voiceless stops that had appeared before the higher vowels.

2.1.5. Voiceless vowels. For similar reasons, if languages exhibit voiceless vowels there is a tendency for them to be high close vowels such as /i/ and

---

[2] For supporting statistical data on this and the following sound patterns as well as their incidence in diverse, unrelated languages, see Ohala (1983) and Maddieson (1984).

/u/ (Greenberg 1969; typically other conditions apply as well, e.g. that the vowels are short and/or appear between voiceless consonants or pre-pausally).

2.2 Circumvent the AVC

Speakers have discovered a number of strategies to circumvent the consequences of the AVC in order to maintain voicing in obstruents. But, as often happens, once implemented the particular strategy may lead to sound changes where other features, which were just consequences of fulfilling the principal feature of voicing, become distinctive.

2.2.1. Make closure durations short. Cross-linguistically the duration of voiced obstruent closures is less than that for cognate voiceless obstruents (Lehiste 1970). A shorter closure duration helps to avoid the buildup of P_o to the point where ΔP becomes too low to support voicing. One consequence of this is that it is voiced stops that are most prone via sound change to become voiced approximants; for example, $b > \beta$ or v, $d > \delta$, $g > \gamma$, and the like.[3] A further consequence of making voiced obstruents short is that the preceding vowel can become long. (Whether this comes about because the vowel now occupies more of the time allotted to the VC sequence or because the longer vowel length creates a useful contrast with the shorter C whose shortness is itself a cue to its identity is an open matter.) In many dialects of English the duration of the preceding vowel is a more salient phonetic feature differentiating minimal pairs conventionally characterized as differing in the voicing of the following obstruent; for example, it is possible with a waveform editor to convert a version of *dice* into *dyes* and vice-versa just by altering the vowel duration.

2.2.2. Prenasalize the voiced stop. Prenasalized voiced stops are found in many languages and are often the only form of voiced stop in opposition to voiceless stops (e.g. in Fijian). Prenasalization is a strategy to circumvent the AVC by venting P_o via the nasal cavity at the onset of the stop closure so that it does not so quickly lead to a reduction in the needed ΔP (Solé, Sprouse & Ohala 2008). Closing the velic valve shortly before the release enables the stop to retain the two features essential to a voiced stop: its voicing and the cues for a stop, a burst and a rapid rise time in the amplitude of the following vowel.

2.2.3. Change voiced stops to voiced implosives. There is abundant documentation of the link between voiced stops and voiced implosives (Green-

---

[3] Voiceless stops may also become fricatives, but in this case it is more often contextually.

berg 1969) as evidenced by diachronic data such as the following, showing the origin of implosives in Sindhi:

(2) Prakrit   Sindhi
     pabba   *paɓuṇi*   'lotus fruit'
     bʰagga   *bʰaːɠu*   'fate'

Even voiced stops are associated with a lower larynx position vis-à-vis voiceless stops (Ewan & Krones 1974). Voiced implosives skirt the AVC by actively creating more volume in the oral cavity to accommodate the accumulating airflow.

2.2.4. Implement voiced apicals as retracted. There is evidence of a link between retroflexion and voicing in apical stops (Greenberg 1969, Hamann & Fuchs 2008). Using the "artificial venting" method of Ohala & Riordan (1979), Sprouse, Solé & Ohala (2008) presented evidence that a retroflex tongue configuration permitted voicing to persist longer than in an api-codental configuration. They hypothesize that the retroflex configuration is more conducive to voicing because it exposes more compliant surfaces of the tongue to the impinging P_o.

2.2.5. Produce stops with [ATR]. Much phonological evidence points to a link between voicing in obstruents and the appearance of [ATR] (Advanced Tongue Root) on adjacent vowels (Stewart 1970, Trigo 1991, Vaux 1996). Diachronically it is evident that it was the [+ATR] on the voiced obstruents that subsequently triggered a change in the adjacent vowels to become [+ATR]. There is also phonetic evidence that the pharyngeal cavity shows expansion during the production of voiced stops (Perkell 1969). Pape et al. (2006) also found a lesser incidence of German voiced stops devoicing me-dially if the coarticulated vowel was a front vowel (which are known to involve tongue root advancement). In addition, visual inspection of my pharynx with a fiberscope revealed quite dramatic movement of the lateral pharyngeal walls synchronized with onset and offset of a voiced stop. It would be precisely the lateral pharyngeal walls that would receive greater exposure with an advancement of the tongue root.

2.3 Interpretation of the Preceding Patterns

Ten ways of adapting to the AVC were discussed; there undoubtedly are more. Those in Section 2.1 essentially adapt by letting the AVC act to pas-sively restrict voicing. The adaptations in Section 2.2 to circumvent the AVC are perhaps more interesting. How did these various strategies come about? I hypothesize that they were serendipitously "discovered" by speak-ers; that is, discovered via random explorations of what could be done with the vocal organs. The fact that there are such different strategies suggests to me that there were no innately specified routes to follow.

Further research is needed to support the scenarios presented. In particular, for the sake of confirming the offered accounts of Sections 2.1.3 (only anterior stops retain voicing), 2.2.4 (retract apical stops), and 2.2.5 (implement ATR), it would be desirable to have a complete map of tissue compliance of all relevant surfaces in the vocal tract for particular stop types as coarticulated with different vowels or sonorants. In addition, quantitative measures on how much additional volume is added to the vocal tract during the production of implosives are necessary.

3 Implications for Phonology

3.1 Explanation, Not Just Description of Patterns

For a phonetically based phonology looking to explain phonological universals (Ohala 1983), the AVC helps to account for a diverse set of sound patterns which, on the surface, would seem to have little in common: closure duration, VOT, implosion, retroflexion, ATR, prenasalization of stops, and so on. It has an explanatory value similar to the "nodes and antinodes" analysis of the standing waves of the resonances in the vocal tract as given by Chiba & Kajiyama (1941).

3.2 Teleology in Sound Change?

There is an issue in diachronic phonology as to whether sound changes are teleologically driven or not—that is, whether changes are purposefully implemented to achieve some goal, for example easier articulation for the benefit of the speaker or greater clarity for the benefit of the listener. My own belief is that neither of these factors plays a role in sound change. But there is some teleology evident in the sound changes in Section 2.2, and that is to *maintain pronunciation according to what the speaker-listener takes to be the accepted norm.* From the point of view of the listener-speakers responsible for implementing the changes mentioned in 2.2, they were doing their best to implement the voiced character of these stops. An unintended consequence (due to how other listeners misinterpreted what they heard) would be the implementation of implosives or retroflex apicals or [+ATR] vowels and so on as new elements constituting a new pronunciation norm. But at its point of origin there would be no teleology for *change*, as such.

Accommodation to the AVC intersects with another issue of whether teleology underlies sound patterns in language. Noting the symmetrical and compact segment inventories that many languages exhibit—manifesting what Ohala (1980) called "maximal utilization of available features",[4] for example, the 4 manners x 5 places of articulation used in Hindi (Table 1)— Clements (2003: 329) proposes that languages exhibit what he called "feature economy" driven by a cognitive principle which "reflects a general predisposition to organize linguistic data into a small number of categories and to generalise these categories maximally". This, again, implies some sort of teleology. But this view neglects another nonteleological route whereby a new series of contrastive sounds emerges via sound change from previously existing sounds.

	labial	*dental*	*retroflex*	*palatal*	*velar*
voiceless	p	t̪	t	t͡ʃ	k
voiced	b	d̪	ɖ	d͡ʒ	ɡ
voicelesss aspirated	pʰ	t̪ʰ	tʰ	t͡ʃʰ	kʰ
breathy voiced	bʱ	d̪ʱ	ɖʱ	d͡ʒʱ	ɡʱ

Table 1. Stop inventory of Hindi

Ohala (1981b) has proposed that sound changes occur when listeners misconstrue or misparse some aspect of speakers' pronunciation (Ohala 1980, especially pp. 189–190). Schematically: To maintain [+voice] during a stop ([-son]), a speaker implements an accessory gesture, [+accessory], as discussed in Section 2.2, which will have its own acoustic-auditory features. From the speaker's point of view, [+accessory] is simply a means to attain [+voice]. But a listener, hearing the complex [-son, +voice, +accessory] may regard the [+accessory] feature as integral to the sound. Necessarily, this [+accessory] feature will only be found in combination with the previously existing [-son, +voice] feature complex. The new feature complex [-son, +voice, +accessory] would be *emergent* in much the same sense as this term is used in evolutionary biology, that is, involving some preexisting elements.

The emergence of such accessory features also occurs in the cultural domain: although there are different theories on the origin of serifs on Roman letters, many agree that they started out as fortuitous ways of terminating the blunt ends of lines (Samara 2004).

3.3 Constraints within Optimality Theory

Optimality Theory (OT; Prince & Smolensky 2004) as applied to phonology also claims to use constraints—even phonetically based constraints—to

---

[4] Acronymized as MUAF by the Grenoble group and studied extensively (e.g. Ménard, Schwartz & Aubin 2008).

guide derivations from an underlying form to a surface form. But there are many questions as to how the sound patterns discussed above would be implemented in OT.

3.3.1. Would OT incorporate the AVC as a *general constraint* motivating all these sound patterns, or would there be separate constraints reflecting each of the sound patterns (e.g. *[+voice, -son])? Would the different strategies for accommodating the AVC be rank ordered such that, for example, prenasalization of a voiced stop would outrank a simple voiced stop? How would such a rank ordering be determined, especially given the considerable variety in how the AVC is accommodated? No doubt with the tools OT has to work with, including the invention of new constraints and the freedom to rank them in whatever way "gives the right output", there would be no difficulty. The important question, though, is: Would that *explain* anything or would it just be an ad hoc exercise to "save the appearances", like the Ptolemaic astronomers' epicycles?

3.3.2. In early OT literature the constraints were claimed to be innate (Tesar & Smolensky 1998). This claim is not defended by all (Boersma 2000, Ellison 2000). There are reasons to reject innateness of constraints; although it is true that certain behaviors may be innately predisposed, these tend to be those that confer some survivability or fitness to those exhibiting the behavior or to their kin, for example, the "broken wing feint" of certain ground nesting birds: it serves to draw predators away from the nestlings but still provide for an escape by the adult bird employing the feint. I do not think anyone has found any selectional advantage to speakers whose languages, say, possess voiced implosives over others that have (simple) pulmonic voiced stops. Nevertheless, it is an essential element of OT to insist that the constraints are part of speakers' grammars: whatever the "input" to what is spoken—morphological concatenations, loanwords, and so on—such forms are supposedly shaped by the constraints. If so, one would have to ask how some speakers happened upon different strategies in accommodating to the AVC. Is the difficulty of producing a sound that is [-son, +voice] just "there", and it is up to the speakers to figure out how to deal with it, there being no prescribed strategy? Are such constraints similar to those in other behavioral domains, for example, *bench pressing > 400 kg, *running the marathon < 2hrs 10mins, or *winning the Nobel Prize in physics?[5] Is it important that these constraints have some sort of cognitive representation or could they, instead, be simply discovered in the course of attempting to accomplish these activities?

---

[5] As challenging as these behaviors may be, some individuals have mastered them.

3.3.3. On that note, it is possible to ask the question: What would be different about the phonologies of languages and the phonological behavior of speakers if OT's claims of these constraints being in the grammar were wrong? The answer is: Nothing. Phonologies would still exhibit the same patterns that they do now. Speakers do not have to "know" the physical and physiological constraints in order to be subject to them. Rocks do not have to know about the effects of gravity in order to be subject to it.

3.4 A "Chicken Little" Inquiry

One might think, however, that the issue of whether these constraints are represented somehow in the speaker's grammar—or, who knows?—in their DNA—is an empirical matter requiring further psychological or genetic study. I propose instead an epistemological inquiry, otherwise known as a "Chicken Little" inquiry (Ohala 1996).

Chicken Little is the principal figure in a children's story familiar to most English speakers. The story, in brief: One day Chicken Little was injured when something struck her head. She then set the entire barnyard into a panic with her claim that the sky was falling. The resolution of the story did not involve experiments testing whether the sky was, in fact, falling; it involved an inquiry as to why Chicken Little *thought* it was falling. The immediate evidence was a swelling on the top of her head. Where was she when the injury occurred? Under an oak tree. A large acorn was found there, very likely what had caused the injury. The moral of the story—not stated quite so explicitly—is that before investing a lot of time and effort in costly experiments evaluating a given hypothesis, one should first look at the motivation for the hypothesis having been made. Then we should ask whether the observation prompting the hypothesis might be accounted for by other, less extravagant, hypotheses.

So what is the motivation for OT? In the late 1960s, Chomsky & Halle (1968) persuaded phonologists that they could discover speakers' grammars—the mental mechanisms used to derive, for example, in English, *obscenity* and *obscene* from the same root via processes that previously were the domain of historical phonology which had no such psychological pretensions. It seems that many phonologists still believe that they can discover psychological elements and mechanisms just by applying the methods of historical phonology and extracting patterns, that is, statistical tendencies in sound patterns. This was an extravagant and empirically unsupported hypothesis in the 1960s and is still so today.

The speculative and empirically vacuous nature of such an approach to phonology has occasionally been recognized:

I do not think anybody actually working on language can doubt … that sooner or later … it is going to be necessary to discover conditions on theory constructions, coming presumably from experimental psychology or from neurology, which will resolve the alternatives that can be arrived at by the kind of speculative theory construction linguists can do on the basis of the data available to them. That is, there will come a point, no doubt, and I think in some areas of linguistics it may already have been reached, where one can set up alternative systems to explain quite a wide range of phenomena. One can think that this or that system is more elegant and much more deep than some other, but is it right? (Chomsky 1967: 100)

Although I reject the idea that linguistics' theories need to be empirically evaluated by other disciplines—this is the responsibility of those who propose the theories—I applaud the recognition that speculative theories based only on observation of raw data need to be empirically tested. The unfortunate thing is this admission was made decades ago and there has been little effort to act on it.

3.5 An Alternative

Is there an alternative to the phonological practice that just offers a translation from informal descriptions into an unnecessarily more complex notation presumptuously labeled "formal"? There is. As for the AVC and also other constraints involving turbulent sounds, there exist aerodynamic models—far more deserving of the label "formal"—which not only explain sound patterns but which can be fruitfully used to explore and discover other sound patterns (Rothenberg 1968, Ohala 1975, Westbury & Keating 1986, Boersma 1995). There are also models that relate the articulatory and aerodynamic of speech to the acoustic output (Chiba & Kajiyama 1941, Stevens 2000). These models are based on well-established, empirically validated physical and physiological principles and thus reduce the temptation to posit "deus ex machina" factors in psychology and genetics as the cause of cross-language sound patterns

4 Conclusion

The AVC, like the bases for other phonological universals, arises from physical and physiological constraints on speech. There is no compelling evidence that such universals require psychological or genetic intervention for their manifestation in human language. It is the adoption of and insistence on empirical support for claims that will help to admit phonology into the family of the natural sciences.

References

Boersma, P. 1995. Interaction between glottal and vocal-tract aerodynamics in a comprehensive model of the speech apparatus. In K. Elenius & P. Branderud (eds.), *Proceedings of the 13th International Congress of Phonetic Sciences, vol. 2*, 430–433. Stockholm: KTH and Stockholm University.

Boersma, P. 2000. Learning a grammar in functional phonology. In J. Dekkers, F. van der Leeuw & J. van de Weijer (eds.), *Optimality Theory: Phonology, syntax, and acquisition*, 465–523. Oxford: Oxford University Press.

Chao, Y.-R. 1936. Types of plosives in Chinese. *Proceedings of the 2nd International Congress of Phonetic Sciences*, 106–110. Cambridge: Cambridge University Press.

Chiba, T. & M. Kajiyama. 1941. *The vowel: Its nature and structure.* Tokyo: Tokyo–Kaiseikan.

Chomsky, N. 1967. Discussion. In F. L. Darley (ed.), *Brain mechanism underlying speech and language*, 100. New York: Grune & Stratton.

Chomsky, N. & M. Halle. 1968. *The sound patterns of English.* New York: Harper & Row.

Clements, G. N. 2003. Feature economy in sound systems. *Phonology* 20: 287–233.

Ellison, T. M. 2000. The universal constraint set: Convention, not fact. In J. Dekkers, F. van der Leeuw & J. van de Weijer (eds.), *Optimality Theory: Phonology, syntax, and acquisition*, 524–553. Oxford: Oxford University Press.

Ewan, W. & R. Krones. 1974. Measuring larynx movement using the thyroumbrometer. *Journal of Phonetics* 2: 327–335.

Greenberg, J. H. 1969. Some methods of dynamic comparison in linguistics. In J. Puhvel (ed.), *Substance and structure of language*, 147–204. Los Angeles: Center for Research in Language and Linguistics.

Hamann, S. & S. Fuchs. 2008. How do voiced retroflex stops evolve? Evidence from typology and an articulatory study. *ZAS Papers in Linguistics* 49: 97–130.

Lehiste, I. 1970. *Suprasegmentals.* Cambridge, MA: MIT Press.

Maddieson, I. 1984. *Patterns of sounds.* Cambridge: Cambridge University Press.

Mathangwane, J. T. 1996. *Phonetics and phonology of Ikalanga: A diachronic and synchronic study.* Berkeley: University of California dissertation.

Ménard, L., J.-L. Schwartz & J. Aubin. 2008. Invariance and variability in the production of the height feature in French vowels. *Speech Communication* 50: 14–28.

Ohala, J. J. 1975. A mathematical model of speech aerodynamics. In G. Fant (ed.), *Speech communication, volume 2: Speech production and synthesis by rule*, 65–72. Stockholm: Almqvist & Wiksell.

Ohala, J. J. 1980. Moderator's introduction to symposium on phonetic universals in phonological systems and their explanation. In E. Fischer-Jørgensen, J. Rischel & N. Thorsen (eds.), *Proceedings of the 9th International Congress of Phonetic Sciences, vol. 3*, 181–185. Copenhagen: University of Copenhagen.

Ohala, J. J. 1981a. Articulatory constraints on the cognitive representation of speech. In T. Myers, J. Laver & J. Anderson (eds.), *The cognitive representation of speech*, 111–122. Amsterdam: North Holland.

Ohala, J. J. 1981b. The listener as a source of sound change. In C. S. Masek, R. A. Hendrick & M. F. Miller (eds.), *Papers from the parasession on language and behavior*, 178–203. Chicago: Chicago Linguistic Society.

Ohala, J. J. 1983. The origin of sound patterns in vocal tract constraints. In P. F. MacNeilage (ed.), *The production of speech*, 189–216. New York: Springer.

Ohala, J. J. 1996. Speech perception is hearing sounds, not tongues. *Journal of the Acoustical Society of America* 99: 1718–1725.

Ohala, J. J. & C. J. Riordan. 1979. Passive vocal tract enlargement during voiced stops. In J. J. Wolf & D. H. Klatt (eds.), *Speech communication papers*, 89–92. New York: Acoustical Society of America.

Pape, D., C. Mooshammer, P. Hoole & S. Fuchs. 2006. Devoicing of word-initial stops: A consequence of the following vowel? In J. Harrington & M. Tabain (eds.), *Towards a better understanding of speech production processes*, 211–226. New York: Psychology Press.

Passy, P. 1890. *Étude sur les changements phonétiques*. Paris: Firmin-Didot.

Perkell, J. 1969. *Physiology of speech production*. Cambridge, MA: MIT Press.

Prince, A. & P. Smolensky. 2004. *Optimality Theory: Constraint interaction in generative grammar*. Malden, MA: Blackwell.

Rothenberg, M. 1968. *The breath-stream dynamics of simple-released plosive production* (Bibliotheca Phonetica 6). Basel: Karger.

Samara, T. 2004. *Typography workbook: A real-world guide to using type in graphic design*. Beverly, MA: Rockport Publishers.

Solé, M.-J., R. L. Sprouse & J. J. Ohala. 2008. Voicing control and nasalization. In P. Warren (ed.), *Laboratory Phonology 11 abstracts*, 127–128. Wellington, New Zealand: Victoria University of Wellington.

Sprouse, R. L., M.-J. Solé & J. J. Ohala. 2008. Oral cavity enlargement in retroflex stops. In R. Sock, S. Fuchs & Y. Laprie (eds.), *Proceedings of the 8th International Seminar on Speech Production*, 429–432. Strasbourg: INRIA.

Stevens, K. N. 2000. *Acoustic phonetics*. Cambridge, MA: MIT Press.

Stewart, J. M. 1967. Tongue root position in Akan vowel harmony. *Phonetica* 16: 185–204.

Tesar, B. & P. Smolensky. 1998. Learnability in Optimality Theory. *Linguistic Inquiry* 29: 229–268.

Trigo, L. 1991. On pharynx-larynx interactions. *Phonology* 8: 113–136.

Vaux, B. 1996. The status of ATR in feature geometry. *Linguistic Inquiry* 27: 175–182.

Westbury, J. & P. Keating. 1986. On the naturalness of stop consonant voicing. *Journal of Linguistics* 22: 145–166.

14

Vowel Height Harmony in Kilimanjaro Bantu: A New Look at the Evidence

GÉRARD PHILIPPSON

1 Introduction

In his seminal article on Vowel height harmony (VHH) in Bantu languages, Larry Hyman (1999; henceforth LH[1]) drew attention to the somewhat bizarre situation exhibited by Chaga dialects, where VHH seems to occur only sporadically. He then went on to use Chaga as a possible witness to what he considered the real diachronic process of VHH in Bantu, namely one where vowels tend to move to peripheral positions (in the cardinal vowel space) when not in the "strong" stem-initial syllable. Based on a number of apparently unusual nonharmonizing situations concerning extension vowels, LH also posited different Proto-Bantu (PB) vowel height for extensions with front vs. back vowels—third degree *-ɛk- and *-ɛd- for neuter and applicative respectively, contrasting with first degree *-is- for causative and second degree *-ʊd- and *-ʊk- for reversive and reversive neuter.[2]

I will start by recalling the main points of LH's analysis. Then I will present the sources for the various languages/dialects dealt with in this

---

[1] It might have been more felicitous to use LMH, including his middle initial, in mindful reference to his lifelong interest in, and contribution to, the theory and practice of tonology (as he himself is fond of recalling, "I never met a tone I didn't like"). However, I will use LH for the sake of brevity.

[2] Note that I use (idiosyncratically) the following transcription for PB vowels: *i, *ɪ, *ɛ, *a, *ɔ, *ʊ, *u. This is a blending of the transcriptions that Hyman (1999: 247) exemplifies in (15b) and (15c) in his paper, and is done for reasons too long to go into here. Note also that little reference will be made to tone, except when it might be needed for the presentation.

Revealing Structure.
Eugene Buckley, Thera Crane & Jeff Good (eds.).
Copyright © 2018, CSLI Publications.

chapter. A description of the various types of harmony with different extensions will follow, and I will conclude by summarizing possible explanations for this complex situation.

2 LH's Analysis

In his 1999 chapter, LH begins by recalling what has been considered as "canonical" VHH in Bantu: It is asymmetrical (i.e. second degree vowels are lowered—or laxed—after both mid vowels in the front series, but only after /o/ in the back series) and applies only stem-internally (i.e. not to the final stem vowel, nor to prefixes). If it is analyzed as a lowering process, it is strange that /a/ does not cause it. Although generally reconstructed to Proto-Bantu (except by Greenberg 1951), this system is in fact only attested in Savanna Bantu languages of central and eastern Africa.

I concentrate on stem-internal processes and leave out the discussion of prefix and final stem vowel harmony, for which the reader is referred to LH's chapter. Exceptions are to be found in the following areas: First, some languages (e.g. Punu, Lengola, and Suku) have no VHH at all. This correlates with the fact that such languages have severe restrictions on which vowel qualities are allowed in stem-internal positions. Second, 7-vowel forest Bantu languages have fully symmetrical harmony. This also applies to the 7-vowel eastern Bantu languages Gusii and Kuria, as well as some 5-vowel languages mostly belonging to the Kongo group (H10).[3] Third, /a/ conditions front VHH in several southwestern Bantu languages (zones K and R). Finally, Southern Bantu (zone S) languages, plus Makua, Mbukushu, and Luyana, have no front VHH: applicatives always have -*e*-, and causatives always have -*i*-. However, back VHH does seem to operate, a fact which leads LH to consider that the two processes are independent.

LH concludes his in-depth examination of the data with the hypothesis that PB did not in fact exhibit VHH at all. Furthermore, he challenges the generally expressed notion that VHH should be considered a *lowering* process—since one would expect it to be also caused by /a/. On the other hand, a *raising* process does not appear very likely, since in this case /a/ would also appear as a source. With great ingenuity, LH rather sees the process as one of peripheralization where vowels tend to move towards less marked positions.[4] The fact that there are differences in the treatment of the applica-

---

[3] According to Cammenga (1994), the process in Kuria is only optional, or perhaps dialectal. Note that Kuria also exhibits a pervasive right-to-left process of raising by first degree vowels.

[4] This analysis makes sense in the case of 5-vowel languages, with the inventory /i, e, a, o, u/, but maybe slightly less in the case of 7-vowel languages, where the most peripheral positions would be /i, u/ rather than /ɪ, ʊ/. Although many 7-vowel languages have symmetrical VHH, which might be considered as a different process, there still remain a number of 7-vowel lan-

tive and stative extensions on the one hand and causatives on the other is due for LH to an original difference in vowel quality (also seen in contemporary 7-vowel languages) between applicative *-ɛd- and stative *-ɛk- on the one hand versus (long) causative *-ıc-i- on the other. Languages of zone S and a few others would thus have retained the original quality, whereas the bulk of the Savanna Bantu languages would have introduced front VHH by the process of peripheralization mentioned above.[5]

Back VHH would thus be very different (as suggested by its different conditioning), with the original (transitive-) reversive and reversive neuter reconstructed with a second degree vowel, *-ʋd- and *-ʋk- respectively. These vowels would then have been subjected to lowering when preceded by a vowel identical in backness and roundness—a very natural assimilation process.

3   LH and Chaga

In LH's analysis, Chaga data (in fact, only from the Mashami dialect, see below) are called upon to show the way the process might have operated. In Mashami, the applicative extension does not harmonize, which has led many observers to believe that there was no VHH in the language. But Hyman's careful examination shows an interesting situation: In complex stems with the structure -(C)VCV(C)- there is complete height and rounding harmony for mid vowels (i.e. no -CoCe-, nor -CeCo-). If the stem contains an extension (possibly fossilized), there is generally no VHH, so that -CeCi-, -CoCi-, and -CoCu- are all attested (as well as -CeCu-, which is of course normal for asymmetrical VHH).

LH's conclusion (p. 272) is that VHH is moribund in Chaga, starting with the applicative, and this loss seems to affect extensions first. Now this is not necessarily a convincing way of looking at things, especially in the light of LH's own analysis of the development of VHH in Bantu. This is apparently felt by LH himself since he notes (p. 285, n. 51) that one should "reponder" the Chaga situation in the light of Southern Bantu.

It would seem from the text that LH cannot visualize "canonical" VHH as not having been present in Chaga, due to the close relationship of Chaga with the other northeastern Bantu languages. However, if we view

---

guages in eastern Africa with "asymmetrical VHH", where /ı, ʋ/ or /e, o/ obtain rather than expected /i, u/—Matuumbi (perhaps with its close relatives, e.g. Ndengeleko) being the lone exception. I do not intend to discuss the point any further in this paper, but it has obvious consequences for the precise reconstruction of the PB vowel system.

[5] Since it is difficult to visualize southern Bantu as genetically distinct from the rest of Savanna Bantu, the spread of front VHH would thus be of an areal nature, as LH himself suggests. Determining the exact locus of the initial innovation would be of great interest, however.

asymmetrical VHH as an innovation which spread from some nondetermined point in Savanna Bantu, it is not entirely inconceivable that Chaga might have escaped it, since it exhibits a number of peculiarities, both phonological and morphological, vis-à-vis its neighbors (see Philippson & Montlahuc 2003).

It thus appears necessary to delve deeper into the question of VHH in Chaga, by taking into consideration as many dialects as possible, as well as geographically adjacent languages, be they genealogically related to Chaga (Dawida, E74a) or only in contact (Asu, G22 and Saghala, E74b).

4 Sources for Data and Problems of Transcription

For the classification of Chaga dialects, the reader is referred to Philippson & Montlahuc (2003). Suffice it to recall that Chaga is divided into four branches: Gweno, and West (WK), Central (CK), and East Kilimanjaro (EK). Chaga has no close relative except Dawida, which, however, exhibits very substantial differences. Following Philippson & Montlahuc (2003), these two languages together form Kilimanjaro Bantu (KB).

There are no extensive Chaga dictionaries apart from Müller (1947) for Mashami (WK). But a reasonable amount of lexical data can be extracted from Raum (1909) and various publications by Gutmann (1922–1923, 1924, 1925) for the Mochi dialect (CK), and from the numerous folktales collected by Stamberg (published between 1932 and 1952) for the Mwika dialect (also CK). Furthermore, word lists of various lengths were collected by Nurse and Philippson for almost all Chaga dialects, as well as for Dawida, Saghala, and Asu. Additional material is available for Gweno in Philippson & Nurse (2000) and for Dawida in Philippson (1983, n.d.). For Saghala, we have Wray (1894) and Philippson (n.d.), and for Asu there are Kotz (1909), Kähler-Meyer (1962), and Kagaya (1989). To all of those must be added recorded texts of various lengths for most lects.

One word of caution must be added as regards Müller, our main resource for lexical data in any Chaga dialect. Müller was active on Kilimanjaro during the German colonial period, and again in the early 1930s, which is when he collected his Chaga material. However, perhaps due to ill health, he could not carry on with the completion of the final version of his dictionary, which was undertaken in turn by various students of Carl Meinhof, to eventually appear after World War II. There are thus a certain number of inconsistencies in the entries; but more than that, the segmental phoneme inventory of the dictionary (tones are hardly mentioned) is sometimes questionable. This does not so much affect vowel quality (the 5-vowel system of Chaga not being open to a great deal of interpretation) as consonants. In particular, Müller distinguishes between dental /d̪/ and /t̪/ whereas more

recent material exhibits only /ṱ/ (alongside implosive /ɗ/, which was cor-
rectly noted by Müller), and this was in fact queried by some of the compi-
lers of the dictionary.[6] Since this opposition is not present in any recorded
material at my disposal, and it is not mentioned in other recent work such as
Rugemalira & Phanuel (2009), one would be tempted to dismiss it out of
hand. It should, however, be mentioned that such a triple opposition /d/ ~ /ɗ/
~ /t/ was discovered by Philippson in Saghala and the northern dialects of
Dawida (see Philippson & Montlahuc 2003), so its former presence in Mashami is not entirely impossible. It is in fact also mentioned by Raum (1909)
for Mochi, where, however, dental /ḓ/ (now universally realized as /ṱ/) appears in an extremely small number of words—whereas it is frequent in
Müller's dictionary. Nevertheless, this putative opposition will be ignored
here and Müller's /ḓ/ will be transcribed as /ṱ/. In addition, Müller has a few
/g/ which have even less credibility than his /ḓ/; they are realized as /k/ in
contemporary materials and will be transcribed as such.[7]

5   Canonical VHH in Saghala

We can take as our starting point the situation in Saghala, since this language (genetically unrelated to Kilimanjaro Bantu, but in contact with
Dawida) exhibits strict asymmetric VHH of the kind found in most other
East African Bantu languages. The shape of the extensions concerned is as
follows: stative *-ika/-eka*, reversive stative *-uka/-oka*, applicative *-ila/-ela*,
reversive *-ula/-ola*, and long causatives *-isa/-esa* and *-iʃa/-eʃa*.[8] Examples
are shown with roots with each vowel in (1)–(5).

(1)   *-ik-* / *-ek-*
      -pay-a 'split' > *-pay-ik-a*
      -riɣ-a 'twist' > *-riɣ-ik-a*   *-kundʒ-a* 'fold' > *-kundʒ-ik-a*
      —   *-ɓon-a* 'see' > *-ɓon-ek-a*

Note that I have no example of *-CeC-ek-* bases. I take this to be an accidental gap, since the pattern in fact occurs in underived bases (*-elek-a* 'carry
on back') and with the causative extension (*-CeC-eʃ-*) in (5).[9]

---

[6] The distinction also appears in the much more succinct handbook by Augustiny (1914),
which, however, makes no reference to /ɗ/, and which sometimes has /ḓ/ where Müller has /ṱ/
and vice-versa.

[7] Augustiny transcribes it as /k/, e.g. *itiko* 'zebra' for Müller's *idigo*.

[8] Differences in the shape of the causatives will be discussed later on.

[9] There is in fact one disharmonic verb in Saghala: *-ḓea* 'do, make' > neuter *-ḓe-ik-a*. Since
this verb is of unknown origin (*-ḓ-* does not appear in stems with a Bantu etymon) and has a
vowel-final root, which is exceptional in Saghala, nothing more will be said about it.

(2) *-uka* / *-oka* and *-ula* / *-ola*
    -ɣal-ul-a 'change'   > *-ɣal-uk-a*
    —   *-dus-ul-a* 'cut rope'   > *-dus-uk-a*
    -gem-ul-a 'drop into' > *-gem-uk-a*   *-ɣol-ol-a* 'straighten'   > *-ɣol-ok-a*

In (2), a gap unexpectedly appears for *-CiC-u(C)-*. I consider it an accidental gap also, since it is a harmonic sequence.

(3) *-ila* / *-ela*
    -pat-a 'obtain'   > *-pat-il-a*
    -lind-a 'protect'   > *-lind-il-a*   *-fum-a* 'come out'   > *-fum-il-a*
    -sek-a 'laugh'   > *-sek-el-a*   *-kot-a* 'ask'   > *-kot-el-a*

(4) *-isa* / *-esa*
    -band-a 'be fat'   > *-band-is-a*
    -zim-a 'quench'   > *-zim-is-a*   *-uk-a* 'wake up'   > *-uk-is-a*
    -el-a   'be clean' > *-el-es-a*   *-ol-a* 'rot'   > *-ol-es-a*

(5) *-iʃa* / *-eʃa*
    -lal-a   'sleep'   > *-lal-iʃ-a*
    —   *-ɲavur-a* 'shake' > *-ɲavur-iʃ-a*
    -kwez-a 'vomit' > *-kwez-eʃ-a*   *-oɣ-a*   'bathe' > *-oɣ-eʃ-a*

In (5), there is no example of *-iʃa* with *-i-*, another accidental gap.

6   VHH in Kilimanjaro Bantu and Asu

If we now turn to Chaga-Dawida (i.e. Kilimanjaro Bantu) and the neighboring but unrelated Asu, the situation is much less clear cut. For instance, consider the neuter form of the Common Bantu root *-bɔ́n-* 'see' (compositionally 'be visible, appear', which has in most Chaga dialects taken on the specialized sense of 'be born'). On the basis of available data, the harmonizing/nonharmonizing behavior cuts across language/dialects irrespective of proximity. So, we find harmonizing *-ßon-ek-a* in Asu, Dawida, Mengwe, and Mkuu (EK), Mochi (CK), and Siha (WK), but nonharmonizing *-ßon-ik-a* in Useri and Mashati (EK), and Kiwoso, Rwa, and Mashami (WK).[10]

The situation exemplified by this stem is fairly typical of what we find across Kilimanjaro Bantu (plus Asu), provided we leave aside Dawida for now, which will indeed turn out to be a "canonical" language, like Saghala, except for a revealing twist. For the other languages, Müller's Mashami dictionary (the one used by LH) is by far the largest and most complete, but we can also turn to grammars of Asu and Mochi for some fairly systematic

---

[10] The *-ßon-ek-a* form is also realized as *-voneka* or *-woneka* according to language/dialect.

information on verbal extensions; as for the rest, this sort of information has to be gleaned rather haphazardly from word lists and text collections.

We have ten extensions or extension combinations to consider: applicative *-ɛd-, reversive *-ʊd-, neuter *-ɛk-, neuter reversive *-ʊk-, long causative[11] *-ıc-i-, causative of applicative *-ɛd-i-, causative of reversive *-ʊd-i-, causative of neuter *-ɛk-i-, and causative of neuter reversive *-ʊk-i-.

Let us first try to clear the question of the applicative (*-ɛd-) and reversive (*-ʊd-), where VHH seems to have entirely disappeared in KB, since it might in fact provide a clue to the whole evolution of VHH. If we look at older transcriptions, Müller (and Augustiny) for Mashami as well as Raum for Mochi consistently transcribe the applicative and reversive extensions as nonsyllabic -y- and -w- respectively. This is due to the fact that eastern Bantu *-l-, which should appear in both of these extensions, gives zero in KB and Asu—in most positions (see Nurse 1999: 25). This has serious consequences for the VHH analysis, since in nonsyllabic positions it is impossible to differentiate between $y < i$ and $y < e$, or between $w < u$ and $w < o$.

These transcriptions would seem to cast doubt on the widely held position that Chaga has no VHH for the applicative, but there are questions as to their accuracy. In contrast to his colleagues, for the Mwika dialect Stamberg transcribes fully syllabic -i- and -u- for the applicative and reversive respectively; the same is true for Rwa in the textbook published by the Lutheran Mission (1931). So, it appears necessary to turn to contemporary material.

For Mochi, texts recorded in the 1970s and in the 1980s clearly have syllabic -i- and -u- practically everywhere, particularly so since, due to the ubiquitous Chaga phenomenon of tone shift (McHugh 1999, Philippson & Montlahuc 2003), a stem H tone is displaced onto an extension that immediately follows it, as seen in the Mochi data in (6).[12]

(6) pfunúo kisimá kyo ...   'uncover the well ...'
     likádamía ihohǔ ...   'it (the baboon) sat on a stone ...'

As examples in (6) show, the H tone originating on the radical (-pfun- and -dam- respectively) is realized on the extension, which is fully syllabic. (Indeed the syllabicity is perceptible even when the extension does not bear a displaced H.)

The same situation obtains in other dialects, and even in Dawida, as in (7) (Philippson n.d.).[13]

---

[11] The difference between "long" and "short" causatives will be explained below.

[12] In these examples, Raum transcribes pfunwo and -damya rather than the forms shown here.

[13] In Saghala, eastern Bantu *-l- is retained everywhere, so the situation does not arise.

(7) *waβémredïa ndee* ... 'he is bringing his father ...'
     waturúa ilaŋga ... 'he has pierced a hole ...'

On the other hand, the situation seems to be different in some dialects, such as Mengwe and Mashati (EK) and above all Mashami, where even contemporary recorded material does not allow one to form a precise idea of the syllabicity of the two extensions.[14] The overwhelming auditory impression, however, is that of nonsyllabicity, which strongly contrasts with Mochi, for instance, although tone shift seems to operate almost identically in the two dialects. So in the Mashami example in (8), the -*y*- is definitely a glide, contrary to what it would be in Mochi (*ndʒïleíβio*).

(8) *ɲfïléé'βyɔ́ mbuχű kyeŋgâ* < *ɲí-ʃi-lé-íβ-i-w-a*
     'a few goats were stolen from me' (passive of applicative)

The case of Dawida suggests that the loss of contrast between desyllabified *i* and *e*, and also that between *u* and *o*, which is certainly present throughout Kilimanjaro Bantu, is not necessarily associated with the disappearance of VHH. As mentioned, Dawida is fully harmonic along the asymmetric VHH pattern *except* in the case of applicative and reversive, where the loss of -*l*- led to desyllabification then resyllabification (perhaps due to the effect of tone shift). Compare the examples of applicatives in (9) and (10).

(9) Saghala: *-lomba* 'beg'
              -lomb-el-a (appl.)

(10) Dawida: **-lómba*
              *-lómb-e(l)-a (appl.) > **-lómb-e-a* > **-lómb-y-a* > *-lomb-i-a*

That this is the correct analysis can be justified by the fact that when the passive extension -*w*- is added to the applicative in Dawida, -*l*- is retained and so is VHH.

(11) Dawida: -*orá* 'sprinkle' > -*oría* 'appease spirits' > -*orélwa* (passive)

We find a similar situation in Mashami when the applicative is added to verb stems ending in *w*, as in (12), and in Mochi, with the intensive form (Raum 1909: 161), as in (13).

(12) Mashami: -*omwa* 'pull'   > -*omuya* (applicative) vs.
               -*ondwa* 'take away' > -*ondoya* (applicative)

(13) Mochi: -*hendya* (appl. of -*henda* 'go') > -*hendelya* (intensive) vs.
             -*ʃiŋgya* (appl. of -*ʃiŋga* 'shut') > -*ʃiŋgilya* (intensive)

---

[14] Interestingly, Rugemalira & Phanuel (2009: 8) make the same remark.

In other words, although the applicative is the extension most frequently mentioned as evidence of the nonexistence of VHH in KB, it is definitely unconvincing, due to the desyllabification process.

Indeed, contrary to Mashami, the Mochi dialect (and presumably the rest of CK) is just as harmonic as Dawida (with the partial exception of the long causative, to which we shall return below), as demonstrated by the examples in (14).

(14) neuter   *-dek-a* 'get lost'   > *-dek-ek-a*

                                       -won-a 'see'   > *-won-ek-a*

      applicative of reversive   *-ond-u-o* 'remove'   > *-ond-oy-a*

      causative of reversive   *-oŋg-u-o* 'burn'   > *-oŋg-ol̯-a*

      intensive (double applicative) *-βed-a* 'wait'   > *-βed-ely-a*

      causative of applicative   *-lem-y-a* 'be heavy' > *-lem-el̯-a*

We thus see that, in spite of the surface loss of VHH in the applicative and reversive (for the reasons detailed above), VHH of the canonical asymmetric type is present in CK. In spite of insufficient data, the same should probably be said of the Useri dialect of EK, which doesn't seem even to have desyllabified the applicative and reversive, as seen in (15).

(15) *-βet-a* 'wait' > *-βet-e-a* (applicative)

        -ol̯-o-a 'stretch' (reversive)

This means that the only languages where serious perturbations of VHH are in evidence are the WK dialects (with the important exception of Siha, the westernmost outlier) and, outside of Chaga, in Asu. But interestingly the pattern in Asu is quite different from that in WK.

7   Neuter Extensions

For the reversive neuter form, that is, LH's *-ok-* (for which information is not plentiful outside of Mashami), we can make the following observations. If the preceding vowel is *-e-* there is no harmonizing in any dialect. If it is *-o-*, there are admittedly few examples, but Asu and the EK and CK dialect groups are entirely harmonic. WK, on the other hand, as exemplified by Mashami (but with the important exception of Siha, the westernmost outlier), offers a mixed situation without visible conditioning. I have found fifteen such verbs in Mashami, eight of them with harmony, seven without. Example (16) is illustrative:

(16)   *-oṯ-ok-a* 'be bent'   *-som-**u**k-a* 'come out, emerge'

It is true that in five of the seven cases with no harmony (e.g. the one just cited), the final stem consonant is a nasal, as rightly pointed out by LH. We will return to this point in a moment. The situation appears the same in Kiwoso and Rwa (-oțoka, -somuka), but not in Siha (-oțoka, -somoka).

In the case of the neuter *-ɛk-, if the preceding vowel is -o-, Mashami never harmonizes or, in LH's terms, always peripheralizes to -ik-; in all other dialects where there is evidence, the situation is mixed (comparable to what was seen for *-bɔ́n-ɛk- in Section 6). In Asu, for instance, the majority harmonize, as in (17); but a minority do not, as in (18), without obvious conditioning (though see the discussion of nasal consonants below).

(17) -kom-a 'bend' > -kom-ek-a   -ŋol-a 'undress' > -ŋol-ek-a

(18) -roŋg-a 'do' > -roŋg-ik-a   -kond-a 'destroy' > -kond-ik-a

The situation is mixed even in Mengwe (EK) which, as we saw above, has -βon-ek-a 'be born', but also has -ʧon-ik-a 'fall'. In fact, variant forms are attested in the same dialect, such as with Siha (WK) -woɭa 'cause to rot' which becomes -woɭ-ek-a or -woɭ-ik-a.

If the preceding vowel is -e-, Asu never harmonizes, as in (19).

(19) -tet-a 'speak' > -tet-ik-a   -hareh-a 'arrange' > -hareh-ik-a

As for Mashami, according to LH it seems to follow a pattern: It is harmonic in nonderived stems, but peripheralizing in derived ones, as in (20). There are exceptions to this pattern, however, as seen in (21).

(20) -telek-a 'be bent'   -ʁeβek-a 'soak (tr.)'
      -sem-a 'pluck feathers' > -sem-ik-a -lem-a 'bend' > -lem-ik-a

(21) -reŋg-a 'notch' > -reŋg-ek-a   -beremik-a 'squeak' (underived)

So the evidence could also be read (as also observed by LH) as the process being affected by the presence of the stem-final -m-, just as for the neuter reversive. This is bizarre on the face of it, since it is not clear what phonological feature of the labial nasal could cause raising of the following vowel; however, the phenomenon is not unknown in East Africa, where, for instance, Sukuma systematically raises the vowel of a noun class prefix when it is preceded by a nasal, as seen in (22), but not otherwise, as in (23).

(22) cl. 1/3 *-mʊ- > mu-   cl. 4 *-mɪ- > mi-

(23) cl. 11 *lʊ- > lʊ-   cl. 15 *kʊ- > kʊ-

Furthermore, there is a strong tendency in Mashami (and indeed throughout KB) to raise a final mid vowel when preceded by a nasal. For instance the deverbative suffix -o always appears as -u in this context (*kikaɓanu* 'fight' < *-kaɓan-o*; *ikwanu* 'meeting' < *-kwan-o*). In addition, the passive suffix *-e* appears as *-i* (*-kami* 'dry (cow)' < *-kam-e*). Also consider *mumu* 'lip' < **mʊ-dɔmɔ*. Although there are a few stems beginning with *-me-*, the only example with *-mo-* is *umo* 'marrow of tree' < **mʊ-ɔyɔ*. The same obtains for *-ne-* (no examples in Müller) and *-no-* (one example).

Whatever the exact phonological conditioning, LH's remark is perfectly on point: The few cases of raising of **-ɛ-* and nonlowering of **-ʊ-* after mid vowels in WK are due to the presence of a stem-final nasal consonant.

8 Causative

As regards the causative, we must first define its forms. There are basically two: the long causative, LH's **-ıc-i*, and the short causative, **-i*, which is mostly revealed, in 5-vowel languages, by its effect on the final stem consonant. As this short causative does not per se affect the quality of the vowels, it should not concern us here. However, it may combine with other extensions: causative of neuter **-ek-i* and **-ʊk-i*, causative of applicative **-ɛd-i*, and causative of reversive **-ʊd-i*. So in certain cases, what appear to be variants of the 'long' causative are in fact causative forms of other extensions (whatever their exact meaning).

By comparing extended and unextended stems, one can deduce what the forms of **C + i* should be. The attested patterns are given in (24).

(24) Saghala: **-d-i- > -z-*   **-k-i- > -s-*
      Asu: **-d-i- > -(d)ʒ-*   **-k-i- > -ʃ-*
      Dawida: **-d-i- > -r-*   **-k-i- > -s-*
      Mashami: **-d-i- > -r-*   **-k-i- > -ţ-*
      Other WK: **-d-i- > -l̦-*   **-k-i- > -ţ-*
      CK: **-d-i- > -l̦-*   **-k-i- > -ts-*
      EK: **-d-i- > -l̦-*   **-k-i- > -s-*
      Gweno: **-d-i- > -r-*   **-k-i- > -ţ-*

If we now try to establish the normal shape of the long causative in languages for which we have sufficient evidence, we obtain the results in (25).

(25) Saghala: *-iʃ-* / *-eʃ-* (fully harmonic); a number of *-iʃ-* / *-eʃ-* (perhaps Dawida influence)
      Dawida: *-iʃ-* / *-eʃ-* (fully harmonic)
      Mochi: *-iʃ-* / *-eʃ-* (?)
      Mashami: *-is-* / *-es-*

In Asu, there are curiously few examples of the long causative in a basic form, the short causative being more common, and the long form appearing most often as *-i(d)ʒ-*, which cannot correspond to **-ıc-i* but rather to

*-ɛd-i-, the causative applicative (perhaps with an intensive meaning). It harmonizes to -edʒ- in some cases (four harmonizing vs. ten nonharmonizing, after both -e- and -o-), without any obvious conditioning—a reverse of the situation for -eC-ek-! A few examples would also point to -if-/-ef-, however, which of course would be indistinguishable from reflexes of *-ɛk-i-, the causative of neuter (note that this is not the case in Kilimanjaro Bantu, where the reflexes are everywhere different, e.g. Mashami *-k-i- > -ʧ-, but long causative -is-, etc.).

The basic behavior of the long causative elsewhere is as follows. In Saghala and Dawida it is fully harmonic (according to asymmetric VHH), as indeed are all extensions, excluding the -l-less applicative and reversive in Dawida discussed in Section 6. In Mashami, the only Chaga dialect with sufficient evidence, it normally never harmonizes, with a few exceptions (in a couple of stems in -e-, and five in -a-, it lowers to -es-). Interestingly, while the long causative does not normally affect the previous stem-final consonant (as it should not, since the second degree vowel *-ɪ- has no such effect), it regularly changes a stem-final -r- (< *-d-i / V) to -ʁ- (*-d-i / C).[15] In Mochi the long causative -if- is well attested, but unfortunately practically never with mid vowels preceding; whatever little evidence there is is inconclusive, as can be seen in (26) below.

(26) -o.la 'germinate'   > -o.l-if-a (causative) (cf. Mashami -ora > -oʁisa)
     -ow-u-o 'be afraid'   > -oβ-ef-a (causative)

As for the causative forms of other extensions, in Mochi (and CK) they are fully harmonic, as with other extensions. In Mashami, the pattern we have already seen for simple extensions applies: There is naturally no VHH in the case of *-ɛC-ʊC-i, nor with *-ɔC-ɛC-i; when the sequences are identical in backness/roundness, harmony applies (with very few exceptions, once again with stem-final -m-). For Asu, see just above.

9 Synthesis

Attempting a synthesis we can make the following remarks. Saghala, which is not a member of KB but rather an outlier of Northeast Coast (see Nurse 1979, Nurse & Philippson 1980), has canonical asymmetric VHH. Dawida, the outlier in KB and in contact with Saghala, has it also. Whether this was

---

[15] I transcribe here the Mashami uvular fricative (which must at one time have been a strong coronal trill, like its counterpart in the other KB dialects) as -ʁ-, although it is most of the time realized with very little voicing, and -χ- would be more exact—especially so since there are no other voiced fricatives in the language. The coronal trill of contemporary Mashami corresponds to the lateral flap of other dialects.

inherited from northeastern Bantu ("Kaskazi" in Ehret's classification, see Ehret 1998), or as a lateral influence from Saghala, cannot be determined.

In Chaga proper, VHH is present in almost canonical form in CK, and for whatever it is worth due to scanty data, in Siha (WK); the poorly documented EK dialects do not give any clear picture, although there would seem to be a preference for harmonizing at least in the northernmost dialect, Useri. The hesitation for claiming harmonization in EK concerns mostly cases where -oC- is followed by a front vowel (cf. WK). As for WK, apart from Siha, it exhibits a quite different harmony pattern, based on backness (or roundness): -eC-u(C)- and -oC-i(C)- vs. -eC-e(C)- and -oC-o(C)- (with the exceptions mentioned), as pointed out by Hyman (1999).

Finally, Asu, though not genetically part of KB, but, like Saghala, a (rather closer) peripheral member of Northeast Coast, offers a very bizarre picture, with VHH operative mostly when the previous mid vowel is back (although there are quite a few exceptions) but not when it is front. This might possibly be an extension of the asymmetric behavior of *-εC-ʊC- (which as we know never harmonizes anywhere), which would have been carried over even to cases where -εC- is followed by front vowel extensions. It would be tempting to attribute this deviant behavior to interference from Gweno, with which Asu-speakers have been in contact for several centuries (see Nurse 1979), were it not for the fact that the very poorly known extension system of Gweno appears more classically harmonizing than Asu. More research is surely needed in this area.

10 Conclusion

So the question remains for Chaga: Are we confronted with a canonical VHH pattern getting gradually displaced (the origin of the loss would then surely be spreading from WK), or is canonical VHH gradually *penetrating* Chaga and displacing a former and different system? In this latter case, the point of entry should be CK, where the most clearly canonical systems are to be found. There is no easy answer to these questions, but it seems obvious that one hypothesis at least has been found invalid: The data examined above clearly show that the desyllabification/resyllabification process of the applicative and reversive extensions following the loss of -l- cannot explain the loss of VHH, since it has affected both Dawida and CK, which otherwise exhibit complete asymmetrical VHH (see (6) above). Assuming VHH to have been present originally in KB would imply its loss first in WK (Mashami/Rwa/Kiwoso) and then the spreading of this loss—more or less haphazardly—to EK, bypassing CK. This is difficult to visualize, although there is a good deal of evidence that EK peoples were in contact with WK either through the path around the northern side of the mountain or through a path situated high above the cultivated zone on the southern side, as attested by Stahl (1964).[16] There is also this quotation, found as an example in Raum's grammar: "As we were going up into the forest we met Chimbii people [i.e. Easterners] crossing the mountain through the high path on their way to Siha" (1909, §183, p. 245; my translation). However, this hypothesis founders on the very fact that the target of both circuits would be the westernmost outlier of WK, that is, Siha, which, for all we know—and this is admittedly not very much—*does* have canonical VHH. So contact between Siha and EK might better support the idea of spread of VHH into Siha, rather than the opposite (recall that Useri, the northernmost EK dialect seems to exhibit more instances of VHH, at least in the applicative, than its immediate neighbors).

Since canonical VHH seems to be at its clearest in CK, it is noteworthy that this is the part of the mountain that was in earliest contact with the outside and indeed the point of arrival of all journeys from the coast since at least the early 1800s. At that time the western and eastern part of the mountain were very much remote outliers.[17] Swahili (which has canonical VHH) seems to have been used from an early date at the Mochi court at least. So I would venture the following scenario: Canonical VHH was not present in early Chaga (for Dawida it is impossible to tell), either through loss (if canonical VHH was inherited from "Kaskazi") or from not having received it from the outside when it spread through northeastern Bantu. The harmonic system found then would have been one similar to that exemplified by Mashami: roundness/backness harmony. Later on, starting with the influence of Swahili (and/or maybe other neighboring languages), canonical VHH spread into CK and from there, somewhat sporadically, into EK and thence to Siha (through the paths mentioned earlier).[18]

It must be admitted that neither hypothesis is unreservedly convincing. Lack of detailed evidence for most dialects makes a thorough com-

---

[16] Stahl (or rather her informant?) goes so far as to assert that the Siha and Useri dialects were mutually intelligible. Now this is certainly wrong as it stands, since the phonology of the two dialects alone would create almost insuperable difficulties to comprehension, even leaving aside the lexical differences. What is true, however, is that a few basic vocabulary items are identical and not found elsewhere in the mountain, which might be due to retention on the one hand, e.g. *mfele* 'woman, wife' (found only in Siha and the East, whereas the other languages including Gweno have *(mndu)mka*), or common borrowings, e.g. *-mu.lo* 'burn (intr.)' found only in Siha, Rwa, and Useri.

[17] See all the historical data in Stahl (1964).

[18] There are many traditions—of fairly dubious validity—of contact between CK and various Northeast Coast groups. For instance, the chiefly line of Mochi claimed to have originated in Usambara, whereas the Mbokom (sub-)chiefdom was said to have inherited its name from the Pokomo people (Tana River in north-eastern Kenya). The languages concerned all have canonical VHH.

parison and reconstruction impossible at present. It should at least be clear that declaring KB to constitute an exception to canonical VHH on the basis of Mashami data alone does not do justice to the complexity of the situation. But the "feel" of the evidence makes one wish to support one of LH's conclusions, namely that "back" and "front" VHH were two independent processes.

References

Augustiny, J. 1914. *Kurzer Abriss des Madschamedialekts*. Berlin: Reimer.

Cammenga, J. 1994. *Kuria phonology and morphology*. Amsterdam: Vrije Universiteit Amsterdam dissertation.

Ehret, C. E. 1998. *An African classical age: Eastern and southern Africa in world history, 1000 B.C. to A.D. 400*. Charlottesville, VA: University Press of Virginia.

Greenberg, J. H. 1951. Vowel and nasal harmony in Bantu languages. *Zaire* 5: 813–820.

Gutmann, B. 1922–1923. Die Kerbstocklehren der Dschagga in Ostafrika. *Zeitschrift für Eingeborenen-Sprachen* 13: 81–109, 205–225, 260–302.

Gutmann, B. 1924. Das Rechtsleben der Wadschagga im Spiegel ihrer Sprichwörter. *Zeitschrift für Eingeborenen-Sprachen* 14: 44–68.

Gutmann, B. 1925. Bruchstücke aus den Kerbstocklehren für Mädchen, nach dem Mreho fo Ljango. *Zeitschrift für Eingeborenen-Sprachen* 15: 1-19.

Hyman, L. M. 1999. The historical interpretation of vowel harmony in Bantu. In J.-M. Hombert & L. Hyman (eds.), *Bantu historical linguistics: Theoretical and empirical perspectives*, 235–295. Stanford: CSLI.

Kähler-Meyer, E. 1962. Studien zur tonalen Struktur der Bantusprachen II. Chasu. *Afrika und Übersee* 46: 250–295.

Kagaya, R. 1989. *A classified vocabulary of the Pare language*. Tokyo: Institute for the Study of Languages and Cultures of Asia and Africa.

Kotz, E. 1909. *Grammatik des Chasu*. Berlin: Reimer.

Lutheran Mission (anonymous). 1931. *Kitabu kya isomisa vana kya Kirwa*. Leipzig: Evangelisch-Lutherische Mission zu Leipzig.

McHugh, B. 1999. *Cyclicity in the phrasal phonology of KiVunjo Chaga*. Munich: LINCOM.

Müller, E. 1947. *Wörterbuch der Djaga-Sprache (Madjame-Mundart)*. Berlin: Reimer.

Nurse, D. 1979. *Classification of the Chaga dialects: Language and history on Kilimanjaro, the Taita Hills, and the Pare Mountains*. Hamburg: Buske.

Nurse, D. 1999. Towards a historical classification of East African Bantu languages. In J.-M. Hombert & L. Hyman (eds.), *Bantu historical linguistics: Theoretical and empirical perspectives*, 1–41. Stanford: CSLI.

Nurse, D. & G. Philippson. 1980. The Bantu languages of East Africa: A lexicostatistical survey. In E. Polomé (ed.), *Language in Tanzania*, 26–67. London: Oxford University Press.

Philippson, G. 1983. Glossaire dawida-français-anglais. *Bulletin des études africaines de l'INALCO* 3: 153–198.

Philippson, G. n.d. Notes on Dawida and Saghala. Unpublished manuscript.

Philippson, G. & M.-L. Montlahuc. 2003. Kilimanjaro Bantu (E60 & E74a). In D. Nurse & G. Philippson (eds.), *The Bantu languages*, 475–500. London: Routledge.

Philippson, G. & D. Nurse. 2000. Gweno: A little-known language of Northern Tanzania. In K. K. Kahigi, Y. M. Kihore & M. Mous (eds.), *Lugha za Tanzania/Languages of Tanzania: A study dedicated to the memory of the late Prof. C. Maganga* (CNWS Publications 89), 233–284. Leiden: CNWS and Dar es Salaam: Mkuki na Nyota.

Raum, J. 1909. *Versuch einer Grammatik der Dschaggasprache (Moschi-Dialekt)*. Berlin: Reimer.

Rugemalira, J. M. & B. Phanuel. 2009. A grammatical sketch of Kimashami. Unpublished manuscript.

Stahl, K. M. 1964. *History of the Chagga people of Kilimanjaro*. The Hague: Mouton.

Stamberg, F. 1932–1933. Märchen der Dschagga (Mwika-Dialekt). *Zeitschrift für Eingeborenen-Sprachen* 23: 202–231, 278–306.

Stamberg, F. 1938–1939. Märchen der Dschagga (Mwika-Dialekt). *Zeitschrift für Eingeborenen-Sprachen* 29: 38–71.

Stamberg, F. 1942–1943. Rätsel der Djaga (Mwika-Dialekt). *Zeitschrift für Eingeborenen-Sprachen* 33: 66–77, 146–156.

Stamberg, F. 1943–1944. Rätsel der Djaga (Mwika-Dialekt). *Zeitschrift für Eingeborenen-Sprachen* 34: 69–76.

Stamberg, F. 1945–1950. Rätsel der Djaga (Mwika-Dialekt). *Zeitschrift für Eingeborenen-Sprachen* 35: 146–157.

Stamberg, F. 1951–1952. Märchen der Dschagga (Mwika-Dialekt). *Afrika und Übersee* 36: 137–143.

Wray, J. A. 1894. *An elementary introduction to the Taita language, eastern equatorial Africa*. London: Society for Promoting Christian Knowledge.

15

Tone Spreading, Tone Shifting, and Tonal Restructuring

RUSSELL G. SCHUH[†]

1 Introduction

Following the classification of Newman (2013), the Chadic languages of Yobe State, Nigeria, fall into two distinct genetic groups: those of the West Chadic A branch (Bole, Karekare, Maka, and Ngamo) and those of the West Chadic B branch (Bade, Duwai, and Ngizim).[1] I will refer to these as the A-Group and the B-Group respectively. The maps in Figure 1 show the location of Yobe State in Nigeria and of the languages within Yobe State, as well as the two dominant linguae francae of the region, Hausa and Kanuri, and also three municipalities in the region (in italics).

[†] The editors and contributors were sad to learn that our colleague passed away on November 8, 2016.

[1] Research on Chadic languages of Yobe State, Nigeria has been supported by National Science Foundation (NSF) grants BCS-9905180 (8/1/1999–7/31/2001), BCS-0111289 (12/1/2001–11/30/2004), and BCS-0553222 (8/15/2006–7/31/2009), Russell G. Schuh, Principal Investigator. Any opinions, findings, and conclusions or recommendations expressed in this material are those of the author and do not necessarily reflect the views of the NSF. Many thanks to all the people I have worked with on these projects, especially my former student, now collaborator and Professor of English at the University of Maiduguri, Dr. Alhaji Maina Gimba. I have, of course, written this paper to honor my friend, Larry Hyman. We started our linguistic lives together as fellow students at UCLA, and our friendship and careers have been intertwined in countless ways for over four decades. A paper on tone seemed appropriate as a tribute to the world's foremost authority on linguistic tone.

In addition to properties these languages have inherited from a common ancestral language, they share areal features (Schuh 2005a), among them aspects of tonal typology.[2] The purpose of this paper is to show (i) that nearly all the tonal alternations in these languages have their source in tone spreading, that is, the tendency of voice pitch to "leak" into the following tonal domain; (ii) how different, even closely related languages, have phonologized the results of tone spreading in significantly different ways; and (iii) an asymmetry between low and high tone in terms of spreading, in particular that low has less tendency to spread and in a sense is inert.

Figure 1. Yobe State, Nigeria (left) and the Yobe Chadic languages (right)

2 LH → LL: Low Tone Spreading

The B-Group languages of Yobe State all have a tone process that can be formulated as in (1).

(1) LH → LL: Low tone spreading
    LH → LL / __]STEM H ...]PHONOLOGICAL PHRASE

That is, a stem-final underlying LH sequence becomes LL when followed by H within a phonological phrase. "Stem" here means root (+ suffix). Phonological phrases for the purposes of this rule include at least those in (2), as exemplified with Ngizim (Ng.) and Western Bade (WB).[3]

---

[2] Editors' note: For an extensive overview of comparative Chadic, see Schuh (2017).

[3] I use the following orthographic conventions: Grave accent (à) = low tone (L); no diacritic = high tone (H); acute accent (á) = downstepped H. The marking on the first mora of a syllable applies to the whole syllable (Càa = a L syllable with a long vowel); a grave accent on the second mora = HL (Caà), i.e. falling tone. Doubled vowels = a long vowel; ə = IPA [ɨ]; y = IPA [j]; j = IPA [dʒ]; sh = IPA [ʃ]; in Ngizim, r = IPA [ɽ], r̃ = IPA [r]. None of the other languages cited here make this distinction, and in those languages r = IPA [r].

(2)   Examples of LH → LL in Ngizim and Western Bade

    verb + object
    Ng.: /zə̀ma gawà/   [zə̀mà gawà]   'he forged an axe'
    WB: /jə̀ dàamə wanáw/ [jə̀ dàamə̀ wanáw] 'we finished the work'

    noun + adjective
    Ng.: /kàayak gangam/ [kàayàk gangam] 'small squirrel'
    WB: /vàvən ɓuwa/   [vàvən ɓuwa]   'red tick'

    noun + noun
    Ng.: /zə̀gər kwaaȓa/ [zə̀gə̀r kwaaȓa] 'leg of a donkey'
    WB: /gwàmaaŋ Kaaku/ [gwàmàaŋ Kaaku] 'Kaku's ram'

    word + 'not'
    Ng.: /bàama bai/   [bàamà bai]   'not gambling'
    WB: /kàyaan pəm/   [kàyàan pəm]   'not a squirrel'

There is one significant difference between the languages. Ngizim, but not Western Bade, applies (1) to nominal subjects. Examples are in (3) with the pitch tracks in Figure 2. The examples are in the subjunctive with a H tone third person proclitic *da*.[4] The relevant portions are underlined.

Ng.: 'it's best that the in-law come'   WB: 'I want that the hoe fall'

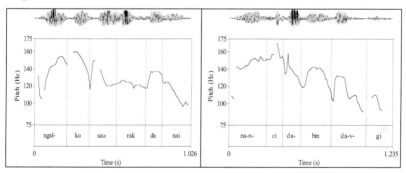

Figure 2. LH nominal subjects with initial H verbs

---

[4] The subjunctive is the only tense/aspect/mood (TAM) with an initial H CV syllable. To elicit the subjunctive, some context is usually necessary, hence, Ngizim *ngalko* 'it's best ...' and Bade *nà nci* 'I want ...'. The downstep on the *dá* in Bade, marked with an acute accent, has a couple of plausible explanations. One may be intonational. Generally in two-tone languages, in phrases that begin with LH, the first H syllable (the syllable *bin* in this case) is boosted in pitch (see Schuh, Gimba & Ritchart (2010) for discussion of this phenomenon in Bole). A second possibility is the tone configuration of *da* + verb. The verb in this TAM is always L. *Da* may be slightly lowered in anticipation of this L, especially in cases like that in (3), where *da* is syllabified with the verb root.

(3) *subject + verb*
    Ng.: /ngalko <u>sàurak da</u> nài/ [ngalko <u>sàuràk da</u> nài]
          'it's best that the in-law come'
    WB: /nà nci <u>dàbin da</u>-vgì/ [nà nci <u>dàbin dá</u>-vgì]
          'I want that the hoe fall'

It is well known that cross-linguistically, subject + verb incorporates a major boundary that generally is not bridged in phonological phrasing compared, say, to verb + object (Hayes 1989). Western Bade conforms to this observation but Ngizim treats this configuration as a phrase for purposes of LH → LL /__H phrasing. This distinction between the languages deserves more investigation, but in listening to recordings while preparing this paper, I found it to be consistent for two speakers of each language, recorded at different times and places and pronouncing a variety of sentences that illustrate the relevant environment.[5]

Another difference between the languages is the effect of consonant types, illustrated in (4) with a negative marker bearing H tone as context.[6]

(4) Ngizim: LH → LL blocked by glottalized or voiceless obstruent
    /__vd. obstruent /mùgba bai/ [mùgbà bai] 'not a Bosc's monitor'
    /__sonorant   /bàama bai/ [bàamà bai] 'not gambling'
    /__glottalized   /àuɗu bai/   no change   'not a grave'
    /__vl. obstruent   /cìita bai/   no change   'not pepper'

    Western Bade: LH → LL blocked by voiceless obstruent only
    /__vd. obstruent /Gàaji pəm/ [Gàajì pəm]   'not Gaji'
    /__sonorant   /kàyaan pəm/ [kàyàan pəm] 'not a squirrel'
    /__glottalized   /wìiɗən pəm/ [wìiɗən pəm] 'not a fart'
    /__vl. obstruent   /tərkaan pəm/ no change   'not an orphan'

    Gashua Bade: LH → LL applies to any LH sequence
    /__vd. obstruent /Gàaji bai/ [Gàajì bai]   'not Gaji'
    /__sonorant   /kàyak bai/ [kàyàk bai]   'not a squirrel'
    /__glottalized   /tə'yi bai/ [tə'yì bai]   'not food'
    /__vl. obstruent   /kùnkus bai/ [kùnkùs bai] 'not charcoal'

The LH → LL /__H rule as stated in (1) requires that the LH sequence be within a stem and that there be a boundary between the two H's, that is, the rule does not apply either in the configuration [...LHH...]_WORD or

---

[5] I do not have relevant data for Duwai or other dialects of Bade in order to say whether they are like Western Bade or like Ngizim.
[6] In Duwai, the most distantly related of the languages in this group, the rule applies to any LH sequence. Gashua Bade and Duwai are geographical neighbors, most if not all Duwai speakers also speak Gashua Bade, and Gashua Bade has had considerable lexical influence on Duwai.

L#HH (where # indicates a boundary). Failure of the rule to apply in the first configuration is shown by many words in all the languages which contain an internal LHH sequence; e.g. Ngizim *shìlaaliyâ* 'skink', *gàdǝk'yik* 'Balsam apple', Western Bade *gàbacǝmǝn* 'rafters made of palm logs', *gàmaďmaďon* 'ringworm'. As an example of the L#HH configuration, in a verb + object construction with the tone pattern [...L]$_{VERB}$ [HH...]$_{OBJECT}$, the initial H of the object is not lowered; e.g. Ngizim *na bùukì baaba* *[na bùukì bàaba] 'that I lack indigo', Western Bade *na-bdì bookaan* *[na-bdì bòokaan] 'that I ask an herbalist'.

In (1), I claim that for the purposes of the rule a stem could consist of root + suffix, that is, a suffix boundary can precede the target H syllable. Of the languages discussed here, only Ngizim has any -CV suffixes that bear H tone. There are two: *-gu* 'the', which can be suffixed to nouns, and *-na* 'totality marker',[7] which can be suffixed to verbs. These suffixes can both serve as the environmental H for the LH → LL / __ H rule, and they are also subject to the rule. The examples in (5) and the pitch tracks in Figure 3 illustrate this.[8]

(5)   Ngizim: /gàrau/   [gàrau]   'goats'
                /gàrau-gu/   [gàrùu-gu]   'the goats'
                /gàrau-gu bai/ [gàrùu-gù bai]   'not the goats'

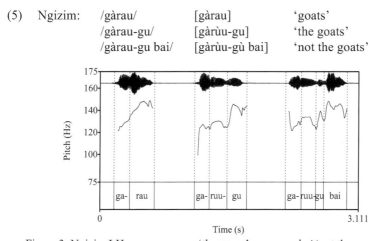

Figure 3. Ngizim LH noun, noun-*gu* 'the NOUN', noun-*gu bai* 'not the NOUN'

Summarizing the situation with regard to boundaries, the environmental H must be preceded by *at least* a suffix boundary, whereas the target H can be preceded *at most* by a suffix boundary.

---

[7] "Totality extension" is the term that Chadicists have generally employed indicating that the action is thoroughly done. In Schuh (2005b) I argue that this extension marks TAM focus.
[8] The alternation *-au* in phrase final position → *-uu* elsewhere (and parallel, *-ai* → *-ii*) is a regular alternation unrelated to particular suffixes or tones.

234 / RUSSELL G. SCHUH

Is the LH → LL / __H rule a phonetically motivated tone spreading rule or is it a *phonological* rule motivated, for example, to avoid a violation of the Obligatory Contour Principle (OCP) by juxtaposing H tones linked to different hosts? Favoring a spreading analysis is the fact that in Ngizim and Western Bade, at least, the rule can be blocked by consonant types that are antithetical to L tone (Tang 2008). A phonological principle such as the OCP would presumably be blind to such segmental effects. Phonetic data also supports a spreading analysis. Note in Figure 3 that in the phrase [gàrùu-gù bai], the syllable [gù] bears a pitch intermediate between the triggering L of [rùu] and the environmental H of [bai]. In fact, recordings of utterances such as those exemplified in (2) and (4) reveal that the target H syllable often is not as low as the conditioning L.[9] This suggests that lowering the H is the effect of leaking of the F_0 of the L into a following syllable rather than a replacement of one phonological tone by another. On the other hand, the process is sensitive to boundaries and the relative placement of boundaries. If lowering the target H were purely the effect of juxtaposing syllables of unlike pitch, why does the rule not apply in […LHH…]$_{WORD}$ or L#HH configurations?

My hypothesis is that LH → LL / __H did start life as phonetically motivated spreading of a L beyond its lexical domain, but as its effects became salient, it was phonologized in somewhat different ways in each language. Some retained blocking across incompatible consonant types, whereas other relaxed this phonetically motivated constraint. All the languages restricted the rule to an intraword domain triggered by a H outside this domain. This is in contrast to H spreading, which, as shown in the next section, works beyond the intraword level.

3   H spreading

3.1   H Spreading in B-Group Languages

Duwai, Ngizim, and Bade all spread H tone across word boundaries within most phrase types unless spreading is blocked by a modally voiced obstruent. A feature typical of these languages is downstepping of a H following a syllable raised by H spreading, which is surely an effect of downdrift combined with effacement of the L. However, downstepping has not been phonologized as it is in languages like Miya (Schuh 1998) or Igbo, where

---

[9] Similarly, the target /H/ sometimes seems to be slightly lower in pitch than the environmental H in cases where the rule should be blocked. For example, a recording of Ngizim *cìita bai* 'not pepper' shows the syllable *ta*, which begins in a voiceless obstruent, to be slightly lower that the environmental H of *bai*.

downstepped H must be recognized as having lexical and morphophonolog-ical status distinct from H and L.[10]

I illustrate H spreading and blocking of spreading with several phrase types from Ngizim and Western Bade, given in (6). Downstepped syllables are marked with an acute accent.

(6)   *subject clitic + verb*

Ng.:	/na kàtau/	[na katáu]	'I returned'
	/na zàdau/	no change	'I arrived'
WB:	/nə tàkwsu/	[nə takwsú]	'I tied'
	/nə dəpsu/	no change	'I hid (it)'

noun subject + verb

Ng.:	/Də̀nda kə̀mau/	[Də̀nda kəmáu][11]	'Dinda heard'
	/Də̀nda gə̀nudù/	[Də̀nda gə̀ńdù]	'Dinda got it'
WB:	/Kaaku tàkwsu/	[Kaaku takwsú]	'Kaku tied'
	/Kaaku dəbàsu/	no change	'Kaku hid'

verb + direct object noun

Ng.:	/na bàku ɗùwai/	[na bàkə ɗuwái]	'I roasted meat'
	/na màsu gàskam/	[na màsə gàskam]	'I bought a rooster'
WB:	/nə ə̀cku ɗacən/	[nə-ckə ɗacə́n]	'I pulled out hair'
	/nə gàfa dùwun/	no change	'I caught a horse'

noun + adjective

Ng.:	/ʒəkəmau màarəm/	[ʒəkəmau maàrəm]	'big camel'
	/ʒəkəmau bə̀lân/	no change	'nice camel'
WB:	/dàbin hə̀rà/	[dàbin hərà]	'new hoe'
	/dàbin dùksi/	no change	'heavy hoe'

Ngizim, at least, seems to apply H spreading to any item that is part of an intonational phrase.[12] For example, a manner adjunct does not form a syntactic constituent with a preceding verb + object, yet Ngizim applies H spreading in such environments, as shown in the pair in (7a), contrasting the unmarked object *kařèe* 'things, stuff, load' with HL citation tones, and

---

[10] Evidence that spreading is not fully phonologized comes from speaker variation. All the speakers with whom I worked during my dissertation research in 1969–1970 and two speakers in their 40s with whom I worked from 2002–2009 applied both L and H spreading as described. However, one speaker, probably in his mid-20s when we started working together in 2002, applies neither rule.

[11] Note that H spreading appears to create the environment for LH → LL /__H, but the latter does not apply (see also the Western Bade example [dàbin hərà] 'new hoe' below). The obvious way to handle this in a rule-based account would be to order LH → LL before H spreading.

[12] I did not specifically record and check Bade or Duwai for spreading across big boundaries other than nominal subject + verb.

the same object with the H suffix *-gu* 'the'. The examples in (7b) are copular sentences, where *bìi tǝku* 'this thing' is the subject and the following noun is the predicate, a boundary at the root node of a full sentence. H spreading applies to *tǝmàaku* 'ewe' whereas it is blocked by the initial voiced obstruent of *vǝ̀ji* 'monkey'.

(7)   H spreading in Ngizim across major syntactic boundaries

    a.   *object + manner adjunct*

/ʐǝmtǝ-naa kařèe wàwài/	[ʐǝmtǝ-naa kařèe wàwài]	'he ruined things on purpose'
/ʐǝmtǝ-naa kařèe-gu wàwài/	[ʐǝmtǝ-naa kařee-gu wawài]	'he ruined the things on purpose'

    b.   *subject + predicate nominal*

/bìi tǝku tǝmàaku/	[bìi tǝku tǝmàakù]	'this thing is a ewe'
/bìi tǝku vǝ̀ji/	no change	'this thing is a monkey'

The domain over which H spreading applies differs between Bade and Ngizim. In Bade, spreading continues to apply until it is either blocked by a voiced obstruent, or the environment __L]_{INTONATIONAL PHRASE} is reached. The latter environment is seen in (6) in the example [dàbin hǝrà] 'new hoe'. In Ngizim, a H spreads only to the first mora of the target. If the target is a light syllable (= one mora), as in most of the cases in (6) and (7), the H spreads to just that syllable. If the syllable is heavy, the spread is only to the first mora, resulting in a falling tone, as in [ʐǝkǝmau maàrǝm] 'big camel' in (6), with a falling tone marked by grave accent on the second mora of [maà]. Compare the sentences in (8) and the corresponding pitch tracks in Figure 4 on the next page. In the Western Bade sentence for 'I pressed', the H spread results in a relatively level pitch throughout the verb. (The final sharp fall is a result of the analysis software package Praat picking up a breathy release, the auditory impression being a relatively level pitch.) In Western Bade 'I learned', the voiced obstruent of the second syllable, *gu*, blocks the H from continuing to spread. Segmentally, Ngizim 'I propped' is like Bade 'I pressed', with each syllable beginning in a voiceless obstruent, but tonally it is like Bade 'I learned' with the second syllable pronounced with a low pitch.

(8)   WB: /nǝ tǝnkǝku/   [nǝ tǝnkǝkú]   'I pressed'
                /nǝ kùzgùzu/   [nǝ kuzgùzu]   'I learned'
      Ng.:   /na tǝnkùsu/   [na tǝṅkùsu]   'I propped'

A final question is whether a boundary is required between the target L and the conditioning H, parallel to the LH → LL / __#H rule, where we saw in Section 2 there must be at least a suffix boundary (#).

Western Bade: 'I pressed'   Western Bade: 'I learned'

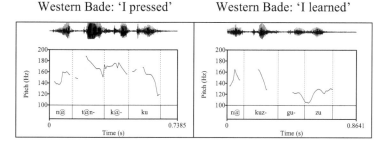

Ngizim: 'I propped'

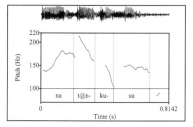

Figure 4. Comparing the domain of H spreading in Western Bade and Ngizim

Cases like Western Bade 'I pressed' in (8) and Figure 4 provide *prima facie* evidence that a boundary is not required: H spreads to the second root syllable of /tǝnkǝku/. Lexical evidence confirms this. First, a search of a Western Bade lexical database (Dagona 2009) reveals that nouns beginning in the patterns HLL vs. HHL are in near complementary distribution: of 29 HLL… nouns, all but 6 have have a voiced obstruent initiating the second syllable (of these, one is a place name, while three involve reduplication and have an ideophonic look); of 22 HHL… words, only two (both borrowed day names from Arabic via Kanuri) have a voiced obstruent initiating the second syllable. Second, most verbs whose first syllable is CVC… or CV_i…, where V_i is not /ǝ/, have a verbal noun with initial H. The tone of the following syllable in the verbal noun is fully predictable: if the second syllable begins in a voiced obstruent, it is L (*kuzgùzan* 'learning'), otherwise it is H (*kurɗyǝmán* 'bending double'). In Ngizim, on the other hand, there are both HLL nouns with a consonant other than a voiced obstruent initiating the second syllable (*santǝr̃àm* 'antimony') and HHL nouns where the second syllable begins with a voiced obstruent (*wangar̃à* 'leather sandals'). Ngizim and Western Bade thus differ in that H spreading in Ngizim applies only to the configuration H#L… (# = some boundary) whereas in Western Bade H spreading applies everywhere unless blocked by a syllable initiated by a voiced obstruent or the last syllable of an intonational phrase.

3.2 H Spreading in Bole

In Bole, an A-Group language, a H tone spreads across a boundary to re-
place a following L (Lukas 1969, Gimba 1998, Schuh & Gimba 2005). Typical cases are seen in (9).[13] See Schuh & Gimba (2005) and Gimba & Schuh
(2015) for extensive discussion and exemplification.

(9)   Bole H spreading

subj cl + v	/mu kàran gam/	[mu karan gam]	'we slaughtered a ram'
n + n gen	/tèmshi làawò/	[tèmshi laawò]	'sheep of a child'
v + do	/ǹ kòna kèɓe/	[ǹ kòna keɓe]	'I will take gypsum'
prep + n	/ndin ko Pìkkà/	[ndin ko Pìkkà]	'he came from Fika'

As in the B-Group languages, H spreading is blocked by a voiced obstruent, e.g. *mu zàla bòkku* *[mu zala bokku] 'we will begin roasting'.[14] In
contrast to B-Group languages, however, Bole H spreading is very sensitive
to syntactic boundaries. It does not, for example, apply between a nonclitic
subject and a verb (e.g. *òoshi lòkkìɗuu gà gàa zòori* *[òoshi lokkìɗuu …]
'the goat became entangled in the rope'), between a noun and a following
adjective (e.g. *tèmshi pèetìlà* *[tèmshi peetìlà] 'white sheep'), nor in several
other cases where the words would otherwise seem to form a close nexus.
Schuh & Gimba (2005) argue that when a word is the head of its XP (where
verb is the head of VP, adjective is the head of AP, etc.), it cannot be the
target of H spreading. Moreover, certain word classes neither condition nor
permit H spreading. Notable classes are proper names as well as interrogative words: *tèmshi Kàkkàaba* *[tèmshi Kakkàaba] 'Kakkaba's sheep', *ko
sòttò?* *[ko sottò] 'from when?'. Finally, there is a phonetic difference between the result of Bole H spreading and the parallel rule in B-Group languages: H spreading in Bole leaves no trace of there having been a L tone.
By contrast, as shown earlier, in the B-Group languages, when a L is raised
by spreading, a following H is typically pronounced as a downstepped H,
and there is often some declination in pitch even on the raised L. Bole has
no phonetic downstepped H tones, and a L that has been raised by
H spreading is pronounced at exactly the same pitch as the triggering H.

In short, in terms of both conditioning environments and phonetic realization, Bole H spreading is essentially part of the morphophonology, serving as a marker of syntactic phrasing. It must have had its origin in the pho-

---

[13] The interpretation of the abbreviations in (9) is as follows: *do* = direct object, *n* = noun,
n gen = genitive noun, *prep* = prepositon, *subj cl* = subject clitic, *v* = verb.
[14] A difference between Bole and Ngizim is that prenasalized obstruents in Bole are treated as
nasals (they allow spreading, e.g. /ka mbàaluwòoyi/ → [ka mbaaluwòoyi] 'you will bury it'),
whereas in Ngizim they are treated as voiced obstruents (they block spreading, e.g.
/ka mbàsənaacì/ → [ka mbàsənaacì] 'you sat down' has no change).

netically based tendency for voice pitch to persist beyond its lexical domain, still evident in the fact that it is blocked by modally voiced obstruents, but in Bole, H spreading has changed character from the more surface-oriented counterpart seen in the B-Group languages.

4 Ngamo

From a phonological point of view, Ngamo, an A-Group language, has by far the most complex tonal system among the Yobe State Chadic languages. Schuh (2009) describes its tone system in detail. Here I outline some central features of Ngamo tone and relate them to the theme of tone spreading.

Ngamo has two dialects, Gudi and Yaya. These dialects differ morphologically and lexically in a number of ways, but the most remarkable difference is a result of what I refer to as the Great Ngamo Tone Shift (GNTS), which has affected Gudi Ngamo alone among all the A-Group languages, including Yaya Ngamo. The GNTS can be schematized as in (10), where T indicates a tone and D symbolizes the domain of a tone, which may range from one mora to multiple syllables. The table in (11) illustrates the GNTS with trisyllabic nouns, where Bole and Yaya Ngamo represent the original tones. H tone is marked with an acute accent here to make the tone shift clear, a circumflex indicates falling tone, (H) indicates a floating H, and items in parentheses have tones that deviate from the expected pattern.

(10) The Great Ngamo Tone Shift (GNTS)

$$
\begin{array}{ccccccccc}
T_1 & \dots & T_n & & L & T_1 & \dots & T_{n-1} & T_n \\
| & | & | & \rightarrow & | & | & | & & \backslash\ (|) \\
D_1 & \dots & D_n & & D_1 & D_2 & \dots & & D_n
\end{array}
$$

(11) The Great Ngamo Tone Shift (GNTS) with trisyllabic words

Orig.	Bole	Yaya Ngamo	Gudi Ngamo	
LLL	*kànkìrshà*	*kànkàrshà*	*kànkàrshà*	'puff adder'
LHL	*àlbásàr*	*àlbásàr*	*àlbàsâr*	'onion'
LLH	*gàlàapí*	*gàlàafí*	*gàlàahì (H)*	'small axe'
LHH	*kàagílmó*	*kàagílmó*	*kàagìlmò (H)*	'garlic'
HHH	(no cognate)	*mándírá*	*màndìrà (H)*	'sesame'
HLH	*ánkàlí*	*hánkàlí*	*hànkálì (H)*	'intelligence'
HHL	*kúrméeshì*	*kúrmásò*	*kùrùmsô*	'biting ant'
HLL	*bíbìdò*	*(bìbìdò)*	*bìibídò*	'like a monkey'
FH	*(pempelì)*	*hîblá*	*híblà (H)*	'wind'

The original tone pattern, as seen in Bole and Yaya, has moved one domain to the right in Gudi, filling in the initial domain with default L. If the final tone was H, it has become a floating H in Gudi. This includes H whose original domain was more than one syllable, as in 'garlic', where

LHH → LLL (H). If the final tone sequence was HL, it has become a F on the final syllable in citation form.[15] Original HLL and FH need some explanation. I interpret the path of 'like a monkey' as *HLL → LHH+L (GNTS) → LHL (reabsorption); that is, the H portion of the H+L on the last syllable was "reabsorbed" into the preceding H, the result being LHL. The proto-Ngamo pattern for 'wind', seen in Yaya, was H+LH, that is, the first H was linked to the first mora of the first syllable and the L to the second mora: *H+LH → L+HL (H) (GNTS). The resultant L+H (= rising tone) is not legitimate in Gudi and was replaced by H (see Leben (1971) for the same process in Hausa).

The source of the GNTS must have been tone spreading, that is, the pitch of each domain encroached on its following neighbor to the point where the new pitch actually took over the full domain. There are two mysteries. The first is how this spreading story accounts for the fact that the spread affected exactly each original domain, whether that domain was one mora or multiple syllables. I have no solution for this mystery, although it makes one a believer in the Obligatory Contour Principle, that is, that the spreading was actually at the level of the tones themselves, not the segmentals that bore the tones.

The second mystery involves words with all H tone, such as *mándírá* 'sesame' in (11) and numerous others, such as Yaya *ló*, Gudi *lò* (H) 'meat' or Yaya *kóoró*, Gudi *kòorò* (H) 'donkey'. In such words, there was no domain to spread to, at least in citation form. Why should the H have moved from its original domain to become a floating H? Thinking back to H spreading in Bole (Section 3.2), I suggest that there *was* a domain, namely the next item in a *phrase*. That is, one should think of the GNTS as being the result of spreading in phrases, not citation forms. Consider the following examples from Bole and Gudi Ngamo, with a verb and following direct object in (12a) and a second-person masculine singular agreement clitic and following verb in (12b). The underlying tones of Bole show the historical tone pattern in this example, and the verbs are in the subjunctive TAM.[16]

---

[15] In Schuh (2009), I interpreted this as reassociation of the displaced final L with the final syllable. I now suspect that final F is simply the unmarked intonation for phrase final H. All words with final F in citation form are realized with final H in nonfinal position, with no trace of there having been a L, historically or synchronically. Nearly all words pronounced with phrase final H are "special", e.g. ideophones, interjections, proper names, and obvious recent loanwords, and even some of these words have F as a phrase final alternant, e.g. the proper name *Tíidá = Tíidâ*. In effect, the GNTS has sent original final L into oblivion!

[16] I don't understand the F on the second syllable of *ngàrî* in the final row of (14). The original tone pattern was LH, which, by the GNTS, should yield ??*ngàrì* (H), and with a noun object, the final vowel elides and a H does appear on the object, e.g. /à ngàr(i) tèmʃì/ > [à ngàr témʃì] 'that he tie a sheep'.

(12)

	Underlying	Bole: H spreading Ngamo: (H) docking	
Bole	/bèsé tèmshí/	[bèsé témshí]	'that he shoot a sheep'
Ngamo	/bèsè (H) tèmshì (H)/	[bèsè témshì]	
Bole	/ká ngòrîi/	[ká ngórîi]	'that you (m.s.) tie'
Ngamo	/kò ngàrî/	[kò ngárî]	

In the modern languages, the surface initial H on [témshí/témshì] 'sheep' and [ngórîi/ngárî] 'tie' must be accounted for by different tonal processes: H spreading in Bole, but floating (H) docking in Ngamo. Historically, however, they had the same source: spreading from a preceding H in the same phrase. What differentiates the languages is the fact that spreading in Bole has not taken place intraword: original lexical tones have remained intact. In Gudi Ngamo, spreading took place across phrases, *including intraword tones*. In Ngamo, the rightward dislocation of tones necessitated a "fix-up" for the abandoned word-initial domains, viz. default L. Pitch tracks presented in this paper (see e.g. Figure 4) show that utterances beginning in a phonological H typically have a "wind-up", starting at a relatively low pitch and rising to a maximum, suggesting that the low portion of this wind-up could itself spread as the source of the now phonologized intial L in nearly all Gudi Ngamo words.

5 Conclusion

The Chadic languages of Yobe State, Nigeria, fall into two rather distantly related genetic groups, but as an areal grouping, they share a variety of tonal processes that all have their source in tone spreading, that is, the tendency of voice pitch to leak from one phonological domain to the next. Despite the natural articulatory basis of this process, the languages have implemented spreading in a variety of ways, some resulting in rather subtle differences, such as sensitivity to different levels of morphological boundaries from one language to another, while others lead to quite radical differences, such as the changing of spreading of surface tones to docking of phonologically abstract floating tones. One notable asymmetry is between H and L tones. In all the languages examined, processes that work across word boundaries involve only H tones. Processes involving L tones are only intraword, and even here there is some question as to whether the processes are best described as spreading. In some languages, a LH → LL / __#H process is potentially describable as a means to avoid an OCP violation. In Gudi Ngamo, imposing a default L on word-initial domains may be the phonologization of the tendency to initiate a phase initial H with a low pitched "wind-up".

References

Dagona, B. W. 2009. *Bade-English-Hausa dictionary (Western dialect)*, 2nd edn. Potiskum, Yobe State, Nigeria: Ajami Press.

Gimba, A. M. 1998. *Low tone raising in Bole*. Los Angeles: University of California MA thesis.

Gimba, A. M. & R. G. Schuh. 2015. *Bole-English-Hausa dictionary and English-Bole wordlist*. (University of California Publications in Linguistics, 148). Oakland: University of California Press.

Hayes, B. 1989. The Prosodic Hierarchy in meter. In P. Kiparsky & G. Youmans (eds.), *Rhythm and meter* (Phonetics and Phonology 1), 201–260. San Diego: Academic Press.

Leben, W. R. 1971. The morphophonemics of tone in Hausa. In C. W. Kim & H. Stahlke (eds.), *Papers in African linguistics*, 201–218. Edmonton: Linguistic Research Inc.

Lukas, J. 1969. Tonpermeable und tonimpermeable Konsonanten im Bolanci (Nordnigerien). *Ethnological and linguistic studies in honour of N. J. van Warmelo*, 133–138. Pretoria: Government Printer.

Newman, P. 2013. The Chadic language family: Classification and name index. http://hdl.handle.net/2022/20964.

Schuh, R. G. 1998. *A grammar of Miya*. Berkeley: University of California Press.

Schuh, R. G. 2005a. Yobe State, Nigeria as a linguistic area. In R. T. Cover & Y. Kim (eds.), *Proceedings of the thirty-first annual meeting of the Berkeley Linguistics Society: Special session on languages of West Africa*, 77–94. Berkeley: Berkeley Linguistics Society.

Schuh, R. G. 2005b. The totality extension and focus in West Chadic. Paper presented at the International Conference on Focus in African Languages, Berlin, Germany, October 6–8. http://www.linguistics.ucla.edu/people/schuh/Papers/ms_2005_Berlin_2005.pdf.

Schuh, R. G. 2009. Ngamo tones and clitics. Unpublished manuscript, UCLA. http://www.linguistics.ucla.edu/people/schuh/Papers/ms_2009_ngamo_tones_and_clitics.pdf.

Schuh, R. G. 2017. *A Chadic cornucopia* (edited by Paul Newman). Oakland, CA: eScholarship, California Digital Library. http://escholarship.org/uc/item/5zx6z32d.

Schuh, R. G. & A. M. Gimba. 2005. Low tone raising in Bole. *Afrika und Übersee* 88: 229–264.

Schuh, R. G., A. M. Gimba & A. Ritchart. 2010. Bole intonation. *UCLA Working Papers in Phonetics* 108: 226–248.

Tang, K. E. 2008. *The phonology and phonetics of consonant-tone interaction*. Los Angeles: University of California dissertation.

16

Compounding in Leggbó

IMELDA I. UDOH

1 Introduction

The Leggbó language is a minority Upper Cross language, under the Benue-Congo subgroup (Faraclas 1989).[1] It is spoken by about 60,000 people living in the present Abi and Yakurr Local Government Areas of Cross River State in south-eastern Nigeria. The variety described here is the Letatama variety spoken in Adadama.

Like many other languages of the world, Leggbó uses compounding to expand its vocabulary, involving combinations such as noun plus noun, noun plus verb, noun plus adjective, etc. Through the combination of these categories, two kinds of compounds can be identified in the language: primary (or root) compounds and synthetic (verbal) compounds. In the creation of compounds, there is an interplay of morphological rules which produce surface forms, including such processes as deletion, harmony, among others.

This paper presents a description of compounding in Leggbó, following Spencer's (1991) classification. The paper is presented in three sections. In Section 1, we present an introduction and overview of the morphophonology of the Leggbó language. Section 2 presents the compounding processes, and we conclude in Section 3.

---

[1] I thank Prof. Larry Hyman, Prof. David Odden, two anonymous reviewers, and Dr. Ogbonna Anyanwu for very useful comments on an earlier version of this paper.

Revealing Structure.
Eugene Buckley, Thera Crane & Jeff Good (eds.).
Copyright © 2018, CSLI Publications.

1.1 An Overview of Leggbó Morphology and Phonology

1.1.1 Leggbó Nouns

The basic Leggbó noun is made up of a prefix and a stem. The prefix may be one of the following: *li-, lɛ-/le-, gi-, gɛ-/ge-, i-, ɛ-/e-, a-, m-/n-/ŋ-*.[2] Vowel-final roots marked with prefixes of the shape *lV-* show final *l*, as well, suggesting a kind of circumfixal class marking. These prefixes are frozen relics of a former noun class system which apparently once supported full agreement, as evidenced by nearby related languages such as Lokəə and Mbembe (see Barnwell 1969a, 1969b, Iwara 1982, Hyman & Udoh 2006). While certain semantic tendencies can be detected in the choice of prefix for a given noun, prefix-noun combinations cannot be said to be predictable. There are also a few nouns with no prefix. Some examples include: *sin* 'hair', *nɔ̀nɔŋ* 'finger', and *kkwàl* 'boat'. The historical prefix in these words may have fused with the stem over time.

The noun stem has a minimum of two syllables. Stems with more than two syllables are either historically reduplicated/compound stems or borrowed.

1.1.2 Leggbó Verbs

The basic Leggbó verb is based on a (possibly complex) stem with a maximum size of two syllables. The stem may additionally be preceded by a reduplicated first syllable and may be followed by an optional pluractional suffix *-azi*. Only such constructions can produce verbs with more than two syllables. Verbs are therefore monosyllabic, bisyllabic, trisyllabic, or quadrisyllabic.

1.1.3 Leggbó Phonology

Leggbó has seven vowel phonemes, /i e ɛ a u ɔ o/, which can appear in short and long forms. The length of the vowel within the syllable is affected by the syllabic prosodies of fortition and lenition. Vowels following fortis consonants are short, while those following lenis consonants are long. The lengthened vowels can be slightly breathy. Long vowels after fortis consonants are only found in cases of morphological concatenation.

The distinction between fortis and lenis consonants in Leggbó bears a heavy functional load lexically and grammatically, as seen in (1).

(1) *nàá* 'take' *ɛnáá* 'he took'
    nnǎ 'shine' *ɛnnái* 'he was taking'

---

[2] Forms separated by slashes represent phonologically predictable alternants based on patterns of vowel harmony.

We have represented the fortis consonants as double, given the importance of this feature in the language. There are twenty-five consonants in the language, and only /m, n, ŋ, l/ can occur in coda positions.

Leggbó has three contrastive level tones—(H)igh, (M)id, and (L)ow—but the tone patterns on nouns and verbs differ slightly. There is a three-way tone contrast on nouns only. The noun prefix generally has an L or M tone.

There is only a two-way contrast in verb roots, with M tone verbs and L tone verbs—that is, there are two lexical tonal classes for verbs. The first has a M tone, while the second has either a H or L tone on the root with the choice being governed by grammatical context. (The L tone is found in the citation form.) For all verbs, surfacing tones are determined by the verb root and a tonal suffix which may be either L or M, as well as by tonal patterns associated with categories like aspect, mood, polarity, and sentence construction type (see Hyman et al. 2002). Six tone melodies can be identified on verbs in total across these configurations: HM, MM, ML, LM, LL, and LHM. In this paper, the high and low tones are marked with acute and grave accents, while mid tones are indicated by diacritic-free vowels.

2 Compounding in Leggbó

Compounds are grammatical units involving at least two roots which may function grammatically as single words. Their constituent members cannot generally be split up, and they cease to independently refer to their original meanings (Dimmendaal 2000: 167). Fabb's (1999: 66) definition of a compound as "a word which consists of two or more words" appears to be one of the most straightforward ones.

Like other words, a compound belongs to a particular syntactic category. It has a head, the morpheme that determines the category of the entire compound. Following this criterion, compounds are often classified as being endocentric or exocentric compounds. The former refers to compounds whose basic meaning is denoted by their head, such as *spoon **feed*** (feed with a spoon) or *tea**spoon*** (spoon for tea); while the latter are compounds whose meanings do not derive straightforwardly from the meaning of their head, such as *red**head*** (not a head which is red, but a person with red hair).

Guevara & Scalise (2008: 107) propose the following schema for compounds:

[X ℜ Y] Z

where X, Y and Z represent major lexical categories, and ℜ represents an implicit relationship between the constituents (a relationship not spelled out by any lexical item).

In other words, the elements involved in compounding must be members of a major lexical category; and the elements of a compound must be linked by either a grammatical or a semantic relationship.

We adopt this schema in our description of Leggbó compounds. The relationship between the compounding elements is linked by both grammatical and semantic relationships. Beyond this, our description of Leggbó compounding is adapts the paradigm of root and synthetic compounds following Spencer (1991). Root compounds (e.g. *houseboat*) consist of concatenations of roots and are directly generated rather than constructed by means of syntactic rules. Synthetic compounds are regarded as verbal compounds, and they are formed from deverbal heads. In this case, the nonhead functions as the argument of the verb which forms the head (e.g. *truck driver* 'one who drives a truck').

Leggbó compounds have one of the following shapes: N1 + N2, Adj + N, Agentive prefix + V + N, N1 *of* N2, and V + N.

2.1 Leggbó Root Compounds

2.1.1 N1 + N2

N1 + N2 compounds are made up of two nouns, the second of which generally loses its prefix (if it has one) in the compounding. However, unpredictably, in some cases this prefix reappears as the prefix of the entire compound, as will be seen in an example like (3a).[3] In others, the original prefix of N1 is maintained (see e.g. (2a)) or an unpredictable prefix appears (see e.g. (2d)). Compounds of this type are right-headed.

In (2a)–(2e), the prefixes are all lost on the nouns in N2 position. In (2b), a nasal deleted from the end of N1 appears to resurface as a velar coda nasal, as though it is functioning as a kind of mobile affix. In (2c) and (2d), a velar prefix is deleted while a velar nasal appears at the end of the compound, perhaps also representing a case of affixal mobility, with a fricative appearing as a nasal due to restrictions on licit coda consonants in the language.

(2) a. *yètti* + *lìkkpal* → *yètti-kkpál*   'bark of tree'
       tree   scale

    b. *ètèn* + *lìkkpal* → *ètè-kkpáŋ*   'skin'
       animal   scale

    c. *yèmmà* + *yèkkpa* → *yèmmà-kkpáŋ*   'lips'
       mouth   cover

---

[3] Iwara (1982: 118–123), reports a similar case in Lokɔɔ (a related Upper Cross language), where the second constituent provides the compound prefix when both constituents have a prefix in isolation.

   d. *èttɔ*   + *yèkkpa* → *ǹttɔ-kkpáŋ*   'roof'
      house   cover
   e. *lèbbòl* + *èttɔ*   → *lèbbò-ttɔ*   'grave, tomb'
      death   house

A prefix which is lost from N2 can reappear as a replacement for the lexical prefix of N1, as seen in the data in (3), though (3b) and (3d) are ambiguous. There are no tonal changes in the compounds in (3), but the prefix on the compound in (3e) shows the influence of vowel harmony, and other, less systematic, processes can be seen in the data as well.

(3) a. *ètti* + *ledùl* → *lè-tti-dùl* 'bundle of sticks'
       stick   bundle

    b. *lɛbɔl* + *ledùl* → *lɛbɔ-dùl*   'fist'
       hand   bundle

    c. *èttɔ* + *ǹzàm*   → *ǹtɔ-zàm*   'backyard'
       house   back

    d. *lèdzìl* + *lèsól* → *lèdzì-só*   'sun, dawn'
       day   face

    e. *yèkkpa* + *ɛttɔ*   → *èkkpi-ttɔ* 'umbrella'
       body   house

The head noun is morphologically more active. For instance, it attracts reduplication or the plural suffix *-bɛ*, as seen in (5) (compare with (4)).

(4) Diminutive nouns

Noun	Diminutive sg	Diminutive pl	Gloss
yètti	*yètti-tti-wɛ*	*yètti-tti-bɛ*	'tree'
lìkkpal	*lìkkpa-kkpal-wɛ*	*lìkkpa-kkpal-bɛ*	'skin'
ledùl	*ledù-dùl-wɛ*	*ledù-dùl-bɛ*	'mound'
ǹzàm	*ǹzàm-zàm-wɛ*	*ǹzàm-zàm-bɛ*	'back'

(5) Diminutive compounds

Noun	Diminutive sg	Diminutive pl	Gloss
yètti-kkpál	*yètti-kkpá-kkpál-wɛ*	*yètti-kkpá-kkpál-bɛ*	'bark of tree'
ètè-kpáŋ	*ètè-kpá-kpáŋ-wɛ*	*ètè-kpá-kpáŋ-bɛ*	'skin'
lè-tti-dùl	*lè-tti-dù-dùl-wɛ*	*lè-tti-dù-dùl-bɛ*	'bundle of sticks'
èkkpi-ttɔ	*èkkpi-ttɔ-ttɔ-wɛ*	*èkkpi-ttɔ-ttɔ-bɛ*	'umbrella'

2.1.2 Adj + N

Another category of root compounds involves the adjective plus noun construction. In phrases, the adjective regularly occurs after the noun, while it appears before the noun in these compounds. Adjectives typically appear with a prefix, often of shape V, as seen in (6). This type of compound sometimes exhibits the pattern seen for N1 + N2 compounds, where the noun prefix is deleted. However, in other cases both prefixes are retained, as seen in (6d). In (6b), the compound contains two adjectives, and an irregular process affects the head noun.

(6)　a.　*ètà + ekkpón*　　　→　*ètà-kkpon*　　'world'
　　　　　big　land

　　　b.　*ètà + ála +gwànɔ*　→　*ètà-là-gwà*　'woman'
　　　　　old　a.bit　female

　　　c.　*ètà + gwànɔ*　　　→　*ètà-gwànɔ*　'old woman'
　　　　　old　female

　　　d.　*èkkà + èdì*　　　　→　*èkkà-edì*　　'truth'
　　　　　real　speech

2.2　Leggbó Synthetic Compounds and Related Formations

2.2.1　Agentive Prefix + V + N

This set of compounds is derived from the nominalization of verb phrases. They consist of a verb followed by a noun, with an initial prefix, and most of them are agentive. The prefix ɛ-/e- is attached before the first component of the compound, the verb. In this type of compound the noun, the second component of the compound, retains its own prefix. There are no tonal changes, but the agentive marker bears a low tone.

(7)　a.　*tto*　　　+　*lìbbol*　→　*è-tto-lìbbol*　　'cry baby'
　　　　　cry　　　　　crying

　　　b.　*kwɔlɔ*　+　*èdì*　　→　*è-kwɔlɔ-èdì*　'preacher'
　　　　　preach　　　speech

　　　c.　*ttùì*　　+　*àtɛèmì*　→　*è-ttùì-àtɛèmì*　'farmer'
　　　　　cultivate　　farm

　　　d.　*dzi*　　　+　*lídzil*　→　*e-dzi-lídzil*　'glutton'
　　　　　eat　　　　　food

　　　e.　*tʃɔ*　　　+　*èdì*　　→　*è-tʃɔ-èdì*　　'talkative person'
　　　　　talk.a.lot　speech

2.2.2　N1 *of* N2

N1 *of* N2 compounds are comprised of two nouns, and each constituent can switch its order to change the meaning of the compound. But with a particular reading, it can be said to be left-headed, as it is the left-hand element that determines what kind of object is being described (and this is the main reason they are grouped here with the synthetic compounds). Formally, they correspond to an associative construction that is also used to express a possessive relationship. The associative marker *awɔ a* 'that of' appears between the two nouns, and this marker is prone to reduction, leading to at least five other variants: *awɔa ~ awaa ~ awɔ ~ aw ~ aa ~ a*.

It has been argued that compounds in some languages contain shrunken link elements that have reduced over time but which correspond historically to 'and'. It is also commonly stated that compounds are a combination of words. But a compound may contain phrasal elements, corresponding to units constructed by syntax. Lieber & Scalise (2006: 10) give the English examples *over-the-fence gossip* and *God-is-dead theology*, showing examples of compounds which involve a phrase and a sentence respectively. Along these lines, we argue that constructions based on the associative construction in Leggbó can be considered compounds, and these constructions are widespread in the language.

Examples of N1 *of* N2 compounds can be seen in (8).

(8) a. *ètèn* + *awɔ* + *ekkpón* → *ètèn-ekkpón* 'animal'
         animal   of   land

     b. *ètèn* + *awɔ* + *àsi* → *ètèn-así* 'fish'
         animal   of   water

     c. *lìzol* + *awɔ* + *èttɔ* → *lìzol-εttɔ́* 'house bird'
         bird   of   house

     d. *èttɔ* + *awɔ* + *lìzol* → *èttɔ-lizól* 'nest'
         house   of   bird

An interesting feature to note with regard to the tonal phenomena associated with this type of compound is that they all end in a MH. While this is not surprising in the case of (8a), even when the second noun has an underlying LM pattern, it surfaces in the compound as MH.

Like the agentive compounds in Section 2.2.1, N1 *of* N2 compounds are also left-headed. Thus *εttɔ-lizól* "house bird" refers to the type of house which belongs to a bird, a 'nest', while *ètèn-así* "animal water" refers to the type of animal which lives in the water, a 'fish'.

In some cases, two N1 *of* N2 compounds can be found using the same nouns, but in the opposite order. For example, beside *εttɔ-lizól* 'nest', there is also *lìzol-εttɔ́*, meaning 'house bird'. In other words, either of the two nouns could be head of the compound, depending on the meaning.

Morphological processes such as reduplication affect the head of the compound. A little bird's house/nest will be *εttɔ-ttɔ-wε lizol*, while a little house bird will be *lizo-zo-wε εttɔ*, in line with the data in (4) and (5), where the right component of the compound was morphologically active. (The *wε* in these forms is a diminutive marker.) This is another trait that compounds of this class share with the other compound structures classified as synthetic here—the compounds are left-headed.

2.2.3 V + N

The final group of compounds consist of a verb followed by a noun, and produce new verbs. The verb, which is the left constituent, carries the argument, and therefore these verb compounds can be said to be left-headed. Examples are given in (9).

(9) a. *yèí*   + *gèkkwe*   → *yei-gèkkwe*   'rest'
         reduce   strength

     b. *dzi*   + *gìta*   → *dzi-gìta*   'bewitch'
         eat   witchcraft

     c. *dzo*   + *ètɛɛm*   → *dzo-ètɛɛm*   'hope'
         keep   heart

     d. *zɔlɔ*   + *àsi*   → *zɔlɔ-àsi*   'baptize'
         pour   water

     e. *bba*   + *ddèn*   → *bba-ddèn*   'to ignore'
         block   eye

3 Conclusion

The data we have presented so far on Leggbó compounding show that compounds in the language can be classified into two groups: root compounds and synthetic compounds. Root compounds exhibit lexical integrity such that morphological processes like reduplication cannot split their constituents. That is, they behave like a single domain in reduplication. This class is made up of compounds with the form Noun + Noun and Adjective + Noun. Their lexical status can be represented as in (10).

(10) a.

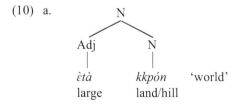

                      N
                    /   \
                 Adj   N
                  | |
                 ètà   *kkpón*   'world'
                 large   land/hill

b.

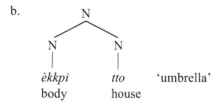

èkkpi   tto   'umbrella'
body   house

Following Spencer's (1991) classification of root and synthetic compounds, we have seen that the Leggbó root compounds are right-headed, and the right constituents are more morphologically active. The synthetic compounds on the other hand, are phrasal in nature and they have compositional meaning, which allows them to interact with morphological processes independently. They have as many domains as there are conjoined elements. Unlike the root compounds, they are left-headed. This class of compounds is made up of Agentive prefix + V + N, N1 *of* N2, and V + N constructions. Their phrasal status can be represented as in (11).

(11) a.

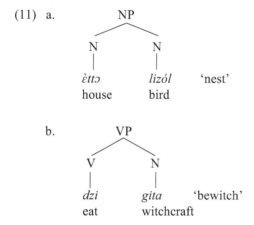

èttɔ   lizól   'nest'
house   bird

b.

V   N

dzi   gita   'bewitch'
eat   witchcraft

Leggbó compounds, therefore, belong to both the lexical and the syntactic domains. A lexical argument draws mainly from the facts of creating new vocabulary items in Leggbó, while a syntactic argument draws on the "headship" of the internal constituents across varying parameters. This study is only a preliminary investigation, however, and the interface relations exhibited by Leggbó compounds merit further investigation.

References

Barnwell, K. G. 1969a. *A grammatical description of Mbembe (Adun dialect): A Cross River language.* London: University College London dissertation.

Barnwell, K. G. 1969b. The noun class system in Mbembe. *Journal of West African Languages* 6(1): 51–58.

Dimmendaal, G. T. 2000. Morphology. In B. Heine & D. Nurse (eds.), *African languages: An introduction*, 161–193. Cambridge: Cambridge University Press.

Fabb, N. 1999. Compounding. In A. Spencer & A. M. Zwicky (eds.), *Handbook of morphology*, 66–83. Oxford: Blackwell.

Faraclas, N. 1989. Cross River. In J. Bendor-Samuel (ed.), *The Niger-Congo languages: A classification and description of Africa's largest language family*, 377–399. Lanham, MD: University Press of America.

Guevara, E. & S. Scalise. 2008. Searching for universals in compounding. In S. Scalise, E. Magni & A. Bisetto (eds.), *Universals of language today*, 101–128. Dordrecht: Springer.

Hyman, L. M., H. Narrog, M. Paster & I. I. Udoh. 2002. Leggbo verb inflection: A semantic and phonological particle analysis. In J. Larson & M. Paster (eds.), *Proceedings of the twenty-eighth annual meeting of the Berkeley Linguistics Society: General session and parasession on field linguistics*, 399–410. Berkeley: Berkeley Linguistics Society.

Hyman, L. M. & I. I. Udoh. 2006. Relic noun class structure in Leggbo. *Studies in African Linguistics* Supplement 11: 75–99.

Iwara, A. U. 1982. *Phonology and grammar of Lokəə: A preliminary study.* London: School of Oriental and African Studies MA thesis.

Lieber, R. & S. Scalise. 2006. The Lexical Integrity Hypothesis in a new theoretical universe. *Lingue e linguaggio* 5(1): 7–32.

Spencer, A. 1991. *Morphological theory: An introduction to word structure in generative grammar.* Oxford: Blackwell.

17

Ejagham without Tense: Historical Implications for Proto-Bantoid

JOHN R. WATTERS

1   Introduction

Two major topics shape this study. One is the structure of the Ejagham verb system.[1] The other is the historic relationship between Ejagham, Bantu, and East Benue-Congo. At the center of both topics is the fact that Ejagham is a language without tense.

The first topic explored is the historical significance of this lack of tense relative to Bantu, Bantoid, and East Benue-Congo. Ejagham is an Ekoid Bantu language, one of seven subgroups within South Bantoid. South Bantoid then joins three other subgroups at its level to form Bantoid. Bantoid then joins with Cross River and a set of other languages to form East Benue-Congo (Williamson & Blench 2000, Schadeberg 2003). Significantly, the South Bantoid group also includes Bantu.

As a South Bantoid language, Ejagham is assumed to share a close genetic relationship with Bantu. This would involve sharing various features and innovations: lexical, phonological, morphological, and so on. Ejagham does bear a close relationship with Bantu when it comes to the lexicon and

---

[1] The primary research for this study was pursued under the University of Yaoundé from 1974–1975 and the Ministry of Scientific Research in Cameroon from 1975–1977 and various periods in the 1980s. Many people participated in the research, too many to list here. However, five key Ejagham people who were consulted in the research in significant ways were Patrick Etta Etta, Martin Obi Ata, Peter Tambe Nchinge, Emmanuel Ndip, and Ayamba Nkiri.

Revealing Structure.
Eugene Buckley, Thera Crane & Jeff Good (eds.).
Copyright © 2018, CSLI Publications.

the noun class system (see Watters 1980, 1981), but not in terms of the verb system. Tense is present in nearly all of Bantu, but Ejagham in contrast does not mark it. So the question is: Did Ejagham lose its tense marking, or did it never mark tense? Nurse (2008: 282–283) suggests that the Bantu languages likely started their development of tense categories some five thousand years ago, before they began migrating east and south from the Bantu homeland along the Cameroon and Nigeria border. Ejagham is found along this border today. So did the ancestral languages of Ejagham not participate in this innovation? Or was tense marking lost along the way? The answer appears to be that Ejagham may be part of a group of languages in the Cross/Manyu River Basin that did not participate in the innovation of tense.

The second topic explored is the structural significance of the Ejagham verbal system, where only aspect and mood are marked and tense is not marked. The focus is on the Eyumojok-Ndebaya subdialect of the Western Ejagham dialect.[2] This is explored in Sections 3–5.[3] The initial focus is on the basic categories and structure of the verb system. This involves identifying what would minimally be reflexes of Proto-South Bantoid verbal morphemes currently found in the Ejagham verb system. Given the basic, inherited structure and categories of the Ejagham verbal system, the question then is: Have these served to guide and possibly limit the development of more recent verbal categories? Or has the language been able to branch out to develop new verbal categories and structure outside the basic structure and categories it may have inherited? Does this branching out include the beginning development of tense? The answer is that Ejagham seems to have verbal material that could have been reinterpreted into tense categories, but this does not happen. The inherited structure has guided all innovation.

---

[2] Ejagham consists of three major dialects: Western Ejagham, Eastern Ejagham, and Southern Ejagham. Southern Ejagham is spoken in the Calabar area by 10,000–15,000 people. Eastern Ejagham is spoken entirely in Cameroon, to the west and southwest of Mamfe, by about 35,000 people. It consists of two subdialects. Western Ejagham is spoken mostly in Nigeria, to the northeast, east, and south of Ikom and also round Akampka, by some 60,000 speakers. It is also spoken by about 10,000–15,000 speakers in Cameroon in the Eyumojok-Ndebaya area. It consists of five or so dialects.

[3] It would be good to add two comments at the outset. The first comment is that what is presented here as the Ejagham verbal system is still a study in progress. More research is needed regarding the full semantic and pragmatic nature of the various categories marked in the system. But there is sufficient information to present its basic structure and categories. The second comment is that the core data point for this study is the Eyumojok-Ndebaya subdialect of the western dialect of Ejagham. Other dialects will be brought into the discussion as they are relevant, but the overall system that will be presented here is based on the speech forms of this particular variety.

2 Verb Systems: Divergence in Verbal Categories

Since Ejagham is shown through lexicostatistical studies, the lexicon, and its noun class system to share some type of common genetic origin with the Bantu languages, how does the comparison in verb systems inform us about this relationship?

Nurse (2003) notes three major features of Bantu verb systems. The first feature is that aspect provides the basic, stable set of categories across Bantu. This stable set includes standard aspects, namely, Perfective, Imperfective, Progressive, Habitual, Anterior (otherwise "Perfect", but see Nurse 2008: 154–155), and Persistive.

The second feature is that Bantu languages generally have an elaborate tense system that makes multiple time distinctions both in the past and the future. The tense categories and their morphological exponents show considerable variation across Bantu. Bantu languages have anywhere from one to five past tenses and one to three future tenses. It is not uncommon for a language to have more past distinctions than future ones.

The third feature is that most Bantu languages have a verb form which is used in discourse as the indicator of the main event line once a timeframe for the discourse or discourse episode is set. It is often a reduced form of the verb and could be labeled "Consecutive". With the Consecutive, the subjects of each clause in a sequence do not have to be coreferential. It is a form that does not occur independently of this discourse context, and the various past tense distinctions are often neutralized. Some languages even allow the Consecutive to have more than just a past reading.

Given these three features of Bantu verb systems, how does Ejagham compare? As for the first feature, Ejagham matches up well. It uses each of the categories noted: Perfective, Imperfective, Progressive, Habitual, Anterior, and Persistive. All but Persistive are expressed by morphological exponents or forms that appear to have a deep historical dimension. This depth is indicated by the fact that tone has become the main exponent distinguishing these categories while the original segmental material has been lost (Watters 2012). The Persistive is expressed by a paratactic construction "subject-*still-be-present* subject-verb-HAB" similar to English *she is still writing* or more literally "she-is-still-present she-writes". The second verb is generally in the Habitual aspect. Is this paratactic construction an indicator that an older form became so reduced that it required this new construction? At this point there is no comparative evidence one way or the other. The aspectual categories will be presented in greater depth below.

As for the third feature (the second feature will be discussed below), Ejagham has the equivalent of the Consecutive. However, it is not a different or simplified form, and it does not seem to bear an etymological relationship with the Bantu consecutive. What the Consecutive contributes in other languages is fulfilled by the Perfective in Ejagham. Whether the discourse is a narrative of past events, a detailed process on how to build a house without any specific temporal context, or an exhortation to the children on how they should behave while their father is away within an irrealis context, the Perfective is the verb form that carries the discourse event line forward, linking one event or situation to the next within the discourse.

This brings us back to the second feature—an elaborate tense system. It is here that Ejagham diverges significantly from Bantu. Ejagham does not mark tense. There are no morphological exponents of time in the verb system. Instead, the temporal setting is set through adverbs or adverbial clauses or a shared understanding of the context between the speaker and hearer.

3   The Basic Ejagham Verbal Categories

If Ejagham inherited a tenseless verb system, the next question is how this feature influenced the innovation of more recent verbal categories in the language. Was there no verbal material that could have been reinterpreted as marking tense? To answer these questions it would be best to start with the basic categories, those with greater historical depth.

As discussed above, Ejagham does have the basic aspects found in Bantu and other South Bantoid languages. These are diagrammed in (1). In the Indicative mood are the Perfective, Imperfective, Progressive, Habitual/Concomitant and Anterior. In the Nonindicative mood, there is the Hortative/Subjunctive, Conditional, and Imperative (Watters 1981: 359–454).

(1)   Basic verbal categories

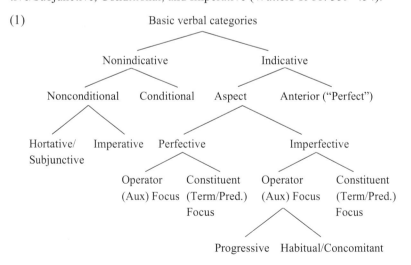

The Operator (Auxiliary) Focus and the Constituent (Term/Predicate) Focus categories are presented in Hyman & Watters (1984) for Ejagham and other languages of Africa. A more detailed presentation of the Ejagham focus categories is found in Watters (2010). An alternative to the Indicative vs. Nonindicative mood distinction is one presented in Watters (1985) using the mood distinctions Indicative vs. Conditional vs. Optative. The Optative would subdivide into the Hortative/Subjunctive and the Imperative.

The morphological structure of the verb follows the schema in (2). The obligatory elements in the fully inflected verb are the person-number subject prefix (PSN) and the root. The one exception is the Imperative form that, as might be expected, is not marked with the person-number subject prefix. Optional slots include a preroot position and a postroot position to mark aspect and mood as well as affirmative and negative polarity. The forms of the preroot position include tonal morphemes of the Perfective, Anterior, Conditional, and Hortative that are manifested only by tone patterns, as well as the segmentally realized Progressive *kí-*. Various negative morphemes also occur in this position. The forms in the postroot position include the Imperfective *-ag* and the (harmonizing) Perfective Constituent Focus suffix *-í`*. The Repetitive (REP) is another preverbal element. It will be presented later.

(2)   VERB

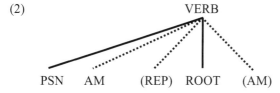

PSN   AM   (REP)   ROOT   (AM)

Examples of the Indicative categories are given in (3), with both affirmative and negative forms.[4] They are given in the third person plural form using only the verb *ràbhé* 'open' which is from the low tone class. In the Affirmative each of the categories is distinguished by a different form. In the Negative the categories formally reduce down to two: the Anterior ("Perfect") is grouped in the same category as the Perfective forms, both using the *ka-* negative prefix; while the Progressive, the Habitual/Concomitant, and the Imperfective Constituent Focus are in a second formal group, all using the *bho-* negative prefix.

---

[4] The Western Ejagham examples will usually be given using the orthographic form used in the written language. Note that the example uses the CVCV root *-ràbhé*. With such roots, when they are suffixed with a vowel-initial suffix, the final root vowel is deleted. For a fuller discussion, see Chapter 6 on the verb in Watters (1981).

(3)

	Affirmative	Negative
Anterior ("Perfect")	á-ràbhè	á-ká-ràbhé
	'they have opened'	'they have not opened'
Perfective Op Focus	á-rábhè	á-ká-ràbhé
	'they opened'	'they did not open'
Perfective Const Focus	á-rábh-'é	á-ká-ràbhé
	'they opened X'	'they did not open X'
Progressive	á-kí-ràbhé	á-bhó-ràbhé
	'they are opening'	'they are not opening'
Habitual/Concomitant	á-ràbh-á	á-bhó-ràbhé
	'they open'	'they do not open'
Imperf Const Focus	á-rábh-'á	á-bhó-ràbhé
	'they are opening X'	'they are not opening X'

The reduction of contrasts among the verbal categories in the Negative that is seen for the Indicative forms in (3) means that we could say that the structure of the Ejagham aspectual system in the Indicative mood is in fact a binary one, contrasting only Perfective and Imperfective, as displayed in (4), rather than Aspect vs. Anterior ("Perfect"), as in (1). The Perfective then consists of the Anterior and Focus-sensitive forms.

(4)

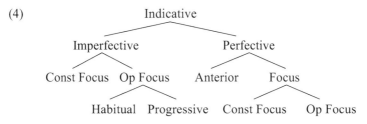

Examples of the basic Nonindicative categories are given in (5).

(5)

	Affirmative	Negative
Hortative/Subjunctive	á-rábh'é	á-kâ-ràbhè
	'they should open'	'they should not open'
Imperative	ràbhê	kà-ràbh'é
	'open!'	'do not open!'
Conditional	á-ràbhé	á-'ró-ràbhé
	'if they open'	'if they do not open'

The Negative form for the Hortative/Subjunctive and the Imperative both use the *ka-* negative prefix found also in the Perfective aspect above.

The difference between the Hortative/Subjunctive and the Imperative *ka-* is the tone: *kâ-* for the Hortative/Subjunctive and *kà'-* for the Imperative. The Negative Conditional uses an entirely different prefix, *ro-*.

4 Possible Reasons for the Lack of Tense

As seen, the major contrast with the system typical of Bantu is that Ejagham does not morphologically mark tense in the verb. Nurse (2008) notes that within Bantu there are also a few exceptions to the generalization that Bantu languages have tense. He points out that three such languages have been heavily influenced by neighboring Cushitic communities. This leaves us with the following questions: Did Ejagham lose its temporal distinctions, changing from a tense-marking language to an aspect-mood-only language through influence of its neighbors? Or has Ejagham always been an aspect-mood-only language? Gaining tense as a major category seems more common than losing tense, but the influence of neighbors like the Cushitic communities elsewhere in Bantu is important to note. At the same time, if Ejagham did lose tense, we would expect to find some residual forms or traces of tense, but none exist. The time depth in the case of Ejagham and Bantu is much greater than that of the Bantu and Cushitic contact. As a consequence, it is more problematic. In addition, today's neighbors are not necessarily yesterday's neighbors. So, where would we look first?

The first place to look would be to the other Ekoid languages. However, insufficient data is available at this time to compare. It will be assumed for now that Proto-Ekoid was also without tense.

The next stratum of neighbors consists of the other Bantoid languages besides Bantu. Watters (1989: 404–413) and Watters & Leroy (1989: 430, 432–438) provide a list of Bantoid language groups that need to be considered: Tivoid, Jarawan, Mbe, Mamfe (Nyang), Beboid, Wide Grassfields, Tikar, Ndemli, and Mbam. Of special interest here would be Mbe, Mamfe (Nyang), and Grassfields. The others would likely have had little or no early impact on the Ejagham verb system. For Mbe, there is insufficient data available at this point. However, for Grassfields languages, the tense system is robust (Watters 2003: 245–247). These languages use from two to five past tenses and two to five future tenses (see examples of such languages in Anderson 1979, 1983, Hyman 1980). These languages would only have encouraged the use of tense.

This leaves the closest geographic neighbors, the Mamfe (Nyang) languages to the east of Ejagham. Of the three Mamfe languages, data is only available for Denya. Abangma (1987: 10–27) states that "in Denya it is difficult to argue convincingly for tense". He initially proposes a distinction between "past" and "nonpast"; however, the data he presents lead him to note that the distinction is really between Perfective and Imperfective. This is not surprising since in minimally marked contexts a Perfective form will be read or interpreted as past tense and an Imperfective form as present tense. Only through investigating various temporal contexts can the lack of tense and the role of aspect be most clearly seen. So essentially, Mamfe (Nyang) Bantu is similar to Ejagham. These neighboring Bantoid languages are without tense.

This finding raises the issue of a larger areal stratum. Within the region of the upper Cross/Manyu River Basin, Ekoid and Mamfe Bantu do not mark tense.[5] Furthermore, it is likely that Proto-Ekoid (Watters 2001: 57–59) speakers lived around what is today Ikom, Nigeria, perhaps 600 to 1000 years ago. Being in the Ikom area, speakers of Proto-Ekoid as well as Proto-Ejagham would most likely have been in contact with speakers of Upper Cross River languages. The likely Upper Cross River languages (Faraclas 1989: 380–385) in the Ikom region would have been the Ikom-speaking people, the Mbembe, and those along the Cross River such as the Loko and Leggbo. It is here that the work of Hyman et al. (2002) is telling. As the authors insist at the outset of their study, "a most striking first fact about Leggbo is that it does not distinguish tense" (Hyman et al. 2002: 399). If this is true of other Upper Cross River languages, it could point to an areal phenomenon for the entire upper Cross/Manyu River Basin involving East Benue-Congo languages sharing the same region. They would have formed a set of languages that were without tense a millennium or multiple millennia before.

A helpful intervention at this point comes from Nurse:

Most Niger-Congo languages can be analysed in terms of aspect alone, having no tense distinctions. They show a classic basic division between perfective and imperfective, with additional aspects. (Nurse 2008: 281)

He goes on to write:

It would seem, assuming the linguistic ancestors of these three communities [Narrow Bantu, Grassfields, and Lower Cross, all with tense], and maybe others, were in the same area of Cameroon and SE Nigeria when the early Bantu moved out, that this [is] the area where tense as a phenomenon started. Whether it started in one of them and spread to the others later, or whether it was an innovation shared at some level of the Bantoid-Cross River tree cannot be determined until we know more of the distribution and nature of tense in Grassfields and southeastern Nigeria ... The in-

---

[5] In Nigeria, the river is named the Cross River, running from the border with Cameroon to its estuary into the Atlantic Ocean. In Cameroon, the river is named the Manyu River from its origin in the mountains of west Cameroon to the border with Nigeria.

novation of multiple tense distinctions characterizes all Bantu languages, but not in the same way. This suggests that once tense distinctions had developed while early Bantu communities and their languages were still in western Cameroon and eastern Nigeria, some five millennia ago, they were then carried and elaborated as communities moved east and south. (Nurse 2008: 282–283)

One implication of these statements is that it is likely that these languages of the upper Cross/Manyu River Basin never lost tense. That is because they never had tense. They form a far eastern remnant of the Niger-Congo aspect-only feature. Unlike other languages in the western Cameroon and eastern Nigeria region such as Bantu, Grassfields, and the Lower Cross River languages, they were not in significant contact with the incipient tense systems in their region five millennia ago, and, as a result, they did not share in this innovation within the larger Bantoid subgroup. This may be because they had already isolated themselves up the Cross/Manyu River Basin and below the steep escarpment on western side of the Bamboutos Mountains in Cameroon. This location could easily separate them from most of the Bantoid languages that began developing tense forms.

At the same time, if newly forming Bantu languages were developing tense forms 5000 years ago along the Nigeria-Cameroon borderland, then the time depth for the languages in the Cross River Basin is far greater than Proto-Ekoid, Proto-Mamfe, or Proto-Upper Cross River. It would have been the ancestors of these proto-languages that were present with the Proto-Bantu dialects and speech forms in the Nigeria-Cameroon borderland.

5   The Origin of the Ejagham Verbal Affixes

At this point it would be important to distinguish those affixes which may have originated from a greater time depth and may be shared with Bantu, South Bantoid, and beyond, and those which have been developed more recently (see Watters 1981: 515–522, 538–541). The ultimate goal is to see how the inherited basic structure of the Ejagham verb system has influenced the development of these more recent innovations. The focus is on the affixes that occur in the AM slots in the schema in (2). Two prefixes and two suffixes are probably inherited from a Proto–South Bantoid era.

The set of older affixes includes the Negative prefix *ka-* that appears as the Negative Perfective and Anterior *kà-*, the Negative Hortative/Subjunctive *kâ-*, and the Negative Imperative *kà´-*. These forms probably derive from a Proto-Bantoid form that Meeussen (1967: 114) recognizes as present in Proto-Bantu, and which he reconstructs as *kà´*. Nurse (2008: 240–246) provides evidence for its distribution and occurrence in Bantu. Its distribution within non-Bantu Bantoid still needs to be determined.

The Progressive prefix *kí*- also probably derives from Proto-Bantoid and is recognized by Meeussen (1967: 109) as likely Proto-Bantu. He reconstructs it as a verbal meaning 'still' in its positive sense and 'no more' in its negative sense. He labels it the "perstitive", a label which Nurse (2008: 145) maintains (as "persistive"). Again, the distribution of *kí*- or its corresponding forms within non-Bantu Bantoid still needs to be determined.

The suffix for the Imperfective Constituent Focus and the Habitual/Concomitant *-ág* likely relates to the possible Proto-Bantu Pre-final element *-ag-* meaning "aspect:imperfective" or "repetitive" or "habitual", which all fit well semantically with the Ejagham use. Even though Ejagham manifests only the consonant *g* as the suffix with CV roots and only the vowel *a* with all other roots, the form and meaning correlation is striking.

Finally, the Perfective Constituent Focus suffix *-ì* might relate to the Final verb element *-ìde* meaning "past" or "perfective" in Meeussen (1967: 110). Nurse (2008) also accepts this correspondence.

What remains are the negative prefixes *bhó*- and *ró*-, as well as the Repetitive (which will be seen below). The Negative Imperfective prefix *bhó*- and the Negative Conditional prefix *ró*- are more recently developed forms that may only date back to Proto-Ejagham or even more recently, especially in the case of *bhó*- since there are five variant forms scattered throughout Ejagham. Nurse notes that, for the Bantu languages:

> A major source of innovation is the constant emergence of forms based on auxiliaries or modals and a main verb which is either in the infinitive or in an inflected form. (Nurse 2003: 93)

This is the case in Ejagham. Certain auxiliary verbs in Ejagham are followed by the class 5 infinitive while others are followed by the class 14 gerund (Watters 1981: 243–251). For the negative prefixes *bhó*- and *ró*-, the main verb used the class 14 gerund prefix *ò-* as its prefix. Thus, for the Negative Imperfective prefix *bhó*-, as depicted in (6), the process went from the original periphrastic construction on the left to the final inflected construction on the right.

(6) *á-bhé''*   *ò-rɔbhé*   →   *á-bhó`-rɔbhé*
     they-HORT:escape 14-opening   they-NEG:IPFV-open
     'they should escape from opening'   'they are not opening'

The auxiliary verb was likely the verb *bhĕ* 'to escape' in the Hortative form. The Hortative and the semantic features of 'escape' developed into a Negative Imperfective prefix (Watters 1981: 519): "they should-be-escaping opening" becoming "they should-not-be opening", which, in turn, became "they are-not opening". For the Negative Conditional the same process took place. In this case the auxiliary verb was probably *rĕ* 'to stop'.

(7) á-rĕ   ò-rɔ̀bhé   →   á-rǒ`-rɔ̀bhé
     they-COND:stop   14-opening   they-NEG:COND-open
     'if they stop opening'   'if they do not open'

A third inflection form that derived from the same construction type is the Repetitive, the final preroot prefix REP in the verb schema (2). The Repetitive (Watters 1981: 404–422) derives from the verb root *kpĕ* 'to add'. What is captured is the iterative meaning of a situation repeating itself again.

(8) á-kpê   ò-rɔ̀bhé   →   á-kpô-rɔ̀bhé
     they-PFV:add   14-opening   they-PFV:add-open
     'they add (again) opening'   'they opened again'

Both forms are attested today. The inflected, prefixed form on the right is the form used in Western Ejagham, while in Southern Ejagham both the periphrastic form on the left and the inflected form on the right serve as acceptable variants. In Eastern Ejagham the inflectional prefix is *kpê*, as in *á-kpê-wùlé* 'they sold again'.

6 Conclusion

Ejagham does not mark tense. This may be evidence that the Cross/Manyu River Basin was an area that did not participate in the development of tense categories that seems to have been actively participated in by the other South Bantoid groups five millennia ago. In addition, the lack of tense development not only characterized the Ekoid and Mamfe Bantoid groups but also the Upper Cross River group within the same river basin. These tense-less languages in this geographic area probably just maintained what they had inherited from Proto–Niger-Congo.

On the question of innovations, Ejagham has shown no tendencies of developing tense categories. All the innovations that have developed in Ejagham fit within the basic inherited system of aspects and moods, each with their own tonal history and characteristics. Even though it would have been possible for Ejagham to reinterpret its inherited forms as tense categories, there do not seem to have been any attempts to do so.

References

Abangma, S. N. 1987. *Modes in Dényá discourse*. Dallas: SIL International.

Anderson, S. C. 1979. Verb structure in Aghem. In L. M. Hyman (ed.), *Aghem grammatical structure: With special reference to noun classes, tense-aspect and focus marking* (Southern California Occasional Papers in Linguistics 7), 73–136. Los Angeles: Department of Linguistics, University of Southern California.

Anderson, S. C. 1983. *Tone and morpheme rules in Bamileke-Ngyemboon*. Los Angeles: University of Southern California dissertation.

Faraclas, N. 1989. Cross River. In J. Bendor-Samuel (ed.), *The Niger-Congo languages: A classification and description of Africa's largest language family*, 377–399. Lanham, MD: University Press of America.

Hyman, L. M. 1980. Relative time reference in the Bamileke tense system. *Studies in African Linguistics* 11: 227–258.

Hyman, L. M., H. Narrog, M. Paster & I. I. Udoh. 2002. Leggbo verb inflection: A semantic and phonological particle analysis. In J. Larson & M. Paster (eds.), *Proceedings of the twenty-eighth annual meeting of the Berkeley Linguistics Society: General session and parasession on field linguistics*, 399–410. Berkeley: Berkeley Linguistics Society.

Hyman, L. M. & J. R. Watters. 1984. Auxiliary focus. *Studies in African Linguistics* 15: 233–273.

Meeussen, A. E. 1967. Bantu grammatical reconstructions. *Africana Linguistica* 3: 79–121.

Nurse, D. 2003. Aspect and tense in Bantu languages. In D. Nurse & G. Philippson (eds.), *The Bantu languages*, 90–102. London: Routledge.

Nurse, D. 2008. *Tense and aspect in Bantu*. Oxford: Oxford University Press.

Schadeberg, T. C. 2003. Historical linguistics. In D. Nurse & G. Philippson (eds.), *The Bantu languages*, 143–163. London: Routledge.

Watters, J. R. 1980. The Ejagham noun class system: Ekoid Bantu revisited. In L. M. Hyman (ed.), *Noun classes in the Grassfields Bantu borderland*, 99–137. Los Angeles: Department of Linguistics, University of Southern California.

Watters, J. R. 1981. *A phonology and morphology of Ejagham*. Los Angeles: University of California dissertation.

Watters, J. R. 1985. The place of morphology in Functional Grammar: The case of the Ejagham verb system. In A. M. Bolkestein, C. de Groot & J. L. Mackenzie (eds.), *Predicates and terms in Functional Grammar*, 85–104. Dordrecht: Foris.

Watters, J. R. 1989. Bantoid overview. In J. Bendor-Samuel (ed.), *The Niger-Congo languages*, 401–420. Lanham, MD: University Press of America.

Watters, J. R. 2001. Some phonological characteristics of Ejagham (Etung), an Ekoid Bantu language of Cameroon and Nigeria. In N. M. Mutaka & S. B. Chumbow (eds.), *Research mate in African linguistics—Focus on Cameroon: A fieldworker's tool for deciphering the stories Cameroonian languages have to tell*, 55–78. Cologne: Rüdiger Köppe.

Watters, J. R. 2003. Grassfields Bantu. In D. Nurse & G. Philippson (eds.), *The Bantu languages*, 225–256. London: Routledge.

Watters, J. R. 2010. Focus and the Ejagham verb system. In I. Fiedler & A. Schwarz (eds.), *The Expression of information structure: A documentation of its diversity across Africa*, 349–376. Amsterdam: Benjamins.

Watters, J. R. 2012. Tone in western Ejagham (Etung): Lexical tone on the "minimal" verb forms. In M. Brenzinger & A.-M. Fehn (eds.), *Proceedings of the 6th World Congress of African Linguistics, Cologne, 17–21 August 2009*, 309–319. Cologne: Rüdiger Köppe.

Watters, J. R. & J. Leroy. 1989. Southern Bantoid. In J. Bendor-Samuel (ed.), *The Niger-Congo languages*, 430–449. Lanham, MD: University Press of America.

Williamson, K. & R. Blench. 2000. Niger-Congo. In B. Heine & D. Nurse (eds.), *African languages: An introduction*, 1–41. Cambridge: Cambridge University Press.

Abbreviations

AM	Aspect or mood marker
COND	Conditional
Const	Constituent
HORT	Hortative
Imperf, IPFV	Imperfective
HAB	Habitual
NEG	Negative
Op	Operator
PFV	Perfective
PSN	Person-number subject prefix
REP	Repetitive

18

Laryngeal Schizophrenia in Washo Resonants

ALAN C. L. YU

1 Introduction

Resonants in Washo—a highly endangered North American language spoken in the area around Lake Tahoe in California and Nevada—have three possible laryngeal settings: glottalized, voiceless (breathy) and modal (see Table 1).[1] Laryngealized (i.e. glottalized or voiceless) resonants are complex consonants involving both supralaryngeal and laryngeal articulations. A glottalized resonant such as [m̰], for example, involves three total articulations. Two of these are oral, namely closure at the lips and lowering of the velum. The third is a sub-oral articulation resulting in creaky voice or a glottal constriction resulting in complete glottal closure. Traditional phonemic analyses (Jacobsen 1964, 1996) assume that voiced and voiceless resonants are contrastive in the language while phonetic glottalized resonants (nasals and approximants) are surface realization of glottal stop plus sonorant sequences. Obstruents, on the other hand, are assumed to exhibit a full three-way laryngeal contrast, although plain obstruents are generally voiced intervocalically, while only the plain series is observed in word-final and preconsonantal positions.[2]

[1] This research would not be possible without the generous support of the Washo elders and their patience. I thank them for sharing their knowledge of the language with me. Portions of this work were supported by NSF Grant #0553675.
[2] The phonemic inventory of Washo according to Jacobsen (1964) excludes the segments in parentheses. Plain consonants are generally voiceless unaspirated, although they are often realized with voicing throughout the stop closure when surrounded by sonorants. Prevoicing may also be observed in word-initial positions but is highly variable. The alveolar plain stop is realized as a flap intervocalically. The sound [s] in one dialect (the variant represented here) corresponds

Revealing Structure.
Eugene Buckley, Thera Crane & Jeff Good (eds.).
Copyright © 2018, CSLI Publications.

plain	p/b	t/d	(ts/dz)	k/g	ʔ
plain		s	ʃ		h
aspirated	pʰ	tʰ		kʰ	
glottalized	p'	t'	ts'	k'	
modal	m	n		ŋ	
voiceless	m̥	n̥		ŋ̥	
glottalized	(m̓	n̓		ŋ̓)	
modal	w	l	j		
voiceless	w̥	l̥	j̥		
glottalized	(w̓	l̓	j̓)		

Table 1. Phonetic inventory of Washo

This paper reevaluates the treatment of laryngealized resonants in Washo in light of recent findings in Washo phonetics and phonology as well as phonological theory more generally. We review phonological and morphophonological evidence in support of an analysis that recognizes a phonemic glottalized sonorant series in Washo.

The structure of this paper is as follows: We begin with a description of the distribution and phonetic realization of the different resonant types in Section 2. The previous analysis of laryngealized resonants is described in Section 3. Arguments for a unitary segment analysis across the obstruent and resonant series are given in Section 4. Complications for the unitary segment analysis are discussed and treated in Section 5. The conclusion appears in Section 6.

2   Resonants and their Distribution

Resonants in Washo include nasals, liquids and glides. Modal voiced resonants may occur in word-initial (1a), intervocalic (1b), word-final (1c), and preconsonantal (1d) positions.

---

to [θ] in the other. For the sake of uniformity, plain stops are generally transcribed below as plain unaspirated in the Washo examples. Voiced variants are shown only when spectrographic evidence is given, as in the case of Figure 4.

(1) Distribution of modal voiced resonants

a. Word-initial

'maːku	'sister's child'
'ŋawŋaŋ	'child'
'napˈːaʔ	'bad'
'lakˈːaʔ	'one'
'waːʃiw	'Washo'
'julːiji	'he's dead'

b. Intervocalic

'tsˈimːel	'beard'
'taːŋal	'house'
't'anːu	'human'
'tilːek	'duck'
'jewːeʃ	'long'
't'iːjeliʔ	'big'

c. Word-final

taw'jatsˈːim	'smoke'
'pojːoŋ	'pine needle'
'ʔutenkʰin	'nighttime'
'tsˈiːpel	'louse'
'p'isːew	'ear'

d. Preconsonantal

tim'laːjaʔ	'my wife'
'tʰaŋlel	'west'
'nent'uʃu	'old woman'
'helmeʔ	'three'
'p'ewlel	'east'

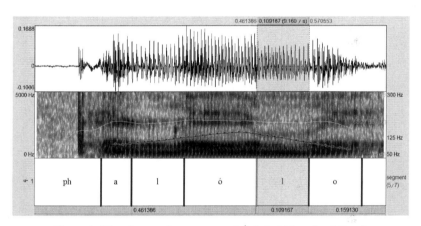

Figure 1. Waveform and spectrogram [pʰaˈlolːo] 'there is a blister'

Voiceless resonants (m̥, n̥, ŋ̊, j̊, l̥, w̥) occur in prevocalic positions and never in coda positions, as in (2). Phonetically, voiceless resonants are never fully voiceless. Consider the resonants in Figures 1 and 2. Figure 1 illustrates the typical acoustic realization of modal voiced liquids in Washo. The light thin line in the spectrogram indicates intensity and the thick dotted line f_0. The word [pʰaˈlolːo] 'there is a blister' contains two laterals, one in pretonic and the other in posttonic position. The liquids show regular periodicity throughout the duration of the modal resonant, with sustained intensity and steady and smooth f_0 movement.[3] In contrast, a voiceless resonant typically begins

---

[3] For ease of comparison, in this and all subsequent figures, the lexical item used, whenever possible, will contain more than one instance of the resonant type of interest. The targeted posttonic

with a period of breathiness (approximately the first 30–50% of the segment), with concomitant reduction in intensity and pitch, and is followed by the resumption of modal voicing for the rest of its duration (see Figure 2). To reflect the phasing relationship between laryngeal configurations, voiceless resonants will be represented from here on with a superscripted aspiration symbol before their corresponding modal resonant symbol, rather than with the voicelessness diacritic (e.g. ʰm vs. m̥). Auditorily and acoustically, voiceless resonants are clearest (with robust and audible breathiness) in pretonic position; the period of breathiness is often weak elsewhere, especially after a long stressed vowel.

(2)   Distribution of voiceless resonants

Word-initial

ˈʰmuʔuʃi	'he's running'
ˈʰleːʔi	'I am'
ˈʰwaːʔi	'he's the one who's doing it'
ˈʰjaːmi	'that's what he's talking about'

Intervocalic

tiˈʰmaːʃ	'my face'
ˈmeːʰlu	'old man'
tiˈʰwaːʔi	'I'm the one who's doing it'
tiˈʰjaːmi	'that's what I'm talking about'

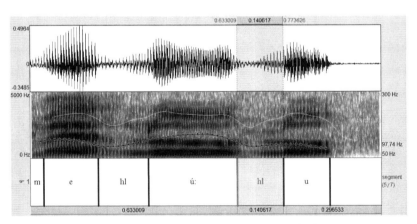

Figure 2. Waveform and spectrogram for the word [meˈʰluːʰlu] 'old men'

While voiceless resonants can appear postvocalically, they are found only after a long stressed vowel or a short unstressed one (3). Voiceless resonants

---

resonant is always highlighted. Segmentation and phonetic transcription is given at the bottom of each spectrogram.

never appear after a long unstressed vowel since long vowels are only found in stressed positions. We shall return to the restriction against voiceless resonants after a short unstressed vowel in Section 5.2.

(3)   Distribution of intervocalic voiceless resonants

   After short vowel
   ti'ʰmaːʃ   'my face'
   ti'ʰwaːʔi   'I'm the one who's doing it'

   After long vowel
   'meːʰlu   'old man'
   't'aːʰjaŋi   'he's hunting'

Glottalized resonants (m̓, n̓, ŋ̓, l̓, j̓, w̓) are found word-initially, intervocalically, word-finally, and in preconsonantal positions (4). However, not all possible glottalized resonants are attested in word-final and preconsonantal positions. The majority of preconsonantal glottalized resonants consist of *Vjʔ* and *Vlʔ* sequences. The *Vjʔ* sequence is often derived from the root *-ájʔ* 'away, out of the way, discarded'. (The reason why the forms in (4a) and (4b) are transcribed as preglottalized, while those in (4c) and (4d) are transcribed as post-glottalized, will be discussed immediately below.)

(4)   Distribution of glottalized resonants 1

a.	Word-initial		b.	Intervocalic
	'ʔmiːkiji	'he sees you'		*'ŋaʔmiŋ* 'baby'
	'ʔnuk'ːupi	'it's no good'		*ta'ʔmoʔmoʔ* 'woman'
	'ʔŋaŋːaʔ	'pillow'		*pʰa'ʔloʔlo* 'butterfly'
c.	Word-final		d.	Preconsonantal
	'palʔ	'cheek'		*tikum'jojʔli* 'I am tired'
	ti'kojʔ	'my father'		*kit'p'ajʔla* 'on his cheek'
	ka'hajʔ	'throw it away!'		*ti'jajʔli* 'I cut it'

Phonetically, glottalized resonants have different realizations depending on their location within the word. Word-initially and intervocalically, glottalized resonants show preglottalization, which can be realized, albeit rarely, with a full glottal stop or, more commonly, with creakiness during the initial portion of the resonant and, in the case of medial resonants, the end portion of the preceding vowel or sonorant if such a segment is present. Glottalization is strongest in posttonic positions, as evidenced by the different acoustic realizations of the pretonic and posttonic glottalized resonants in Figure 3. That is, glottalization is generally very weak in pretonic positions (e.g. slight drop in intensity and f_0) and is often undetectable; robust creakiness is observed in the posttonic resonant, as evidenced by the sudden drop in intensity and irregularity in the glottal pulse intervals and f_0 realization. In word-final

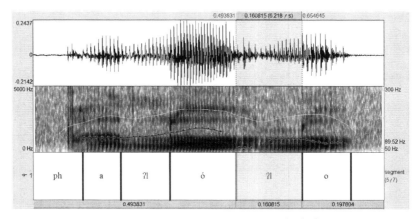

Figure 3. Waveform and spectrogram for the word [pʰaˈʔloˈʔlːo] 'butterfly'

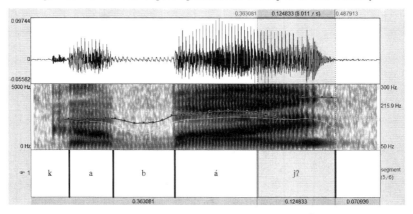

Figure 4. Waveform and spectrogram for the word [kaˈbajˀ] 'take it off'

(Figure 4) and preconsonantal (Figure 5) posttonic positions, these resonants are realized with post-glottalization, which generally means there is strong creakiness during the later portion of the resonant.[4] Word-final and preconsonantal glottalized resonants are not found after an unstressed vowel. This type of variable glottalization in resonants has been reported in a variety of languages, such as Yowlumne (Plauché et al. 1998) and Kwak'wala (Howe & Pulleyblank 2001). The difference in phasing relationship between glottalization and the resonant depending on the position of the resonants has been argued to be a consequence of perceptual optimization (Silverman 1997, but see Howe & Pulleyblank 2001). To indicate this difference in pre- and post-glottalization, the Washo examples from (4) and onward are transcribed with

---

[4] Glide segmentation is notoriously difficult and given in Figure 4 only for general guidance.

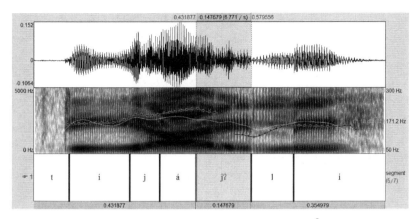

Figure 5. Waveform and spectrogram for the word [tiˈjajˀli] 'I cut it'

the superscripted glottal stop notation (i.e. ^{ˀ}R or $R^{ˀ}$), instead of the $R̥$ notation shown in Table 1.

3 Previous Analysis

The previous analysis of Washo phonology advocates a distinct treatment for voiceless and glottalized resonants (Jacobsen 1964, 1996). Phonemically, glottalized resonants are treated as sequences of glottal stop and modal resonant while voiceless resonants are seen as underlyingly unitary segments. The main argument for this diverging treatment comes from the issue of contrast. Jacobsen (1964: 78) argues that "[i]t is not possible to analyze the voiceless resonants as clusters of voiced resonants either preceded or followed by /h/, as such clusters also occur in contrast to the voiceless resonants".

In the same vein, Jacobsen (1964) rejects the unitary segment analysis for glottalized resonants based on the observation that there is no contrast between glottalized resonants (- ^{ˀ}R-) and clusters of a glottal stop followed by a voiced resonant (- $ʔR$-).[5] Glottal stops, which are found initially (5a)[6] and finally (5b), may also appear before (5c) and after obstruents (5d), in contrast to ejectives ([ˈt'apˈːil] 'its tail', [ˈpikˈːus] 'cradle basket'), which do not appear

---

[5] We return to the issue of contrast between glottalized resonants and glottal stop + resonant sequences in Section 5.3.

[6] Word-initial glottal stops in Washo have two origins. All words begin with a consonant in Washo. Underlyingly vowel-initial words are realized with a glottal stop when no consonantal prefix is attached. There are, however, roots that begin with an underlying initial glottal stop. The existence of underlying root-initial glottal stop is evidenced in prefixal allomorph selection. For example, the first-person pronominal prefix has two allomorphs, *ti-* and *l-*. Underlying vowel-initial roots take the *l-* variant (/aʃːaŋ/ 'to bleed' → [ˈʔaʃːaŋi] 'he's bleeding', [ˈlaʃːaŋi] 'I am bleeding'), while roots that begin with a consonant, including those beginning with a glottal stop, take the *ti-* variant (/jaliʔ/ 'stand' → [tiˈjalːiʔi] 'I am standing'; /ʔaːka/ → [tiˈʔaːkaji] 'I am scraping (paint)').

before another consonant. Jacobsen (1964) found no evidence that glottalized resonants could contrast with clusters of a glottal stop followed by a voiced resonant.

(5)   Distribution of glottal stop

 a. Word-initial
  ˈʔajːis 'antelope'
  ˈʔoːkal 'mountain sheep'

 b. Word-final
  ˈtimːeʔ 'water'
  ˈtsʼalːiʔ 'cottontail rabbit'

 c. Preconsonantal
  taˈlaʔka 'on the mountain'
  ˈmaʔka 'on the wood'

 d. Postconsonantal
  kitˈʔiːsa 'his older sister'
  kitˈʔaːtʼu 'his older brother'

Considerations of contrastivity aside (we shall revisit this issue in Section 6), there is ample evidence in support of a uniform treatment of voiceless and glottalized resonants in Washo. This is the topic of the next section.

4 A Unified Treatment of Laryngealized Resonants

4.1 Two Strands of Evidence

In this section, we argue for a unified treatment of laryngealized resonants. In particular, we contend that glottalized resonants, like voiceless resonants, are best viewed as unitary segments, based on distributional and morphophonological evidence.

4.2 Distributional Evidence

Washo has no word-initial clusters, at least in the native lexicon. As Jacobsen (1964: 117) noted, "[t]he only initial two-consonant clusters that occur in indigenous words are of the type /ʔ/ plus voiced resonant. All other examples are found in loanwords from English". Word-final clusters and word-medial triconsonantal sequences are likewise impossible in Washo. When such sequences are derived due to morphological concatenation, /i/ is epenthesized in between the first two consonants in such a sequence (6). Note that the post-tonic consonant before the epenthetic vowel is also lengthened as a result of postgemination (see Section 5.2 for more discussion).

(6)   Vowel insertion

Root		Prevocalic		Before C/word-final	
-alŋ-	'arm'	't'alŋa	'on her arm'	'lal:iŋlu	'with my arm'
-aʃk-	'back'	'kaʃka	'on its own back'	't'aʃ:ik	'her back'
-iʃm-	'to sing'	'ʔiʃmi	'he's singing'	'keʃ:im	'sing!'

The only exception to this ban on triconsonantal sequences is when the medial consonant is a glottal stop and when at least one of the flanking consonants is a resonant (7).[7]

(7)   Distribution of glottalized resonants 2

kit'ʔma:ʃ	'his pinenut territory'
'k'aw'ʔlak	'a type of owl'
teʔil'ʔjinɨjini	'varicolored'
ʔum'ʔŋaŋ:aʔ	'your pillow'

Under a bi-consonantal sequence analysis, the distribution of glottalized resonants is anomalous from the perspective of Washo phonotactics. On the other hand, by treating glottalized resonants as unitary segments, a more uniform phonotactic description of the native Washo lexicon is obtained.

4.3   Evidence from Reduplication

Washo employs partial reduplication to denote plurality in nouns and pluractionality in verbs (Jacobsen 1964, Winter 1970, Yu 2006). The reduplicant (underlined) is generally CV in shape. The left edge of the reduplicant must coincide with the left edge of the stressed syllable (8). In other words, the reduplicant must be part of the stressed syllable and the onset of the reduplicant must be the onset of the stressed syllable.

(8)   Plural reduplication

Singular	Plural	Gloss
'taʔa	ta'ʔaʔa	'mother's brother'
'ʔel:el	ʔe'lel:el	'mother's father'
'kew:e	ke'wew:e	'coyote'
'pik':i	pi'k'ik':i	'grandmother's sister'
'sukʰ:uʔ	su'kʰukʰ:uʔ	'dog'

Since stress, which is a property of stem, falls predominantly on the penultimate syllable, the reduplicant appears infixing on the surface. The infixal nature of this reduplicative process is most obvious when the reduplicative stem contains a medial consonantal sequence, as in the example in (9a). From the perspective of the present discussion, what is noteworthy about the data in (9)

---

[7] See Section 5.3 for more discussion on word-final clusters in Washo. In order to maintain transcription uniformity throughout the paper, the glottal stop of interest is given in (7) in the raised notation, rather than in Jacobsen's CʔC format.

is the fact that the shape of the reduplicant remains CV. The medial consonant sequence is not copied as part of the reduplicant. For example, the plural of ˈʔewʃiʔ 'father's brother' is ʔeˈʃiwʃiʔ, not *ʔewˈʃiwʃiʔ. This pattern extends to the voiceless resonants, as illustrated in (9b).[8] The only exception to this generalization once again would come from glottalized resonants. If ʔR were treated as a consonant sequence, the whole sequence would have to be copied (9c), which is against the general morphophonological pattern of this process.

(9)   Reduplication with stems with internal consonant sequences

	Singular	Plural	Gloss
a.	ˈʔewʃiʔ	ʔeˈʃiwʃiʔ	'father's brothers'
	ˈnentʼuʃ	neˈtʼuntʼuʃu	'old women'
	ˈsaksak	saˈsaksak	'father's father's bother'
b.	ˈmeːʰlu	meˈʰluːʰlu	'old men'
	(jeːʰlu)	jeˈʰluːʰlu	'elders'
c.	ˈŋaʔmiŋ	ŋaˈʔmiʔmiŋ	'baby'
	taˈʔmoʔmoʔ	taˈʔmoˈʔmoʔmoʔ	'woman'
	pʰaˈʔloʔlo	pʰaʔloˈʔloʔlo	'butterfly'

Given the exceptional behavior of glottalized resonants under a consonant sequence analysis, a unitary segment analysis is more desirable if an economical and uniform treatment is to be achieved. There are, however, two apparent complications to the unitary segment analysis for all laryngealized resonants. This is the topic of the next section.

5   Some Complications for the Single-Segment Analysis

5.1   Two Cases of Mistaken Identity

There are two main complications to the unitary segment analysis of laryngealized resonants in Washo, both involving what appear to be instances of segmental fission (Blevins 2003). In this section, we confront these two problems head-on and provide explanations for their seemingly exceptional behavior.

5.2   Segmental Fission to the Rescue

The first complication concerns the distribution of voiceless resonants. Recall that Jacobsen argues against treating voiceless resonants as clusters of voiced resonants either preceded or followed by /h/ because such clusters also occur in contrast to the voiceless resonants. This characterization is not entirely accurate, however. Sequences of h + resonant have a very restricted distribution

---

[8] This word for jeˈʰluːʰlu 'elders' is always attested in the plural; the singular form is given in parentheses to indicate that it is the presumed singular counterpart, but is not attested in our corpus.

and they appear in a predictable way. While h + resonant sequences are attested (e.g. [ˈlahla] 'in my leg', [waˈmahmi] 'it's cloudy'), they are found only after a short stressed vowel, precisely the position where voiceless resonants are banned. The segment /h/ is not found in word-final or preconsonantal positions elsewhere in the language. Thus, the fact that preconsonantal /h/ is only observed before a resonant after a short stressed vowel—the very environment where voiceless resonants are never found—strongly suggests that voiceless resonant and /h/ + resonant clusters are in complementary distribution and that they should be treated as allophones of the same phoneme. How might an /h/ + resonant sequence be related to a voiceless resonant?

Here, we contend that the complementary distribution between voiceless resonants and /h/ + resonant sequences in posttonic position follows from more general properties of stress realization in Washo. Stressed syllables in Washo must be heavy (Yu 2006; cf. Hyman 1985), meaning that the stressed syllable must contain either a long vowel (10a) or a short vowel (10b) followed by a coda consonant (i.e. CVV or CVC). When the stressed syllable does not contain a long vowel and the posttonic consonant is not followed by a hetero-organic consonant, the posttonic consonant is geminated (10b). A geminated consonant is on average about 50% longer than its singleton counterpart (Yu 2008).

(10) Distribution of singletons and geminates

a.	V:C		b.	VC:	
	ˈjaːsaʔ	'again'		ˈjasːaɲi	'it's hot'
	ˈwaːʃiw	'Washo'		ˈtaʃːaŋ	'blood'
	ˈpaːmuʃ	'muskrat'		ˈtamːuʔ	'skirt'
	ˈʔaːni	'red ant'		ˈtʰanːiw	'Miwok'
	ˈkʼaːŋi	'it's roaring'		ˈkʰaŋːa	'cave'
	ˈwaːlaʃ	'bread'		ˈʃalːaʔ	'pitch'
	ˈpʼaːwa	'in the valley'		ˈtawːal	'buckberry'
	timˈlaːjaʔ	'my wife'		ˈʔajːis	'antelope'

In light of the evidence for posttonic gemination, the fact that, after a short stressed vowel, only /h/ + resonant sequence is found, and never a voiceless resonant, suggests that the appearance of the so-called /h/ + resonant sequence is a consequence of posttonic gemination. Recall that nonmodal phonation in voiceless resonants never extends over the entire laryngealized segment; nonmodal phonation (breathiness) always precedes modal phonation. Due to a stress-to-weight requirement in Washo (Yu 2006), the posttonic segment is lengthened if the stressed vowel is underlyingly short. What is different between a complex segment, like a voiceless resonant, and other simple segments is that, when a voiceless resonant is lengthened, the window of breathiness phonation is timed in such a way that it appears to decouple, perhaps completely, from the modal resonant. The gemination-induced phase separation between nonmodal and modal phonations thus presents itself phonetically as a sequence of a glottal fricative followed by a resonant with modal phonation.

5.3   Echo Vowel Insertion

The other, perhaps more serious, complication concerns the existence of glottalized resonants that correspond to a genuine glottal stop + resonant sequence. For example, the glottalized glide in *ta²wa* 'in the lake' appears as modal voice when the word occurs without a suffix, *'ta²aw* 'lake' (see also (11b)). The vowel that separates the glottal stop from the modal resonant comes from a process of echo vowel insertion. That is, the vowel that intervenes between the glottal stop and the following consonant is always a copy of the vowel preceding the glottal stop (11a); the echo vowel is inserted when the glottal + consonant sequence appears word finally.[9]

(11)   Distribution of echo vowel insertion; echo vowel is bolded

a.	ta'la?ka	'on the mountain'	ta'la?ak	'mountain'
	'te?ka	'on the rock'	'te?ek	'rock'
	'ma?ka	'on the wood'	'ma?ak	'wood, stick'
	t'i?pa	'at his navel'	'?i?ip	'navel'
b.	'ta²wa	'in the lake'	'ta?aw	'lake'
	wes'k'i²mi	'it's windy'	we'k'i?im	'wind'

Echo vowel insertion specifically targets glottal stop + consonant sequences. As shown in (12), other consonant sequences are broken up via the insertion of /i/ (see also (6)).

(12)   Distribution of default vowel insertion

-aŋ-	'to lick'	'k'alŋi	'he's licking it'	'kaliŋ	'lick it!'
-iʃm-	'to sing'	'?iʃmi	'he's singing'	'keʃim	'sing!'
-alŋ-	'arm'	't'alŋa	'on her arm'	'laliŋlu	'with my arm'
-aʃk-	'back'	'kaʃka	'on his own back'	't'aʃik	'her back'

Functionally, both echo vowel epenthesis and default vowel insertion prevent the formation of word-final consonant clusters. To this end, it is noteworthy that there exist words with glottalized resonants in Washo that do not appear to trigger echo vowel epenthesis (13).[10]

---

[9] It is unclear if the glottal stop participates in consonant gemination in the context of the inserted echo vowel. As noted earlier, glottal stops are often realized as creakiness. The glottal stop that occurs in the echo vowel context is no exception. Since vowel length is never contrastive before a glottal stop, there is unfortunately no way to establish whether the glottal stop or interval of creakiness is lengthened or not.

[10] Recall that post-glottalized resonants are positional allophones of the preglottalized resonants; see Section 2.

LARYNGEAL SCHIZOPHRENIA IN WASHO RESONANTS / 279

(13) Word-final glottalized resonants

ʼkojʔ	'father'
kaˈʰmojʔ	'run away!'
gaˈlajʔ	'wipe it!'
pʼalʔ	'cheek'

How should we reconcile the fact that there exist some word-final glottalized resonants that trigger echo vowel epenthesis (11) while others do not (13)? Here, we propose that glottalized resonants in Washo come from two sources. The type of surface final glottalized resonant seen in (13) is best treated as a unitary segment in light of the fact that Washo generally does not tolerate word-final consonant clusters. The type of surface glottalized resonant that is associated with echo vowel insertion must be treated as an underlying glottal stop + resonant sequence. Thus the underlying form for 'father' is /kojʔ/, with a unitary glottalized resonant, while the underlying form for 'lake' would be /taʔw/, which has an underlying glottal stop + glide sequence.

6 Conclusion

As Hyman's work often reminds us, it is only through a close examination of the patterning in language that a deeper understanding of the underlying system is revealed. The analysis of laryngealized resonants in Washo presented in Jacobsen (1964), which advocated for distinct treatments between voiceless resonants and glottalized resonants, relies on the claim that voiceless resonants contrast with *h* + resonant sequences, while glottalized resonants do not contrast with *ʔ* + resonant sequences. This observation, to be sure, was highly insightful. Yet, it misses the mark as it fails to take into account the behavior of the rest of the system. That is, voiceless resonants can be shown to be in complementary distribution with *h* + resonant sequences; the allophonic realization of voiceless resonants as *h* + resonant sequences can be explained by independently motivated requirements of stress realization in the language. By contrast, glottalized resonants can be shown to be in contrast with *ʔ* + resonant sequences based on evidence from echo vowel epenthesis.

The uniform treatment of laryngealized resonants in Washo advocated in this paper (i.e. the existence of both unitary glottalized resonants and voiceless resonants in the language) has significant ramifications for our understanding of the Washo phonemic system. In particular, the proposed phonemic inventory, presented in Table 2, is far more symmetric than the one proposed in Jacobsen (1964). Rather than a reduced set of laryngeal contrasts in the resonants (see sounds not in parentheses in Table 1), the three-way laryngeal contrast in the obstruents (i.e. plain vs. aspirated vs. glottalized) now finds an analog in both the nasals as well as the approximant series (i.e. modal vs. voiceless vs. glottalized).

plain	p	t		k	ʔ
aspirated	pʰ	tʰ		kʰ	
glottalized	p'	t'	ts'	k'	
plain		s	ʃ		h
modal	m	n		ŋ	
voiceless	m̥	n̥		ŋ̊	
glottalized	m̓	n̓		ŋ̓	
modal	w	l	j		
voiceless	w̥	l̥	j̥		
glottalized	w̓	l̓	j̓		

Table 2. Phonemic inventory of Washo

References

Blevins, J. 2003. The phonology of Yurok glottalized sonorants: Segmental fission under syllabification. *International Journal of American Linguistics* 69(4): 371–396.

Howe, D. & D. Pulleyblank. 2001. Patterns and timing of glottalization. *Phonology* 18(1): 45–80.

Hyman, L. M. 1985. *A theory of phonological weight*. Dordrecht: Foris.

Jacobsen, W. H., Jr. 1964. *A grammar of the Washo language*. Berkeley, CA: UC Berkeley dissertation.

Jacobsen, W. H., Jr. 1996. *Beginning Washo*. Carson City, NV: Nevada State Museum.

Plauché, M. C., R. Beam de Azcona, R. Roengpitya & W. F. Weigel. 1998. Glottalized sonorants: A phonetic universal? In B. K. Bergen, M. C. Plauché & A. C. Bailey (eds.), *Proceedings of the twenty-fourth annual meeting of the Berkeley Linguistics Society: General session and parasession on phonetics and phonological universals*, 381–389. Berkeley, CA: Berkeley Linguistics Society.

Silverman, D. 1997. *Phasing and recoverability*. New York: Garland.

Winter, W. 1970. Reduplication in Washo: A restatement. *International Journal of American Linguistics* 36(3): 190–198.

Yu, A. C. L. 2006. Quantity, stress and reduplication in Washo. *Phonology* 22(3): 437–475.

Yu, A. C. L. 2008. The phonetics of quantity alternation in Washo. *Journal of Phonetics* 36(3): 508–520.

Index